Dialogues/Dialogi

LITERARY AND CULTURAL EXCHANGES

BETWEEN (EX)SOVIET AND AMERICAN

WOMEN

DIALOGUES/DIALOGI

LITERARY AND CULTURAL EXCHANGES

BETWEEN (EX)SOVIET AND AMERICAN

WOMEN

❖

SUSAN HARDY AIKEN

❖

ADELE MARIE BARKER

❖

MAYA KORENEVA

❖

EKATERINA STETSENKO

DUKE UNIVERSITY PRESS   Durham and London   1994

Library of Congress Cataloging-in-Publication Data

Dialogues = Dialogi : literary and cultural exchanges between (ex)Soviet
and American women / Susan Hardy Aiken . . . [et al.] p. cm.
Includes bibliographical references and index.
ISBN 0-8223-1375-8 (alk. paper).—ISBN 0-8223-1390-1 (pbk. : alk. paper)
1. Literature, Comparative—Russian and American.   2. Literature, Comparative—
American and Russian.   3. Russian fiction—Women authors.   4. American fiction—
Women authors.   5. Russian fiction—20th century—History and criticism.
6. American fiction—20th century—History and criticism.   7. Intercultural
communication.   8. Feminism and literature.
I. Aiken, Susan Hardy, 1943– . II. Title: Dialogi.
PG2981.U6D5   1994 891.73'4099287—dc20
93-8650   CIP

FOR OUR MOTHERS

Grateful acknowledgment is made

for permission to reprint or translate the following:

Toni Cade Bambara, "Witchbird," from *The Sea Birds Are Still Alive*, pp. 166–186 (New York: Random House, 1977). © 1977 Toni Cade Bambara. Reprinted by permission of Random House (U.S.) and by permission of The Women's Press Ltd. (British Commonwealth).

I. Grekova, "Damskii master," from *Novyi mir*, no. 11 (1963), pp. 89–120. Translated by permission of the author.

Elena Makarova, "Ryba-Igla," from *Perepolnennye dni: rasskazy: povesti*, pp. 57–68 (Moscow: Sovetskii Pisatel', 1982). Translated by permission of the author.

Anna Nerkagi, excerpts from *Aniko iz roda Nogo*. © 1977 Molodaia Gvardiia. Translated by permission of the publisher.

Tillie Olsen, "Tell Me a Riddle," from *Tell Me a Riddle*, pp. 72–125 (New York: Delacorte Press/Seymour Lawrence, 1961). © 1961. Reprinted by permission of the publisher.

Liudmila Petrushevskaia, "Takaia devochka," from *Bessmertnaia liubov'*, pp. 144–158 (Moscow: Moskovskii Rabochii, 1988). © 1988 Moskovskii Rabochii. Translated by permission of the author.

Jayne Anne Phillips, "Home," from *Black Tickets*, pp. 7–25 (New York: Delacorte Press/Seymour Lawrence, 1979). © 1979 Jayne Anne Phillips. Reprinted by permission of Delacorte Press/Seymour Lawrence (U.S.) and by permission of ICM (British Commonwealth).

Leslie Marmon Silko, "Storyteller," from *Storyteller*, pp. 17–32 (New York: Seaver Books, 1981). © 1981 Leslie Marmon Silko. Reprinted by permission of the author.

Contents

Acknowledgments

We always read the acknowledgments first, that window into the author's private world where we are afforded a glimpse of how the book took shape. *Dialogues* was the work of many hands. At every turn colleagues, friends, and family members both in the United States and in the former Soviet Union helped us on our way.

A Steinfeld Grant, a Women's Studies Advisory Council Award, and a grant from the provost's office at the University of Arizona helped finance the early stages of the project, while a summer salary stipend from the Graduate School at the University of Washington provided much-needed time for writing. A generous Interpretive Research Grant from the National Endowment for the Humanities, together with additional funds from the Faculty of Humanities and the office of the Vice President for Research at the University of Arizona, enabled us to complete the book. Lynn Fleischman, grantwriting adviser extraordinaire, assisted us at every stage of the process. Our two NEH program officers, Irving Buchen and George Lucas, have been steady sources of wisdom, practical help, and encouragement, as has Ken Wissoker, our editor at Duke. Valerie Millholland graciously stepped in when we needed her, and Pam Morrison caught our errors and made the job of copyediting almost tolerable. Margo Dutton at the University of Arizona disentangled budgetary intricacies, and Angie Moreno, Linda Stapleton, and Janet Kania ran expert administrative interference for us. Josephine Sarchiapone at Dell Books went out of her way to help us with permissions.

We are deeply grateful to Liudmila Betekhtina, editor at the University of St. Petersburg Press, for encouraging us to begin this project, and to Steve Cox, Director of the University of Arizona Press, for arranging the occasion of our first meeting with her. Bill Ferris, Director of the Center for the Study of Southern Culture at the University of Mississippi, provided pivotal assistance at the outset of our enterprise and has graciously continued to offer us hospitality, advice, and support. Hunter Cole, of the University Press but in their infinite wisdom also knew precisely when to take us away.

Susan Aiken and Adele Barker
Washington Pass, Washington
May 23, 1993

Preface

SUSAN HARDY AIKEN AND ADELE MARIE BARKER

This book has been written over the course of the last four years, a period that has witnessed the most rapid and dramatic transformations in the former Soviet Union since the revolution. Beneath the surface of our text lie the vestiges of that history, as well as the choices, debates, and deliberations that have characterized our dialogues.

In developing a comparative study of contemporary Soviet and American women writers, we sought a structure that would allow their voices to speak to each other in multiple, mutually illuminating ways. In each of the book's major sections two stories, one by a contemporary (then)Soviet woman and one by a contemporary American woman, become the focus of two interpretive essays, one by an American, one by an (ex)Soviet scholar. These dialogues are juxtaposed, in turn, with another set of encounters—those of the American and Soviet coauthors. In the introductory chapter, we trace the personal and intellectual journeys involved in the book's making by telling the story of our own evolution in the process of working together, and each section concludes with brief segments of our transcribed discussions. For those who want more information on the social contexts from which contemporary women's writings have emerged, we have included an afterword that situates the stories and essays by sketching the history and implications of women's authorship in both countries.

Perhaps our most difficult decision was which Soviet and American authors to include. Our choices were dictated by the combined pressures of aesthetic, social, and historical considerations—and inevitably, as well, by personal preferences. In considering our alternatives, we faced an abundance of riches: during the past thirty years women have authored much of the greatest fiction in the United States, and in the former Soviet Union women's fiction, initially overshadowed by women's poetry, has become increasingly visible and influential. Given the range and quality of that work, even extensive anthologies could not begin to represent fully the multiplicity of the current literary scene nor exhaust its critical possibilities, and this book is not an anthology. Still, we hope our selections at least begin to suggest something of the manifold interests, generations, cultural origins, and ethnic backgrounds of women writing in each country, as well as the exquisite stylistic and thematic variety of their work. We wish to demonstrate the fruitfulness of the comparative approach we adopt, not to exhaust its possibilities.

Though standards of literary value are inevitably contingent on cultural and historical contexts, we nevertheless wanted to include fictions whose richness of signification and significance seemed to us to invite many levels of response, texts that were, in our judgment, likely to endure the vicissitudes of those forces that help determine any work's survival: not only its own aesthetic qualities but also the vagaries of production and dissemination in an increasingly market-driven arena, the critical evaluations and politics that determine who's in, who's out at any given moment, and all the complex social and psychological factors that motivate shifts in public preferences.

We did not include some of the most recent Russian fiction. In a market glutted with new writing since the demise of censorship, we felt it was still too early to determine who among the new writers will emerge as the enduring representatives of this generation. Though the case of Liudmila Petrushevskaia may seem a departure from this standard, in fact she is not, strictly speaking, a new writer, simply a recently (re)discovered one. Because many of her first prose works found their way into print only in smaller provincial journals, many Soviet readers remained unfamiliar with her work until the mid-1980s.

Among the Russian writers, we also chose not to include some, such as the brilliant Tatiana Tolstaia, who had already received wide exposure abroad. Nevertheless, our dialogues and our thinking were often influenced by powerful voices like hers and by others in both Russia and America who have made their mark on women's writing in their respective countries: Kathy Acker, Natalia Baranskaia, Rita Mae Brown, Sandra Cisneros, Louise Erdrich, Maia Ganina, Nina Katerli, Maxine Hong Kingston, Barbara Kingsolver, Paule Marshall, Toni Morrison, Valeria Narbikova, Gloria Naylor, Lily Promet, Francine Prose, Amy Tan, Viktoria Tokareva, Larisa Vaneeva, Alice Walker, and Joy Williams, to name only a few.

Many readers will undoubtedly come to this book wondering why the concerns they most champion have not been represented. Some, for example, may remark on the apparent lack of explicitly lesbian writers. While lesbian fiction and theory are among the most exciting developments in the West, lesbian issues continue to be both underrepresented and repressed even in the new Russia, and have yet to find an explicit voice among fiction writers. We would argue, however, that there are powerful lesbian elements in Petrushevskaia's "That Kind of Girl" and Bambara's "Witchbird."

Some of our most volatile dialogues revolved around the pairings of the stories. We limited our choices to works written since the 1960s and divided our pairings according to generation, ethnicity, and theme. We chose to compare I. Grekova and Tillie Olsen as representative of an older generation of contemporary writers in both countries whose works have arguably attained the status of canonical classics. Elena Makarova and Jayne Anne Phillips are younger writers who, despite their cultural differences, deal in comparable ways with questions of sexuality and alienation common to their generation. We juxtaposed Toni Cade Bambara and Liudmila Petrushevskaia as writers who speak for and about marginalized groups in both countries, either because of race, as in the case of Bambara, or of class, as in the case of Petrushevskaia. Finally, we chose to pair Anna Nerkagi and Leslie Marmon Silko as representative of indigenous women's voices in our two countries— voices increasingly suppressed, in Russia, in the wake of the Soviet Union's collapse and the growth of Russian nationalism.

Obviously, we could have constructed the pairings otherwise. In fact, as we originally conceived them, they were configured slightly differently from the current arrangement. Most notably, at the outset of the project Adele and Susan had placed Bambara alongside the Jewish writer Makarova in order to highlight the visions of women from ethnic groups marginalized by the dominant cultures in their respective countries. Katya and Maya strongly objected to this pairing, seeing in it an implicit equation between the situation of blacks in America and Jews in Soviet and post-Soviet Russia. They noted that Jews were not the only ethnic group to suffer under tsarist and Soviet rules and that Russian Jews had never been subjected to the severe oppressions American blacks had endured. Maya and Katya were all too aware that despite the gains wrought by glasnost, the issue of Jewishness remains a sensitive one in Russia; they felt more comfortable placing Makarova in a context in which the Jewish theme would not be highlighted. Reluctantly, Adele and Susan deferred to them on this issue.

The book that has resulted from our collaborative efforts is a kind of hybrid. A conflation of genres, it is neither solely a collection of fiction nor solely a work of criticism. It is autobiography as well as cultural analysis, memoir as well as explication. We have tried to reach across received boundaries not only in its subjects but also in its generic form. As the preceding account of the positional shifts of the Makarova and Bambara stories suggests, this crossing of borders ultimately includes the opening up of the artificial boundaries established by the pairings in their present arrangements. Like our own voices, the stories all speak in many registers to each other. Thus, for example, the issues of sexuality and isolation raised by Phillips invite comparison not only with the concerns of Makarova but with those of

Petrushevskaia or Silko. The gendered implications of class pervade Olsen and Grekova as well as Phillips and Petrushevskaia. Self-reflexive treatments of the artist in "Ladies' Hairdresser" resonate with comparable concerns in "Needlefish" and "Storyteller." Confrontations with mortality conjoin Olsen and Nerkagi. Discursive experimentation marks the fictions of Makarova and Olsen. And always the experience, construction, and creations of woman as Other reverberate across the disparate lives and writings of all these women.

Like the events against whose background this book evolved, our dialogues took us in directions we could scarcely have predicted. Over the past four years we have come to appreciate in new ways how infinitely complex, how replete with unexpected permutations true dialogue is. Our exchanges were seldom directly hampered by language barriers: we slipped back and forth between Russian and English, with Adele usually serving as the mediating voice between us, and Maya and Katya alternately clarifying questionable English locutions for each other and elucidating the nuances of Russian for Susan. Yet the very fact that English was the dominant language of our discussions meant that Maya and Katya always carried the heavier linguistic burden. Despite their fluency, speaking in a nonnative language inevitably placed them at a certain disadvantage, raising questions of linguistic colonization that no translated text or dialogue can escape.

Further, the very nature of our discussions, interweaving both personal and scholarly material foreign to the cultural milieux of one pair of coauthors or the other, created another arena for potential misunderstandings. Thus Katya observed that Russians regard the personal life as at once too private and too fundamentally irrelevant to be incorporated into social and political concerns, while Adele and Susan questioned the very opposition of the categories "personal" and "political," considering them to be intricately interwoven and inseparable. Because it was important to us that we not infect each other with our critical assumptions, thereby homogenizing all the essays, in transcribing our dialogues and translating and editing the essays we deliberately retained expressions and turns of phrase which suggest the gulf that still separates most Russian and American critical discourses. Thus, for example, Maya and Katya use the terms "hero" and "heroine," while Susan and Adele refer to "character," "protagonist," or "subject," terminologies that embody strikingly disparate theoretical assumptions. Whereas Susan and Adele might favor the term "psychological," Katya and Maya are likely to speak more often of "spiritual." In the last set of essays Katya and Adele use the word "civilized" differently. In both Russian and English, Katya and Maya still employ "man" and "his" as generic references to the human race or the individual, whereas Susan and Adele, influenced by current feminist linguistics, use gender-neutral language and inclusive pronoun forms. And throughout our dialogues, we were all struck by our different perceptions of the words "nature," "natural," and "sex." Each of our linguistic choices reflects not only our theoretical divergences but also the effects of our distinctive cultural positionings—the subtle strength of those social, historical, and ideological assumptions that shape all perception but that we ourselves can only begin to analyze—and inevitably, as well, our personal idiosyncrasies.

In all our discussions, despite linguistic and cultural barriers, we strove for as much equity as possible. We had originally hoped that the book would appear simultaneously in both English and Russian. Later we would discover that Soviet presses were hesitant to publish such a study, claiming, incredibly, that a book about women would not find sufficient interest among the Russian reading public. (Ironically enough, anthologies aplenty of Russian and Soviet women's writing had begun to appear in the USSR by the late 1980s, perhaps as much in response to pressure from Western feminism as to that from Soviet readers. Unfortunately a number of publishers seem to think that they must publish romance novels in order to appeal to a female audience. In 1992 Raduga Publishers signed a contract with Harlequin, thereby introducing the public to the Harlequin romance [Lowe 5]). In any case, it was our intention that no one voice should dominate our conversations or our essays. Thus in "Beginnings," written primarily by Adele and Susan, we have frequently interjected windowed quotations of Katya's and Maya's words, so that the gaze of the reader could be at least momentarily shifted from our perspective to theirs. If, in one sense, we saw Katya and Maya not only as coauthors but as subjects of study, so too they regarded us. We wanted the reader to see us through their eyes as well, as through a kind of reversed lens.

Although we deliberately retained the moments that reflect our diversity, a certain homogenization inevitably occurred as we became more comfortable with each other's perspectives. Katya in particular came increasingly to regard certain texts through more feminist eyes, so that Susan often kidded her that she was rewriting de Beauvoir's *Le Deuxième Sexe* without ever having read it.

Did we, out of deference to each other, avoid debate or discussions that we might otherwise have pursued had all of us come from the same cultural background? By way of answer, we might note that the most vehement debates, sometimes outright arguments, took place not between the Soviet and American sides but between Katya and Maya themselves, over issues as diverse as how to read a text, whether or not the Russian revolution was inevitable, or what ethical judgments were appropriate to contested historical events. Recalling how many times she had witnessed similar heated exchanges running far into the night in Russian kitchens, Adele felt that there was a cultural specificity to this propensity for passionate dispute. The sustained intellectual intensity, the fervor and sheer tenacity of Maya's and Katya's critiques of the system and of each other's ideas, appear more rarely in American academic circles. Moments like these reminded us that whatever elusive thoughts we might entertain about a convergence of our critical discourses, we could never fully escape those intangibles of land and culture that have engendered us and continue to inform our ways of seeing.

Finally, the fact remains that despite our best efforts at collaboration, the book appears only in English. That the Russian stories and essays have been translated into a foreign tongue is a disquieting reality for all of us. To presume to speak for the other is always perilous, an act of hubris that no amount of good will and honest intention can completely efface. Translation, never more than partially successful, distorts even as it discloses what would otherwise go unheard. That such translation transcends mere semantics, attempting to bridge world views so disparate that in some cases no genuinely mutual understanding may ever be achieved, goes without saying. What is perhaps most remarkable is that out of such diverse histories, assumptions, and experiences, we four were able to reach the level of understanding which, despite all our differences, we did attain.

Note on Transliteration and Editing

We have generally adhered to the Library of Congress system of transliterating Russian. We have made exceptions in cases where a "y" rather than an "i" in proper names (Tolstoy, Dostoyevsky, Marya, Galya) makes reading easier for an English-speaking audience.

Editorial comments have been enclosed in brackets. Asterisked footnotes in the Russian stories were added by Aiken and Barker.

Beginnings

SUSAN HARDY AIKEN AND ADELE MARIE BARKER

WITH MAYA KORENEVA AND

EKATERINA STETSENKO

The history of any set of events can never be more than a summary, made up of memories and composed, necessarily, after the fact. So shaped and pruned, summaries are always deceptive, concealing beneath their smooth surfaces and seeming certainties all the disheveled realities, the disjunctions, elisions, complexities, and conundrums of lived experience. This book is the finished product of our exchanges, but that finish—in the sense of both closure and veneer—belies the vagaries of its development. In what follows, then, we have tried to recapture some of the vital density of our encounters by juxtaposing transcripts of our discussions with the story of how they came about. By including moments from our actual dialogues within our account of their unfolding, we hope to share with the reader some of the immediate quality of our conversations, with all their ragged edges, their gropings, hesitations, reservations—and their laughter.

It is not often that one knows precisely where a book begins, but with this book that beginning was unforgettable. It happened in Tucson, Arizona, on one of those hot, interminable July days when the sun scintillates off the pavement, cicadas buzz, and the world seems to hang in a dust-choked state of suspension. It was the summer of 1988, some two years after the inception of glasnost, and we sat in the dining room of the Arizona Inn, a beautiful old rose-colored hotel built in the 1930s to house movie moguls and their entourages filming westerns in the Sonoran desert. We had been invited by Steve Cox, the director of the University of Arizona Press, to a luncheon with a group of Soviet editors, who had come to this country as part of a groundbreaking project to open communications with selected American presses.

As we sat conversing over starched linen tablecloths and crisp salads, we began to realize that this group was unlike the delegations usually sent currents of change spreading with increasing rapidity out of Moscow had touched her as they had so many others in the West. Thus she had eagerly accepted the invitation to meet with Soviet editors.

The idea for this book came into being between two and six that afternoon. Within an hour after our discussions at the luncheon, Adele called Susan to propose a collaborative project. In multiple telephone conversations and rapidly scribbled notes, we generated the concepts that would become its framework. What we envisioned was a comparative study of contemporary Soviet and American women's fiction, a book coauthored by American and Soviet critics, addressed to both American and Soviet audiences, and published in both English and Russian. We wanted a format that would ensure many levels of exchange between Soviet and American writers and critics—dialogue that would go beyond the mere formal juxtaposition of essays to genuine conversation.

In addition to its focus on women's writings, we wanted the book to explore how differing cultural contexts, ideologies, and histories help shape the ways human beings perceive and represent their experiences. While attending to the specifically literary qualities of the stories, we would also consider how racial, ethnic, and class affiliations, as well as issues of gender and sexuality, were articulated within the strikingly disparate social and political systems of the Soviet Union and the United States.

Literary texts constitute a particularly fertile ground for exploring these subjects, especially in the case of Soviet literature, which traditionally served as a preliminary forum for broaching social issues that only much later could be addressed in other public discourses. Moreover, despite the striking increase in the United States of attention to so-called minority or Third World literatures (both problematic terms which reinforce the ethnocentric perspective of dominant, often imperialistic cultural groups), many "mainstream" critics in 1988 were still only beginning to attend to the profound formative effects of race, ethnicity, or sexual orientation on the production of literary works. While Soviet criticism had considered class and, occasionally, race earlier than most U.S. criticism, it had done so from ideological perspectives no longer accepted even by Soviet critics themselves. Thus, for instance, serious study of "Negro" writers began much earlier in the Soviet Union than in the United States, partially in response to a party mandate to depict the West in the most unflattering terms possible. Thus black authors such as Langston Hughes, whose revulsion at the racism of American society in the 1930s and 1940s led them to socialism, were eagerly published in the Soviet Union and lauded by Soviet criticism. Currently, however, black writers receive little attention there, and the theoretical analysis of race and ethnicity now well advanced in the United States has yet to affect Russian criticism.

As our ideas for the project took shape, we became increasingly intrigued by its possibilities. What sorts of dialogues, we wondered, might develop between literary critics from countries with histories of mutual political antagonism—critics whose own thinking was grounded in radically different social and ideological systems—and between the literary and critical texts these traditions produce? What problems might such attempts at dialogue encounter, and what might those difficulties reveal about our different forms of blindness or insight? We hoped for discussions that might cross over hitherto impassable borders, stimulating future Soviet-American exchanges by opening up critical avenues for further investigation.

There were many reasons why such a book had never been attempted. Most obviously, the sort of close collaboration we envisioned would have been almost unthinkable before the advent of glasnost. Mikhail Gorbachev came to power in March 1985. While the issue of a new openness in Soviet society had its roots as far back as the Brezhnev era, it was not until 1986 that the principles of glasnost began to have widespread effects.[2] The concept was first proclaimed to the literary world that summer, at the Eighth Writers' Union Congress in Moscow, by the poet Andrei Voznesensky. Since the Writers' Union had long been a major arm of the central government, no one doubted that Voznesensky's defense of glasnost and call for the publication of previously forbidden literature had official sanction and had originated with Gorbachev.[3]

The radical changes Voznesensky heralded made possible extraordinary new opportunities for cooperation between Soviet and Western scholars. By the summer of 1988, a few books had begun to appear that included essays by both Soviets and Americans, but these were almost all in the sciences and social sciences; in literature, virtually nothing of the sort had ever been undertaken. American and Soviet scholars had, of course, met for many years at international congresses of Slavicists, where their papers were sometimes published in joint volumes, and the Gorky Institute of World Literature had hosted Western scholars at several symposia on specialized topics. Soviet critics, most often from the Gorky Institute, had also occasionally attended conferences in the United States. But real dialogue at such gatherings was generally limited by the nature of the delegations permitted to travel outside the USSR and by the formal, carefully controlled circumstances under which discussions took place. If meaningful exchanges did occur unofficially, they were not recorded in the published proceedings. Given the tremendous pressure to which Soviet writers were subjected prior to glasnost, contributors to joint volumes were always potentially at risk.[4]

Even after glasnost, pragmatic concerns impeded collaborations. Soviet writers and critics now became preoccupied with their newfound freedom to study and publish their own literature. Prior to glasnost many of their own classics, suppressed at home, had been known only in the West. Other works had either been published in incomplete or censored versions or circulated underground to a small select audience. Still others had been written, as the Soviets put it, "for the drawer"—that is, with no immediate hope of publication or circulation. Suddenly, with the advent of glasnost, material formerly banned became available on the open market—works such as Boris Pasternak's *Doktor Zhivago*, Alexander Solzhenitsyn's *Arkhipelag gulag* (*Gulag Archipelago*), Evgeniia Ginzburg's *Krutoi marshrut* (*Journey into the Whirlwind*), Andrei Platonov's *Chevengur* and *Kotlovan*, or Nadezhda Mandelshtam's *Vospominaniia* (translated into English as *Hope against Hope*). Works like Chingiz Aitmatov's *Plakha* (*The Executioner's Block*) and Viktor Astafyev's *Pechal'nyi detektiv* (*The Sad Detective*), treating social and political problems unacknowledged by the party, also began to appear. And hitherto unpublishable manuscripts—Anatolii Rybakov's *Deti Arbata* (*Children of the Arbat*) and Alexander Bek's *Novoe naznachenie* (*The New Assignment*), for example—were printed for the first time. Given this intellectual ferment, Soviet scholars were understandably more concerned, at least in the initial stages of glasnost, with responding to changes at home than with seeking collaborative projects abroad.

But even leaving aside the obvious political and pragmatic constraints on collaborative work, theoretical differences constituted a potential obstacle. Now that the doors were beginning to open, critics from both sides felt an uneasy, often unspoken concern about what we might make of each other— about whether, after all, the profound differences in our social histories and critical training might preclude the possibility of finding sufficient common ground for fruitful discussions. For historical reasons, little critical exchange had occurred between the two countries, with the notable exceptions of Russian Formalism and, more recently, of the Tartu school (Yury Lotman, Boris Uspensky) in the West, or of the formalist methods of America's (now old) New Criticism in some academic quarters in the USSR. Mikhail Bakhtin, the Russian theorist who had perhaps exercised the single greatest influence on Western critical theory, had until recently been regarded far more highly in the United States than in his own country. While comparisons are always problematic, it seems valid to say that by the summer of 1986, the theories and methodologies that predominated in the Soviet Union, even those not primarily shaped, as most were, by the tenets of Socialist Realism, resembled those prevalent in America during the 1930s, 1940s, and 1950s—traditional literary history, biographically oriented studies, or formalist criticism. An important exception to this generalization was structuralism, which had influenced Soviet criticism since the sixties and formed the basis for much of the work done by the Tartu school. Yet even these theories had by no means affected all Soviet critics.

There were other differences. Until 1989, for example, the texts of Freud were virtually unobtainable in the USSR. Hence Soviet critics had little access to even rudimentary psychoanalytic literary criticism, much less to the many post-Freudian schools, from object relations to Lacanian theory, that had flourished in the West for several decades.[5] The formative texts of deconstruction, a movement now widely regarded as passé in the West by new historicists and cultural critics who have built on many of its premises, were virtually unknown in the Soviet Union, as were the works of Foucault. Gay and lesbian theory, currently burgeoning in the United States, was at best nascent in the Soviet Union, where homophobia carried even greater force of official sanction than in America (see Afterword). And even the forms of Marxist criticism that had circulated most widely in the West had followed a course markedly different from that of Soviet Marxism.

Feminism, when it was discussed at all in the USSR, was treated reductively as a monolithic movement, with virtually no recognition of the extraordinary complexity and diversity that have marked its development over the past two decades, or else as merely a bourgeois phenomenon, a historical stage through which Soviet society had long since passed. Soviet writers and critics, both male and female, still disregarded gender as an analytic category, tending to approach "exceptional" writings by women as if they were de facto male authored: that is, as if "man" (*chelovek*)—that putatively generic reference which in both English and Russian has historically concealed the male-specific bias that forms its unacknowledged foundation—were in fact the norm, and "woman" essentially invisible or irrelevant.[6] When gender issues did receive attention in literary circles, it was generally negative. Thus, although the official literary establishment typically denigrated "women's writing" (*zhenskoe rukodelie*, literally "women's handwork") as "silly" and "trivial"—a kind of embroidery, as *rukodelie* suggests—these pejoratives were never applied to respected writers such as Galina Nikolaeva, Margarita Aliger, Olga Berggolts, or Vera Panova. The disparaging designation "women's writing" was also used selectively over the years to malign those women who were perceived as unruly, recalcitrant, or transgressive, reluctant to stay on the right side of the party line. Both Anna Akhmatova and I. Grekova, for example, have at times suffered such denigration (see Afterword).

Finally, as we have already suggested, ethnic and racial studies, among the most provocative developments on the American critical scene when they were pursued at all in the USSR, had assumed a somewhat monolithic form. The limited analysis of racial questions reflected not only the force of an ideology that construed all conflicts as manifestations of social and class struggles, but also the propagation of a homogeneous, even imperialistic vision of the "great Soviet family of nations."[7]

Yet despite the constraints on Soviet literary criticism, we knew that there were also critics who, while undertaking approaches different from those in the West as well as from each other, managed to elude simple conformity to dominant ideological prescriptions and to produce work of exemplary quality and originality even during periods of extreme repression—Igor Zolotusky, Galina Belaia, Igor Vinogradov, and Lydiia Ginzburg, for example.[8] We hoped to locate critics like this for our project, scholars amenable to frank, flexible discussions.

We would follow similar principles in selecting fiction writers. Though many Soviet authors had been persecuted for what they wrote, even before glasnost there were those who managed to elude the dictates of Socialist Realism, writing eloquently and honestly without capitulating to the party line. Thus, for example, when asked by an American how his writing had changed under the influence of glasnost, Anatoly Kim, one of the most radically experimental novelists in Russia, responded that it had not changed at all, since he had never written according to the dictates of political ideology (personal communication, 1990). Such a statement might appear politically naive in the West, at least in the academy, where cultural theorists have demonstrated the ineluctable entanglements of writing and ideology (though these connections are still hardly self-evident to the broader reading public or even to many academics). But within a Soviet context, given the repressiveness of a system within which, until recently, conformity or resistance to official tenets was sometimes literally a matter of life or death, Kim's assertion evokes another interpretation. While writing never exists in an ideological vacuum, historical contexts nevertheless do render some ideological positions more courageous than others. Even before glasnost, gifted writers were able to elude or subtly subvert official codes without necessarily identifying themselves explicitly as dissidents. In looking for women writers, we wanted to locate those who had managed to produce this sort of work.

That evening, at the party for our Soviet guests, we described our ideas to Liudmila Betekhtina. Her response was enthusiastic: such a book had never been attempted; now, for the first time, it might just be possible. We should definitely do it. But we should do it quickly, given the uncertainty of the political climate and the unpredictability of future Soviet-American relations.

In addition to Liudmila's concerns, we had several of our own, beginning with the subject and focus of the book. It was far from clear how the Soviets would feel about having their scholars participate in a joint project on women.

After all, according to the official view, what was there to write? The party and even popular opinion held that women had long since received equal rights with men, and for the Soviet critical establishment, gender issues and women's writing were a nonsubject: either a thing of the past, a notion projected onto Soviet society by the bourgeois imaginations of Western feminists, or a triviality beneath the notice of any serious scholar. One of our primary reasons for writing the book was to counter these widespread assumptions.

Then there was money. Genuine collaboration would be prodigiously expensive, entailing not only several trips back and forth between the two countries but the prohibitive costs of telephone and telefax, especially since the Soviet postal service was so inefficient that ordinary airmail letters might take up to three months for delivery or go astray altogether. We would spend much of our time during the first two years writing a seemingly interminable succession of grant proposals to help get the project underway. As a result, the book itself was always several steps ahead of our finances, sustained by a series of small grants and, for the most part, out of our own pockets. Until receiving a grant from the National Endowment for the Humanities in 1991, we never knew where funds would come from next or even whether we could continue.

We had other concerns as well. We ourselves came from radically different critical backgrounds. Susan was strongly grounded in gender theory, Anglo-American literatures, and comparative literary studies, but she did not speak Russian and had no specialized training in Russian studies; she would be, in effect, the experimental subject in our translation project, depending on Adele as a consultant on the linguistic and stylistic elements of the Russian stories. Adele, a specialist in Russian language, literature, and culture, had little background in gender criticism and narrative theory, and at least initially, despite her growing interest in women's writing, she shared the prevalent Soviet view that gender and writing were not importantly related. She would be relying heavily on Susan's theoretical background. Given these discrepancies, how well would we work together?

And given the differences between American and Soviet criticism in general, could we hope to find two critics sufficiently sympathetic and open-minded to collaborate productively with us? Although we recognized that some Soviet critics had managed to do work of high quality under appallingly difficult circumstances, we wondered whether they could make the transitions necessary to enable their work to speak meaningfully to an American audience. We wondered too, considering the low regard in which the Soviet intelligentsia held women's writing, whether any of them would be willing to devote themselves solely to analyses of women authors. Would we not, in sum, encounter intellectual chasms too wide to bridge?

There were practical considerations as well. Since Susan did not speak Russian, we would have to conduct our discussions in English, a fact that already shifted the balances of the coauthorship in problematic ways. But even had Susan been fluent in Russian, we would still have needed at least one coauthor with a strong command of English because some of the American stories were written in highly colloquial language, vernacular, or disjunctive experimental prose. We needed a critic able to follow their nuances and, if necessary, to assist our second collaborator with English translations, as well as to engage in theoretical discussions with us. Assuming such critics existed, how might we find them?

Thus began our search for our Soviet colleagues. It was far from simple. As we discovered after several false starts and faulty leads that consumed the better part of a year, we would need not only critics with theoretical range and fluency in English but at least one whose knowledge of American literature and society could complement Adele's knowledge of Russian and Soviet culture. Adele knew a number of Soviet Americanists, but all were men. To find the sorts of women we sought, she queried colleagues in departments of Slavic languages and literatures across the country. Her quest, ranging from California to Indiana, from Chicago to Cambridge, Massachusetts, ended at a destination neither of us could have predicted. Speaking one day to a colleague at Harvard, she received the pivotal lead: "You're not going to believe this, but the person who knows more about Soviet Americanists than anybody else in this country is not a Sovietologist at all. He's the director of the Center for the Study of Southern Culture at the University of Mississippi. His name's Bill Ferris. Call him. You won't be disappointed."

We weren't. Bill's work with Soviet scholars of American literature dated from the beginning of the eighties, when, through his initiative, the Center for the Study of Southern Culture had signed an agreement with the Gorky Institute of World Literature providing for an exchange of scholars for conferences and symposia—no mean feat at that time. Since then, he himself had hosted many Soviet scholars and had been back and forth to the USSR on many occasions; he knew virtually every Soviet critic engaged in American studies. He was enthusiastic about our project and suggested that we get in touch with Maya Koreneva and Katya Stetsenko, whose open-mindedness, geniality, and scholarly abilities he could vouch for.

Encouraged by Bill's recommendations, Adele made an appointment to confer with Maya during a trip to the Soviet Union in the fall of 1989. They met at the Gorky Institute one windy October morning amid the rubble of reconstruction, the seemingly endless renovation to which this old bastion of the literary establishment seems subject. There, amid constant interruptions, the incessant comings and goings well known to anyone who has ever tried to conduct business at the Institute, the two of them worked out an internal proposal which they presented at day's end to Peter Palievsky, deputy director of the Institute, requesting his approval of Maya's and Katya's participation in the project.

Not until two years later, during one of our meetings in Tucson, would we realize the full import of what had happened that day in Moscow. "I never understood it," Maya would recall. "We just walked in there and got what we needed from them. It *never* works like that. Usually it's, 'Well, come back in three months. The proposal has to go to so and so.' Then in three months you come back, and it's another three months. Sometimes a year can pass like that." Why this did not happen to us, why we so readily received those essential permissions for a project which to this day certain members of the institute regard with suspicion, none of us can say. But it was in that office, on that autumn afternoon, that the possibility for our joint project became a reality.

Back at Maya's apartment, Adele and Maya continued their discussions far into the night, surrounded by the books and boxes Maya had recently moved from her former flat. Like the Institute, her dwelling was also undergoing major renovation (*kapital'nyi remont*). But amid the chaos of both places Maya remained unperturbed.

At the time of this initial meeting, Katya, Maya's younger colleague at the institute, was in the United States attending a Hemingway conference in Ohio—her first trip to America. She had published essays on Twain, Thomas Wolfe, Faulkner, Margaret Mitchell, and William Styron and was now at work on a book about the modern American novel. But like Maya, she too was interested in Russian and Soviet culture and had written on Chekhov and Pushkin.

Katya's perspectives would be important to our project for another reason as well: as a native Ukrainian, she had historical antecedents and cultural values sometimes at odds with those of Russians. Born in Kiev in 1946, Katya was a descendant of the intelligentsia who had shared the fate of the upper classes after the revolution. The family had preserved its traditions through stories: of ancestors who had participated in the turbulent events of Ukrainian history, of life on the country estates, of the atrocities of the civil war and Stalin's terror. Like most longtime inhabitants of Kiev, Katya was brought up with an acute sense of time. In this ancient city, the capital of old Russia, many of the buildings on the streets where she walked had been designed by her great-grandfather. It was no accident that her first work on American literature, her candidate's dissertation, addressed "The Problem of Time in the Southern School of American Literature," or that Faulkner was one of her favorite authors.

Katya's father was a civil engineer, her mother a biologist who had abandoned her career after witnessing the destruction of genetics, under Stalin, by Lysenko and his school of pseudoscientists. Though the family lived a modest life typical of the Soviet middle class, it managed to preserve the old cultural habits inherited from prerevolutionary ancestors: the two small rooms in the communal apartment were jammed with books; vacations were devoted to traveling all over the country; and Katya's education encompassed the arts, literature, and foreign languages.

Her decision to study literature was easy; she found in books the ideas and ideals sorely lacking in the society she inhabited. Though both her parents strenuously objected to her choice of the humanities as a profession, fearing that it would be impossible for her, as a scholar in the Soviet Union, to write what she really thought, she insisted on entering the Philological Faculty at Kiev University.

Katya: At that time, for one who didn't belong to the Soviet elite, it wasn't an easy task to enter the department, which was considered extremely prestigious among the girls of the upper class. I'm not sure that they were deeply in love with Shakespeare's plays or Melville's novels or that they were even eager to devote themselves to academic literary studies. Rather, most of them followed the widespread conviction that the privileged people were those who had the possibility to work with foreigners and to travel abroad.

Taking into account the limited number of students at this department, it was absolutely impossible for me to hope to win the competition—not of "talents" but of "parents." [Katya is referring to the system of privilege in the USSR whereby children of the Soviet elite generally had easier access to the universities than did others.] That's why I managed to enter only the evening division, from which, after the first year, because I had the highest marks in all disciplines, I was lucky to move on into the regular department.

Susan: Were there many men in your class?

Katya: We had one faculty for foreign languages, divided into two departments. The linguistics and literature department was available to both men and women, but the second department was only for men. It trained interpreters who would go abroad, so many men tried to get into it.

Adele: There was also an assumption that interpreters were often involved in intelligence work. But the official reason for keeping women out was that they were supposedly not as well suited for the "hardships" of travel as men.

Susan: So in a sense, Katya, your possibilities were doubly limited—by your family's position outside the Soviet elite and by gender.

Katya: Yes. When I graduated in 1972, even though I had my degree *cum laude* and was recommended for postgraduate courses, I had no chance to pursue my goal of literary scholarship immediately—again, for the reasons I mentioned earlier. So I had to struggle on my own for my professional future. I earned my living by working as a teacher of English at the secondary school for a year and then as a translator of technical texts at one of the research institutes for three years. The only way for me to become a scholar of literature was to write the thesis on my own, so at night and during holidays I studied, did research, and wrote.

The person who helped me choose the subject of my thesis was Tamara Denisova, a specialist in American literature from the Shevchenko Institute of Literature of the Ukrainian Academy of Sciences. She had taught the course I took on the American novel at the Philological Department and had noticed my work then, so now I turned to her for advice. The two of us decided on a theme which not only required sound scholarship but which also seemed as distant as possible from ideological matters.

Tamara Denisova also introduced me to her colleague Dmitry Zatonsky, a famous scholar in the field of Western literature, who became my official mentor. Thus, due to these generous people, I got the perspective to obtain a scientific degree and the possibility of publishing several articles, though unfortunately without a great chance to find a job corresponding to my scholarly interests.

But at this point in my career my circumstances changed radically. I married a Moscovite and moved to Moscow, where I had the opportunity to be accepted in 1977 as a junior researcher at the Gorky Institute. There I met Maya, who would become not only my colleague but also my close friend.

Although Katya and Maya eagerly accepted our proposal to collaborate on the book, they too had initial reservations about doing a joint project. Both felt concerned, though for different reasons, about the content of the book and their contributions to it. Neither, after all, claimed any specialization in women's writing, though both had written about individual American women and Maya had translated Denise Levertov and edited the Russian volume of her selected poetry. Unlike most Soviets, Katya and Maya had also followed some of the developments of Western women's movements by reading U.S. journalistic accounts, which had provided a somewhat less reductive coverage than had the Soviet media. Still, both women remained uneasy about feminism, less perhaps as a political commitment than as a critical methodology, and both tended to regard it as a single, monolithic dogma.

Maya in particular felt that writing could not and indeed should not be gender specific, that the power of literature transcended both the sex of the author and the gender arrangements of the author's culture. She viewed such a position as clearly antifeminist. Yet her ideas on this issue, as Susan would later point out, were not unlike various feminist theories about the dangers of essentializing authorial gender. And feminist speculations about the possibilities of reading literary texts against the grain of traditional interpretations— discovering alternative possibilities formerly overlooked by male-centered critical perspectives—were based on the assumption that literature always exceeds the scope of any single interpretive framework.[9] A crucial difference between these premises and Maya's was that her critical assumptions reflected prefeminist traditions with their own historic specificity, traditions which, assuming maleness as the human norm, valued most highly the woman who "transcended her sex"—that is, who "wrote as well as a man," disregarded the subordination of women, and denied the entanglements of writing with the material, social, and psychological formations of gender.

Yet Maya was acutely aware of other political pressures that impinge on literary texts, a perception honed by years of her own writing in defiance of dominant Soviet ideologies and of having her criticism attacked as politically suspect. "I've never thought," she told us in one of our last conversations, "that you can teach literature merely from an aesthetic perspective. All the aspects of a work of art should be represented according to the views presented in it. In the sixties I wrote a book on Arthur Miller. The editor who was working with the manuscript said, 'You write about Miller as if you were writing about us.' I was never tied simply to aesthetics."

Maya's views also reflected her family background. Born into the Moscow intelligentsia in the 1930s, she had grown up longing for a career in the theater but found her ambitions thwarted by a variety of disappointments. Instead, she took up the study of English and American literature at Moscow State, the most prestigious university in the USSR, where among her classmates were many who are now leading figures in the Russian literary establishment. She herself would eventually become one of the Soviet Union's most distinguished analysts of American drama.

Maya: I entered the university in 1953, the year Stalin died. But all my life I wanted to be an actress—I really did—so I tried to enter theater school. And I failed. I had been so much in love with the Moscow Art Theater [MKHAT], and I knew everything about it and Stanislavsky. But I was offended by the way the preaudition was conducted at the MKHAT, and so I went to the school of Malyi, even though I knew that I would never be accepted there because their kind of acting still has this trace of pre–Moscow Art Theater.

Both my parents started as schoolteachers. My mother was Polish and taught at the Polish *tekhnikum* [technical school], but after the war all Polish schools in Moscow were closed. Before the war she was a student in the History Department at Moscow State University. Her studies were interrupted by the war. Finally she got her degree in Polish history.

My father wanted to be a historian but was not permitted to enter the History Department of the University because history was considered a sensitive subject and his father had been a priest. So he taught geography at school until the war broke out. He was lucky: he was the only one of his brothers who survived the war. Afterwards he entered the university history department for postgraduate studies because a new law had been passed granting admission to veterans of the war. He specialized in Russian history and culture, particularly the eighteenth century. Both my parents then taught in the History Department at MGU [Moscow State University].

When I couldn't get into acting school, my mother urged me to study literature at the university. She said that I could study drama there as well. I followed her advice. It wasn't hard for me to get in, since I had graduated from school with a silver medal. I had this rather long talk, maybe an hour, with the head of the English department. It was informal, but I was asked all sorts of questions about English literature and the nature of my interest in it.

When I graduated from the university in 1958, they said that none of the students could be accepted to do postgraduate work without first working for two or three years. But there was no real work for any of us. Four persons got positions, but all of them were linguists. Three were hired by military organizations as English interpreters, and the other one, I think because of his father, got a position at the Gorky Institute reading articles in literary magazines to pass along to people at the head of the institute so that they could stay informed.

At that time, I still wanted to be an actress, and joined an acting troupe. But by then I was married. My husband was an actor, and that was terrible, because he was desperately against me going on the stage; he believed that an actress could not be a moral person. Then my mother arranged that I would meet one of the members of the Moscow Art Theater, who would audition me. But I had to consider my husband's opposition. Finally I decided, without saying anything to him, that I would just not go to the audition. I just didn't go.

We were separated soon after that, and I continued with another acting group. The original one had by then disbanded; some had gone on to the theater school, and some had gotten married. The girls would have liked to continue, but because of the other demands on their lives, most of them couldn't manage it.

By then I had my daughter to support, so after a while I had to look for a job. One of my former teachers at the university got me a position at the Academy of Sciences, and for two years I translated technical texts on welding and forging. When I do something, I do it really thoroughly, and then I remember it for years; I can still tell you about welding and forging!

This continued for two years. Meanwhile I had my daughter with me. At that time

Professor Samarin was the head of the Western Literature Department at the [Gorky] Institute and at the university, and since the girls who graduated from our class at the university were better students than the boys, he suggested that I try to enter the Gorky Institute for postgraduate work. And so I continued working with the theater group and did my research on American drama. After I did my postgraduate work, I was kept on at the Institute as a member of the staff.

Studying American literature in the USSR during the fifties, sixties, and seventies was still fraught with professional complications, especially in the critical context that had evolved during the Cold War era. Condemning America's capitalism, its strained racial relations, and its bourgeois way of life, the official line also treated most American literature as no more than an embodiment of those repudiated values—a decadent, bourgeois, corrupt corpus antithetical to everything the party stood for. American texts, particularly those considered ideologically and artistically suspect, were taken off the shelves of the libraries and made accessible only to those with special permits.

Given this context, many scholars who chose to enter this highly sensitive area did so not only out of curiosity about America but also, self-servingly, to defend the party line. Emphasizing the negative features of American culture and exalting the glories of the Soviet Union, they procured rapid professional advancement. Yet even while approaching American studies with a carefully honed political agenda, these critics were also able to catch a tantalizing glimpse of American life usually off limits to Soviet citizens. Ironically, then, the very project designed to reinforce the Soviet system also had the paradoxical potential to undermine it, providing a matrix within which other, less doctrinaire critics might gain an otherwise unattainable opportunity to study American culture and literature.

Some of these scholars, in order to justify their studies, chose to work on those few writers whom the party considered acceptable—Theodore Dreiser, Jack London, and Sinclair Lewis, for example—because their texts appeared either apolitical or pro-Soviet; that is, they focused on those negative aspects of capitalist society that could be used to reinforce authorized Soviet views. Yet among this same group of scholars were those who, by a process of camouflage and double reference, easily recognizable to Soviet readers long practiced at reading between the lines, were able to bypass literal-minded censors. Appearing simply to condemn the American system, they used their critique as a double-edged discourse to challenge the Soviet system as well.[10]

By the late 1950s this set of complex historical conditions had rendered the field of American studies relatively safe—provided it was approached in the correct way, via the acceptable party line. In fact, though this issue is still disputed, Maya and Katya maintain that in pre-glasnost days it may even have been easier to write creative criticism on American than on Soviet literature because the standards of Socialist Realism were applied less stringently to foreign texts.

Thus the ground was laid for critics like Maya, who chose to work with American literature because she loved it. The history of her career epitomizes the Byzantine complexities Soviet scholars encountered in attempting to study American culture from a Soviet perspective in the three decades prior to glasnost. In choosing to work on figures the party still regarded as suspect, Maya charted a subversive course, placing her career and herself in potential jeopardy.

Maya: I was very slow in having my thesis defended because I wrote it on American drama since World War II. I finished it in the mid-1960s. My advisor wasn't happy with it because he was of the older generation. He didn't like my interpretation of authors such as [Edward] Albee and [Tennessee] Williams, who were then called "modernists" in the USSR, which made them completely unacceptable. I was expected to blame them, to accuse them of all kinds of aesthetic sins. I refused.

Then came the Arab-Israeli war of 1968, and my interpretation of Arthur Miller, which had once satisfied my dissertation advisor, no longer satisfied anyone. Miller was then head of PEN and made certain statements regarding the war and politics that made him persona non grata in the USSR. But I refused to change my interpretation of him. I still have a book in galleys on Miller, which passed the censors but then was stopped by the lady editor [at the publishing house] because she didn't think it was politically correct. It has never been published.

So, I was asked to change my work, particularly on Miller. I said no. Then a new director arrived at the institute, who said to me, "Why do you persist in studying drama in the twentieth century? It's hopeless. Why not start another dissertation?" I refused again. I simply put it away, where it lay for ten years. I didn't want to be put into a cell and told to do that, or that, or that. Had I been willing to, I would have had my dissertation earlier, my degree earlier, other promotions earlier. But I wouldn't follow that line. I just don't pay attention to such pressures. I seek to feel right.

Maya's interest in Faulkner took a comparable course. Though he was regarded as the epitome of American decadence, her great admiration for his art compelled her to translate his works.[11] She was not alone in her interest in Southern literature. Russian critics have long felt peculiarly intrigued by the

American South, perhaps in part because they perceived certain similarities between the antebellum social order that underlay Southern literary history and the social arrangements of prerevolutionary Russia. In both, a veneer of high civilization at once rested on and glossed over fundamentally heinous systems: in Russia, a privileged class of landowning gentry, whose very existence depended on the serf system, produced a leisured intelligentsia whose way of life invited comparison with that of many Southern plantation owners dependent for their identities and livelihoods on slavery. For Soviet critics like Maya and Katya, Faulkner became the preeminent example of the dilemma of attraction and repulsion that would plague many later white Southern writers, whose complex nostalgia for lost roots was interwoven with aversion to the system from which they sprang.

In light of these conjunctions, it seemed at once peculiarly appropriate and intensely ironic that we should first come together in Oxford, Mississippi, that quintessentially Southern town where Faulkner was born and died, the matrix from which he would construct his myth of the South, embodied in Yoknapatawpha County. Oxford is now a thriving repository of Faulkner memorabilia. His grave lies discreetly in the local cemetery just off the square, sharing a rolling hillside with the (white) Revolutionary War and Civil War dead; on the other side of town, amid cedars and magnolias, stands his white-columned home Rowan Oak, carefully preserved and open to public view. Oxford is also the site of the annual Faulkner and Yoknapatawpha Conference, a lively event organized by the Center for the Study of Southern Culture and held on the campus of the University of Mississippi. It was this conference that became the occasion for our initial meeting.

We had been invited there by Bill Ferris, who had long used the Faulkner Conference as a major occasion for hosting Soviet scholars. In the early years, Bill had been forced to accept the delegations the Soviets were willing to send, and the participants had all been male. Only in 1987, in response to a specific request from the Center, had the first women been included. One of these was Maya. By the summer of 1990, the group included more women than men. Having helped us locate Maya and Katya, Bill now helped coordinate the details of our initial meeting with them.

We arrived at the university on a steamy afternoon in late July, driving past restored nineteenth-century houses set well back from streets lined with oak, dogwood, and magnolia. Looking for the Alumni House, the conference center where we were to stay, we drove through the handsome Georgian campus of Ole Miss, one of the earliest white universities in the South, and past row after row of sorority and fraternity houses. The walls of the elegantly decorated foyer in the Alumni House were hung with larger-than-life portraits of the past presidents (male) of the alumni association, facing the equally spectacular photographs of smiling former students (female) who had gone on to become Miss Americas. It was against this unlikely backdrop that our discussions on women's creativity would unfold.

That night we met briefly with Maya and Katya. None of us really knew what to expect. Beneath our formal cordiality, mixed feelings surged—curiosity, anticipation, anxiety—heightened by the awareness that for all the surface changes wrought by glasnost, Maya and Katya were still part of a formal delegation whose members were far more comfortable with each other than they could ever be with us. Though Adele had already met both women, she had no idea how we would all get along, nor what it would be like for them to be with us on American soil. Over years of traveling to the Soviet Union, she had often been struck by the cultural and personal splitting such visits engender, by how one tends to develop two distinct, nonintersecting personalities appropriate to each place and each language. Knowing how much her own behavior altered within a Soviet context, she wondered whether the same would be true in reverse for Katya and Maya in America. Susan was equally apprehensive. Although she had known several Soviets well as a result of student exchange programs, she had never been to the Soviet Union and had encountered Soviet academics under only the most formal circumstances.

Maya and Katya: We also had mixed feelings, though for somewhat different reasons. Maya, convinced that literature is an integral entity that should be treated in aesthetic rather than in "sexual" terms, was concerned about her coauthors' theoretical assumptions. She believed that a feminist approach to literature and culture in general led, together with other factors, to further fragmentation of man and society, which already suffer fragmentation. Katya was more positive about feminism, considering that gender psychology is, in one way or another, reflected in all the writings of both men and women. But she was embarrassed by the possibly condescending reaction of Soviet colleagues, most of whom believe that no serious scholar would take part in such a trivial study. Both of us were also afraid that our American colleagues might be fanatical feminists. Nevertheless, we had decided to accept the invitation to work with them. Both of us were attracted to the originality of the project and the opportunity to present our views on matters long neglected in Soviet literary criticism. It was also a time when everybody was celebrating the fall of the Iron Curtain and trying to establish new contacts, looking for possibilities to study the newly found America and Americans, their psychology, their culture, their way of life.

None of us admitted our misgivings during our early discussions; we were too conscious of the fragility of our connection to risk jeopardizing it. Not until our second visit a year later, when we had become more comfortable with each other, would we acknowledge the depth of our initial apprehensions.

Maya and Katya: Acquaintance with Adele and later with Susan dispelled whatever remaining doubts we might have had. Our fear that they might be fanatical feminists turned out to be groundless. We found them to be undogmatic, open to our ideas and opinions, easy to communicate with.

Our Soviet colleagues were in general indifferent to the project. Some showed no interest at all in the unpopular subject. Others were mildly attracted by the unusual idea and structure of the future book. Most, particularly men, as was to be expected, were ironic about the project, which they considered of minor importance. They advised us to concentrate rather on the institute's major projects and to work on this one on women without expending too much time and effort. In fact, although the book was included in the Gorky Institute's program of cooperation between Soviet and American scholars, it has never been officially included among our annual work assignments.

And then both of us had quite a lot to do in connection with this project, since neither of us had studied much Soviet literature, ethnic literature, or feminist criticism. We had to read many books on these subjects, some of them sent by Adele and Susan.

Our qualms first began to dissipate when the four of us were finally able to sit together in the quiet of our room in Oxford and talk at length. We spoke of the stories, debating the selections and the pairings, comparing our evaluations. Our discussions of theory led to the discovery that our differences sometimes allied us across national boundaries: occasionally Adele or Susan seemed to have more in common with Katya or Maya than with each other. Thus, for example, Susan's sense of the manifold ways in which Western societies have constricted women, and her suspicion that similar forms of discrimination, both subtle and overt, existed in the Soviet system despite official claims to the contrary, resonated with Katya's perception of gender inequities in the USSR. Adele, on the other hand, had initially felt that the concepts of Western feminist criticism were virtually inapplicable to Soviet society. Here her views seemed closer to Maya's. Yet Adele had long recognized the gender inequities in both her own and Soviet society, and by the time we met in Oxford, she found herself in a state of transition, having gradually begun to question many of her own earlier assumptions.

These conversations spilled over into others: accounts of growing up in our respective societies, of our schooling and early experiences, the vicissitudes of our graduate careers and professional lives, our families, our tastes in food and in people, our views on the salient political and social issues of our times. We ranged from the abstractions of literary theory to the nature of the graffiti littering the walls of Soviet apartment buildings, from global politics to the permutations of Russian obscenities. Always these discussions returned to our distinctive experiences as women.

Katya: I can't complain about the way my professional and private life turned out, but still I have always felt some derogatory attitudes towards me because of my gender. It's certainly connected with a specific social and male psychology formed during the ages. Though man considers his main goal to be self-realization as a human and social being, he doesn't usually apply such notions to woman, whom he rather considers as an object and a function, occupying a certain limited place in his life. It's difficult for him to realize that she is an individual, equal to him and having her own destiny. In love he conquers her. In private life he expects her to create for him family and home, but at the same time he looks at the domestic occupations as trivial and trifling, secondary and minor spheres of reality.

This attitude is transferred to a social life, and thus it's not easy for a woman to be taken seriously as a professional. It will take you a long time to convince your colleagues that you're not "just a girl." It was much more so in our country because everything was politicized there, and politics was always thought of as a man's field. More than that, our society, unfortunately, still bears a heavy weight of patriarchal traditions, which influence even the younger generations.

Maya: I think it's more complicated than that, because most men would consider home care and child care as belonging to the sphere where woman is to be the major force according to social norms. I wouldn't say that all men wouldn't recognize talent or originality in the women they see around them. It's another thing what they make of it! [Laughter]

Adele: How many researchers are in the Gorky Institute?

Katya: More than four hundred.

Adele: How many women?

Katya: At least half of them.

Adele: What about the organizational structure of the institute? Who runs it? Is it all men at the top?

Maya: We have a director and two vice directors, all men, although a woman once held the position of vice director. It is not impossible for women to occupy these top positions, but it is rare. We have a secretary of the institute, who is a woman, and that position has been held by a woman before.

air, momentarily terminating our conversation. Here and elsewhere our own lives reverberated with the same contradictions as those that unfold in "Tell Me a Riddle" and "Ladies' Hairdresser," whose female protagonists also feel themselves torn between the conflicting demands of home, family, and their own creative lives. "I do not," writes Toni Cade Bambara, "have anything profound to offer mother writers or worker writers except to say that it will cost you something" (Tate 1983b). Many times in the course of our discussions we felt the truth of those words and longed for that room of one's own that Virginia Woolf insisted was necessary for women's writing to flourish.

Yet our thinking about that room also shifted, moving from the literal sense of a need for space and solitude to the realization that this book could actually proceed amid the constant interruptions and demands of family life, in studies that often doubled as playrooms. Those familial responsibilities, the children's voices always in the background, their insistence and their relentless vitality, provided not only stress but solace. Watching Maya befriend our children, hearing her speak lovingly of her grandson, we were again reminded of how thoroughly these two forms of creativity become intertwined. As Olsen says, motherhood always leaves its marks on writing, but rather than the inevitable dichotomy some critics have posited between mothering and creativity, we found that the two can also nourish each other. If children bring professional anguish, a lack of peace and privacy—and this they do with great regularity—they also bring a kind of shine, an amplitude of energy and spirit that can enrich as well as retard creative work.

Pondering the inescapable contradictions inherent in mothering the child while seeking to mother the mind, we thought too of that other, bleaker side to the room of one's own. As Susan discussed with Adele the psychological and political implications of the cramped space Marya Vladimirovna inhabits with her two sons in "Ladies' Hairdresser," Adele was suddenly struck by how descriptions of Moscow apartments had assumed very different psychological dimensions in Grekova's other works. She recalled "No Smiles" ("Bez ulybok"), a story written in 1970, in which the narrator describes her life in a home now bereft of children.[13] Sitting in Grekova's high-ceilinged, spacious Moscow flat one evening, Adele had asked whether it had served as the prototype for any of the dwellings Grekova describes in her works. "I reared my children here," Grekova replied. "And here we lived throughout the terror. My husband Dmitrii Alexandrovich was a ballistics expert. Like me, he taught at the Zhukovsky Academy. One day at a faculty meeting, during the height of the purges, he said something that was construed as anti-Soviet. From then on, we would sit in this living room late into the night, unable to sleep, listening to the sounds of feet on the stairway. I am still amazed that we survived those years." Now, having outlived both her husband and one of her children, she spends much of her time alone in that space once inhabited by so many.

We had originally planned that our second meeting with Maya and Katya would take place in Moscow, but cascading changes in the Soviet Union forced us to defer that visit. The sense of optimism that had characterized the early days of glasnost and perestroika had now given way to skepticism, frustration, and despair. By the beginning of 1991 the Soviet army had entered Lithuania, coal miners from Vorkuta and the Donbas had gone on strike, and at least six major Soviet republics had voted against the all-Union treaty. With the dismantling of the old centralized economy, no viable alternative in place, and Gorbachev's sometime ally and chief rival Boris Yeltsin mounting a campaign of his own for more radical economic reforms, the Soviet economy rapidly disintegrated. With growing food shortages, transportation slowdowns, and the reluctance of farmers to harvest and deliver crops without higher compensation, people in the cities began experiencing serious privation. Food disappeared from market shelves in Moscow, lines lengthened, and obtaining even the basic staples became a precarious affair. While no one was actually starving, most city dwellers endured months of bare subsistence. Maya and Katya would recall weeks when they could obtain nothing but potatoes and cabbage. This, together with the general disarray of Soviet society, led us to alter our plans. Rather than traveling to Moscow, we would bring Maya and Katya to Tucson.

Even that was no easy matter. In addition to the bureaucratic red tape there were new difficulties with Aeroflot, then the state airline of the USSR and the only carrier most Soviet travelers could use after other national airlines refused to accept payment in rubles. Egregious increases had put airfare beyond the means of most Soviet citizens, but even those few lucky enough to have amassed the necessary funds had to camp out on the floor of Sheremetovo airport for days, waiting for the possibility of purchasing an elusive ticket. Then came the chaos of boarding, the struggle between the officiousness of customs inspectors and the predations of the Mafia rings that regularly looted checked baggage.

It was thus not until 1:00 A.M., a day before their scheduled arrival, that we heard that Katya and Maya had finally managed to lay hold of tickets and were definitely on their way, having endured the usual irritating last-minute humiliations endemic to boarding an Aeroflot flight: leaping over stranded suitcases and their frustrated owners destined for Beirut, into whose line Maya and Katya had been mistakenly deposited by an airport official; elbowing their way through the jumble of passengers waiting for other destinations; dashing across the tarmac to the plane, terrified lest their seats already be taken; hurrying up the stairs and through the door—only to discover that the flight was virtually empty.

Tucson in May sits poised, waiting for summer to begin. It is still possible to linger in the sun in that last month before the fierce heat descends and the dry desert winds begin to blow. For Katya, who had spent many summers in the eastern Crimea, there was something strangely familiar in our climate, and in the desert hills something that felt like home. It was Maya, the native Moscovite, who suffered most as the temperatures soared toward 100 degrees Fahrenheit.

But if the heat proved less than hospitable, the desert landscape did not. Maya and Katya, expecting a topography like the deserts of Turkmenia— naked sand dunes nudging the edges of town and rolling away to the horizon—were enchanted by the wild profusion of the Sonoran desert: mesquite groves, yellow blossoming palo verde trees, and leathery gray-green cacti bursting incongruously with exotic flowers of saffron, magenta, and lilac. Seeing birds, plants, and animals hitherto encountered only in books, Maya delightedly named each one, while Katya recorded them in her small black travel journal.

We had arranged for them to stay in the guest house of the Poetry Center, a small, stuccoed adobe cottage with airy rooms, a shady back ramada, and a desert garden where salvia blooms drew hungry hummingbirds. Recently redecorated, the house had been purchased to replace the original cottage, which had been sacrificed to university expansion two years before. On the kitchen wall of that first dwelling, every major contemporary American poet and many of the best fiction writers of our time had made their marks: poetic graffiti, playful verses tossed off after midnight, humorous testimonials designed to make permanent their author's brief presence there. That memorial wall had been lost along with the rest of the cottage, but some of the spirit of the place lingered on in the house that had succeeded it. There we set up our tape recorders, our portable computers, our pads and pencils, and, every day for a week, met together to work.

Our discussions ranged from shared commentaries on each others' essays to more general concerns: literary theory and critical practice; the pressures of ideology; the problems and possibilities of translation; the intersections of race, ethnicity, and writing; the histories of women in both countries; the relation of gender and genius; the social constructions of sexuality; political censorship and methods of subversion. These topics, at once abstract and intensely concrete, intermingled with moments of personal revelation: discussions of our own experiences as women, of what we have gained and lost as a result both of massive historical upheavals—the revolution, the purges, the civil rights movement, Vietnam—and of the slower changes engendered by various legislative and social reforms in both countries. We spoke, too, of the textures of our everyday lives, of bearing and rearing children, or choosing not to, of aging, sexuality, freedom, power, risk, and loss—all those phenomena that shape life more intricately and ineluctably than events commonly regarded as historically significant.

These issues took on a larger resonance in the context of our discussions of what Russians call *byt*. The Soviet writer Yurii Trifonov has accurately described *byt* (literally, "daily life") as "perhaps the most enigmatic, multidimensional, incomprehensible word in the Russian language." The term signifies the "everyday domestic round"—cleaning, "toiling over the stove, and down to the laundry, and round to the shops"—but it also extends much further, encompassing "a precise context of place and relationships, of family customs and historical associations":

> how husbands and wives get on together, and parents and children, and close and distant relations—that, too. And people being born, and the old men dying, and illnesses, and weddings. . . . And the interrelationships of friends and people at work, love, quarrels, jealousy, envy—all this, too, is *byt*. This is what life consists of! . . . We are all enmeshed in *byt*, in our own network of everyday concerns. . . . We are located in a tangled and complex structure of *byt*, at the intersections of a multiplicity of connections, views, friendships, acquaintances, enmities, psychologies, and ideologies. (102)

What Trifonov does not say here is that while everyone is enmeshed in the network of *byt*, it is women who are expected to hold that network together. In the former Soviet Union as in the West, women, conditioned from birth by the gender ideologies that undergird both the concept and the lived experience of *byt*, still assume primary responsibility for the everyday functioning of life, not only the domestic chores but the entire web of relationships and responsibilities Trifonov describes. If, as he maintains, *byt* is "the great ordeal," the stage on which "morality . . . is manifested and tested," then woman is the matrix—in every sense—of its web. And its primary victim. "A choice has perpetually to be made, something to be decided upon, overcome, sacrificed. You're tired? Never mind—you can rest in another world. In this world *byt* is a war that knows no truce" (102).

Maya: Akhmatova and Tsvetaeva had husbands, had children, whom they nursed, whom they lost. So there were personal feelings they had as women, but I don't think it made a great difference to their writing, even to Tsvetaeva, who hated *byt*—who felt she had this burden more than anyone else in the family. She tried to avoid it, yet in her writing it was *byt* that was the obstacle, not her female role.

Susan: Why should she have had more responsibility for *byt* than anyone else? Isn't that because of "her female role" as her culture defined it?

Maya: Well, we can say that she was burdened with all these responsibilities. She hated *byt,* she felt it to be an obstacle to her creative freedom, but I don't think she felt there was some specific woman's role. It was natural for her, somehow. She hated it, but not as part of a woman's fate. Also Akhmatova suffered, but mainly from social developments.

Susan: From the imprisonment of her son?

Maya: Yes, and her loss of her husband. But the man would have suffered too if she had been assassinated.

Katya: But he would never have been called a "whore." This attitude is typical of reactions to woman's writing.[14]

Susan: And what about the idea that for women to take primary responsibility for domestic matters is somehow "natural"—that loaded term used so often throughout our history to justify the oppression of one group by another?

Throughout our entire project we remained acutely aware of the tenuousness of our undertaking, of the ever-shifting ground on which we stood. This sense of ephemerality had a particularly forceful effect on our discussions of censorship, which revealed differences between Maya and Katya that were often more profound than those between their perspectives and ours. Toward the end of their visit, we asked them to what degree censorship still influenced their lives. Maya answered that while no one can be wholly free in a totalitarian state, she remained convinced that whatever decisions she made were ultimately her responsibility. She felt that she had always transcended political pressures and repression, even when these were a way of life in her country. Katya disagreed, arguing that while external strictures had indeed dramatically decreased, Soviet citizens still maintained deeply ingrained habits of self-censorship, internalized constraints produced by long exposure to repression and practiced for decades as a necessary means of survival. So insidious and pervasive were these acculturated responses that they were virtually beyond eradication. Indeed, in many cases, repression had operated for so long that its mechanisms eluded conscious awareness altogether. Some of the sharpest debates between Maya and Katya revolved around this issue, especially with reference to questions of gender.

Katya: A year or two ago, we had a meeting with a delegation of American women, fifteen or so, from a women's association: some black, some white—even one from South Africa—and one Native American. We openly discussed our problems as women, since we were only women there. One of them complained about how awful her child-bearing was; another said we shouldn't deal with feminism, we should just live according to our own convictions, and not impose our intentions on others, on men. Just try to live our inner lives, not try to change things immediately or by force.

Susan: Is that what you've been saying, Maya?

Maya: No—you *can* oppose things, but as far as power or dominance is concerned, to be free a person should be free of power, too, free of private property, like Thoreau. I think all this strife for power is another way of enslaving oneself. It's the everyday choices you make: you either conform to the demands of society or you don't. You write your books, either following your own ideas, or you take the ideas that are conventional for society. As a physician, you treat everyone, like Chekhov, or you have an office only in the richest area of town, and build your career thus. I'm not so much bothered by the power problem. Maybe I'm wrong, but I think to be free is the most important. But then, there are as many ideas of freedom as there are people.

Katya: Obviously I too think that we should not seek power. But I don't think that living by one's own inner life would be enough, because there are those that are weak and can't oppose oppression, and we should help them—children, young girls, young women. We shouldn't just find shelter in our inner world; we should struggle to change things. But it depends on the means of the struggle. Perhaps it shouldn't be direct but oblique. Your struggle may even be your own behavior. You live as an example for someone, and that is your struggle. If I had to choose, I would choose mainly this.

Adele: I guess that sometimes, among both men and women, the struggle for power, to find one's place, to get what we think is ours is seen as a struggle against outside forces, but often that desire for power reflects something deep within us. In my own life the hardest thing has been to see what it is in myself that leads me sometimes to want power, because I think that having that kind of power takes us away from ourselves. We may gain in the outside world, but lose a tremendous amount within. Sometimes I think that generally, as we try to gain power that we believe should be ours, run businesses, become heads of departments or corporations—all those things that men have been—we also pay a price for it. Maybe if this were a better world, we could get power without the price. But maybe when we find out what it's like to get power, we may turn back.

Susan: You're bringing up an important and difficult point. Ironically, women who rise to power in male-dominated systems may well have had to internalize the values of those systems in order to do so. On the one hand, what's needed to change the dominant orientation of the system is more women in positions of influence. Yet there's a danger for women who enter positions of power in hierarchically structured institutions that are still primarily controlled by men and biased toward their interests. The risk is that in becoming a part of any institutional system, instead of changing it, we may become coopted by it, since its well-being demonstrably affects our own, both professionally and personally.

Katya: In our society this problem of power—or changes that take place in a person who attains power—may apply not only to women but to the intelligentsia as a whole. Some people who have never had power are rapidly acquiring it, and demonstrate the same ways of thinking and acting as their recent opponents. There is something in the very nature of power that corrupts a person.

Susan: As many social commentators have said. That's one reason some contemporary theorists have argued that the qualities traditionally thought of as feminine—nurturing, intuitiveness, sensitivity, openness—may be part of the mentality produced when one is socialized as a member of a subordinated group. Alternatively, it's worth noting that members of subordinated groups are often routinely feminized by dominant groups—a sad commentary on how gender codes may permeate even those social interactions where gender is presumably not operative. In both cases, you see assumptions driven by certain essentialist and oppositional definitions of what constitutes masculinity and femininity.

After a week of work, interrupted long enough for trips into the mountains and the grasslands of Patagonia, we saw Katya off at the airport, on her way to the University of Mississippi for another literary conference. Maya stayed on for a few days longer, becoming increasingly absorbed into the routines of our family lives. Sitting at the kitchen table, she and Adele worked on translations, arguing semantic nuances, making suggestions, throwing them out. Driving back and forth to buy presents for her family, Maya and Susan discussed the history of women writers in both countries and the vagaries of critical theory. Through it all, our intellectual discussions were often precipitously interrupted by the demands of *byt*—searching for a child's lost shoe, debating the proper way to dress a salad or to catch the lizard that had invaded Maya's bedroom.

Maya was alternately appalled by the superficiality of American half-hour news programs, the excesses of shopping malls and billboards, and the swelling numbers of homeless people seeking aid on street corners, and quizzically delighted by distinctively American phenomena—iced tea, the Olympic-sized pool in the university recreation center, clerks who said "please" and "thank you," and the ubiquitous restaurant doggie bags that gradually accumulated in her refrigerator. Like Katya, she was intrigued by the mix of peoples who make up the Tucson community—Native Americans, Mexican Americans, Anglos, Blacks, Asians—and by the richly interwoven texture of the culture they had created.

Just after dawn on 15 May, we stood in the parking lot near the empty university stadium, waiting to put Maya on the airline transport van to Phoenix. She would travel to other conferences—first to the University of California at Riverside, from there to Nashville and Durham, North Carolina, and finally to Washington, D.C. As we saw her off, we remembered standing at the airport security checkpoint the week before as Katya, shouldering her luggage, disappeared down the corridor, gradually absorbed into the throng of other passengers. That Soviet citizens had finally earned the right to mingle freely with American travelers seemed to us then, as now, a sign of how far glasnost and perestroika had come since 1985.

When Katya and Maya left Tucson at the end of May, we scarcely imagined what lay ahead for the Soviet Union in August. Instead, we grieved over personal losses—Adele's mother died in July—and over Adele's imminent move to the University of Washington in Seattle, which would take her far from the world that had bound us and our friendship so solidly together over the years since we began our joint work. By the beginning of August, *Dialogues* sat in packing boxes labeled "STUDY," and we came to realize that our own personal dialogues were acquiring the same long-distance dimensions as those with Maya and Katya.

On the morning of 19 August, we were each in separate cities. Katya and her husband Volodya were tying up loose ends in Moscow as they prepared to leave for their summer holiday in Kiev. Maya was in Perm, in Central Russia, staying with her grandson in the home of friends. Adele's possessions had arrived in Seattle without her, since she and her son Noah had remained for a month in West Virginia with her father. Susan was in Tucson preparing for the start of the fall semester.

When the news hit—the putsch, Gorbachev's arrest, Yanaev's pronouncements at the press conference—we waited out the events like millions of others and confronted the real possibility that the reforms that had made this book possible could, in a moment, be rescinded.

Maya: I was there in Perm, alone in the house of my friend for the whole day, and I turned on the radio and couldn't understand anything, just anything at all.

Adele: What do you mean?

Maya: Well, you know there are certain programs that are on at certain times and suddenly they were not on, yet there was nothing special that replaced them. So I thought there might be something amiss, but I didn't think it might be so serious. I thought there might be some disruption on the local radio station.

Adele: But in the past, when leaders die, there is also an interruption of scheduled programs with somber classical music.

Maya: There was some classical music.

Adele: Did you think that someone had died?

Maya: No, I didn't, because the music was not so very sad. They played Tchaikovsky's adaptations of folk music, but not his *Pathétique* or something from Chopin.

Susan: Did you have any suspicion that the coup was about to happen?

Maya: No, no, nothing. Well, for half a year there had been rumors, so everyone was talking about it, but there was nothing specific.

Susan: Yes, I remember last May when you and Katya said that you were afraid the hard-liners might ally themselves with the military to overthrow Gorbachev.

Maya: Yes, but you expect when something like this happens it will take some sort of grim, sordid aspect from the beginning. But nothing of the sort happened.

At 6:30 on the morning of the nineteenth, Katya and Volodya were awakened by a call from Volodya's aunt: "Something is wrong. Switch on your radio. Gorbachev is out. There is a coup." Katya had an appointment at the Gorky Institute that morning and, partially against her better judgment, set out to keep it. Her trip took her to the center of Moscow, where the apparent normality of her own neighborhood gave way to a scene of tanks slowly moving down the street, away from the Parliament building.

Katya: And the first thing that frustrated and astonished me were the people on the bus. All of them immediately started speaking in low voices—they whispered. They had been trained by years of experience, so now they stopped discussing things with people they didn't know and only talked in hushed tones between themselves. Fortunately the situation would change in a few hours, but at this moment I was deeply shocked by such an immediate return to the old way, and I began to cry.

On 22 August Mikhail Gorbachev returned to Moscow, a leader no longer in control of the party, his power now dwarfed inexorably by Yeltsin's. If the failure of the coup was greeted with a collective sigh of relief in the West, for Katya and Maya and many others the events it set in motion have had an insidious and long-term effect, far beyond the mere fact of food shortages. As their society sheds its former structures while being yet unable to accommodate itself to new ones, much that once provided Soviet citizens with a secure and predictable existence is simply no longer there. There are no certainties, no givens anymore.

These changes have particular ramifications for writers and critics.

Maya: For me, one noticeable change has been my relationship with the publishing houses. I had some commissioned translations that were ready to be published. Now I bring these manuscripts to the publisher who had invited them, and no one wants to speak about them. They say, "Oh, all right, we will inform you when we decide. We have no money, we have no paper; probably your editor will leave the publishing house," and so on and so forth.

Katya: Yes, it's a difficult situation. I am free in my writing now; it has been so since glasnost. Before, I never wrote what I didn't want to write, but there were some things I *couldn't* write. It can sound paradoxical, but maybe now it is even worse because I can write what I want, but I can't publish it. I am now starting my second book but am not at all sure that it will ever be published. And about my traveling, things turned worse as well. A year ago I could travel, for I could afford it, but now tickets to the United States cost ninety-eight thousand rubles, to Paris forty-eight thousand, and so on—and I get no more than six hundred rubles a month for salary. There is more freedom but no means. What oppresses me most of all is my own personal feeling of instability. I am not sure anymore about the fate of my institute, my department, myself. For half a year now I do not even know exactly how much money I earn.

Susan: Do you have a contract?

Maya: No, nothing. And lately the sum we receive has varied every month.

Katya: My family felt ourselves members of what the Americans call the middle class, so we lived decently by our standards. Now I think that this is questionable. In spite of the fact that my husband and I work at the Academy of Sciences, I feel we will be on a lower rung of society than we used to be and than many younger people going in for business will be. But I hope that there will not be a full catastrophe, for if I lose my job so will others, and if I am not able to buy food, this means that 80 or 90 percent of the population will be in the same situation. If this many people are in the streets hungry, the situation won't last a week.

You know, all we want is to live a decent life. We are not ambitious; we don't want fancy cars or dachas or lavish possessions. We live very modestly by American standards. But we would like to maintain the way of life we have been used to. And frankly, I have to say that this year I have almost lost that hope.

These conversations took place during our final meeting in April 1992. Given the instability and economic crisis in Russia, it was sheer good fortune that the meeting could be arranged at all. As it happened, Maya received a Fulbright fellowship that spring to teach at the Center for Southern Studies at Mississippi, and Katya was awarded a Newberry Library Fellowship to do research in Chicago. Thus we four were able to spend a week together in Seattle, where Adele was now on the faculty of the University of Washington. By then, keenly aware that our joint work was nearing its conclusion, all of us felt a certain poignancy, ironically intensified by the flamboyant signs of spring all around us—the streets lined with flowering cherry, dogwood, and azalea, the yards overgrown with tulips, hyacinths, and daffodils, the moist air heavy with fragrance. We did not dwell on the probability that this might be our last meeting for a long time. Instead, we compared notes on our ideas over the last year, speculated about political developments in both our countries, debated critical perspectives, edited each other's essays, worked on translations, made meals for each other, took a round-trip ferry across Puget Sound, and laughed a lot. One night, over dinner in a waterfront tavern, we made plans for a trip to Moscow in the fall, after the book was completed, to draft an updated conclusion about a situation so volatile now that no one dared predict its future directions.

Repeatedly, our conversations turned to the implications of all these issues for our own lives. Pondering the personal changes we had experienced in the course of our collaborations—the new levels of comprehension and communication, the permanently altered perspectives—the four of us returned again and again to the far more massive changes that have swept through the former Soviet Union since we began this book. Our dialogues have spanned the period of the most rapid and radical social transformations to transpire there since the revolution. We have witnessed the best Gorbachev's reforms had to offer, as well as the complete dismantling of the USSR, and we have felt at every turn the fragility of our connection.

Much of our conversation focused on the persistence of the old guard, the tenacity of figureheads who pay lip service to reform only in order to reconsolidate the power they had amassed under the old regime. That topic led to the larger questions of power and to discussions of the intransigence of institutions and the difficulty of effecting real, lasting, and fruitful transformations in any society. For Katya and Maya, this phenomenon undermines the effects of any change that might be heralded by the movement toward a new social or economic order. Finally, the new technology, the new economy, and the new political and social structures remain all too often in the hands of those who have opposed reform from the start. But even if they did not, even if the changes now underway could be guaranteed eventually to produce a better society, that hope cannot diminish the immediate agonies of the transition. And, of course, there is no such guarantee.

None of us at this point can hazard predictions of what the next years may bring in a country that no longer even has a stable name. But for us, at least, there can be no reversal of these dialogues. Pondering the changes that our countries and our lives have undergone, we have been reminded repeatedly of the need to abandon the security of single perspectives, to risk unsettling mobility, to shuttle between apparently contradictory positions— literally to inhabit (at least) two places at once.

On our last day in Seattle, Maya was the first to leave. As she and Adele pulled out of the driveway for the airport and we caught a final glimpse of each other's faces through the fogged windows of the truck, we thought how far we'd come together. We could never have envisioned, as we began our initial discussions that July day in 1988, what fruit Gorbachev's reforms would bear in the next four years. By historical coincidence, our project spanned the dissolution of the Soviet Union. In that volatile context, our meetings took us far beyond the literary topics that initiated them. As catalysts for wide-ranging political discussions and mutual, deeply personal insights, our encounters, begun as academic exchanges, concluded as friendships. Retrospectively, our dialogues seem a lens, one part of a larger, multifaceted and shifting prism, in which individual reflections both focus and embody events of historic magnitude.

Notes

1. Interestingly enough, I. Grekova would later write an article for the Soviet paper *Literaturnaia gazeta* (19 June 1991, 10) in defense of Solzhenitsyn. Grekova acknowledges the weakness of Solzhenitsyn's depiction of women, who generally function only to illuminate the male protagonist.

2. The word *glasnost* (openness) first gained currency in nineteenth-century Russia under the tsars, when its proponents advocated that decisions affecting the lives of the people be arrived at publicly. The concept of more openness in Soviet society has come about gradually since the 1960s, often affecting specific areas of Soviet life before Gorbachev promoted it for society as a whole. Under Brezhnev, scientists were finally freed from the crippling effects of Lysenkoism, a bogus form of genetics named after the Soviet agronomist supported by both Stalin and Khrushchev.

According to Richard Pipes, however, the application of glasnost to society at large has surprised many Sovietologists. "It had been generally thought that major economic reforms were unavoidable, and that they would be accompanied by some liberalization of the political system. But the experts were convinced that the 'sur-reality' the regime had placed on the population since 1917 would be kept in place because the lies of which it was woven were essential to the regime's survival. The founders of the Soviet state knew that once the citizens were permitted to raise questions, they would be unlikely to keep within prescribed limits. In retrospect, it appears that the experts did not make adequate allowance either for the disastrous state of the Soviet system or for the political exigencies of perestroika. In order to justify the contemplated changes, which faced entrenched opposition, the govern-ment had to tell the population the truth about the country's condition. For if the Soviet Union was indeed the most progressive and prosperous country in the world, as Soviet propaganda has been claiming for decades, why change?" (1989, *National Review* 41.10: 42).

3. Several days before the Writers' Congress opened in late June 1986, Gor-bachev called a meeting at the Kremlin of about thirty writers and editors to tell them that he needed their help in creating more openness: "We have no opposition [party]. How then are we going to control ourselves? Only through criticism and self-criticism; but most importantly through glasnost. No society can exist without glasnost." Thus, when Andrei Voznesensky took the platform at the Writers' Congress, it was obvious that his daring proposals had official sanction (see Garrard and Garrard 203–8).

4. In the 1970s and especially the early 1980s, a large number of bilateral sym-posia on topics in the social sciences were organized by the USSR Academy of Sciences and its counterpart organizations, such as IREX, in other countries. Some of these resulted in volumes or special journal issues. In legal studies there were also sev-eral collaborative volumes; see, for example, Butler and Kudriavtsev. Since glasnost, other works have appeared in the sciences and social sciences which draw heavily on Soviet sources but are not actually collaborative; see, for example, Cohen and Vanden Heuvel; and Edberg and Yablokov. A year after we began work on this book, *Cana-dian Woman Studies/Les cahiers de la femme* published a special issue on "Soviet Women," with literature and criticism by both Western and Soviet women, but the format was only implicitly dialogical. In 1990, a group of American and Soviet schol-ars began plans for a joint collection of essays, tentatively entitled *Culture/Kul'tura: Soviet and American Dialogues on Literature and Culture*, ed. Chances, Elliot, and Maguire, forthcoming from Duke University Press. And in 1992, The University Press of Mississippi, in conjunction with the Gorky Institute of World Literature, published *Russian Eyes on American Literature*, ed. Chakovsky and Inge.

5. In the early days of literary ferment following the 1917 revolution, Freud was widely studied in the Soviet Union, though Lenin pronounced his works "complete nonsense." Indeed, many prominent Soviet psychologists and psychiatrists, including A. R. Luria, I. P. Pavlov, and K. N. Kornilov, pursued Freud's ideas in studies on per-sonality development and the role of the unconscious. But by the early 1930s, Freud's works, though they continued to be published, were denounced as idealistic, bour-

geois, and reactionary. As psychoanalysis of all sorts came to be actively discouraged, attempts to use psychoanalytic methods of treatment met with repressive measures. Perhaps the most famous of these cases was that of Professor I. S. Sumbayev, punished by the authorities for using psychoanalysis to treat homosexual patients. Although the Soviet Union was not unique in banning Freud in the thirties (in Germany in 1933, Goebbels also committed Freud's work to the flames "in the name of the nobility of the human spirit"), Freud was anathema to the leaders of the Soviet state because his theories of the unconscious and the role of the irrational in human behavior threatened their exaltation of the triumph of reason and human perfectability. Since Stalin's death in 1953 the reception of Freud in the USSR has undergone numerous permutations; a partial revival of research in the mid-fifties was followed by another period of condemnation and suppression as Freud continued to be viewed as representative of all that was most pernicious in bourgeois Western culture. And even when Freud again became a permissible subject of study in the mid-fifties, access to his work was all but impossible. Mark Popovskii, in his study of sex in the Soviet Union, recalls going to the Lenin Library in Moscow to do research on Freud for a biography about famous figures in medicine. Denied permission to the books, he went to the assistant director of the library, "a glum looking woman," who also refused his request, declaring that since Freud was not one of "the heroes of medicine," Popovskii could not possibly need to read him. Thus Popovskii was unable to gain access to Freud until after emigrating to the West (Popovskii 15). Only in recent years have Freud's works begun to be reissued; see his *Vvedenie v psikhoanaliz* (*Introduction to Psychoanalysis*), 1989; *Izbrannoe* (*Selected Works*), 1989; and *Ostroumie i ego otnoshenie k bessoznatel'nomu* (*Wit [Humor] and Its Relation to the Unconscious*), 1991. Apart from Freud, selected works by Eric Fromm are available, and those of Adler are likely to appear soon. For more information on the resurgence of psychoanalysis in the former Soviet Union see Rancour-Laferriere 1991. Our thanks to him for much of this background information.

6. The theoretical work on the inherent male bias of such so-called generic terms as "man" and "he" as substitutes for "humanity" or "human being" is too extensive to document here, but see, for example, Spender.

7. Russian historians are increasingly coming to link the notion of Russian national consciousness with imperial consciousness, a phenomenon which has its origins in pre-Petrine Russia. According to Evgenii Anisimov, a senior researcher at the Institute of the History of the USSR Academy of Sciences, there are certain key beliefs which have governed this notion of imperial consciousness: "the inalienable right of Russia to meddle in the affairs of its neighbors; the idea of a 'great enemy' of the empire; the pan-Slavic ideal of uniting all Slavic peoples under Russian leadership; the conviction that the various lands of the empire had voluntarily 'chosen' to join it; the complex of Russian national superiority and colonial ingratitude; the notion of the Russian army as a civilizing, enlightening force; the patriarchal stereotype of the state; the stereotype of the Russian people as being without sin; and a centralized hierarchical world view with Moscow at its center" (Anisimov, n. pag.).

8. Glasnost has given Soviet critics an opportunity to complain openly about the appallingly low level of literary criticism in their country; see Ivanova 1988a and 1988b.

9. On the question of essentializing gender, see, among many examples, Kamuf; Miller 1982; Kristeva 1981; Jardine; and Fuss. On alternative ways of reading, see Showalter 1981; Fetterley; and Flynn and Schweikart.

10. In the early days of the Bolshevik state, when censors were appointed as political favors or in reward for military service, critical sophistication was not a criterion for the position. Unfortunately for Soviet writers, over the years the censors became considerably more astute, and by the 1960s it became far more difficult to get around them until the demise of censorship. Soviet writers often chastised American critics for making the job of the Soviet censor easier by emphasizing the political context of subversive writings.

11. Faulkner was first translated into Russian in 1934, when "That Evening Sun" appeared in a Soviet anthology of American short stories. Subsequently, as a result of the purge trials in the USSR and the rise of fascism in Europe, Faulkner, like many other writers (foreign as well as Soviet), "disappeared completely from Soviet publications" because "those who made Soviet literary politics regarded only those writers who shared their ideological bias" as "suitable" for publication. By the late 1940s Faulkner's *Intruder in the Dust,* as well as Eugene O'Neill's *The Iceman Cometh,* "were denounced by the Soviet literary establishment as the embodiment of all that was negative, decadent, perverted, and antihumanistic in contemporary American literature" (Koreneva). Even when Faulkner's works began to be published anew in Russian in the late 1950s, some critics still denounced his novels as "repulsive" in content and "difficult" stylistically. Most Soviet critics regarded his reputation in America as "inordinately inflated" (Kashkin 177). Ironically, while Faulkner has been regularly denigrated even in the best of times in the Soviet Union, he has had an undeniable influence on writers from the former USSR, particularly Fazil Iskander, Chingiz Aitmatov, and Anatolii Ananyev.

12. VAAP (All-Union Association of Authors' Rights, the official Soviet copyright agency) was established in 1973 to collect royalties for authors within the USSR and to try to control the flow of manuscripts abroad. Under Soviet law contracts by Soviet authors with foreign publishers were invalid if not made through VAAP. However, foreign countries never recognized this rule, which violated their ideas of authors' rights and freedom of the press. Beginning in January 1991, VAAP was transformed into the USSR State Agency on Copyright and Related Rights. Much of this reorganization resulted because VAAP had long been the target of criticism from its own authors for carrying out many functions inappropriate for a copyright agency, such as collecting taxes and witholding royalties from the authors. Under the new organization authors now have independent control of their own copyrights and can assign them to whatever agency they wish. Thus the authors themselves will have the option of asking either VAAP, the publishing houses, or other authorized agencies to act on their behalf. For more on the reorganization see Ivanov.

13. "No Smiles" ("Bez ulybok") was written shortly after the prolonged period of

chastisement (*prorabotka*) to which Grekova was subjected at her institute for having written a work critical of the Red Army (*Na ispytaniiakh* [*On Maneuvers*], 1967). In it the narrator describes coming home to her apartment alone every night, drawing strength from the writings of Russia's nineteenth-century political dissidents.

14. Katya is referring to a well-known statement by Stalin's cultural chief, Andrei Zhdanov, who accused Akhmatova of being "half nun, half whore, writing poetry in which she flitted indiscriminately between the chapel and the bedroom." Zhdanov was making perverse use of images from a famous essay on Akhmatova by Boris Eikhenbaum (1923), who praised the poet for "not using metaphor yet going outside the boundaries of everyday language" by employing the rhetoric of church and biblical traditions." Thus the image of the heroine is not just the passionate whore, not just the poor nun who prays to God for forgiveness, but the paradox of the doubleness of them, and, more specifically, their oxymoron (Eikhenbaum 429–30).

1

I. Grekova

❖ ❖ ❖ ❖

Tillie Olsen

I. GREKOVA ❖ Born Elena Sergeevna Dolgintseva in 1907 in Revel' (now Tallin) into a family of prerevolutionary intelligentsia, the woman who would later adopt the pen name I. Grekova followed her father's example and became a mathematician, graduating from the University of Leningrad in 1929. In 1930 she married D. A. Ventsel, a ballistics expert, and together they taught at the Zhukovsky Military Aviation Academy in Moscow until his death in 1955. They had three children. Asked how she has been able to combine motherhood with her professional life, she responded, "I haven't. Something always suffers. In my case, it has been my children" (1981).

The author of numerous textbooks on probability theory, Grekova became one of the few women in the Soviet Union to earn the prestigious *doktorat* degree. She began her career as a fiction writer in 1960, crafting the feminine pseudonym I. Grekova from the sign that stands for the mathematical symbol "Y"—literally, in Russian, "an unknown quantity." She continued to teach at the Zhukovsky Academy until 1967, when, because of the furor caused by her story "On Maneuvers" ("Na ispytaniiakh"), a scathing portrait of the Red Army, she resigned her research position. She has authored numerous short stories and novels, which have appeared in the collections *Pod fonarem* (*Under the Street Lamp*, 1966), *Kafedra* (*The Department*, 1983), *Porogi* (*Thresholds*, 1985), and *Na ispytaniiakh* (*On Maneuvers*, 1990). Widely recognized as the originator and grande dame of contemporary Russian women's fiction, Grekova now lives and writes in Moscow.

Ladies' Hairdresser

I. GREKOVA

I came home from work dog tired. The boys were playing chess—what else is new! It's some sort of peculiarly male disease.

"What the hell is this?" I said, "That stupid chess game again! How long this time?"

On the table there was the usual mess—an ashtray full to overflowing with cigarette butts, beer bottles in which oversize bubbles slowly swelled and burst.

"Regular pigs in a sty!" I said, "Don't you have anything better to do, with your exams starting tomorrow?!"

"Let's have a paw," Kostya said ingratiatingly.

"No paw for you. Pigs, that's all you are. I may as well be coming home to a public tavern. Couldn't even empty one ashtray after yourselves! Do I, an older woman, really. . ."

"Objection!" said Kolya.

"Cut the crap!" I shouted.

"Paw!" Kolya demanded.

I shouldn't have smiled, but my lips somehow started to part, and I gave him my hand.

"Not that one!" Kolya yelled like one possessed, "The left one, the left one!"

(The left one is prized more highly because of the birthmark on it.)

"The right one's just fine for us commoners," Kostya said.

I gave him the right one. Each kissed his respective hand. Two lowered heads, one yellow as straw, the other black as coal. My little fools, my sons. But don't think you got off the hook that easily. I'm still angry.

"Clear off the table this instant!" I shouted, trying to stand my ground.

Kostya, groaning, loaded the ashtray onto his shoulders while Kolya started wiping off the table with someone's trousers.

I was as hungry as a horse.

"Have you eaten?"

"No. We were waiting for you."

"Is there anything in the house?"

"No. We'll run and get something now."

"Some hell of a reception!" I said, working myself into a rage. "Do I really . . ."

"Do you, *an older woman*, really . . ." Kolya prompted helpfully.

"That's right, damn it! An older woman!" I yelled. "A working woman! A woman trying to raise you two fools!"

"Note with only limited success," Kolya interjected softly.

"Yeah, unfortunately—with limited success! My whole life's shot to hell and I have nothing to show for it!"

"Take it easy, girl" said Kostya, playing the peacemaker.

I grabbed a bottle and wanted to throw it on the floor, but didn't do it.

"I've had enough of this roadhouse! I'm leaving. You can live by yourselves."

"Live and let live," Kostya advised in that same quiet, even voice of his.

"Enough of your idiotic observations! I'm dead serious—life isn't a circus!"

"What was that?" Kostya asked, "Life isn't a circus? Permit me to write that one down!"

He took out a notebook, licked the point of his pencil and took aim.

"You know . . . life . . . isn't . . . a circus," he wrote down.

"What's more," I broke in loudly, "I'm sick and tired of all this! Sick and tired! Got it? I'm going to Novosibirsk. No—better yet, I'll get married!"

"Aah—that's a good one!"

"What's that supposed to mean—you think I can't marry anyone at my age?"

"Only a lion tamer," Kolya said.

To hell with it!

I went into the kitchen, slamming the door behind me.

Even a glass of milk would do . . . I opened the refrigerator. It was empty and dirty, with one solitary withered radish on the second shelf. More like a crypt than a refrigerator. No milk in sight, naturally. There was some this morning . . . "Down the hatch," the kids' wet nurse used to say.

I've had enough of this, I thought, combing my hair and angrily tearing out whole clumps. Those two idiots can't even take care of themselves, to say nothing of their mother. . . . "Let's have a paw"—what nonsense! They lie around stuffing themselves while their mother goes hungry. I'm sick and tired of it. . . . And my stupid, neglected hair, half-grown-out and all over the place. So many gray hairs coming in, all in ridiculous places, like behind my ears—not the way to go gray with dignity, at the temples. Stupid—I can't even do that properly. And those home-cut bangs! Stupid old woman—

you rolled them on curlers yourself. Now I can't sleep with them, it hurts too much.

I'm not cooking dinner for them any more. Let them fend for themselves . . .

But I've got to do something with this hair. Get it cut, maybe? It'd be too bad—I've spent years growing it out, all that work down the drain. . . . No, enough. I'll get it cut. "I'll get a haircut and get started" my father always used to say. My father lived a troubled life, wanted to "get started" right up to the very end. "Get a haircut and get started . . ."

"I'm going out," I said to the boys.

"Where?" Kostya asked.

"To get married," Kolya answered.

1

Still, it was lovely outside—everything was covered with fresh raindrops, and the newborn leaves of the linden trees were bright, lacquered. A street cleaning truck made its way down the street—for some reason watering the already wet asphalt—a rainbow sparkling in its mist. I bought an ice cream and as I walked took small bites from the hard candy rose that decorated its top. My teeth ached slightly, but I enjoyed eating on the go like this. Like when I was in school.

My legs are still sprightly, the spring day's not over yet, people walking, hurrying places, lots of pretty faces—I'll get a haircut and get started.

And here's a hair salon. In the enormous window display, photographs of girls three times larger than life, each one taking great pains to preserve her hairdo. The sign reads: "All styles, no appointment necessary. First come, first served."

Now or never. I opened the tall, heavy door with the word "PULL" written vertically on it. Inside it smelled of cheap perfume, burnt hairs and something else disagreeable. There were about two dozen women standing and sitting around.

God, what a line! Maybe I should leave? No—I've made up my mind, I'll stick it out.

"Who's last?" I asked.

Several heads turned toward me without answering.

"Would you be so kind as to tell me who's last?"

"There are no last ones here," joked a dark, Southern-looking woman with a big front tooth.

"You're looking for the end of the line, dear?" an older woman in light blue socks with a gray mop on her head asked me. "I thought the last person was in the place behind me, but she seems to have left."

Her red, overworked hands lay heavily between her knees.

"Then I'll be behind you if it's all right. What do you think, comrades, how long will it be?"

"About two hours at the worst," the older woman answered.

The others were silent. One of them, an imposing woman with bleached hair, rotated her swan-like neck in my direction, looked me over with piercing blue eyes, and turned away.

I'm not a particularly shy person, but for some reason I'm shy around women. Especially when there are a lot of them and they're all involved in some kind of peculiarly female ritual. It always seems to me that they should be judging me. For what? For whatever—for my respectable age (she's here to make herself beautiful, too!), for my glasses, for the English book visible in my net shopping bag. In this particular group I immediately gravitated toward the older woman with the socks. It was obvious that she had also noticed me. Two grandmothers. She moved over on her chair to make room for me.

"Have a seat, why don't you? Standing there won't get you anywhere, as they say."

I perched myself carefully on the edge of the chair.

"Don't worry, go ahead and sit on your whole bottom. We'll both fit; all the juice has gone out of mine, anyway."

We both sat down.

"I want to have a six-month perm done, a firm curl," she told me. "I'm afraid my husband won't go for it. Lately he's started paying visits to a younger woman."

"Do you have any children?"

"Sons, two of them."

"Same here."

"And does your husband fool around?"

"I don't have one."

She fell silent.

"Everyone's got their problems," she said, having given the matter some thought. "Mine fools around, but at least he doesn't drink, and you don't have one at all. Well, don't you give up. Keep your hopes up. You're not all that old, you've still got some meat on your bones."

"I'm not giving up," I told her.

"Next!" a fattish man in a white labcoat and bright green tie shouted through the doorway.

The dark woman with the tooth jumped up and darted forward.

All the women started yelling:

"It's not her turn!"

"Don't take her!"

"I'm here for a firm curl," she hurled back, trying to defend herself.

"Just like everyone else!"

"I'm here for the same!" I squeaked.

"It says out there 'all styles' . . ."

"It also says 'first come, first served'! Were you here first?"

The line was shouting and agitated.

"Don't make a scene, lady," the fat one said. "We'll be sure to get to every single one of you."

The dark woman slipped into the salon. The racket continued.

"He's sleeping with her," the bleached one with the swan's neck said.

"So what if he is? A line's a line. Who cares who's sleeping with whom? . . ."

"We'll demand the complaints book . . ."

"Where's the manager?"

"Get the manager out here!"

A graying elderly lady sitting behind the counter of the coat room took up her knitting. A redhead in a blinding white labcoat sitting in the cashier's booth yawned, took out a small mirror and, frowning, began layering on mascara.

The mascara did it. My shyness evaporated instantly. I went up to the cashier's booth.

"The complaints book, please."

She gave me a hostile look. "Whadd'ya need the complaints book for?"

"None of your business. A patron has the right to ask for the complaints book at any time."

The line began to rumble, but this time it was directed at me.

"Didn't take *her* long . . ."

"One person out of turn and she goes for the complaints book . . ."

"She writes a complaint and someone else catches it . . ."

"She should understand herself, people are trying to make a living here . . ."

There's no love lost on complainers around here. But the fat was already in the fire.

"Ma'am," I said in a police officer's voice, "if you don't hand over the complaints book this instant . . ."

"I'll get the manager for you," the woman said, leaving the booth.

A moment later a hulk with black, curly hair who looked like he belonged in a butcher shop appeared. "Whadd'ya need, lady?"

I explained to him that they'd just taken someone out of turn. I gestured toward my witnesses, who remained silent. He heard me out without reacting then called back toward the salon, in the same way people call their dogs, "Rosa!"

A pockmarked woman wearing a muslin turban came out.

"Take this lady next, Rosa."

"Very well, Ruslan Petrovich."

"That's not why I came up here! You think I wanted to get in first?" I said, getting upset.

Ruslan turned and left the room.

"Rosa," I said, turning toward her, "please. This has nothing to do with me. I just want things to be orderly."

"It's you thoughtless people who cause the disorder around here yourselves," said Rosa, also leaving the room.

I returned to my place in line. The women were silent. Even the older one in the socks was planted firmly on her chair and didn't move over.

Fine . . .

Still a long wait. My thoughts wandered as I stood leaning against the cool, glossy surface of the wall.

. . . Still, it might be nice to move to Novosibirsk. I could get a one-bedroom apartment, or, even better, a room in the hotel where I stayed the last time I was there. . . . It's such a sweet and quirky little place, all different colors, green here, pink there. . . . Forest all around, dense, green grass up to my neck. Birds singing everywhere, sidewalks full of mathematicians, physicists, people wearing glasses, people with beards, young people, happy people. . . .

. . . And maybe it would be nice to surprise them all, to marry my old friend from school and move to his place in Evpatoriia. He's loved me his whole life, loves me to this very day, I know it. He's already over the hill—but how much older than I can he be? Ten years? As the saying goes, anyone ten years your senior is over the hill. But why not? Why not up and marry him? Let them learn to take care of themselves. And what about work? I'll find something easier. Or, I'll just live without working. Take swims in the ocean, plant flowers in the garden, raise chickens. . . . And what about it? There'll be plenty of washing, I'll hang out the laundry to dry in our sunny pebbled courtyard. . . . Soapy hands, hair all wet and mussed up, I'll brush it out of my face with my elbow. . . . Then he'll come up and touch me on the shoulder: "Are you tired, dear? Take a break, honey." "No, I'm just fine." What raving nonsense!

"Who wants to be next?" a shrill, boyish voice rang out.

I came down to earth.

"It's too early to call me an artist, but if I go on in this field I hope to become one."

"Thank you, thank you very much! How much do I owe you?"

"Five rubles at the cashier. Anything over that amount is the patron's choice . . ."

It was hard to tell from his face whether he was satisfied with the "patron's choice" on this particular occasion. He simply took the money and said a dry "Thank You."

"Goodbye, Vitaly," I said. "Would it be all right if I came back to see you some time?"

"I'm quitting here and going back to my old location," he answered. "I've already gotten everything I can from the master hairdressers here."

"Where is your old location?"

He gave me the address and telephone number. I wrote them down.

"Vitaly . . . who?"

"Vitaly Plavnikov."

"Vitaly Plavnikov," I wrote down. "I'll keep it in mind. You're a good kid, Vitaly Plavnikov. Let me introduce myself. I'm Marya Vladimirovna Kovaleva."

"I got something out of this, too," he said, shaking my hand.

2

I went home. It was quiet in the apartment (those lousy bums must have gotten so hungry they fell asleep), but the light was on in my room. I went in. On the round table under my old-fashioned orange lamp there was a bouquet of flowers surrounded by bottles of milk. Several sandwiches were arranged with care on a large plate. My God, what sandwiches!—with ham, sturgeon, caviar. . . . In the bouquet there was an envelope, in the envelope—a letter. Repentant little devils!

I took out the letter. It was typewritten, two pages. What is this nonsense?

"All pigs of the earth are similar both in body structure and disposition. The typical sound of a pig is a strange grunting noise which can hardly be termed pleasant, even when it is used to express satisfaction or inner contentment . . ."

The devil take it—what a bunch of nonsense!

"The female of the species is not as irritable as the male, but does not yield anything to it in courage. Although it is incapable of inflicting serious wounds with its small fangs, nevertheless it is no less dangerous than the latter, in that it never retreats from the object of its anger, trampling it and tearing out large pieces of flesh . . ."

So that's where this is heading!

"The young piglet is actually very endearing. Its youthful agility and liveliness contrast sharply with the indolence and sluggishness of the adult. The mother takes very little care of her young, often neglecting even to build a nest for them. Frequently, having tired of her brood, she will eat several of them, usually strangling them first . . ." (Brem, *Animal Life,* vol. 2, pp. 731–745).

"Oh, those scoundrels! Scoundrels!" I groaned, but I couldn't help laughing to the point of tears.

Something fell in the boys' room, and a sleepy Kostya in undershorts appeared in the doorway.

"Well?" he asked. "Did that do the trick?"

And suddenly, noticing my hair, he cried out, "Mother! What a haircut! Stunning! Nikolai, get in here quick! Take a look at our mother!"

Kolya, also in undershorts, crawled in.

"On behalf of the reviled piglets . . ." he mumbled, then suddenly froze, saying only, "Well, well, well! Let's have a paw!"

I gave them each a hand—Kostya the right one and Kolya the left one. Again they both kissed their respective hand, while I looked at their heads: one yellow as straw, the other black as coal . . .

. . .My dear little fools—how could I ever leave you? . . .

3

The next day I went to work as usual. Well, not quite as usual: on my shoulders I had a head, and on my head I had a hairdo, which I carried with me to work. My secretary, Galya, looked at me in astonishment (with delight, I would have liked to believe), but said only, "Oh, Marya Vladimirovna, someone just called from somewhere, the Council of Ministers maybe, or maybe the Cybernetics Council—I've forgotten now . . ."

"What did they say?"

"I've forgotten that, too. I think they wanted you to call them back . . ."

"At what number?"

"I didn't ask."

"Galya, how many times do I need to repeat it: if you can't remember a number, write it down."

"I didn't have time to, they hung up so fast."

Galya was embarrassed. Her huge, watery blue eyes had a guilty look.

"Shall I buy some for you too, Marya Vladimirovna?"

"Absolutely not."

"I'll be off, then . . ."

"Go. Only come straight back."

Bad timing. Her help's not worth anything, but today of all days I wanted the telephone to be busy. I needed to think. The one essential requirement for living is just to *think* sometimes.

Actually, it's been a long time since I've done any scientific work. I knew when they foisted this institute job on me that my research was over, and told them as much. "Don't be silly, Marya Vladimirovna, we'll take care of everything for you, we'll get you a first-rate deputy," they said. My "first-rate deputy" is off sulking at the moment—hopefully not for long.

If you think in terms of absolute, astronomical time, I suppose I'm not even as busy as all that. I could tear myself away for an hour or two to do research. But it never works out. A scientific problem demands all your concentration, and mine has been shattered into tiny pieces. To take some random examples: there's no plywood for partitions. It's been discovered that the engineer Skurikhin has two wives. The police have asked for a talk on current issues in cybernetics. Where will you put the cars when the garage is torn down at the end of the week?

Shattered concentration, shattered time. Maybe I have more of it than I think—it's just that it never comes in a whole chunk. As soon as I get down to work, there's a visitor at the door. It's pointless sending him to Lebedev, he'll just bounce him back. It used to seem as though things in the Institute were about to settle down, and that I'd get my big chunk of time. Then it became obvious that this was just a utopian fantasy—that I would never have the chunk of time I hoped for.

And today, as if out of spite, the specter of my old familiar math problem, my lifelong friend and enemy who's been laughing at me for eight years now, rose up before me.

It had started with a dream I'd had about it. Of course, the dream was all nonsense, but waking up and analyzing it, it seemed as though I'd thought up a new approach, one less simplistic than all the previous ones. I had to try, and thus desperately needed a large chunk of time. No such luck: the telephone was having seizures. I tried to work, from time to time answering the calls. Still, it seemed like something was falling into place. . . . Could it be true? . . .

There was a knock at the door. A girl from the dispatcher's office poked her head in.

"Please excuse me, Marya Vladimirovna. Galya's not in, and I have a document for you. They said it was urgent . . ."

"Okay." I took the note. It read:

"On 21 May 1961 at 22.00 on Gorky Street citizen Mikhail Nikolaevich Popov was detained in an irrational state. Citizen claims to be employed as a lab assistant at the Institute of Computers. On being brought into custody, citizen relieved himself on the wall and surrounding area . . ."

"Fine, I'll take care of it," I said.

The girl went out. I tried to get my concentration back. There was a faint glimmer. And then the telephone again. The devil take you, damned epileptic! I picked up the receiver:

"Yes?"

"Get me Lebedev, miss, and hop to it," said an arrogant voice.

"You listen to me:" I said, "before you call someone a 'miss,' find out if she really is one!"

"Wha-a?" the voice said.

"Here's what," I said with malicious delight. "You're speaking with the director of the Institute, Professor Kovaleva, and I can assure you that I'm no 'miss.'"

There was a slight gulp. I hung up. A minute later there was another call. The phone rang for a long time, demanding to be answered. I didn't answer it. Of all the nerve—he wants to apologize. Let him worry.

. . . Still, I shouldn't have been so rude with him. It's not really his fault. And that haughty tone—"The director of the Institute, Professor Kovaleva." Foolish, vain old woman. When will you learn? "I'll get a haircut and get started." I got my hair cut, but didn't get started.

After that call I calmed down a bit and answered the phone quietly, saying politely, "Marya Vladimirovna isn't in at the moment, would you like to leave a message?" and writing everything down—in a word, playing the ideal secretary I would have liked Galya to be. Come to think of it, she never came back, Lebedev too. It was harder with visitors. I couldn't say "Marya Vladimirovna isn't in" to *them,* and each one had his little problem that stuck to me like electrical tape. My time had been shattered again, but still I worked, wrote, my free hand in my hair, crumpled paper, crossed out, wrote some more. . . . And then the calls stopped, it was evening. When I came to, it was ten o'clock. I did it!

I double-checked my calculations. They were all correct. My God, it's minutes like these that make life worth living. . . . I've had a long life and can report with authority that nothing on earth—not love, not motherhood, nothing—has brought me as much happiness as these minutes.

In all the confusion I'd forgotten to eat again.

I locked the safe and went down to the lobby. Everyone had left long ago, even the coat checker. My frayed raincoat hung all by itself. I stopped in front of the mirror. Just great—a pale, old face with circles under the eyes. Not a trace was left of my wind-tousled hairdo. It looked more like the work of a pack of monkeys than of the wind.

I put on my coat and went home. A light rain tap-danced on the new leaves. And, as usual, I splashed the backs of my stockings.

4

It was a terrible idea to get that haircut. It was just something else to worry about. It was easy before: I'd just pin it up and that would be it. But now . . . The first time I washed my hair before bed, I woke up the next morning with a head of chicken feathers. It looked like someone had ripped open a pillow. I called Vitaly.

"Vitaly, something's happened with my hair—it's standing on end."

"Did you wash your hair?" he asked sternly.

"Of course I washed it. Did you think I wasn't ever going to wash my hair again?"

"There's washing and there's washing. Your hair requires care. You should use egg yolks. . . ."

"I'm sorry, Vitaly, but I can't listen to that now. I have to give a talk at the Ministry today, and with hair like this. . . ."

"Come over and I'll fix you up."

Thus I found Vitaly at his old location and started going to him nearly every week. It was a small, sleepy place, with no long lines or fancy window displays. Just two old chairs in a shabby salon.

There was only one other hairdresser besides Vitaly there: the old Moisei Borisovich, whose hands trembled and head nodded. How did he manage to work with those hands? Still, he managed, and superbly at that. True, he didn't like cold sets. His specialty was curling irons.

"Curling irons are the things to use," he said. "It takes time, but you get results."

Several elderly ladies came to him regularly. I liked them—they were gray, stern, and indomitable. One was especially beautiful, with dark, piercing eyes, a haughty profile and a thick, heavy, bluish-gray head of hair. When she let it down, it looked as though a blue cloak were hanging on the back of the chair. She sat as straight as can be, pursing her small pale lips and never averting her gaze from the mirror. What a beauty she must have been! Moisei Borisovich would fiddle with the curling irons, twirl them by the handle, bring them close to his lips, twirl them again and finally plunge them decisively into the blue hair, making a precise wave that was almost too perfect. The whole time he nodded his head, as if agreeing with something.

"Do you know how to work with curling irons?" I asked Vitaly once.

"Why shouldn't I? We learned all types of procedures in school: pin curls, air waves, spiral perms. . . . Only none of those things are appropriate nowadays. These days you need to know how to work with big rollers, a razor and brush, and know the shape of the head. A master hairdresser, if he has any respect for himself, has to know all the peculiarities of a client's head. If a client has a flat head, the hairdresser should suggest a hairdo that will conceal the flatness. Sometimes a client's head is unusually large or her neck is too short. You have to take all of this into account and compensate for it with the hairdo. If I had a place to live, I could work on developing my technique there. Now I don't have any such opportunity."

"Where are you living?"

"I'm forced to rent a corner in an old woman's apartment. I'm registered at my sister's,* but she has a husband who smokes and drinks, plus two children. Their room is a hundred-square-foot walk-through, so that people are literally living on top of each other, with no privacy at all. The atmosphere was so tense that I rented this other place, even though it's at the expense of material comforts."

"Can't you live with your parents?"

"With my father and stepmother? Not desirable. My father drinks away his whole salary and then some. Living with them, not only would I not get any support from them, but I'd even be forced to give up part of my earnings for my father's liquor. The thought of that doesn't appeal to me."

5

As I said, I saw Vitaly every week. He worked slowly and pensively, and we spent a good deal of time together. One might even say that we became friends. He was a vector I didn't feel orthogonal to. We had things to talk about. From time to time I helped him with his "plan of general development," and finally convinced him to put off his study of Belinsky until a later time. Sometimes he would bring specialized hairdressers' magazines in German and English and I'd translate them from cover to cover, including the advertisements and marriage announcements, such as:

---

*In the Soviet Union people had to be registered to live in a specific apartment. However, many lived illegally in apartments where they were not registered.

"26-year-old male hairdresser, 5′5″, 130 lbs., looking for 20 to 50-year-old female hairdresser with experience in perming and her own salon for eventual marriage . . ."

Sometimes I would correct his stress. He would listen to me attentively, and I never knew him to repeat a mistake. I taught him to say "food" instead of "grub," "going to" instead of "gonna." Occasionally he would borrow small sums of money from me—five or ten rubles—always returning them the next time we met.

He often asked me about my sons. Apparently the thought of them interested him. Once in a while he would throw out a question:

"Are your sons in college?"

"Yes—Kolya's already almost done, and Kostya's a sophomore."

"What are they studying to be?"

"Engineers. Kolya's in automation and Kostya's in computers."

"Did they choose their fields on their own or did you advise them?"

"They chose them themselves."

"And did they experience difficulties in choosing a specialty?"

"To tell the truth, I don't know. I guess not."

"Are your sons good students?"

"They're different. The older one's all right, the younger one could be a lot better."

"If I had the kind of advantages your son has, I wouldn't allow myself to do badly."

"I don't think you would."

Sometimes he was concerned with more complicated issues:

"How did you manage to make sure that your sons turned out well?"

"How did I manage? By not trying too hard."

"Did you talk to them?"

"No, I guess I didn't . . ."

Time passed, and little by little changes started happening.

First of all, Vitaly took the master hairdresser exam. When I asked him about it, he said: "You can't even call it an exam, it's such a joke. My demands on myself go far beyond the bounds of that exam."

Secondly, there began to be lines, not only before holidays, but on weekdays too. And they were all for Vitaly.

"Vitaly, you're gaining popularity."

"I couldn't care less about that kind of popularity, to tell the truth. I'm interested in building a reliable clientele that I can get something out of. For example, I was recommended to the wife of a military man. A woman doctor came back from East Germany and brought a completely new type of roller with her. These, though"—he gestured scornfully toward the line—"they couldn't care less whether they look like sheep or not."

. . . It's amazing how fast one's psychology changes with the circumstances. What I mean is this: when I was waiting outside the salon and that fat hairdresser in the green tie took someone out of turn, I would scream and yell. Now as I went through to Vitaly without waiting in line, people behind me would scream and yell, sometimes demanding the complaints book. Back then I looked up to those who were served out of turn; now I look down at the people standing in line. Completely different perspectives. It's the same old story: the ones with the privileges are desperate to keep them, and everyone else wants to take them away. I was ashamed of my own privileges, and in my heart I was there with the people who were screaming and yelling, but the rest of me sat down in the chair without waiting in line. What could I do? I was terribly short of time . . .

"This lady has to give a talk at the Ministry today," Vitaly said once to a particularly pushy young woman. She had shiny, defiant eyes that looked like pools of water.

"Who cares where she has to give a talk? A line's a line."

Absolutely true. . . . My heart was on the young woman's side.

"All right, I'll wait."

But, as always happens in such situations, voices began to protest all around me.

"Maybe she really does have to give a talk."

"She's an older woman, an intellectual, obviously . . ."

"It's not like we can't wait for one person . . ."

Thus, on a wave of popular support I was borne into the chair. I wasn't giving any talk at the Ministry that day. God, was I ashamed!

. . . Still, I did have to give talks at the Ministry from time to time, and sometimes—even worse—attend receptions. For those I couldn't do without Vitaly. On the day of one such reception (the devil take it!), I went to the salon without calling in advance. Moisei Borisovich wasn't there. Vitaly was all alone. He was sitting in his salon chair, lost in thought, with the tools of his trade—different-sized rollers, clamps, various liquids, locks of hair—spread out before him. He didn't notice me right away, and when he did he was unusually cold.

"Ah, Marya Vladimirovna, it's you. . . . I was just getting down to work. I was taking advantage of being alone. I'm trying to figure out the specifics of one procedure as they relate to hair quality . . ."

"The telephone was busy . . . I'll leave if you don't have the time now."

"Why should you leave? As long as you're here, I'll serve you. Only you'll have to wait."

He started cleaning up his station, and I sat down in the corner with a book. Oh, how many times have I tried to persuade myself to drop reading in bits like this. You don't absorb anything anyway. It's just a bad habit, like shelling sunflower seeds. . .

Opposite me a little radio crackled, distracting me from my reading like a kid acting up. Tchaikovsky's violin concerto was being broadcast. I like most of the thing, but at that moment they were playing my least favorite part, where the unaccompanied violin practically chokes itself on double notes in a hopeless attempt to simulate the orchestra. Come on, come on, finish up this part, I prodded the violin in my head. All right, let's have a full voice. . . . And it obeyed. The violin broke into song, but was suddenly accompanied by a second instrument. Could it be a flute? Since when was there a flute in the Tchaikovsky violin concerto? I raised my head. It was Vitaly whistling.

He was cleaning up the counter and whistling. Moreover, he was moving to the music. He darted about between the counter and cabinet, light, skinny, with his boy's pointed elbows, and whistled. His careful, subtle accompaniment at times assented (yes, yes, yes), at times dissented (no, no, no) with the violin, receded and swelled up again. I marked my page with my finger and listened in astonishment, a shiver running down my spine.

Suddenly there was a click. Vitaly had turned off the radio.

"Have a seat, Marya Vladimirovna. I'm ready."

"My dear Vitaly, that's wonderful! Who taught you to whistle like that?"

"To whistle? I taught myself. In my old place, where conditions were better, I was always listening to the radio and learned a lot of pieces by heart."

"Do you know what you were just whistling?"

"Of course—the concerto for violin and orchestra in D major of Pyotr Iliich Tchaikovsky."

"Listen, Vitaly, you're very musical! You should take lessons . . ."

"I thought about that, but decided not to. To obtain a piano you have to be set up with a place to live first."

. . .Vitaly worked away while I sat in silence, obediently lifting and lowering my head. He started the conversation up again himself:

"I was interested in music from my earliest years, even in the orphanage. I remember a band playing while we were out on a walk. I got separated from the group, and, noticing I was missing, they started looking for me. I was standing glued to the spot in front of the band. Another time the governess brought us some wind instruments, small ones. Maybe there were big ones, too, but I only remember the small ones. They had castanets, cymbals, a regular drum and also those semicircular ones, what do you call them?"

"You mean kettledrums?"

"Right, exactly. Kettledrums. I started playing those kettledrums and made such a racket that she got furious and really went at me, started beating and stamping on me. I've never forgotten it and even now I cry when I remember how she stamped on me."

"How dreadful! Was it usual for them to beat you in the orphanage?"

"No, they never beat us."

"How did you end up in an orphanage? Didn't you say you have a father?"

"My father wasn't able to raise me. And my mother—I never knew her, never even saw a picture of her—she died when I was around two weeks old. I never saw her, but gather from what people say that she was an intelligent woman. My father couldn't feed me—I had two older sisters, too—so he put me into a home for abandoned babies, and after that I ended up in the orphanage."

"Did you know that you had a father?"

"I wouldn't have known, but something happened so that I found out. A delegation was visiting the orphanage. They took a liking to me, and took pictures of me in a toy airplane that looked like a piano. Then they brought me into the sleeping area and started taking pictures of me sleeping. They put a box of 'Sadko' chocolates under my pillow and told me that if I lay there like I was asleep, I would get the box. I actually did fall asleep from fatigue, but when I woke up the chocolates were gone. I sobbed like crazy. When I had been falling asleep, I had overheard their conversation. The director of the orphanage said that I had a father and two sisters. I remembered that.

The next year—it must have been sometime around New Year's since they were decorating a tree—I saw one woman giving her son a present. I suddenly remembered that I had a father and two sisters. That night I came into the room and started shaking the tree. I don't even know myself why I started shaking it. But the administrators came in and saw me shaking the tree. I don't remember myself what measures were taken against me, but I didn't care. When that woman gave her son that present, I suddenly remembered everything, the governess stamping on me, everything . . ."

Vitaly abruptly stopped working and went over to the window. A minute later he came back.

"Please excuse me, Marya Vladimirovna. It happens to me sometimes. I remember something from my life and can't help crying."

"Don't think about it, it's too hard on you. I'm sorry I asked you so many questions."

"No, I feel better when things are completely clear. Go ahead and ask."

"How did you get out of the orphanage?"

"Oh, that was later, when Anna Grigorievna wanted to adopt me."

"Who's Anna Grigorievna?"

"The head of a factory who often visited the orphanage. I don't know why, but she took a liking to me and decided to adopt me instead of having a son of her own. But at first she didn't notify anyone about it, even me. She would just bring me to her house as a guest to try things out. I never swiped anything and was a quiet and neat guest, so that she became even more attached to me. I really wished that she would take me. But instead one day she brought . . . she brought my father and sister along with her. And my stepmother, too. They showed me to my stepmother and she said: 'let him live with us. Maybe he won't eat us out of house and home.' So I started living with them, and each day was worse than the one before it."

"But where did Anna Grigorievna find your father and sister?"

"I found that out only later. When she wanted to adopt me, she went to the director of the orphanage and asked them to let her have that child, Vitaly Plavnikov. The director told her that I had a father and two sisters. She located them, thought she'd make me happy. But after that she didn't even want to look at me. If I can't get him as son, then I don't want to look at him, she probably thought."

"And you never saw her again?"

"No, never again."

"Was it bad living at home?"

"I wouldn't say it was bad. It was satisfactory. But I was very upset."

"Was your stepmother abusive?"

"No, I can't complain about my stepmother. If I remembered my own mother, of course, I might complain. But things being as they were I even called my stepmother 'mama,' although I fought against her religiosity. No, I was upset because I couldn't forget Anna Grigorievna."

6

Galya came in to see me.

"Marya Vladimirovna . . . Please excuse me, but . . ."

"What is it, Galya? Stretchable stockings again?"

"No, no, nothing like that. Marya Vladimirovna, I want to talk to you about something personal, but it's kind of awkward . . ."

"Well, let's have it."

"Marya Vladimirovna, I've wanted to ask you for a long time: where do you go?"

"Where do I go?" . . .

"I mean, for your hair."

"Oh, that. I didn't understand right away."

"You'll excuse me, Marya Vladimirovna, but believe it or not we and the other girls have been looking at you and are amazed. Not very many people of your age look after themselves like you do. Honestly, I'm not just saying that, I really mean it. Ask the girls if you want."

"All right, all right. Get to the point."

"I'd like to know who does your hair so well, Marya Vladimirovna, and if you might arrange an appointment for me with him. I'd really appreciate it, that is if you don't mind . . ."

"Why should I mind? I'd be glad to talk to Vitaly."

"Your hairdresser's name is Vitaly? Is he very old?"

"Terribly old, about your age."

"What do you mean? For a girl I'm not young any more, I'm almost twenty-four," Galya sighed.

"You said it," I said. "Old age."

"No, I'm serious, Marya Vladimirovna. Nowadays men consider a girl young only if she's seventeen or eighteen, maybe twenty, but no more. And even then only if she dresses well."

I cast an approving glance at Galya. I'm terribly fond of her. Of course, she was dressed well. Where on earth, by what extraordinary instinct, do our girls learn all this? It's incomprehensible to me. Everything on her was clean, short, simple, without a single superfluous button, brooch, or bead. Everything was in its place, and she walked tiptoe in her needle-sharp high heels. A man would probably like to pick up a little thing like that by the waist with two fingers and move it around from place to place.

"You're dressed beautifully, Galya. No one could take you for over eighteen or twenty."

"You're joking, Marya Vladimirovna."

"It's the honest truth."

. . . It's true, I'll never be able to believe that there's a difference between eighteen and twenty-three . . .

"Well, thanks," Galya said. "Please do ask your Vitaly if he'll do my hair. We're having a party on Saturday. You won't forget?"

"I won't forget."

I didn't forget. The next time I was sitting in front of the mirror at Vitaly's, I said:

"Vitaly, I have a favor to ask of you. I know this one girl, Galya. She's my secretary. A very sweet girl, by the way. Well, she would very much like for you to do her hair. She liked my hairdo very much."

"What kind of hair?" Vitaly asked dryly.

"Hers? How can I describe it . . . light chestnut, I guess. She's almost blonde."

"The color is irrelevant. Is it short, long? . . ."

"Closer to long."

"If she needs a teased look, then you can tell her I don't do them. This style doesn't interest me. The majority of girls have it now, and if you ask me it's a mistake. That back-combing only gives the appearance of a thick head of hair, when in reality it's fluffed up and split. Some girls get teases and don't comb their hair for two whole weeks. Doesn't do the hair any good."

"No, Vitaly, she didn't say anything to me about a teased look. Do something pretty for her, something that you like yourself."

"Is she an interesting girl?" Vitaly asked matter-of-factly.

"I think she's very interesting."

"I asked because sometimes I allow myself to serve interesting girls without any thought of material gain. I'm interested in the problem of choosing a hairdo depending on the size of the forehead, the length of the neck, and other factors. It's easier to test things out on young girls than on my older clients. Often my older clients don't have the right kind of hair, their features aren't as well-defined, and besides, they want a specific style for themselves, not the one I offer them as a hairdresser. On the other hand, by working on young girls a lot I risk not making enough to live on. But from time to time I have to test my theories on them."

"Well, then, test them on my Galya."

"Okay."

"I'll tell her, then. She'll call you."

"Better that I call her myself. Number?"

"My office number."

"Excellent. I'll call her."

7

Saturday is a short day for some people. It turned out to be a long one for me, though. I was even late for the young people's party. By the time I arrived at the youth center, the dances had already started. I enjoy looking at the legs of people dancing. Often they say more than the faces. And footwear? Little shoes, little shoes, little shoes, imported ones, pointed ones, weightless ones with narrow, almost non-existent heels. I congratulate those who can walk on those fine non-existences without stumbling—I certainly can't. And next to the little shoes, men's loafers, or sandals, or boots. . . . And so many—God, how many!—girl-girl pairs, little shoes with little shoes. They dance gracefully, deliberately, aloof, as if they didn't need anything more. My poor, poor girls. The war's long over, a new generation's grown up, and still there are too many of you . . .

Among the many fashionable shoes, the ones in the minority, the simpler ones, are especially noticeable: women's sandals, even slippers. Slippers even look nice if the legs are sprightly and straight. . . . A pair of green canvas sandals especially caught my eye. How they hustled, tapped, darted! To each beat of the music they went through not one, not two, but around ten blurred steps. I wonder who the owner of those sandals is? I slid my gaze northward along the plump calves and saw a girl of around seventeen with curls stiff as oakum. Vitaly would call her a sheep. Everything about her was squat and firm, like a small turnip. Her narrow, flashy-gold, brocaded dress ended above her knees and tightly hugged her small, protruberant rear end. She was studiously dancing the man's part with a thin, languid young woman almost a head taller than she. I like girls who dance with each other. You can rely on them . . .

Also among the mass of dancing footwear a pair of enormous yellow loafers with monstrously thick, wavy soles attracted my attention. They reminded me of something, but of what? Oh, I know. Dandies—not the ones today but the old-fashioned ones, from around 1956—used to dance in that kind of work loafer. It was as if he was straight off the pages of *Krokodil*,* with his baggy, checkered jacket and short, pipe-like trousers, those huge feet on ribbed soles, that mussed-up hair. . . . An old-fashioned dandy!

But where's my Galya? I'll try to locate her by her feet. It turned out not to be difficult. I immediately spotted two graceful feet in gray shoes with sword-like tips. I wonder what kind of hairdo Vitaly gave her? I raised my eyes to her face and realized right away that Galya was a beauty. Not just a nice, cute girl, but a real beauty. Or was it the hairdo? Her thick, dark golden locks flowed over her head like honey, there's no other way to put it. She was dancing with some fellow, looking at him spellbound, her enamel eyes melting. But who is that fellow? Is that really Volodya? But . . . but that's Vitaly!

Why didn't I recognize him before? In that black suit he looked different, not so thin, even imposing, I'd say. Looking sternly over the magnificent honey-like hairdo, oblivious to his legs, he almost imperceptibly stepped with them to the rhythm, shaking his knees a little. Apparently that's the modern way to dance: staying in one spot.

It's a miracle! Galya and Vitaly . . .

The radio sputtered and fell silent. The couples went off in various directions, dragging pieces of streamers behind them. But then the music started up again, this time it was a waltz.

There's one that never goes out of style! How many dances have come

* Soviet humor magazine.

and gone in my lifetime, but the waltz is still around. It's my favorite dance. Pairs of whirling dancers flashed by me. Next to me Lebedev popped up out of nowhere.

"Marya Vladimirovna, one dance!"

"God, no, Vyacheslav Nikolaevich. I haven't danced for years."

"You're not dancing, but it's obvious you want to."

"Why is it obvious?"

"Because your whole being is keeping time: *one*, two three, *one*, two, three. . . . What do you say?"

I moved away. "Really, it's not worth it. Some other time, in some other place."

"What a coward!"

He grabbed some girl and started spinning her around. The old man dances well. It's enviable and sad.

. . .Just stand here and watch the waltz spinning past you . . .

8

The music stopped, the waltz was over. They hooked up a microphone. Zina—our high priestess of culture, an athletic-looking girl with thin, tanned arms bare up to her elbows—went into the center of the hall and spoke into the microphone:

"Good evening, comrades!"

"Go-od Eve-ning," the crowd droned back.

"We'll now begin the second part of our officially organized youth gathering. On the program we have an evening of laughs and group games in store."

"Not group games *again!*" an annoyed female voice whined.

"Don't interfere, comrades. Comrades! Please make room for the group games. Be orderly about it, comrades!"

People moved off the dance floor toward the walls. At first I was pushed toward the back, but then someone recognized me:

"Please go ahead, Marya Vladimirovna."

"You first, Marya Vladimirovna!"

"There's no need," I retorted. "I'm fine here."

"But you won't see anything from here."

"I'll be able to see, really."

The devils pushed me into the front row anyway.

Zina was fussing about in the middle of the open dance floor. They brought in a bag. She started taking one inflatable, pre-inflated rubber rabbit after another out of the bag. Each rabbit was about the size of a cat. She solemnly planted them side by side on the floor. I counted them automatically—there were fifteen. The crowd was silent.

After all the rabbits had been taken out, guns emerged from the bag: one, two, three, four toy guns, as well as some mysterious objects made of cardboard—masks, probably. One of them was pink.

"Your attention, comrades! I will now explain the game. Two pairs participate in this group game, two girls and two young men."

Everyone laughed.

"A little more discipline, comrades! You'll laugh later. The game is called 'rabbit hunting.' Who wants to participate?"

The crowd squeezed together. No one volunteered.

"Come on, comrades, let's go. Show some initiative."

"Well, why not?" one girl shouted, and shot into the center of the room.

It turned out to be the same one, the one in the gold dress. Good for you, turnip!

That was the beginning of the end. Another girl—one I knew, the lab assistant Tonia—followed after the turnip, and then two boys, both of them from our institute. One was slightly shorter than the other, with a flushed, blotchy face, the other was as tall as could be, with unkempt hair and in jeans. It looked like Sasha Lukianov, but I wasn't sure. If it is Sasha, I've already signed two official reprimands against him. This fellow's legs were too long, and he kept shifting around on them, bending first one knee, then the other.

"Once again, your attention, comrades. I shall now explain the object of 'rabbit hunting.' Four people participate in the game. Each person must wear his gun over his shoulder."

Giggling shyly, the kids climbed into the shoulder straps of the toy guns.

"Fine. Next, the assignment of corners. Each of you four take a corner. The rabbits are in the middle of the hall. Do you see them?"

"Why wouldn't we see them? We're not blind, you know," the short one said.

A funereal silence reigned. The rabbits sat despondently in single file with their soft, cold ears hanging down. One of them was about to fall on its side. Zina was trying to straighten it up.

"Each of you has to shoot as many rabbits as possible, and bring them back to your corner. Do you understand? You take your gun off your shoulder, take aim at a rabbit, and execute the shot. Of course, they won't be real shots, since they're only toy guns and aren't even loaded, in the interests of safety. Once you have killed a rabbit, you take it to your corner. Do you understand?"

"We understand," the tall one said sadly, this time bending his right knee.

"Now I shall put masks on you. In order that you don't see anything, the eye slits have been covered. Do you understand?"

"What's there to understand? We're not three-year-olds," said the turnip.

"Attention. I'm now putting on the masks."

The tall fellow got the mask of a dejected drunk, with ears that stuck out and a bulbous purple nose. The short one got something yellow and flat that looked like it was sniffing at something. An ugly old mug wrapped in a kerchief was strapped on Tonia. But the most awful of all was the female mask that the gold turnip received. It was a puffed-up, bluish-pink woman's head with almost no eyes, only one ear, and a crooked mouth that was permanently paralyzed open. The face of a clinically certified idiot. The masked quartet stood, guns hanging from their shoulders, in the opposite corners of the hall, looking like they'd just stepped out of some drunkard's nightmare.

"Attention, we're all ready. At my signal, the players will commence the game of rabbit hunting. On your mark, get set, go!"

Zina, half training coach, half police officer, blew into her whistle. The first one to move was the gold turnip with that pink horror instead of a head. She took down her gun, painstakingly took aim, shot at the invisible rabbits, and, stepping heavily, set out for her prize. It must have been hard to keep your sense of direction when you couldn't see anything. She strayed too far to the right, passing by the rabbits, squatted down, and began to grope around on the bare floor, uselessly shaking that idiotic head. Isolated chuckles could be heard in the audience.

"How awful," I thought. "Why are they doing this? . . ."

Now the lanky fellow in jeans and with the drunkard's face grabbed his gun. Was it Sasha Lukianov or not? Apparently he was trying to add his own touch to the number: he took a shot, said "bang, bang," and headed toward the rabbits in goose step, throwing his legs high up in the air. He calculated the distance fairly well. At first he stepped on the rabbits, breaking up the row, then oriented himself and sat on the floor, felt out two of them, and, grabbing them by the ears, took them back to the wrong corner.

"Not here, not here!" the audience yelled at him.

Many people were already laughing out loud when a couple of whistles rang out. Zina tried to intervene and restore order, but no one was listening to her anymore. The remaining masks entered into the game. . . . In several minutes the unthinkable was happening. The masked quartet, forgetting to shoot, stumbled senselessly around the dance floor, tripping, bumping into and groping at each other, haphazardly seizing the ill-fated rabbits and dragging them from place to place. Everyone was laughing. No one understood what was happening, but they only laughed harder because of it. I didn't

understand what there was to laugh about—it was a terrible scene—but suddenly felt that I couldn't bear it any more, felt myself laughing along with the
others . . .

"What the hell is this?" said a dark-skinned, big-shouldered fellow standing next to me, then stuck two fingers in his mouth, and let loose a deafening whistle—a real Nightingale-Robber.* A couple of protracted whistles
answered him from the far ends of the hall.

"Comrades, please maintain order!" the high priestess of culture wailed
into the microphone.

Someone grabbed me by the leg. I looked down and saw the frightful,
contorted mug of an idiot. The girl had lost her way and was groping at the
legs of the spectators.

"Take off that mask at once!" I said sharply.

She stood up and pushed the mask off to one side. A pretty face, flushed
and sweaty, looked out at me.

"You shouldn't be doing this, honey," I said to her.

She burst into tears.

God, as if everything else weren't enough . . .

I went up to Zina. "Put an end to this disgraceful spectacle immediately!"

"What happened?" Zina asked, but at that moment recognized me,
grabbed her whistle and emitted a long, piercing blast. "Attention, comrades!
The rabbit hunting game is over! The first prize—an assortment of postcards
of Moscow—is awarded to. . . . What's your name, comrade?"

But the "comrade," the tall fellow with the unkempt hair, had already
torn off his mask and hurled it like a football into the opposite end of the hall.
The two others also took off their masks and threw them into the air, where
they fluttered and danced above people's heads. The crowd, laughing and
shouting, threw the masks back and forth. They tore the nose of the drunkard
part way off, and it wiggled dejectedly as if protesting.

Zina came up to me, wringing her hands.

"What should I do? The youth gathering is off course . . ."

"You mean to say there's more?"

"In the plan we were supposed to bob for apples . . ."

"Let me use the microphone," I said.

"Be my guest . . ."

. . . What will I say to them? I don't know. But I absolutely must say
something. When I went up to the microphone, the hall fell silent. I didn't
even recognize my own voice. And the things I said! . . .

"Kids," I said. "Boys and girls! My dear boys and girls. . . . Please excuse

* A mythical character from Russian oral epic.

me for referring to you in this way. I have two sons your age. The older one is twenty-two, the younger is twenty . . ."

. . .What am I doing? But it was already too late to stop. A mass of eyes was looking up at me, and it was absolutely quiet.

"My dear boys and girls," I said, "you were laughing just now. You were laughing involuntarily, you couldn't help it. I know this from myself, I was also laughing along with you. But was this really fun? Sometimes it's fun to drink vodka, for example. My son calls it 'chemically-induced.' What you were just having was also 'chemically-induced' fun . . ."

"Right on, right on!" several voices cried out.

Someone whistled, others hissed.

"I don't know how to explain to you what's going on here, but I have the feeling that this kind of fun is bad. How should I put it? You know, sometimes little boys throw stones at a dog and laugh about it. . . . But are they really having fun?"

Now Zina started crying.

I got up my courage and said: "Only don't even think of blaming Zina. She's not at fault, I alone am. Forgive me. We'll think about this some more. We'll think of a way to have genuine, good fun. And until we think of it, let's dance. A waltz, please!"

And immediately, as if by magic, the record player started playing a waltz. I was covered with sweat. Tried to make a speech when I had nothing to say . . .

That same tall fellow in jeans came running up to me. "Marya Vladimirovna, may I have this dance?"

I nodded and gave him my hand. Anyway, I had nothing to lose after humiliating myself like that. He led, whirling me around so that the dresses, jackets, shirts, and faces all merged into one blurred circle in which a little round rear end would occasionally spin by with a bright flash . . .

"Are you Sasha Lukianov?" I asked my dance partner.

"That's me," he answered.

We didn't say anything more to each other. The waltz ended. The kids surrounded me . . .

"Marya Vladimirovna, please, may I have the next dance?"

"No, I was here first! . . ."

"That's enough," I said, and went out into the foyer.

I wasn't feeling well. My heart, probably. A person goes along living his life without realizing that he's carrying such a weight inside, and then one day he finds out. . . . What you can do . . .

"Marya Vladimirovna, what's wrong? You're so pale . . ."

Ah, it's Galya. And Vitaly's with her.

"Galya, dear, could I please have some water?"

Galya brought a glass of water. She's kind of pale herself. Do I really mean something to her? I'd have never guessed . . .

I drank the water and said: "It's nothing. My head was just spinning. I haven't danced for a long time. I'll be fine in a minute."

9

Actually, I'm stupid. This is absolutely clear to me, but others, even my closest friends, don't believe me for some reason. They think I'm putting on airs.

Take that party, for example. It's hard to imagine behavior stupider than mine. Probably everyone knows the stabbing feeling when, alone, you shake your head and groan at some shameful recollection. So I shook my head and groaned, recalling my performance at the party. It was still possible that I'd have to answer to some authority for creating a "public disturbance." But that was the least of my worries.

When I went to see Vitaly the next week, he was cold and laconic with me.

"Well, how did you like our party?" I asked him, to break the silence.

"The party was fine, of course. I'm generally against parties like that, though. I go to them only because I want to study social strata. But I didn't find anything of interest to me in that stratum. Even if I didn't finish high school, and many of them are already in college, I don't see anything so outstanding about them compared to me . . ."

When you're ashamed of something, you want to pick at your wounds:

"What did you think of my speech?"

"Please don't be offended at me, Marya Vladimirovna, but your speech didn't satisfy me—it was too simple, the wording was wrong. One might have expected a more profound analysis from the head of an institute."

"Don't tell me you liked those rabbits?!"

"The rabbits!" He waved his hand with contempt. "Who said anything about rabbits? A stupid game, for mind and body."

"Well, what should I have said, in your opinion?"

"I can't give you any pointers. I don't have enough education for that. But I would use clearer wording. And to then dance with a fellow who, if you'll excuse the expression, didn't think twice about coming to a party in jeans . . . in my opinion it's not in keeping with your respected position . . ."

So that's the verdict . . .

Of course, everything gradually got smoothed out. I even apologized to Zina and offered her my help in organizing a second party. We even brought it off. . . . The kids themselves helped a lot, especially Sasha Lukianov. He turned out to be an amazing fellow, he had something special in that head of his. Humor issued from him like oxygen does from a plant. You needed only to see how he raked his smooth hair back with his wide, shovel-like hand, then pointed a threatening finger at it (stay there!), to understand that he had a first-rate wit.

There are different kinds of humor. The kind that Sasha had was the most puzzling of them all. What did he actually say? If you were to repeat it yourself, it wouldn't be funny. But there everyone is in stitches, with tears in their eyes. He could bend his knee and his audience would die laughing.

Sasha Lukianov and I spent many electrifying evenings preparing for the party. Our inventions knew no bounds. In order to fit them all in, the party would have had to last a whole day. We were forced to limit ourselves. We called it a "cybernetics party," and brought in mechanics and engineers to design it. . . . Everything was based on semiconductors. The guests were met by a robot-host, built specially for the occasion, whose eyes blinked and who bowed and cried out greetings. . . . There was machine-composed poetry and music, and a cybernetics lottery. Double-coded congratulatory telegrams were exchanged and deciphered. . . . That's not to say there weren't hitches: the robot-host promptly stopped working, one of its eyes went out and it began repeating ". . . elcome" nonstop. Then Sasha Lukianov hit it over the head with a hammer, and it shut up . . .

On the whole, the party was a success, though a fairly limited one, especially in proportion to the energy spent on planning it. I myself felt as if what we had done was not exactly right. . . . The next day I called in Seryozha Shevtsov, the president of the Young Communists. He's kind of slow, but he's well-liked, and, most importantly, he won't lie to me.

"Well? Were the kids satisfied with the party?"

"Sure, I guess," he said without enthusiasm.

"Well, what are they saying?"

"There are differing opinions. Some people are satisfied, some are saying it used to be better."

"What, like those rabbits?"

"Who cares about the rabbits?" He waved his hand like Vitaly had done. "No one fell for that. They laughed just because they had nothing better to do. No, they're saying there used to be more time for dancing . . ."

"Fine, Seryozha. We'll keep that in mind."

Yes, I thought after he had left, there's nothing more mysterious, more elusive than laughter. What's the secret to it? Funny to one, just plain stupid to another. Funny to one, frightening to another. Funny to one, boring to another. . . . Maybe we should have just let Sasha Lukianov on stage and had him bend his knee . . .

Thus concluded my work on the side as social organizer—not completely ignominiously, but certainly not in triumph . . .

10

One more thing happened as a result of the first, failed party: Galya and Vitaly started going out together. It wasn't hard to figure out. Often, picking up the telephone receiver, I would hear Vitaly's high, shrill voice and Galya's dove-like cooing on the line. Well, what's wrong with it? It's good for her. Vitaly's a serious young man. And Galya seemed happy. Every three or four days she would appear with a new hairdo, the envy of all the girls in the institute. Sometimes it would be a fantastic tower that made her face look haughty and ethereal. Sometimes her glossy-smooth hair would be pulled back in the style of the nineteenth century and tied in a thick, heavy bundle on her neck. And sometimes she'd have girlish locks scattered gently over her shoulders and uneven bangs above her blue eyes. . . . And every time her face was different, every time she seemed happier than she was before . . .

Only it didn't last long. The intervals between hairdos gradually lengthened: a week, two weeks. . . . Then one day I came to work and Galya was crying.

"Galya, dear, what's wrong?"

She cried like a child, sniffling loudly, oblivious to everything around her.

"Galya, what happened?"

She shook her head.

"Come on, darling. Please tell me what's the matter. Is it something to do with Vitaly?"

She shook her head again as if to say "no," but it was clear she meant "yes."

"Come on, sit down and wipe your nose, and we'll talk."

I could just barely make sense of what she was saying:

"He doesn't love me."

"Why would you think that? Why, everything was going well for you two . . ."

"No, Marya Vladimirovna, you're wrong. He doesn't love me, I know it."

"And do you love him?"

"I love him. Before I didn't think I was capable of such serious feelings. But now I've fallen for him. . . . Wouldn't you know it . . ."

More tears.

"Marya Vladimirovna, my life isn't so happy, either. Don't think just because I'm cute that it is. No man will fall in love with me."

"What about Volodya?" I asked. I couldn't help myself.

"What *about* Volodya? He's a married one. He only went out with me as long as his wife was expecting . . ."

What to say to her? My heart goes out to her, but I know that I can't say what she needs to hear. Damn orthogonal projections.

I patted Galya on the head.

"Now, now, calm down. Maybe things aren't really so bad. Would you like me to talk to him?"

"Oh, please, Marya Vladimirovna! He'll listen to you, I know it. He has great respect for you. You can believe it or not, but whenever we see each other, he talks about nothing but you."

Flattering, but ridiculous.

11

"Vitaly," I said, "you and I need to have a serious talk."

He frowned. "Is this about Galya?"

"Absolutely right."

"I've been anticipating this conversation for a long time. But it's no fault of mine, after all. I was interested in Galya as a suitable subject for hair-dressing. She's got healthy, vibrant hair that keeps its shape no matter what styling tools you use on it. I tried various kinds of rollers on her. But now I've exhausted the possibilities of her hair, it's not interesting to me anymore, and I have to develop my skills further. I can't work on one kind of hair all the time."

"How can you not understand that hair isn't the issue here!"

"And besides, you should understand yourself that I'm not ready to tie the knot yet. I'm too young and can't support anyone else. I still have to take the high school equivalency exam, to say nothing about college, and I have no permanent place to live. If she had an apartment herself I might be interested, but she lives in a single room with her mother and sister."

"Vitaly, how can you? It's awful what you're saying! To let something like that depend on an apartment. . . . Don't you understand how cynical that is?"

He looked at me with such sincere bewilderment that I was ashamed.

"For me the apartment question has great relevance. If I get married some day, it'll only be if my wife and I have decent living conditions. Where would I take Galya? To my corner? That's not very respectable. Besides, I would make one main demand on my wife: that she not keep me from moving ahead, but on the contrary help me. For example, I spend a lot of time preparing my breakfast, lunch and dinner, and this takes away from my personal time. It's quite possible that if I married Galya she would hinder me in my personal development."

"Oh, Vitaly! What on earth are you saying! Is all that really important?"

"What's important if that isn't?"

"One thing: do you love her or not?"

Vitaly stopped to think.

"It's possible that I love her. I'm still young, you know, I don't know myself whether I love her or not."

He fell silent and began working on my hair. I was also silent.

"Marya Vladimirovna, I'd like to ask you one question. May I?"

"Of course."

"Marya Vladimirovna, in all seriousness, I think your level of intellectual development is very high, and respect you even more than my own stepmother. . . . Of course, you've had a lot of experience. I wanted to ask you: how can you tell if you love someone or not, what signs are there?"

So that's the question! I'll have to answer. I gave it some thought.

"That's a hard question, but I'll try to answer it. I think the main indication is a permanent feeling of presence. She's not with you, and yet she is. You come home at night, open the door, the room's empty, but she's there. You wake up in the morning, she's there. You open up your cabinet, take out your styling tools, and she's there."

"That I understand," said Vitaly.

"Well, that's good, then!"

We were silent again, this time for longer. Finally he said:

"Marya Vladimirovna, you've explained the signs very clearly, and now I know for certain that, according to such an understanding of love, I don't love Galya."

"Well, did you talk to him?" Galya asked the next morning.

"Yes."

Here Galya should have asked "well?", but she didn't bother to, she had understood without words. She's a sharp one, my Galya!

Female grief. It's always the same, and there's nothing you can do to ease it . . .

12

In midwinter the chair next to Vitaly became empty—Moisei Borisovich had fallen ill and died. Too bad, he was a nice old man. . . . People continued to ask for him on the telephone for some time—probably those beautiful old ladies with blue hair—and then that thread was cut, and everyone forgot about the old master.

Toward spring a new figure appeared over the neighboring chair, a woman hairdresser by the name of Lyuba. She was as big and heavy as a draught horse, with brazen, peroxide-damaged hair. She took an immediate dislike to Vitaly—and how! No one wanted to be served by her, they all wanted him. While Vitaly worked she would file her bright purple nails with feigned indifference and sing some tralala tune with no melody. Once in a while she would saunter up to the people waiting in line and, as if she was just happening by, throw out an invitation: "How's about we fix you girls up?"

"No thanks, we'll wait."

She ended up for the most part with first timers, women from the country with white wrinkles on their brown faces who shyly took plastic colored combs out of their hair and asked "Do you do firm curls here?" Lyuba served them grudgingly, pursing her toxic red lips so they looked like a worm.

She didn't like me, either. For example, I would always say hello to her, but she wouldn't reply. One time I stayed late translating an English magazine for Vitaly and heard her talking to the cashier:

"She has grown children, she'll have grandchildren soon, and she's hanging out with small fry. And she thinks she's good-looking. Well, lah-de-dah. There's nothing good-looking about her, she's a fat witch."

Vitaly started getting more and more agitated, would treat the ladies besieging him more and more rudely. "There's twenty of you and only one of me," he would say.

And then one day I came into the salon and found him crying. If it's possible to cry without tears, then that's exactly what he was doing. He shook as he cleared off his counter, crying silently and bitterly and squeezing his eyelashes together. Oh, my kids. First one, then the other. I went up to him.

"Please excuse me, Marya Vladimirovna, but I can't serve you now."

"What happened, Vitaly?"

"Nothing in particular happened, only I have to go home now."

"But what on earth's wrong? I'm not letting you go until you tell me."

"I should have seen it coming."

"Seen what coming? Here, sit down and tell me the whole story."

He sat down.

"Marya Vladimirovna, I knew they wouldn't let me work in peace."

"Who is 'they'? Lyuba?"

"Yes, Lyuba, and others came forward in solidarity with her, the hairdresser from the men's section, and Alevtina Petrovna, the cashier. I've been getting on their nerves with my work for a long time. I have my own customers, I allow myself to spend a lot of time on each one, the quota doesn't get filled, they're always having to call me to the phone . . . all this makes them bitter toward me. Also, I have a lot of people wanting to see me. But I'm simply not capable of serving all those people, it's not worth it even from an economic standpoint. Why should I do every customer's hair? They come three times a year at the most, for the May and November holidays, maybe for New Year's. In choosing customers for myself, I always look at whether I can get something out of them for my professional development. I don't want to serve every last person who comes in. They get offended, file complaints. I already have several against me, but I don't care, because I'm interested in the work and the work alone."

"But what upset you so much today?"

"The following thing happened. They stole the address book, where all my clients' names and numbers are written down, out of my pocket, and passed it on to the union for the investigation of my case."

"What case? Do you mean to tell me you're not allowed to write down any address you please?"

"Of course, technically I am, but in fact those women's addresses show that I have my own customers, and that's strictly forbidden. I'm supposed to work at the same rate as everyone else and fulfill the quota. I don't allow myself to do that, because if I did I'd unintentionally slip into hackwork. Now, for example, little bangs are in fashion. You have to think out those kinds of bangs, I spend more time on them than on a whole permanent. This doesn't conform to existing standards. So, based on all these things—the address book, the complaints, the unfulfilled quota—they plan to manufacture a whole case against me."

"Let's think, Vitaly. Can't someone help you?"

"I've already thought about it, and it would be difficult to help me. The thing is, our director is unfit for her job—she's rude, she insults the hairdressers, she literally curses at us. Besides, Matyunin's against me."

"And who might Matyunin be?"

"He's the director of the hairdressing section of our Personal Services Administration."

"And why is he against you?"

"For my speeches. They nominated me secretary of the local branch of the Young Communists. I accepted even though I had so little time. I have to move forward in my personal development, to gain some prestige. I don't have a lot of prestige, but not so little, either, an average amount. So I made a speech at a meeting of Young Communists calling attention to one problem. So I'm up there talking away about it . . ."

"What was it you were calling attention to?"

"Worn-out tools. I asked when the question concerning the disgraceful situation with monetary compensation for worn-out tools would be raised. I won a lot of prestige by saying it, but Matyunin didn't like it, of course. He's not interested in paying out compensation . . ."

"Why is that?"

"He profits directly from not paying."

"You mean he steals?"

"He doesn't literally steal, he takes advantage of the situation."

"Don't tell me there's nothing you can do about it?"

"It's very difficult. To put it crudely, the personal service enterprises scavenge off the government. Matyunin and others like him take advantage of the fact that up to now the government, with all its other obligations, has had no time to enforce the law in this business. Take the use of materials, for instance. There's a certain operational norm. But someone doesn't distribute everything here, switches things there, some people even manage to redistribute used materials. All this is money lost. I also allowed myself to call attention to the problem of rude service. It's better to get a bad haircut from a gracious hairdresser with a pleasant appearance than the same bad haircut from a boor. That turned the hairdressers who still haven't mastered the art of gracious service against me . . ."

"Listen, Vitaly," I said. "What if I call him?"

"Call whom?"

"Matyunin, damn him."

"I'd be very grateful to you."

"Give me the phone, then."

I dialed the number. A smooth, sensual bass voice answered.

"Matyunin speaking."

"Comrade Matyunin? This is the director of the Institute of Computers, Professor Kovaleva, speaking."

"How do you do," the bass replied.

"Comrade Matyunin, there's a young hairdresser working in one of your salons by the name of Vitaly Plavnikov . . ."

Matyunin was silent.

"Are you listening?"

"I'm listening," he answered dryly.

"Right. Well, I've been coming to him for a year now and must tell you that he's an outstanding hairdresser, a real artist . . ."

"All of our hairdressers are good," Matyunin said in a metal voice.

"But this hairdresser. . . . You know, he's besieged by customers . . ."

"I don't see anything special in Mr. Plavnikov. In our system all hairdressers are qualified, they've all fulfilled the technical requirements, they can all perform any type of operation. And this Plavnikov is always getting complaints—he's rude with customers, he doesn't fulfill the quota . . ."

"But you can't talk about quotas when it's a question of artistry."

"That's what you think. All of our people are artists. Should we all not have to fulfill the quota?"

"Still, I would urge you to take my comments into account. I'm probably not the only one you've heard from."

"That's for sure, but I hear mostly complaints. And besides, how do I know who I'm talking to?"

I slammed the receiver down.

"I knew it," said Vitaly. "He's also against me because I don't bring him money. I act like I don't know about it."

"Know about what?"

"There's this unwritten rule—of course, it never gets mentioned—that every hairdresser who wants to work in peace has to bring him money. Not very much, just enough—three or four rubles a month."

"Good God, Vitaly! What are you saying! Can this be true?"

"Why not? In our neglected sector such things happen in administration. The salary is low, there are no gratuities, they try to improve their lot. Why else would he, with a higher education, be in a job like that?"

"That scoundrel has a higher education? In what?"

"In law. By the way, I like law school, that is of course if it's used according to its intention. I'd be happy to go to law school . . ."

"Fine, but that's in the future. Right now it would be nice to expose Matyunin."

"Matyunin? He's extremely clever. And where are your witnesses? Besides, as long as I'm employed in this sector, stepping forward so directly like that could do harm to my work, it could really make it impossible."

Then suddenly he said:

"But, Marya Vladimirovna, I want to leave."

"Leave this location, you mean?"

"I mean leave this profession."

"What are you talking about? Think about it: you've got a ready-made career in your pocket, and, most importantly, you love your work and have talent."

"That kind of talent isn't suitable for our times. And I'll tell you also, Marya Vladimirovna: I don't mind the pay in terms of quantity, but I don't like it in terms of quality. I'm dependent on the good wishes of customers whom I don't even respect."

"I understand. Only don't you rush it. Would you like me to talk to the people at the film studio about you? Maybe they'll have something for you."

"I've already made some inquiries. The film studio requires special education, a degree from an art institute. It's not important how you do there, you just need that piece of paper . . ."

"We'll see, maybe something will work out. Only don't rush, okay? I'll see you later, Vitaly. Don't get too upset."

Vitaly got up.

"My mood's already reversed. I'll do your hair . . ."

. . . Nothing with the film studio was as simple as I, in my naiveté, had assumed. First of all, there were no positions. Besides that, they really did require that piece of paper. But they promised to think it over; I implored them for Vitaly's sake. With some reluctance I even passed him off as my step-nephew (is there any such thing?).

"Only at your request, and even then it's unlikely," the administrator said.

13

At home there was the usual circus with the boys. I can never manage to convince them that my anger is for real. They turn everything into a farce.

"Clowns!" I said.

"Are you really a person? No, you're a clown!" Kolya yelled in a repulsive voice.

"What are you yelling about, you fool?"

"It's the music from Leoncavallo's opera *Pagliacci!*"

Oh, how I want to punch him in the nose sometimes, for some reason him in particular, not Kostya.

"You know, youth requires a certain attentiveness, a sensitivity, you might say . . ." Kostya submitted.

The telephone rang. Kolya answered it.

"It's for you, your highness. Whoever it is, I pray for his soul!"

I grabbed the receiver. "Yes?"

I didn't recognize Vitaly's voice right away. It was almost singing.

"Marya Vladimirovna," he shouted. "Marya Vladimirovna, congratulate me! I'm no longer a hairdresser! I'm finished with that profession!!"

"What do you mean? So soon? But I told you not to rush. . . . Someone promised me something . . ."

"I don't need anything, Marya Vladimirovna. I want to be responsible to myself alone."

"What did you do, leave your job? Where will you work?"

"At a factory as a metalworker's apprentice. I'm very, very happy!"

"But how . . . why so suddenly?"

"I don't do anything suddenly. My plan has been thought out to the last detail. I'll work in the collective, take the high school equivalency exam, then the college admission exam. But I'll always be willing to make an exception for you and do your hair, Marya Vladimirovna. I can even come to your house, even though it'll be difficult in terms of time."

"Thank you, Vitaly. Thank you very much. I wish you luck. If you ever need any help, you know . . ."

"I understand. I'll call you."

"Please do. All the best to you. Thank you . . . thank you . . ."

I hung up the phone and stood there staring at my palms. There's something here I must have missed . . .

"What happened? Is it good or bad?" Kostya asked.

"I don't know myself. Good, I suppose."

Well, then . . . a pleasant journey to you, Vitaly!

1963

Translated by Brian Thomas Oles

© *Miriam Berkley, by permission*

TILLIE OLSEN ❖ Born in Nebraska in 1913, Tillie Olsen dropped out of high school to work at a variety of odd jobs in order to help support her family. She soon became a social and political activist, organizing packinghouse workers in Omaha and Kansas City, joining the Young Communist League, and aligning herself with the San Francisco labor movement. In 1943 she married Jack Olsen, also a labor activist, and continued her political work while holding temporary jobs ("someone else's work") and rearing four children. Olsen began writing as a young woman, but the demands of this "triple life," as she has called it, continually interrupted her progress. Finally, as she notes in *Silences,* her creative work "died." Olsen resurrected it only in the 1950s, when her youngest daughter entered school. She published the celebrated collection *Tell Me a Riddle* in 1961, followed by the novel *Yonnondio: From the Thirties* (1974)—a book begun many years earlier and long left unfinished—and *Silences* (1978), which explores the relationship of class, race, and sex to "the unnatural thwarting of what struggles to come into being." The recipient of several honorary degrees and of awards from the Ford Foundation, the National Endowment for the Arts, and the Guggenheim Foundation, she has been writer-in-residence at a number of universities, including Amherst, Stanford, and the Massachusetts Institute of Technology. She now lives in California.

Tell Me a Riddle

TILLIE OLSEN

"These Things Shall Be"

1

For forty-seven years they had been married. How deep back the stubborn, gnarled roots of the quarrel reached, no one could say—but only now, when tending to the needs of others no longer shackled them together, the roots swelled up visible, split the earth between them, and the tearing shook even to the children, long since grown.

Why now, why now? wailed Hannah.

As if when we grew up weren't enough, said Paul.

Poor Ma. Poor Dad. It hurts so for both of them, said Vivi. They never had very much; at least in old age they should be happy.

Knock their heads together, insisted Sammy; tell 'em: you're too old for this kind of thing; no reason not to get along now.

Lennie wrote to Clara: They've lived over so much together; what could possibly tear them apart?

Something tangible enough.

Arthritic hands, and such work as he got, occasional. Poverty all his life, and there was little breath left for running. He could not, could not turn away from this desire: to have the troubling of responsibility, the fretting with money, over and done with; to be free, to be *care*free where success was not measured by accumulation, and there was use for the vitality still in him.

There was a way. They could sell the house, and with the money join his lodge's Haven, cooperative for the aged. Happy communal life, and was he not already an official; had he not helped organize it, raise funds, served as a trustee?

But she—would not consider it.

"What do we need all this for?" he would ask loudly, for her hearing aid was turned down and the vacuum was shrilling. "Five rooms" (pushing the sofa so she could get into the corner) "furniture" (smoothing down the rug) "floors and surfaces to make work. Tell me, why do we need it?" And he was glad he could ask in a scream.

"Because I'm use't."

"Because you're use't. This is a reason, Mrs. Word Miser? Used to can get unused!"

"Enough unused I have to get used to already. . . . Not enough words?" turning off the vacuum a moment to hear herself answer. "Because soon enough we'll need only a little closet, no windows, no furniture, nothing to make work, but for worms. Because now I want room. . . . Screech and blow like you're doing, you'll need that closet even sooner. . . . Ha, again!" for the vacuum bag wailed, puffed half up, hung stubbornly limp. "This time fix it so it stays; quick before the phone rings and you get too important-busy."

But while he struggled with the motor, it seethed in him. Why fix it? Why have to bother? And if it can't be fixed, have to wring the mind with how to pay the repair? At the Haven they come in with their own machines to clean your room or your cottage; you fish, or play cards, or make jokes in the sun, not with knotty fingers fight to mend vacuums.

Over the dishes, coaxingly: "For once in your life, to be free, to have everything done for you, like a queen."

"I never liked queens."

"No dishes, no garbage, no towel to sop, no worry what to buy, what to eat."

"And what else would I do with my empty hands? Better to eat at my own table when I want, and to cook and eat how I want."

"In the cottages they buy what you ask, and cook it how you like. You are the one who always used to say: better mankind born without mouths and stomachs than always to worry for money to buy, to shop, to fix, to cook, to wash, to clean."

"How cleverly you hid that you heard. I said it then because eighteen hours a day I ran. And you never scraped a carrot or knew a dish towel sops. Now—for you and me—who cares? A herring out of a jar is enough. But when I want, and nobody to bother." And she turned off her ear button, so she would not have to hear.

But as he had no peace, juggling and rejuggling the money to figure: how will I pay for this now?; prying out the storm windows (there they take care of this); jolting in the streetcar on errands (there I would not have to ride to take care of this or that); fending the patronizing relatives just back from Florida (at the Haven it matters what one is, not what one can afford), he gave her no peace.

"Look! In their bulletin. A reading circle. Twice a week it meets."

"Haumm," her answer of not listening.

"A reading circle. Chekhov they read that you like, and Peretz. Cultured people at the Haven that you would enjoy."

"Enjoy!" She tasted the word. "Now, when it pleases you, you find a reading circle for me. And forty years ago when the children were morsels and there was a Circle, did you stay home with them once so I could go? Even once? You trained me well. I do not need others to enjoy. Others!" Her voice trembled. "Because *you* want to be there with others. Already it makes me sick to think of you always around others. Clown, grimacer, floormat, yesman, entertainer, whatever they want of you."

And now it was he who turned on the television loud so he need not hear.

Old scar tissue ruptured and the wounds festered anew. Chekhov indeed. She thought without softness of that young wife, who in the deep night hours while she nursed the current baby, and perhaps held another in her lap, would try to stay awake for the only time there was to read. She would feel again the weather of the outside on his cheek when, coming late from a meeting, he would find her so, and stimulated and ardent, sniffing her skin, coax: "I'll put the baby to bed, and you—put the book away, don't read, don't read."

That had been the most beguiling of all the "don't read, put your book away" her life had been. Chekhov indeed!

"Money?" She shrugged him off. "Could we get poorer than once we were? And in America, who starves?"

But as still he pressed:

"Let me alone about money. Was there ever enough? Seven little ones—for every penny I had to ask—and sometimes, remember, there was nothing. But always *I* had to manage. Now *you* manage. Rub your nose in it good."

But from those years she had had to manage, old humiliations and terrors rose up, lived again, and forced her to relive them. The children's needings; that grocer's face or this merchant's wife she had had to beg credit from when credit was a disgrace; the scenery of the long blocks walked around when she could not pay; school coming, and the desperate going over the old to see what could yet be remade; the soups of meat bones begged "for-the-dog" one winter. . . .

Enough. Now they had no children. Let *him* wrack his head for how they would live. She would not exchange her solitude for anything. *Never again to be forced to move to the rhythms of others.*

For in this solitude she had won to a reconciled peace.

Tranquillity from having the empty house no longer an enemy, for it stayed clean—not as in the days when it was her family, the life in it, that had seemed the enemy: tracking, smudging, littering, dirtying, engaging her in endless defeating battle—and on whom her endless defeat had been spewed.

The few old books, memorized from rereading; the pictures to ponder (the magnifying glass superimposed on her heavy eyeglasses). Or if she wishes, when he is gone, the phonograph, that if she turns up very loud and strains, she can hear: the ordered sounds and the struggling.

Out in the garden, growing things to nurture. Birds to be kept out of the pear tree, and when the pears are heavy and ripe, the old fury of work, for all must be canned, nothing wasted.

And her one social duty (for she will not go to luncheons or meetings) the boxes of old clothes left with her, as with a life-practised eye for finding what is still wearable within the worn (again the magnifying glass superimposed on the heavy glasses) she scans and sorts—this for rag or rummage, that for mending and cleaning, and this for sending away.

Being able at last to live within, and not move to the rhythms of others, as life had forced her to: denying; removing; isolating; taking the children one by one; then deafening, half-blinding—and at last, presenting her solitude.

And in it she had won to a reconciled peace.

Now he was violating it with his constant campaigning: *Sell the house and move to the Haven.* (You sit, you sit—there too you could sit like a stone.) He was making of her a battleground where old grievances tore. (Turn on your ear button—I am talking.) And stubbornly she resisted—so that from wheedling, reasoning, manipulation, it was bitterness he now started with.

And it came to where every happening lashed up a quarrel.

"I will sell the house anyway," he flung at her one night. "I am putting it up for sale. There will be a way to make you sign."

The television blared, as always it did on the evenings he stayed home, and as always it reached her only as noise. She did not know if the tumult was in her or outside. Snap! she turned the sound off. "Shadows," she whispered to him, pointing to the screen, "look, it is only shadows." And in a scream: "Did you say that you will sell the house? Look at me, not at that. I am no shadow. You cannot sell without me."

"Leave on the television. I am watching."

"Like Paulie, like Jenny, a four-year-old. Staring at shadows. *You cannot sell the house.*"

"I will. We are going to the Haven. There you would not hear the television when you do not want it. I could sit in the social room and watch. You could lock yourself up to smell your unpleasantness in a room by yourself— for who would want to come near you?"

"No, no selling." A whisper now.

"The television is shadows. Mrs. Enlightened! Mrs. Cultured! A world comes into your house—and it is shadows. People you would never meet in a thousand lifetimes. Wonders. When you were four years old, yes, like

Paulie, like Jenny, did you know of Indian dances, alligators, how they use bamboo in Malaya? No, you scratched in your dirt with the chickens and thought Olshana was the world. Yes, Mrs. Unpleasant, I will sell the house, for there better can we be rid of each other than here."

She did not know if the tumult was outside, or in her. Always a ravening inside, a pull to the bed, to lie down, to succumb.

"Have you thought maybe Ma should let a doctor have a look at her?" asked their son Paul after Sunday dinner, regarding his mother crumpled on the couch, instead of, as was her custom, busying herself in Nancy's kitchen.

"Why not the President too?"

"Seriously, Dad. This is the third Sunday she's lain down like that after dinner. Is she that way at home?"

"A regular love affair with the bed. Every time I start to talk to her."

Good protective reaction, observed Nancy to herself. The workings of hos-til-ity.

"Nancy could take her. I just don't like how she looks. Let's have Nancy arrange an appointment."

"You think she'll go?" regarding his wife gloomily. "All right, we have to have doctor bills, we have to have doctor bills." Loudly: "Something hurts you?"

She startled, looked to his lips. He repeated: "Mrs. Take It Easy, something hurts?"

"Nothing. . . . Only you."

"A woman of honey. That's why you're lying down?"

"Soon I'll get up to do the dishes, Nancy."

"Leave them, Mother, I like it better this way."

"Mrs. Take It Easy, Paul says you should start ballet. You should go to see a doctor and ask: how soon can you start ballet?"

"A doctor?" she begged. "Ballet?"

"We were talking, Ma," explained Paul, "you don't seem any too well. It would be a good idea for you to see a doctor for a checkup."

"I get up now to do the kitchen. Doctors are bills and foolishness, my son. I need no doctors."

"At the Haven," he could not resist pointing out, "a doctor is *not* bills. He lives beside you. You start to sneeze, he is there before you open up a Kleenex. You can be sick there for free, all you want."

"Diarrhea of the mouth, is there a doctor to make you dumb?"

"Ma. Promise me you'll go. Nancy will arrange it."

"It's all of a piece when you think of it," said Nancy, "the way she attacks my kitchen, scrubbing under every cup hook, doing the inside of the oven so I can't enjoy Sunday dinner, knowing that half-blind or not, she's going to find every speck of dirt. . . ."

"Don't, Nancy, I've told you—it's the only way she knows to be useful. What did the *doctor* say?"

"A real fatherly lecture. Sixty-nine is young these days. Go out, enjoy life, find interests. Get a new hearing aid, this one is antiquated. Old age is sickness only if one makes it so. Geriatrics, Inc."

"So there was nothing physical."

"Of course there was. How can you live to yourself like she does without there being? Evidence of a kidney disorder, and her blood count is low. He gave her a diet, and she's to come back for follow-up and lab work. . . . But he was clear enough: Number One prescription—start living like a human being. . . . When I think of your dad, who could really play the invalid with that arthritis of his, as active as a teenager, and twice as much fun. . . ."

"You didn't tell me the doctor says your sickness is in you, how you live." He pushed his advantage. "Life and enjoyments you need better than medicine. And this diet, how can you keep it? To weigh each morsel and scrape away each bit of fat, to make this soup, that pudding. There, at the Haven, they have a dietician, they would do it for you."

She is silent.

"You would feel better there, I know it," he says gently. "There there is life and enjoyments all around."

"What is the matter, Mr. Importantbusy, you have no card game or meeting you can go to?"—turning her face to the pillow.

For a while he cut his meetings and going out, fussed over her diet, tried to wheedle her into leaving the house, brought in visitors:

"I should come to a fashion tea. I should sit and look at pretty babies in clothes I cannot buy. This is pleasure?"

"Always you are better than everyone else. The doctor said you should go out. Mrs. Brem comes to you with goodness and you turn her away."

"Because *you* asked her to, she asked me."

"They won't come back. People you need, the doctor said. Your own cousins I asked; they were willing to come and make peace as if nothing had happened. . . ."

"No more crushers of people, pushers, hypocrites, around me. No more in *my* house. You go to them if you like."

"Kind he is to visit. And you, like ice."

"A babbler. All my life around babblers. Enough!"

"She's even worse, Dad? Then let her stew a while," advised Nancy. "You can't let it destroy you; it's a psychological thing, maybe too far gone for any of us to help."

So he let her stew. More and more she lay silent in bed, and sometimes did not even get up to make the meals. No longer was the tongue-lashing inevitable if he left the coffee cup where it did not belong, or forgot to take out the garbage or mislaid the broom. The birds grew bold that summer and for once pocked the pears, undisturbed.

A bellyful of bitterness and every day the same quarrel in a new way and a different old grievance the quarrel forced her to enter and relive. And the new torment: I am not really sick, the doctor said it, then why do I feel so sick?

One night she asked him: "You have a meeting tonight? Do not go. Stay . . . with me."

He had planned to watch "This Is Your Life," but half sick himself from the heavy heat, and sickening therefore the more after the brooks and woods of the Haven, with satisfaction he grated:

"Hah, Mrs. Live Alone And Like It wants company all of a sudden. It doesn't seem so good the time of solitary when she was a girl exile in Siberia. 'Do not go. Stay with me.' A new song for Mrs. Free As A Bird. Yes, I am going out, and while I am gone chew this aloneness good, and think how you keep us both from where if you want people, you do not need to be alone."

"Go, go. All your life you have gone without me."

After him she sobbed curses he had not heard in years, old-country curses from their childhood: Grow, oh shall you grow like an onion, with your head in the ground. Like the hide of a drum shall you be, beaten in life, beaten in death. Oh shall you be like a chandelier, to hang, and to burn. . . .

She was not in their bed when he came back. She lay on the cot on the sun porch. All week she did not speak or come near him; nor did he try to make peace or care for her.

He slept badly, so used to her next to him. After all the years, old harmonies and dependencies deep in their bodies; she curled to him, or he coiled to her, each warmed, warming, turning as the other turned, the nights a long embrace.

It was not the empty bed or the storm that woke him, but a faint singing. *She* was singing. Shaking off the drops of rain, the lightning riving her lifted face, he saw her so; the cot covers on the floor.

"This is a private concert?" he asked. "Come in, you are wet."

"I can breathe now," she answered; "my lungs are rich." Though indeed the sound was hardly a breath.

"Come in, come in." Loosing the bamboo shades. "Look how wet you are." Half helping, half carrying her, still faint-breathing her song.

A Russian love song of fifty years ago.

He had found a buyer, but before he told her, he called together those children who were close enough to come. Paul, of course, Sammy from New Jersey, Hannah from Connecticut, Vivi from Ohio.

With a kindling of energy for her beloved visitors she arrayed the house, cooked and baked. She was not prepared for the solemn after-dinner conclave, the too probing in and tearing. Her frightened eyes watched from mouth to mouth as each spoke.

His stories were eloquent and funny of her refusal to go back to the doctor; of the scorned invitations or her stubborn silence or the bile "like a Niagara" of her contrariness: "If I clean it's no good how it's cleaned; if I don't clean, I'm still a master who thinks he has a slave."

(Vinegar he poured on me all his life; I am very marinated; how can I be honey now?)

Deftly he marched in the rightness for moving to the Haven; their money from social security free for visiting the children, not sucked into daily needs and into the house; the activities in the Haven for him; but mostly the Haven for *her:* her health, her need of care, distraction, amusement, friends who shared her interests.

"This does offer an outlet for Dad," said Paul; "he's always been an active person. And economic peace of mind isn't to be sneezed at, either. I could use a little of that myself."

But when they asked: "And you, Ma, how do you feel about it?" could only whisper:

"For him it is good. It is not for me. I can no longer live between people."

"You lived all your life *for* people," Vivi cried.

"Not with." Suffering doubly for the unhappiness on her children's faces.

"You have to find some compromise," Sammy insisted. "Maybe sell the house and buy a trailer. After forty-seven years there's surely some way you can find to live in peace."

"There is no help, my children. Different things we need."

"Then live alone!" He could control himself no longer. "I have a buyer for the house. Half the money for you, half for me. Either alone or with me to the Haven. You think I can live any longer as we are doing now?"

"Ma doesn't have to make a decision this minute, however you feel, Dad," Paul said quickly, "and you wouldn't want her to. Let's let it lay a few months and then talk some more."

"I think I can work it out to take Mother home with me for a while,"

Hannah said. "You both look terrible, but especially you, Mother. I'm going to ask Phil to have a look at you."

"Sure," cracked Sammy. "What's the use of a doctor husband if you can't get free service out of him once in a while for the family? And absence might make the heart . . . you know."

"There was something after all," Paul told Nancy in a colorless voice. "That was Hannah's Phil calling. Her gall bladder. . . . Surgery."

"Her *gall* bladder. If that isn't classic. 'Bitter as gall'—talk of psycho-som——"

He stepped closer, put his hand over her mouth, and said in the same colorless, plodding voice. "We have to get Dad. They operated at once. The cancer was everywhere, surrounding the liver, everywhere. They did what they could . . . at best she has a year. Dad . . . we have to tell him."

2

Honest in his weakness when they told him, and that she was not to know. "I'm not an actor. She'll know right away by how I am. Oh that poor woman. I am old too, it will break me into pieces. Oh that poor woman. She will spit on me: 'So my sickness was how I live.' Oh Paulie, how she will be, that poor woman. Only she should not suffer. . . . I can't stand sickness, Paulie, I can't go with you."

But went. And play-acted.

"A grand opening and you did not even wait for me. . . . A good thing Hannah took you with her."

"Fashion teas I needed. They cut out what tore in me; just in my throat something hurts yet. . . . Look! so many flowers, like a funeral. Vivi called, did Hannah tell you? And Lennie from San Francisco, and Clara; and Sammy is coming." Her gnome's face pressed happily into the flowers.

> It is impossible to predict in these cases, but once over the immediate effects of the operation, she should have several months of comparative well-being.
> *The money, where will come the money?*
> Travel with her, Dad. Don't take her home to the old associations. The other children will want to see her.
> *The money, where will I wring the money?*
> Whatever happens, she is not to know. No, you can't ask her to sign papers to sell the house; nothing to upset her. Borrow instead, then after. . . .
> *I had wanted to leave you each a few dollars to make life easier, as other fathers do. There will be nothing left now. (Failure! you and your "business is*

from her, so that he wails. And a long shudder begins, and the sweat beads on her forehead.

"Hush, shush," croons the grandfather, lifting him back. "You should forgive your grandmamma, little prince, she has never held a baby before, only seen them in glass cases. Hush, shush."

"You're tired, Ma," says Vivi. "The travel and the noisy dinner. I'll take you to lie down."

(*A long travel from, to, what the feel of a baby evokes.*)

In the airplane, cunningly designed to encase from motion (no wind, no feel of flight), she had sat severely and still, her face turned to the sky through which they cleaved and left no scar.

So this was how it looked, the determining, the crucial sky, and this was how man moved through it, remote above the dwindled earth, the concealed human life. Vulnerable life, that could scar.

There was a steerage ship of memory that shook across a great, circular sea: clustered, ill human beings; and through the thick-stained air, tiny fretting waters in a window round like the airplane's—sun round, moon round. (The round thatched roofs of Olshana.) Eye round—like the smaller window that framed distance the solitary year of exile when only her eyes could travel, and no voice spoke. And the polar winds hurled themselves across snows trackless and endless and white—like the clouds which had closed together below and hidden the earth.

Now they put a baby in her lap. Do not ask me, she would have liked to beg. Enough the worn face of Vivi, the remembered grandchildren. I cannot, cannot. . . .

Cannot what? Unnatural grandmother, not able to make herself embrace a baby.

She lay there in the bed of the two little girls, her new hearing aid turned full, listening to the sound of the children going to sleep, the baby's fretful crying and hushing, the clatter of dishes being washed and put away. They thought she slept. Still she rode on.

It was not that she had not loved her babies, her children. The love—the passion of tending—had risen with the need like a torrent; and like a torrent drowned and immolated all else. But when the need was done—oh the power that was lost in the painful damming back and drying up of what still surged, but had nowhere to go. Only the thin pulsing left that could not quiet, suffering over lives one felt, but could no longer hold nor help.

On that torrent she had borne them on their own lives, and the riverbed was desert long years now. Not there would she dwell, a memoried wraith. Surely that was not all, surely there was more. Still the springs, the springs were in her seeking. Somewhere an older power that beat for life. Some-where coherence, transport, meaning. If they would but leave her in the air now stilled of clamor, in the reconciled solitude, to journey on.

And they put a baby in her lap. Immediacy to embrace, and the breath of *that* past: warm flesh like this that had claims and nuzzled away all else and with lovely mouths devoured; hot-living like an animal—intensely and now; the turning maze; the long drunkenness; the drowning into needing and being needed. Severely she looked back—and the shudder seized her again, and the sweat. Not that way. Not there, not now could she, not yet. . . .

And all that visit, she could not touch the baby.

"Daddy, is it the . . . sickness she's like that?" asked Vivi. "I was so glad to be having the baby—for her. I told Tim, it'll give her more happiness than anything, being around a baby again. And she hasn't played with him once."

He was not listening. "Aahh little seed of life, little charmer," he crooned, "Hollywood should see you. A heart of ice you would melt. Kick, kick. The future you'll have for a ball. In 2050 still kick. Kick for your grandaddy then."

Attentive with the older children; sat through their performances (command performance; we command you to be the audience); helped Ann sort autumn leaves to find the best for a school program; listened gravely to Richard tell about his rock collection, while her lips mutely formed the words to remember: *igneous, sedimentary, metamorphic;* looked for missing socks, books, and bus tickets; watched the children whoop after their grandfather who knew how to tickle, chuck, lift, toss, do tricks, tell secrets, make jokes, match riddle for riddle. (Tell me a riddle, Grammy. I know no riddles, child.) Scrubbed sills and woodwork and furniture in every room; folded the laun-dry; straightened drawers; emptied the heaped baskets waiting for ironing (while he or Vivi or Tim nagged: You're supposed to rest here, you've been sick) but to none tended or gave food—and could not touch the baby.

After a week she said: "Let us go home. Today call about the tickets."

"You have important business, Mrs. Inahurry? The President waits to consult with you?" He shouted, for the fear of the future raced in him. "The clothes are still warm from the suitcase, your children cannot show enough how glad they are to see you, and you want home. There is plenty of time for home. We cannot be with the children at home."

"Blind to around you as always: the little ones sleep four in a room be-cause we take their bed. We are two more people in a house with a new baby, and no help."

"Vivi is happy so. The children should have their grandparents a while, she told to me. I should have my mommy and daddy. . . ."

"Babbler and blind. Do you look at her so tired? How she starts to talk and she cries? I am not strong enough yet to help. Let us go home."

(To reconciled solitude.)

For it seemed to her the crowded noisy house was listening to her, listening for her. She could feel it like a great ear pressed under her heart. And everything knocked: quick constant raps: let me in, let me in.

How was it that soft reaching tendrils also became blows that knocked?

C'mon, Grandma, I want to show you. . . .

Tell me a riddle, Grandma. (*I know no riddles.*)

Look, Grammy, he's so dumb he can't even find his hands. (Dody and the baby on a blanket over the fermenting autumn mould.)

I made them—for you. (Ann) (Flat paper dolls with aprons that lifted on scalloped skirts that lifted on flowered pants; hair of yarn and great ringed questioning eyes.)

Watch me, Grandma. (Richard snaking up the tree, hanging exultant, free, with one hand at the top. Below Dody hunching over in pretend-cooking.)

(*Climb too, Dody, climb and look.*)

Be my nap bed, Grammy. (The "No!" too late.)

Morty's abandoned heaviness, while his fingers ladder up and down her hearing-aid cord to his drowsy chant: eentsiebeentsiespider. (*Children trust.*)

It's to start off your own rock collection, Grandma.

That's a trilobite fossil, 200 million years old (millions of years on a boy's mouth) and that one's obsidian, black glass.

Knocked and knocked.

Mother, I *told* you the teacher said we had to bring it back all filled out this morning. Didn't you even ask Daddy? Then tell *me* which plan and I'll check it: evacuate or stay in the city or wait for you to come and take me away. (Seeing the look of straining to hear.) It's for Disaster, Grandma. (*Children trust.*)

Vivi in the maze of the long, the lovely drunkenness. The old old noises: baby sounds; screaming of a mother flayed to exasperation; children quarreling; children playing; singing; laughter.

And Vivi's tears and memories, spilling so fast, half the words not understood.

She had started remembering out loud deliberately, so her mother would know the past was cherished, still lived in her.

Nursing the baby: My friends marvel, and I tell them, oh it's easy to be such a cow. I remember how beautiful my mother seemed nursing my brother, and the milk just flows. . . . Was that Davy? It must have been Davy. . . .

Lowering a hem: How did you ever . . . when I think how you made everything we wore . . . Tim, just think, seven kids and Mommy sewed everything . . . do I remember you sang while you sewed? That white dress with the red apples on the skirt you fixed over for me, was it Hannah's or Clara's before it was mine?

Washing sweaters: Ma, I'll never forget, one of those days so nice you washed clothes outside; one of the first spring days it must have been. The bubbles just danced while you scrubbed, and we chased after, and you stopped to show us how to blow our own bubbles with green onion stalks . . . you always. . . .

"Strong onion, to still make you cry after so many years," her father said, to turn the tears into laughter.

While Richard bent over his homework: Where is it now, do we still have it, the Book of the Martyrs? It always seemed so, well—exalted, when you'd put it on the round table and we'd all look at it together; there was even a halo from the lamp. The lamp with the beaded fringe you could move up and down; they're in style again, pulley lamps like that, but without the fringe. You know the book I'm talking about, Daddy, the Book of the Martyrs, the first picture was a bust of Spartacus . . . Socrates? I wish there was something like that for the children, Mommy, to give them what you. . . . (And the tears splashed again.)

(What I intended and did not? Stop it, daughter, stop it, leave that time. And he, the hyprocrite, sitting there with tears in his eyes—it was nothing to you then, nothing.)

. . . The time you came to school and I almost died of shame because of your accent and because I knew you knew I was ashamed; how could I? . . . Sammy's harmonica and you danced to it once, yes you did, you and Davy squealing in your arms. . . . That time you bundled us up and walked us down to the railway station to stay the night 'cause it was heated and we didn't have coal, that winter of the strike, you didn't think I remembered that, did you, Mommy? . . . How you'd call us out to see the sunsets. . . .

Day after day, the spilling memories. Worse now, questions, too. Even the grandchildren: Grandma, in the olden days, when you were little. . . .

It was the afternoons that saved.

While they thought she napped, she would leave the mosaic on the wall (of children's drawings, maps, calendars, pictures, Ann's cardboard dolls with their great ringed questioning eyes) and hunch in the girls' closet on the low shelf where the shoes stood, and the girls' dresses covered.

For that while she would painfully sheathe against the listening house, the tendrils and noises that knocked, and Vivi's spilling memories. Sometimes it helped to braid and unbraid the sashes that dangled, or to trace the pattern on the hoop slips.

Today she had jacks and children under jet trails to forget. Last night, Ann and Dody silhouetted in the window against a sunset of flaming man-made clouds of jet trail, their jacks ball accenting the peaceful noise of dinner being made. Had she told them, yes she had told them of how they played jacks in her village though there was no ball, no jacks. Six stones, round and flat, toss them out, the seventh on the back of the hand, toss, catch and swoop up as many as possible, toss again. . . .

Of stones (repeating Richard) there are three kinds: earth's fire jetting; rock of layered centuries; crucibled new out of the old (*igneous, sedimentary, metamorphic*). But there was that other—frozen to black glass, never to transform or hold the fossil memory . . . (let not my seed fall on stone). There was an ancient man who fought to heights a great rock that crashed back down eternally—eternal labor, freedom, labor . . . (stone will perish, but the word remain). And you, David, who with a stone slew, screaming: Lord, take my heart of stone and give me flesh.

Who was screaming? Why was she back in the common room of the prison, the sun motes dancing in the shafts of light, and the informer being brought in, a prisoner now, like themselves. And Lisa leaping, yes, Lisa, the gentle and tender, biting at the betrayer's jugular. Screaming and screaming.

No, it is the children screaming. Another of Paul and Sammy's terrible fights?

In Vivi's house. Severely: you are in Vivi's house.

Blows, screams, a call: "Grandma!" For her? Oh please not for her. Hide, hunch behind the dresses deeper. But a trembling little body hurls itself beside her—surprised, smothered laughter, arms surround her neck, tears rub dry on her cheek, and words too soft to understand whisper into her ear (Is this where you hide too, Grammy? It's my secret place, we have a secret now).

And the sweat beads, and the long shudder seizes.

It seemed the great ear pressed inside now, and the knocking. "We have to go home," she told him, "I grow ill here."

"It's your own fault, Mrs. Bodybusy, you do not rest, you do too much." He raged, but the fear was in his eyes. "It was a serious operation, they told you to take care. . . . All right, we will go to where you can rest."

But where? Not home to death, not yet. He had thought to Lennie's, to Clara's; beautiful visits with each of the children. She would have to rest first, be stronger. If they could but go to Florida—it glittered before him, the never-realized promise of Florida. California: of course. (The money, the money, dwindling!) Los Angeles first for sun and rest, then to Lennie's in San Francisco.

He told her the next day. "You saw what Nancy wrote: snow and wind back home, a terrible winter. And look at you—all bones and a swollen belly. I called Phil: he said: 'A prescription, Los Angeles sun and rest.'"

She watched the words on his lips. "You have sold the house," she cried, "that is why we do not go home. That is why you talk no more of the Haven, why there is money for travel. After the children you will drag me to the Haven."

"The Haven! Who thinks of the Haven any more? Tell her, Vivi, tell Mrs. Suspicious: a prescription, sun and rest, to make you healthy. . . . And how could I sell the house without *you?*"

At the place of farewells and greetings, of winds of coming and winds of going, they say their good-byes.

They look back at her with the eyes of others before them: Richard with her own blue blaze; Ann with the nordic eyes of Tim; Morty's dreaming brown of a great-grandmother he will never know; Dody with the laughing eyes of him who had been her springtide love (who stands beside her now); Vivi's, all tears.

The baby's eyes are closed in sleep.

Good-bye, my children.

3

It is to the back of the great city he brought her, to the dwelling places of the cast-off old. Bounded by two lines of amusement piers to the north and to the south, and between a long straight paving rimmed with black benches facing the sand—sands so wide the ocean is only a far fluting.

In the brief vacation season, some of the boarded stores fronting the sands open, and families, young people and children, may be seen. A little tasselled tram shuttles between the piers, and the lights of roller coasters prink and tweak over those who come to have sensation made in them.

The rest of the year it is abandoned to the old, all else boarded up and still; seemingly empty, except the occasional days and hours when the sun, like a tide, sucks them out of the low rooming houses, casts them onto the benches and sandy rim of the walk—and sweeps them into decaying enclosures once again.

A few newer apartments glint among the low bleached squares. It is in week. They have never been? She will come to them for dinner tomorrow and they will all go together.

So it is that she sits in the wind of the singing, among the thousand various faces of age.

She had turned off her hearing aid at once they came into the auditorium—as she would have wished to turn off sight.

One by one they streamed by and imprinted on her—and though the savage zest of their singing came voicelessly soft and distant, the faces still roared—the faces densened the air—chorded into

children-chants, mother-croons, singing of the chained love serenades, Beethoven storms, mad Lucia's scream, drunken joy-songs, keens for the dead, work-singing

> *while from floor to balcony to dome a bare-footed sore-covered little girl threaded the sound-thronged tumult, danced her ecstasy of grimace to flutes that scratched at a cross-roads village wedding*

Yes, faces became sound, and the sound became faces; and faces and sound became weight—pushed, pressed

"Air"—her hands claw his.

"Whenever I enjoy myself. . . ." Then he saw the gray sweat on her face. "Here. Up. Help me, Mrs. Mays," and they support her out to where she can gulp the air in sob after sob.

"A doctor, we should get for her a doctor."

"Tch, it's nothing," says Ellen Mays, "I get it all the time. You've missed the tram; come to my place. Fix your hearing aid, honey . . . close . . . tea. My view. See, she *wants* to come. Steady now, that's how." Adding mysteriously: "Remember your advice, easy to keep your head above water, empty things float. Float."

The singing a fading march for them, tall woman with a swollen leg, weaving little man, and the swollen thinness they help between.

The stench in the hall: mildew? decay? "We sit and rest then climb. My gorgeous view. We help each other and here we are."

The stench along into the slab of room. A washstand for a sink, a box with oilcloth tacked around for a cupboard, a three-burner gas plate. Artificial flowers, colorless with dust. Everywhere pictures foaming: wedding, baby, party, vacation, graduation, family pictures. From the narrow couch under a slit of window, sure enough the view: lurching rooftops and a scallop of ocean heaving, preening, twitching under the moon.

"While the water heats. Excuse me . . . down the hall." Ellen Mays has gone.

"You'll live?" he asks mechanically, sat down to feel his fright; tried to pull her alongside.

She pushed him away. "For air," she said; stood clinging to the dresser. Then, in a terrible voice:

After a lifetime of room. Of many rooms.

Shhh.

You remember how she lived. Eight children. And now one room like a coffin.

She pays rent!

Shrinking the life of her   into one room   like a coffin   Rooms and rooms like this   I lie on the quilt and hear them talk

Please, Mrs. Orator-without-Breath.

Once you went for coffee   I walked   I saw A Balzac   a Chekhov to write it   Rummage   Alone   On scraps

Better old here than in the old country!

On scraps   Yet they sang like like   Wondrous! *Humankind one has to believe*   So strong for what? To rot   not grow?

Your poor lungs beg you. They sob between each word.

Singing.   Unused   the life in them.   She in this poor room with her   pictures   Max   You   The children   Everywhere un-used   the life   And who has meaning?   Century after century   still all in us   not   to grow?

Coffins, rummage, plants: sick woman. Oh lay down. We will get for you the doctor.

"And when will it end. Oh, *the end.*" *That* nightmare thought, and this time she writhed, crumpled against him, seized his hand (for a moment again the weight, the soft distant roaring of humanity) and on the strangled-for breath, begged: "Man . . . we'll destroy ourselves?"

And looking for answer—in the helpless pity and fear for her (for *her*) that distorted his face—she understood the last months, and knew that she was dying.

4

"Let us go home," she said after several days.

"You are in training for a cross-country run? That is why you do not even walk across the room? Here, like a prescription Phil said, till you are stronger from the operation. You want to break doctor's orders?"

In a half-whisper: "Like Lisa she is, your Jeannie. Have I told you of Lisa who taught me to read? Of the highborn she was, but noble in herself. I was sixteen; they beat me; my father beat me so I would not go to her. It was forbidden, she was a Tolstoyan. At night, past dogs that howled, terrible dogs, my son, in the snows of winter to the road, I to ride in her carriage like a lady, to books. To her, life was holy, knowledge was holy, and she taught me to read. They hung her. Everything that happens one must try to understand why. She killed one who betrayed many. Because of betrayal, betrayed all she lived and believed. In one minute she killed, before my eyes (there is so much blood in a human being, my son), in prison with me. All that happens, one must try to understand.

"The name?" Her lips would work. "The name that was their pole star; the doors of the death houses fixed to open on it; I read of it my year of penal servitude. Thuban!" very excited. "Thuban, in ancient Egypt the pole star. Can you see, look out to see it, Jeannie, if it swings around *our* pole star that seems to *us* not to move.

"Yes, Jeannie, at your age my mother and grandmother had already buried children . . . yes, Jeannie, it is more than oceans between Olshana and you . . . yes, Jeannie, they danced, and for all the bodies they had they might as well be chickens, and indeed, they scratched and flapped their arms and hopped.

"And Andrei Yefimitch, who for twenty years had never known of it and never wanted to know, said as if he wanted to cry: but why my dear friend this malicious laughter?" Telling to herself half-memorized phrases from her few books. "Pain I answer with tears and cries, baseness with indignation, meanness with repulsion . . . for life may be hated or wearied of, but never despised."

Delirious: "Tell me, my neighbor, Mrs. Mays, the pictures never lived, but what of the flowers? Tell them who ask: no rabbis, no ministers, no priests, no speeches, no ceremonies: ah, false—let the living comfort themselves. Tell Sammy's boy, he who flies, tell him to go to Stuttgart and see where Davy has no grave. And what? . . . And what? where millions have no graves—save air."

In delirium or not, wanting the radio on; not seeming to listen, the words still jetting, wanting the music on. Once, silencing it abruptly as of old, she began to cry, unconcealed tears this time. "You have pain, Granny?" Jeannie asked.

"The music," she said, "still it is there and we do not hear; knocks, and our poor human ears too weak. What else, what else we do not hear?"

Once she knocked his hand aside as he gave her a pill, swept the bottles from her bedside table: "no pills, let me feel what I feel," and laughed as on his hands and knees he groped to pick them up.

Nighttimes her hand reached across the bed to hold his.

A constant retching began. Her breath was too faint for sustained speech now, but still the lips moved:

When no longer necessary   to injure others
Pick   pick pick   Blind Chicken
As a human being   responsibility

"David!" imperious, "Basin!" and she would vomit, rinse her mouth, the wasted throat working to swallow, and begin the chant again.

She will be better off in the hospital now, the doctor said.

He sent the telegrams to the children, was packing her suitcase, when her hoarse voice startled. She had roused, was pulling herself to sitting.

"Where now?" she asked. "Where now do you drag me?"

"You do not even have to have a baby to go this time," he soothed, looking for the brush to pack. "Remember, after Davy you told me—worthy to have a baby for the pleasure of the ten day rest in the hospital?"

"Where now? Not home yet?" Her voice mourned. "Where *is* my home?"

He rose to ease her back. "The doctor, the hospital," he started to explain, but deftly, like a snake, she had slithered out of bed and stood swaying, propped behind the night table.

"Coward," she hissed, "runner."

"You stand," he said senselessly.

"To take me there and run. Afraid of a little vomit."

He reached her as she fell. She struggled against him, half slipped from his arms, pulled herself up again.

"Weakling," she taunted, "to leave me there and run. Betrayer. All your life you have run."

He sobbed, telling Jeannie. "A Marilyn Monroe to run for her virtue. Fifty-nine pounds she weighs, the doctor said, and she beats at me like a Dempsey. Betrayer, she cries, and I running like a dog when she calls; day and night, running to her, her vomit, the bedpan. . . ."

"She needs you, Grandaddy," said Jeannie. "Isn't that what they call love? I'll see if she sleeps, and if she does, poor worn-out darling, we'll have a party, you and I: I brought us rum babas."

They did not move her. By her bed now stood the tall hooked pillar that held the solutions—blood and dextrose—to feed her veins. Jeannie moved down the hall to take over the sickroom, her face so radiant, her grandfather asked her once: "you are in love?" (Shameful the joy, the pure overwhelming joy from being with her grandmother; the peace, the serenity that breathed.) "My darling escape," she answered incoherently, "my darling Granny"—as if that explained.

Now one by one the children came, those that were able. Hannah, Paul, Sammy. Too late to ask: and what did you learn with your living, Mother, and what do we need to know?

Clara, the eldest, clenched:

>*Pay me back, Mother, pay me back for all you took from me. Those others you crowded into your heart. The hands I needed to be for you, the heaviness, the responsibility.*
>
>*Is this she? Noises the dying make, the crablike hands crawling over the covers. The ethereal singing.*
>
>*She hears that music, that singing from childhood; forgotten sound—not heard since, since. . . . And the hardness breaks like a cry: Where did we lose each other, first mother, singing mother?*
>
>*Annulled: the quarrels, the gibing, the harshness between; the fall into silence and the withdrawal.*
>
>*I do not know you, Mother. Mother, I never knew you.*

Lennie, suffering not alone for her who was dying, but for that in her which never lived (for that which in him might never live). From him too, unspoken words: *good-bye Mother who taught me to mother myself.*

Not Vivi, who must stay with her children; not Davy, but he is already here, having to die again with *her* this time, for the living take their dead with them when they die.

Light she grew, like a bird, and, like a bird, sound bubbled in her throat while the body fluttered in agony. Night and day, asleep or awake (though indeed there was no difference now) the songs and the phrases leaping.

And he, who had once dreaded a long dying (from fear of himself, from horror of the dwindling money) now desired her quick death profoundly, for *her* sake. He no longer went out, except when Jeannie forced him; no longer laughed, except when in the bright kitchenette, Jeannie coaxed his laughter (and she, who seemed to hear nothing else, would laugh too, conspiratorial wisps of laughter).

Light, like a bird, the fluttering body, the little claw hands, the beaked shadow on her face; and the throat, bubbling, straining.

He tried not to listen, as he tried not to look on the face in which only the forehead remained familiar, but trapped with her the long nights in that little room, the sounds worked themselves into his consciousness, with their punctuation of death swallows, whimpers, gurglings.

Even in reality (swallow) *life's lack of it*
Slaveships   deathtrains   clubs   enough
The bell   Summon what enables
78,000 in one minute (whisper of a scream) *78,000*
human beings   we'll destroy ourselves?

"Aah, Mrs. Miserable," he said, as if she could hear, "all your life working, and now in bed you lie, servants to tend, you do not even need to call to be tended, and still you work. Such hard work it is to die? Such hard work?"

The body threshed, her hand clung in his. A melody, ghost-thin, hovered on her lips, and like a guilty ghost, the vision of her bent in listening to it, silencing the record instantly he was near. Now, heedless of his presence, she floated the melody on and on.

"Hid it from me," he complained, "how many times you listened to remember it so?" And tried to think when she had first played it, or first begun to silence her few records when he came near—but could reconstruct nothing. There was only this room with its tall hooked pillar and its swarm of sounds.

No man one   except through others
Strong   with the not yet   in the now
Dogma dead   war dead   one country

"It helps, Mrs. Philosopher, words from books? It helps?" And it seemed to him that for seventy years she had hidden a tape recorder, infinitely microscopic, within her, that it had coiled infinite mile on mile, trapping every song, every melody, every word read, heard, and spoken—and that maliciously she was playing back only what said nothing of him, of the children, of their intimate life together.

"Left us indeed, Mrs. Babbler," he reproached, "you who called others babbler and cunningly saved your words. A lifetime you tended and loved, and now not a word of us, for us. Left us indeed? Left me."

And he took out his solitaire deck, shuffled the cards loudly, slapped them down.

Lift high banner of reason (tatter of an orator's voice)
justice   freedom   light
Humankind   life/worthy   capacities
Seeks (blur of shudder) *belong   human being*

moved, of being one and indivisible with the great of the past, with all that freed, ennobled. Package it, stand on corners, in front of stadiums and on crowded beaches, knock on doors, give it as a fabled gift.

"And why not in cereal boxes, in soap packages?" he mocked himself. "Aah. You have taken my senses, cadaver."

Words foamed, died unsounded. Her body writhed; she made kissing motions with her mouth. (Her lips moving as she read, poring over the Book of the Martyrs, the magnifying glass superimposed over the heavy eyeglasses.) *Still she believed?* "Eva!" he whispered. "Still you believed? You lived by it? These Things Shall Be?"

"One pound soup meat," she answered distinctly, "one soup bone."

"My ears heard you. Ellen Mays was witness: 'Humankind . . . one has to believe.'" Imploringly: "Eva!"

"Bread, day-old." She was mumbling. "Please, in a wooden box . . . for kindling. The thread, hah, the thread breaks. Cheap thread"—and a gurgling, enormously loud, began in her throat.

"I ask for stone; she gives me bread—day-old." He pulled his hand away, shouted: "Who wanted questions? Everything you have to wake?" Then dully, "Ah, let me help you turn, poor creature."

Words jumbled, cleared. In a voice of crowded terror:

"Paul, Sammy, don't fight.

"Hannah, have I ten hands?

"How can I give it, Clara, how can I give it if I don't have?"

"You lie," he said sturdily, "there was joy too." Bitterly: "Ah how cheap you speak of us at the last."

As if to rebuke him, as if her voice had no relationship with her flailing body, she sang clearly, beautifully, a school song the children had taught her when they were little; begged:

"Not look   my hair   where they cut. . . ."

(The crown of braids shorn.) And instantly he left the mute old woman poring over the Book of the Martyrs; went past the mother treading at the sewing machine, singing with the children; past the girl in her wrinkled prison dress, hiding her hair with scarred hands, lifting to him her awkward, shamed, imploring eyes of love; and took her in his arms, dear, personal, fleshed, in all the heavy passion he had loved to rouse from her.

"Eva!"

Her little claw hand beat the covers. How much, how much can a man stand? He took up the cards, put them down, circled the beds, walked to the dresser, opened, shut drawers, brushed his hair, moved his hand bit by bit over the mirror to see what of the reflection he could blot out with each move, and felt that at any moment he would die of what was unendurable.

Went to press the buzzer to wake Jeannie, looked down, saw on Jeannie's sketch pad the hospital bed, with *her;* the double bed alongside, with him; the tall pillar feeding into her veins, and their hands, his and hers, clasped, feeding each other. And as if he had been instructed he went to his bed, lay down, holding the sketch (as if it could shield against the monstrous shapes of loss, of betrayal, of death) and with his free hand took hers back into his.

So Jeannie found them in the morning.

That last day the agony was perpetual. Time after time it lifted her almost off the bed, so they had to fight to hold her down. He could not endure and left the room; wept as if there never would be tears enough.

Jeannie came to comfort him. In her light voice she said: Grandaddy, Grandaddy don't cry. She is not there, she promised me. On the last day, she said she would go back to when she first heard music, a little girl on the road of the village where she was born. She promised me. It is a wedding and they dance, while the flutes so joyous and vibrant tremble in the air. Leave her there, Grandaddy, it is all right. She promised me. Come back, come back and help her poor body to die.

> *For two of that generation*
> *Seevya and Genya*
> *Infinite, dauntless, incorruptible*
> *Death deepens the wonder*

1961

Stages of Dissent: Olsen, Grekova, and the Politics of Creativity

SUSAN HARDY AIKEN

Where is she, where is woman in all the spaces he surveys,
in all the scenes he stages?—Hélène Cixous, "Sorties"

Staging Protest: The Carnival of Revolution

When the Berlin Wall collapsed in December 1989 and the ensuing communal celebrations became instant media icons—politics replayed as global spectacle—the festive insurgency at the site of that monumental breakthrough
seemed a striking reenactment of Mikhail Bakhtin's concept of carnival as a
vehicle of antitotalitarian movements, a "liberation from the prevailing truth
of the established order" and "a suspension of all hierarchical rank, privileges, norms and prohibitions" (1984, 10). It is now a critical commonplace
that Bakhtin's idealized configuration of carnival as "the true feast . . . of
becoming, change, and renewal," developed during the Stalin era, encodes
social protest within literary theory, mounting a tacit challenge to totalitari-
anism (Eagleton 144). But as students of revolution have long recognized,
and as subsequent events in Eastern Europe and the former Soviet Union
have amply proven, whatever the emancipatory potential of carnivalesque
protest, its consequences are disquietingly unpredictable: political upheavals
begun in the name of liberation can rapidly become catalysts for fresh violence and new forms of oppression. It is hardly surprising, then, that the
euphoria these events engender commonly intermingles with anxiety, simultaneously concealed and expressed through the turbulent performances of
the celebration.[1]

Almost three decades before the wall's collapse, Tillie Olsen and
I. Grekova, from opposite sides of the world, were pondering precisely these
contradictions. Written within a year of one another, both "Tell Me a Riddle"
and "Ladies' Hairdresser" portray the human spirit in resistance and represent festive, carnivalesque moments as sites of incipient transformation. Both
stories rise toward the climactic rupture of boundaries, at once literal and

psychological, by an insurgent energy that mocks repressive structures, challenges official authority, and blurs the boundaries between protest and play.

Yet the authors evoke quite different meanings from these carnivalesque moments. In Olsen the carnival spirit, begun in the "community sing" and continued in Eva's dying monologues—a mélange of revolutionary songs, slogans, speeches, meditations, and snatches of dialogue, all mingling in an overflow of pent-up recollection—signifies a transformative vision of hope, maintained against the odds of bankrupt lives, a diseased society, and ultimate dissolution, literally embodied in Eva's metastasizing cancer and mortal agony. Olsen's story of death and dying ends with an affirmation of rebirth, evoked by the final figure of Eva as a peasant child in Russia, momentarily transcending her wretched poverty as she whirls in a festival of renewal: "It is a wedding, and they dance."

But for Grekova's Marya the swirling energy of the carnival spirit, climactically erupting in the disastrous communal party, is more ambiguous, its figures of dissolution simultaneously alluring and sinister. Through Marya's ambivalence Grekova enacts her own, implying that the release of suppressed energies, while potentially liberatory and transformative, also threatens the precarious orderliness and restraint that may serve as defenses against both anarchy and the mundane tyrannies of a repressive social order.

This faith in order finds a parallel in the discursive control of the conventional narrative structure Grekova favors—a "style," as she puts it, approximating "exact sciences rather than pure fiction."[2] Her chronologically linear first-person narration, externalized representation of characters, and uncomplicated syntax position her fiction firmly within Russian realist traditions with nineteenth-century roots. How striking, even in translation, is the difference between the straightforward Aristotelian progressions of "Ladies' Hairdresser" and Olsen's fragmentary, discontinuous text—a linguistic stew peppered with multiple histories, voices, and levels of consciousness.

We might read these obvious differences not only in light of Olsen's and Grekova's positions within their respective societies and of their differing theories of artistic production, but, more generally, in light of their views on the place of women writers of their generation in each country. Olsen's story appeared in 1961, at a point of gathering crisis in the American national consciousness. The McCarthy era, during which Olsen herself had come under surveillance, had ended, the civil rights movement was underway, and the first stirrings of a renewed feminist consciousness had begun. A longtime socialist activist, Olsen was also one of the pioneers of the contemporary women's movement: "Silences," her eloquent exploration of the "relationship of circumstances—including class, color, sex" to "the unnatural thwarting" of creativity, was first presented as a lecture in 1962. The emergent ideologies of resistance to the bourgeois status quo found a counterpart in the insurgent spirit animating Olsen's prose, and Eva's dying monologue echoes Olsen's own radical social vision.

Grekova began writing equally late in life, but her stated attitudes toward her art diverge strikingly from Olsen's. Her authorial career began near the end of the Khrushchev regime, on the eve of the Brezhnev era, the period of *zastoi* (stagnation), when literary censorship intensified, forcing many talented writers underground. Despite official Soviet proclamations of women's equality, widespread inequities persisted. Grekova's public position on these discrepancies is contradictory: on the one hand she seems to accept unproblematically the official line, insisting that "women in the Soviet Union have long enjoyed equal rights with men. We are not discriminated against economically or socially, so there is no question of any 'struggle for equal rights.' Equality has, to all intents and purposes, been achieved" (1990, 9–10). Yet immediately afterward she details the staggering array of women's "problems" stemming "from the fact that while we have been granted equal rights with men, we have not been relieved of traditional feminine duties." Grekova neither questions the ideology of "traditional feminine duties" nor acknowledges the inconsistency of her own position, which becomes most conspicuous when she turns to women writers: "They are not discriminated against in any way. Each works as much and as well as her ability, talent, and free time allow. Free time, however, is a commodity in catastrophically short supply for most women. . . . How many women writers are there in the Soviet Union? There are comparatively few. . . . But the same is true of other creative occupations, [in which] women are vastly outnumbered by men" (11). Where Olsen probes the material and ideological circumstances responsible for this inequity, Grekova evades them: "It is not for me to explain the reasons for this state of affairs. But that's the way it is" (11). Such denial lends salience to Olsen's summation: "Proclaiming that one's sex has nothing to do with one's writing" is a sure indication of a woman writer's unconscious "coercion" by the dominant symbolic order (1965, 250).

Similarly, Grekova's use of a pseudonym may indicate not only her recognition of the problematic status of all writers in the Soviet Union of the early sixties, but specifically her concern about cultural censure of women writers. As feminist scholars have shown (e.g., Showalter), the disparagement traditionally inflicted on women writers within androcentric societies has led many of them to adopt pseudonyms as what Olsen, in *Silences*, called "camouflage." At the very least Grekova's decision to use a pseudonym underscores her ambivalence about her belated decision to become a writer. Her reputed reply when the editor of a major journal first urged her to take up full-time authorship reflects (perhaps ironically) the traditional association of female authorship with another female profession socially marked as illicit: "What me, a respectable mother of three? I might as well go on the streets" (Barker, "Reluctant Artist" 6). Given her historical circumstances, Grekova's defensiveness about her own writing, the inconsistencies of her public pronouncements about women's authorship, and her reluctance to be typecast as a "woman writer" are hardly surprising.

Yet such a reading of the authors' respective positions would be misleadingly reductive. For the America of the early sixties might also be called a period of stagnation: despite undercurrents of dissent and incipient social change, the conservative ideologies that were dominant throughout the 1950s on matters of race, gender, class, and political affiliation still prevailed throughout much of the country. Rather than moving with the mainstream, Olsen was still resisting the current of received opinion. On the other hand, the Soviet Union, even under Brezhnev, experienced a creative ferment in the arts. Writers like Solzhenitsyn, Siniavsky, and Grekova herself began speaking for the first time about subjects previously unmentionable: the camps, Soviet failures during the war, and the repressive mechanisms employed by the state to ensure conformity to its policies.

Moreover, rather than simply replicating the party agenda or condoning gender inequities as her essays appear to do, Grekova's fiction stages many forms of dissent. For all its elements of conventional Socialist Realism, "Ladies' Hairdresser" rightly brought her recognition as a major new voice in Soviet letters. The narrative deploys a covert protest, appearing to conform to the tenets of Socialist Realism and the system that maintained them, while in fact subverting both. Though less explicitly than Olsen and with considerably more ironic distance from her characters, Grekova too questions dominant social constructions and oppressive ideologies. She too implies that their stultifying effects are not restricted to public policies but are played out in the most intimate personal interactions, the most intricate textures of consciousness. And despite Grekova's overt repudiation of gender differences and her deliberate self-distancing from other women writers, she, like Olsen, represents woman's body and subjectivity as primary sites where the dialectics of power—that interplay of domination and resistance undergirding all larger political structures—are enacted.

The stories begin with a common image: two households, one obsessively tidied, scrubbed, dusted, the other a "pigsty" (svinstvo); one a site of hard-won "solitude" and "reconciled peace," the other the epitome of disruption. Yet both are places of entrapment for the women who inhabit them. Constricted by ideologies of motherhood that in both Western and Slavic traditions celebrate female selflessness, idealize female suffering, and define female creativity primarily as a function of biological reproduction, both Marya and Eva (their very names recalling the two preeminent mothers of Judeo-Christian tradition) struggle for creative self-expression amid soul-stifling social conditions. In representing the sites of domesticity that open both narratives, Grekova and Olsen launch an implicit critique of the politics of space whereby home is at once literal enclosure and emblem of woman's oppression, a place to which she is symbolically tied but in which she is per-petually *not at home*. The double meaning of "vacuum," that appliance that figures so prominently as an instrument of domestic purification in "Tell Me a Riddle," suggests the hollowness at the core of such spaces.

Significantly, it is only outside the domestic confines that Eva and Marya find the loci of self, security, and creativity that home commonly signifies in both America and Russia. Yet the stories also question whether there really is a clearly definable outside. For both Grekova and Olsen locate in the decaying family a sign of wider social disorder, exposing the link between the oppressions associated with the domestic realm and those of the outside world. In evoking the continuum between official public institutions and the microstructures that subtend them, the stories reveal the far-reaching politi-cal dimensions of such ostensibly privatized constructs as home, motherhood, sexuality, and selfhood.[3] In what follows I want to look more closely at the effects of these configurations in each story, focusing on the implications of their differences and convergences.

Undoing the Permanent

"Ladies' Hairdresser" seems deceptively simple: a middle-aged professional woman meets, mentors, and mothers a gifted young apprentice hairdresser, whose creative drive and passion for self-improvement offer stark contrast to the inertia of her own two "clownish" (*duraki*) boys. In their mutually benefi-cial alliance, she promotes his artistic and intellectual development while he, through his own creative labors, remakes not only her hairdo but herself. In the charged dynamics of their relationship, he becomes at once symbolic son and quasi-lover, his jealousy and devotion no less romantic for the absence of explicit sexual expression. Yet despite the dialectics of creativity their friend-ship engenders, he ultimately abandons his art, capitulating with shocking enthusiasm to the pressures of a system that blocks his inspiration and balks his creativity.

In this context Vitaly's story might be seen as a parable of the artist's plight in a social order that enforces uniformity, sanctions similarity, and regards with suspicion all individual departures from the norm. He thus becomes a fictional counterpart to Grekova herself. But in choosing a hairdresser "as the persona through whom she explores the dilemmas of the artist," she expands her story "beyond the privileged classes to include virtually anyone with talent and imagination who must also labor within the confines of socialist canons" (Barker, "Reluctant Artist" 24). From this perspective, the story is social critique with an oedipal twist: in the failed artistry and the flawed relationship of Vitaly and Marya, Grekova explores the fate of difference in a world governed by the law of the Same.

Such a reading is reinforced by the vivid realistic surface of the story, a lively, often satiric depiction of many segments of Soviet life—the long waits for simple services, the dearth of consumer goods, the overcrowded communal apartments, the quotas and enforced camaraderie imposed by the party apparatus, the relentless minor irritations spurred by an economy of perpetual scarcity. Even at this level Grekova depicts with poignant accuracy the gender inequities of her society, especially the notorious double bur- den of women in a system where the politics of domesticity remain virtually unaltered despite the state rhetoric of equality.

She depicts, too, the persistence of traditional gender codes regulating female appearance. "Little has been written," Olsen observed at about the same time, "on the harms of instilling constant concern with appearance; the need to please" (*Silences* 28). Grekova too suggests that profound connections exist between the construction of woman's body and the structures of the body politic. The opening scenes of "Ladies' Hairdresser" sketch with bril- liant irony the "peculiarly female ritual" of the beauty parlor where women wait for "six-month perms," conforming to an ideology of the female body that prevails despite official Party images of women as energetic, virtually asexual workers. The window display of the salon, lined with "photographs of girls, each one taking great pains to preserve her hairdo," become a comic metaphor for the rigidities of a social system based on a fundamental contra- diction: acculturated to become active members of the labor force, equal with men, women are also implicitly encouraged to remain fetishized sexual ob- jects of the male gaze. Grekova underscores the irony of this sociosymbolic (dis)order: in the very process of seeking self-enhancement through a process of corporeal beautification, attempting to make *permanent* the artificial illu- sion of seductiveness embodied in cultural stereotypes, women are turned, in fact as in photographs, into simulacra—replications of replications, reduced to sameness by "firm curls" administered to an endless "line" that signifies not uniqueness but endless imitation.[4] This representation of women as in- finitely interchangeable parts becomes explicit in Grekova's later depiction of Vitaly's narcissistic relationship with Galya, whom he sees merely as "a suitable subject for hairdressing," subsequently expendable.

The confining social apparatus inherent in notions of artificial female beauty also pervaded the ideology of marriage that undergirded the Soviet state. The commiserations Marya receives upon admitting that she has no husband are illuminated by Ekaterina Alexandrova's analysis of how ideologies of marriage in the former Soviet Union reinforced both gender inequities and social control: "In our country, official or civil marriage is considered . . . perhaps the most important achievement in a woman's life, no matter how educated or independent she is and no matter how successful. . . . Formal civil marriage is supported officially . . . in the highest degree. The desire for marriage is actively inculcated . . . by the authorities" (31). Alexandrova notes that such support was actively pursued as a means of social regulation, maintained by systems of surveillance that afflicted Soviet citizens with "a 'precautionary fear' of crossing the boundaries . . . of what is permitted" (36–37). Under such mechanisms, "anyone not married" was assumed to be "leading an incomplete, second-hand life" (38).

The wry double entendre with which Marya eludes her fellow client's commiserations—"I'm not giving up"—does not necessarily refer to the promised fulfillment of conjugal bliss but suggests the extent to which Marya, like her author, resists the stereotypical constructions of commodified femininity embodied in both versions of "the permanent": hairdo and marriage. Grekova represents Marya as a woman who, like her author, eludes rigid gender positions. At ease in her authoritative role as head of the institute, she alternately mothers her staff as a surrogate family and behaves in ways her coworkers consider "un-ladylike." Similarly, she feels uncomfortable amid the "peculiarly feminine rituals" of the salon, yet delights in the renewed feminine image produced by her new hairdo.

This gender fluidity is most pronounced in her exchanges with Vitaly, who has severed himself from normal filial ties (16). Even as she mothers the motherless youth, she is also a surrogate father, overseeing both his education and his growth into manhood, symbolically renaming him by replacing the "baby talk" diminutive *Vitalik* with its mature and virilizing root: "the Latin word for 'life.' "

Nevertheless, their relationship initially seems to reenact traditional gender ideologies: his work advances; her appearance improves. And for all her skepticism about marriage, she is more deeply affected by the ideologies of femininity than her tart response to her fellow client reveals. As Grekova implies through Marya's opening reflections—both her literal encounter with her mirrored self and the rueful musings on her appearance it inspires—her very presence in the salon is a confession of shame and self-doubt, driven by subliminal acceptance of stereotypical womanhood. Regarding herself as an inadequate woman, a castoff, bedraggled and unlovable, she implicitly identifies with the "solitary wilted radish" lying desolately in the "crypt"-like refrigerator of her chaotic apartment.

Here and elsewhere, Grekova uses setting expressionistically to externalize psychological dynamics. Thus, once outside the house, Marya feels regenerated, a transition figured by the "fresh" springtime world of budding linden trees bathed with rain, "bright," "newborn." The images prefigure her later budding relationship with Vitaly, which will literally *revitalize* her self-image. In the creation scene evoked by Grekova's description of his labor ("he was tired, and all across his narrow brow . . . beads of sweat stood out"), Marya becomes at once a new-made Eve and the Galatea to his Pygmalion.

Yet such a reading oversimplifies both Marya's character and Grekova's purpose. For Marya too is an artist, self-sustaining and powerful in ways she herself, with her internalized cultural stereotypes, often fails to appreciate. And in the complex Pygmalion myth evoked by her relationship with Vitaly, she is as much creator as created. Her own generative power appears not only in the way she shapes Vitaly but most importantly in the climactic scene in which she achieves the long-sought solution to a thorny problem of theoretical math. The fierce surge of creative energy she experiences is at least as intense as Vitaly's joy at solving the aesthetic "problem of choosing a hairdo" for a particular head. Gesturing toward Grekova's own double career as mathematician and writer, this scene is a vivid reflexive reprise of its author's creative process.

Yet, like Vitaly, Marya too finds her creativity blocked by the pressures of the system. Grekova's depiction of her susceptibility to constant interruption is a fictional parallel to Olsen's analysis of the plight of women artists who labor as both mothers and members of the work force: "Circumstances for sustained creation are almost impossible. Not because the capacities to create no longer exist, or the need . . . but the need cannot be first. . . . It is distraction, not meditation, that becomes habitual; interruption, not continuity; spasmodic, not constant, toil. Work interrupted, deferred, postponed makes blockage—at best, lesser accomplishment. Unused capacities atrophy, cease to be" (1965, 33). As Grekova herself lamented, "The woman has a much harder time than the man who works by her side. The man usually carries one load (his job), while the woman carries three (her job, her children, her home). . . . This burden, combined with work—which alone demands a woman's full output—is almost unendurable (as I know from my own experience, being a mother of three children and a grandmother of four)" (1990, 10).

Marya's artistic productions, like Vitaly's, are represented as transgressive, covert activities, unsanctioned and necessarily pursued *off limits:* Vitaly designs hairstyles "behind a screen" in "a tiny back room" of the salon, a site of "sorcery" and "suspicious" transactions, while Marya seeks her solution—in more than one sense of the word—in stolen moments outside the bounds of her official administrative duties. In this context Marya's collusion with Vitaly to resist the prescriptive system of "the quota" (tantamount to a minor insurrection, as his later dismissal suggests) is not merely a gesture of motherly support but a form of symbolic self-assertion. The "natural" hair style he gives her, fluid and free as if "the wind had just tousled" it, suggests an alternative way of being supremely dangerous to the mechanized, rigidified codes figured by both the stiff uniformity of the "firm curl" and the larger social conformities of "the quota."

In depicting the subversive alliance of Marya and Vitaly, Grekova weaves a profound psychological parable of the relation of sexuality to creativity, exploring the limitations of a world that treats both as threats to the dominant order. The ambiguous, charged relationship of the aging woman and the younger man underscores the connections between mothering and artistic generation. Grekova breaks with traditional ideologies, which connect the two phenomena primarily by appropriating motherhood as a metaphor for artistic production in the well-worn trope of the (male) author's labor to "give birth" to art (Aiken 1990, 3–25). In "Ladies' Hairdresser" maternity and artistry appear not as mutually exclusive but as potentially parallel forms of creativity, both requiring mutable, multiple perceptual positions that challenge the totalizing, monolithic categories of dominant ideologies.

Marya's ambivalence about these contradictions generates the story's most vivid tensions. Drawn toward the creative transgressiveness Vitaly signifies, she also remains fearful of its anarchic possibilities. As her response to music suggests, it is dissonance, when uniformity is disturbed and certainties unsettled, that makes her most uneasy: she dislikes the passage in the Tchaikovsky concerto "when the solo violin chokes itself on double notes." Those ambiguous musical moments converge with Vitaly's image: "The violin broke into song, but was suddenly accompanied by a second instrument. Could it be a flute? . . . I raised my head. It was Vitaly whistling." Simultaneously daunted and dazzled ("My dear Vitaly, that's wonderful!"), she simultaneously longs for and fears the wild, dissonant, liberating energies the music signifies—energies she projects onto Vitaly but must ultimately recognize in herself. For while Vitaly finally repudiates his own "wild" gifts and capitulates to the forces of conformity, Marya, despite her anxieties, remains critical of those forces. It is she, ultimately, who retains the vitality he abdicates.

Grekova's discursive practice reenacts these contradictions. As in the household of the opening scene, so in Grekova's house of fiction, disorder continually erupts. From the outset, Grekova undermines her own conventionally realistic narrative mode with a metaphoric subtext that works in excess of what the representational plot contains, a carnivalesque discourse that travesties and transforms official lines of all sorts and writes another story. Just as the contradictory "double notes" of the Tchaikovsky concerto "choke" the dominant "voice" of the solo violin, so in this subversive subtext grotesque and monstrous figures disrupt the surface plot, invading the apparent orderliness of its narrative voice and progression with transgressive elements, textual equivalents to the wildness Marya both seeks and fears. Here human and animal, order and disorder, male and female shift and change places, mocking the standardizing, regulatory categories by which the dominant culture maintains itself.

Thus, in the opening episode, the realistic depiction of a domestic scene between mother and sons becomes, at the metaphoric level, a surreal, topsy-turvy "circus" (tsirk), in which nothing is as it seems. Both boys and mother are "fools"; ordinary conversation yields to a frenzy of shouts, groans, and invective, shot through with metaphors that dehumanize the human occupants: the boys devolve into "pigs," Marya into a "dog" or a "wolf," hands into "paws." And "home" moves through a series of dizzying metaphoric transmutations, becoming successively a pigsty, a mock courtroom in which Marya is parodically addressed as "Your Honor," and a "saloon" (kabak)—an apt figure for the linguistic intoxication which, like the beer bubbles rising in the bottles that litter the table, bursts through and de-forms the surface narrative. While some of these figures—notably the image of "paws" (lapy)—accurately render the idioms of everyday Russian familial conversation, within the broader metaphoric context we see Grekova underscoring the element of grotesquerie that inhabits ordinary domestic interchanges.

The site of Marya's first meeting with Vitaly is similarly unsettling. The salon is at once a literal place and a bizarre, liminal space where boundaries are breached and reality takes on monstrous overtones. Grekova configures the female customers with bawdy zest, turning the ostensible sanctuary of beauty into an anatomical freak show: women are "sheep," teeth protrude, hair becomes "a gray mop" and grotesque "bottoms" jostle each other in the overcrowded room. Despite insistent invocations of "order" (poriadok), the scene continually threatens to dissolve into anarchy: "The line was shouting and agitated."

As with the domestic "circus" she has fled, Marya reacts to this social disarray with mingled humor and horror. Ironically, it is precisely in trying to restore "order" by "policing" the place when things get "out of line," that she herself is labeled as an agent of chaos: "It's you thoughtless people who cause disorder."

Her encounter with Vitaly intensifies these discordances. It is no accident that his first words to her bear the comic threat of "disfiguration." Grekova presents him as a feral creature with "wild" eyes and "sharp, white teeth." The screened back room where he practices his art is "musty and stuffy," like an animal's den. Yet this metaphoric descent into the "wild" yields a masterpiece of beauty—"Well, well, well. So that's a permanent wave . . . a shining, vital mass of dark hair"—that immediately devolves again into the animal world: "It looked more like expensive fur than a head of hair." Grekova here prefigures later theoretical speculations in America and Europe on women's peculiar relationship to the "wild space" outside the bounds of dominant culture (e.g., Cixous; Showalter). This space is not simply a place of isolation and powerlessness inhabited by marginalized groups, but potentially a place of subversive creative power, its very ex-centricity offering another way of being and seeing.

In the scene of the institute party, Marya's ambivalent, discordant subjectivity and the dissonant elements in the text converge in a spectacular climax. In this collision of inner and outer worlds, plot and metaphoric subtext, Grekova reveals the consequences of social and psychological repression— the explosive release of accumulated forces, at once creative and destructive, in lives too rigidly bounded. In the "spinning" (vertiashchiesia pary) figures of the dance, as with Grekova's own spinning figures of speech, a carnival spirit erupts. Boundaries dissolve and the world turns upside down as women "dance the man's part," anatomical members—feet, legs, "protuberant rear ends"—take the place of full human bodies, and the dancers are comically distorted into nonhuman shapes—shoes, sheep, or turnips. At once yearning to participate in the exuberant festivities and incapable of overcoming her own internal restraints ("I haven't danced for years"), Marya looks on, envious and wistful, "watching the waltz spinning past."

The metaphoric and literal play of transformation culminates in the "group game" of "rabbit hunting." But now the joyous insurgencies of the dance disintegrate into "horror" as human beings, trapped behind grotesque, sightless masks, become monstrosities, like figures "in some drunkard's nightmare." Comic confusion merges with a chilling spectacle of blind aggression that implicitly recalls the Great Terror: the purges, the camps, the entire system of violence and victimage that once formed the unspoken nightmare of Soviet life.

Tatiana Tolstaia has pertinently remarked on the "terrifying feeling, well known to Europeanized Russians, of coming into contact with what we call the absurd, a concept in which we invest far greater meaning than Western people do" (1991, 3). In this context the eyeless masks become signs of a deeper blindness of terrifying proportions. It is no coincidence that the "game" ultimately reduces the masked participants to a state of utter abjection, roaming "stumbling senselessly, . . . tripping, bumping into and groping at each other." To this disorienting vision of social and psychic chaos, the audience responds with the automatic reflex of anxiety: "Everyone was laughing. No one understood what was happening, but they only laughed harder. . . . it was a terrible scene!"

The resounding release of pent-up emotions precipitates Marya's own crisis: "Suddenly [I] felt that I couldn't bear it anymore, felt myself laughing along with the others." Terrified by her own potential complicity, she moves to contain chaos, invoking her maternal authority: "Put an end to this disgraceful spectacle immediately! . . . My dear boys and girls. . . . Excuse me for referring to you in this way. I have two sons your age. . . . I have a feeling that this kind of fun is bad."

At this crucial moment, Grekova too moves beyond disorder, suggesting the creative possibilities it may enable. Paradoxically, only in re-calling order does Marya acknowledge her own involvement with the insurgent energies she has feared: "I was laughing along with you." In so doing she liberates herself from repression in a way previously impossible, for by acknowledging the forbidden insurgency within herself, she frees herself into the creative dimensions of the carnivalesque—the "whirling" of the dance, both literally and symbolically—becoming a part of the vitality that she has so long resisted: "My head was just spinning. I haven't danced for a long time."

Grekova makes explicit the subversive implications of this event, and implicitly relates it to her own writing, in Marya's subsequent concerns that her speech will be construed by the authorities as an attempt at "creating a 'public disturbance.'" Ironically, it is Vitaly, hitherto the very figure of transgression in her eyes, who now takes on the role of censor: "I'm generally against parties like that." The moment marks a reversal in their positions in the narrative. As Vitaly contracts himself by limiting his horizons and abandoning his art, Marya opens outward. For her the "whirling" power of the dance persists in a new acceptance of the grotesque and comic elements in life, the liberating force of carnival laughter. This transformation is figured in her growing appreciation of Sasha Lukianov: seeing him at first as repulsive, grotesque, even frightening, she now perceives him as "an amazing fellow": "Humor issued from him like oxygen does from a plant." With him she becomes another kind of artist, the cocreator of a carnival world: "our inventions knew no bounds": "There's nothing more mysterious, more elusive, than laughter."

If Marya's situation figures Grekova's, we might read these scenes of carnival and its consequences as a reflexive expression of Grekova's own ambivalent relation to her subversive artistic productions. In "Ladies' Hairdresser," she too creates a kind of festive comedy, a "dance" of language that releases the "mysterious" power of creative laughter. It is Vitaly's loss that he, not unlike some of Grekova's own readers, is unable to accept the implications of the "wild" forces he himself has embodied. Finally, it is Marya, not Vitaly, who understands the liberating power of art, while remaining fully aware of the ephemerality of its subversive moments.

Yet at the conclusion of the narrative, Marya's accumulated small gestures of protest appear to have come to nothing; the story ends, in effect, with her bemused, dismissive shrug, and the forced cheerfulness of her wry farewell seems to cover a profound resignation: "Well, then . . . a pleasant journey to you, Vitaly!" (*Schastlivogo puti tebe, Vitalii!*). While her last words may appear to signify both her own and her author's capitulation—Marya's to the pressures of the status quo, Grekova's to the sort of forced, optimistic ending imposed by the tenets of Socialist Realism—the earlier events of the story give the line another meaning. For if Marya is resigned, she is also, by virtue of the story, re-signed—refashioned, by both herself and her author, in terms other than those condoned by the dominant symbolic order.

In comparable ways, if Grekova appears to capitulate to a repressive tradition by concealing herself behind a pseudonym, resigning herself to the dominant economy in which artists, especially women, are suppressed, in fact she uses that gesture to re-sign herself: as she herself explains, *I. Grekova* is a play on *Igrek*, the mathematical sign used in Russian to denote an unknown quantity (1990, 14). Thus it is precisely in Grekova's seeming self-effacement under the disguise of the "unknown woman" that she most strikingly asserts herself, revealing the woman behind the cipher as a figure of resistance to the order that would relegate contestatory writers to nonentity. As the unknown quantity effecting an uncanny return in the traces of her own erasure, she also gestures toward the violence, the massive repression, necessary to the maintenance of what the state calls reason, law, and order—those supports of "self-evident meaning"—and of the liberating possibilities inherent in even momentary challenges to that regime.

Reading Riddles

This subversive subtext of "Ladies' Hairdresser" invites comparison with that in "Tell Me a Riddle." Like Grekova, Olsen sees the domestic space as a site of repression, a sign of gender politics that relegate to women the primary responsibility for domestic work, child care, and those other essential human functions that society both depends on and devalues. But in Olsen's narrative, home is an even more contradictory, multivalent construct than in Grekova's, for unlike Marya, Eva has seldom had the opportunity of escape into a world beyond the house. Most of the events of the narrative take place within domestic enclosures, which become progressively more constricted as the story develops, "shrinking" at last into "one room like a coffin."

As the narrative opens, over fifty years after Eva's revolutionary activism in Russia propelled her emigration to America with David, she has been so long confined within the house that any other alternative seems literally unthinkable. Now the place that for decades has entrapped her has become a kind of womb, a symbolic extension of her own body, shielding her from a world she loathes and fears. As her belatedly chosen haven, the house stands in ironic opposition to that other "Haven" to which David would forcibly remove her—a home for "the aged," its commercial promises of "happy communal life" resounding like a banal echo of the communality for which they had fought unsuccessfully in the Russia of their youth.

If the house signifies for Eva a last vestige of order and security in a life that has seldom been hers to control, it is also the matrix on which she practices the remnants of her blocked creativity: obsessive cleaning is the negative version of what might have been her art. Staving off disorder and dirt becomes for her an implicit evasion of the mortality they symbolize: "'Soon enough we'll need only a little closet, no windows, no furniture, nothing to make work, but for worms.'" Loss of the house, then, for her represents the final displacement in a long life of dislocations. In depicting her refrain-like plea to "go home" after she and David depart on their last journey together, Olsen poignantly captures the complexities of Eva's agonized relation to the place that is both her prison and her refuge.

In Eva and David, Olsen unfolds the implications of both literal and psychological exile. Jewish-Russian refugees like Olsen's own parents, they have lived their entire lives as displaced persons. Having lost their native land, where they were marginalized by class oppression, they seek in America a better society, but find instead a world that masks oppression and injustice with commercialized stereotypes of success and glib slogans about freedom and equality, a world where grinding poverty exists side by side with crass materialism and where gender and class remain powerful determinants of privilege. In the plight of Eva and David, as in *Silences*, Olsen exposes the economic and social inequities of the so-called classless society, revealing a nightmare at the heart of the American dream.

Their differing responses to these circumstances create the forty-seven-year quarrel that has riven them apart. Like Vitaly, David capitulates to social pressures: despite a lifetime of incessant labor and disappointed hopes, he still believes the myth of the American dream and subscribes to the value system of bourgeois capitalist society. Gregarious and witty, he uses humor as a defense, willfully blinding himself to the corruptions of his adopted country, his own collusion with its crasser values, and the woman who relentlessly calls his attention to both.

As site and sign of their conflict, the house becomes a figure of the marriage itself, a prison where they live "shackled . . . together" in a relationship that is at once bond and bondage. Olsen suggests that their differing perspectives are most prominently shaped by gender: for all his class-bound disadvantages, as a man David still enjoys social privileges from which Eva is excluded—not least the freedom to abandon her to incessant childcare and housework while he goes out to "meetings." As in the Soviet Union Grekova criticizes, where "bearing and raising children, running the house, and taking care of a host of time-consuming daily chores are still the woman's responsibility" (1990, 10), so in America. Underscoring the connection between the mundane oppressions of marriage and the broader oppressions of the sociopolitical system it supports, Olsen represents the inequitable relationship of Eva and David as a microcosmic embodiment of all those other forms of alienation and coercion the story represents.

In making her protagonist a former Russian revolutionary, Olsen underscores parallels between the political situation in the United States of the early sixties and that in Russia in the early twentieth century. Notably, many of the leaders of the 1905 uprising were women—iconoclastic figures for whom Eva and Lisa become fictional equivalents. In revealing the falsity of the American dream—suggesting that the vaunted "land of the free" is also a place of repression, of material and spiritual penury—Olsen discloses the links between the overt injustices of the regimes against which Eva and David rebelled in youth and the more subtle but still pervasive injustices of a male-dominated capitalist social order.

A perpetual outsider, alienated from both the country where she sought refuge and from her husband, Eva ultimately finds that her only recourse is "to live within." In that internal dwelling, through the liberating power of memory, music, and words, she recalls the Russia of her youth, not as a literal state but as a state of being—the core of visionary selfhood she has lost. Ultimately it is a return to this spiritual home, not simply to a literal house, for which she pleads.

Only in forced ejection from the house (as both physical edifice and symbolic structure), only by leaving "home" as defined by bourgeois culture, does she begin to find freedom. The farther she moves from the domestic enclosure, the closer she draws to home in its other, more profound implications. In Olsen's poetics of space, the narrative unfolds as a series of journeys, moving Eva progressively westward, in the process transforming both Eva and the images of home and motherhood that have defined her. "Motherhood truths," Olsen writes in *Silences*, are "not yet incorporated into literature and other disciplines, let alone into psychiatric theory and practice" (253). In her fiction she seeks to voice those unspoken truths. Instead of depicting home as simply a prisonhouse where a woman is condemned for life to hard labor, or motherhood as simply a sacrificial bondage in which a woman, caught in the "maze" of her own needs (93), is virtually cannibalized ("warm flesh like this that had claims and nuzzled away all else and with lovely mouths devoured"), Olsen also represents home and mothering as symbols of human connection, generativity, and creative transcendence.

Traveling westward, Eva literally moves back toward Russia, that "motherland" which, as a figure of her lost childhood and revolutionary past, remains her crucial reference point, the home toward which she perpetually yearns because there, despite oppression, she was most fully and freely herself. She moves also toward the sea, "mother" of "life as it first crawled toward consciousness millions of years ago." Drawn by its "far ruffle," she is for a moment regenerated: " 'There take me,' and though she leaned against him, it was she who led. . . . Already the white spray creamed her feet." The scene poignantly prefigures that final westward movement toward death, a homeward journey in which Eva will again outstrip David. It is in dying, paradoxically, that she ultimately finds liberation from the confinements that have held her, both the multiple systems of power she has spent her life contesting and that frail dwelling Anglo-Saxons called the "bone house."

In the figures of Lisa and Jeannie, Olsen extends these redefinitions. For if "home" is Mother Russia, or the maternal sea, or death itself—"mother of beauty," in Wallace Stevens's stunning phrase—"going home" also signifies Eva's imagined reunion with Lisa, symbolic mother/mentor of her youth, who continues to haunt her recollections as the figure of her highest ideals. That idealism is reembodied in Jeannie, whose psychological kinship with her grandmother structurally replicates Eva's youthful relationship with Lisa. In these connections Olsen evokes a female genealogy of the spirit as powerful as biological bonds. The text implies that through passing on her stories to Jeannie, who will replicate them in both words and drawings, Eva insures for both Lisa and herself a kind of immortality. It is a pattern reflexively suggestive of the effects of Olsen's own narrative, which, in retelling the stories of all three women, places Olsen implicitly in the line of generation they embody.

Eva's journey, then, like the narrative progression of the story, is not simply toward oblivion; it is also a movement toward renewal and reconciliation, culminating in the great prose poem of Eva's dying monologues. Here Olsen conjoins past with present and future, the personal with the global, as Eva moves at once backward, via memory, and, forward, in prophecy, toward

Russia, at once literal land of her youth and symbolic revolutionary landscape of her imagination.

Olsen marks the stages of that progression through the imagery of stones, figures inseparable from the multiple meanings of the story's title. In the house of her daughter Vivi, whose very name, like Eva's, embodies the traditional image of life-giving, nurturing mother, Eva encounters both rocks— *"igneous, sedimentary, metamorphic"*—and riddles in her grandchildren's importunities: "Tell me a riddle, Granny." "I know no riddles."

Yet she does, of course, "know riddles." Her life has unfolded an unending series of them, from the global enigma of human inhumanity to the intimately personal paradox of maternity, that conjunction of love and violence: *"How was it that soft reaching tendrils also became blows that knocked?"* "Sheathing" herself against those seductive blows, she meditates on stones: "Had she told them . . . of how they played jacks in her village. . . . Six stones, round and flat, toss them out, the seventh on the back of the hand, toss, catch and swoop up as many as possible." The passage recalls not only her childhood, but her children, the seventh lost in combat during a war that epitomizes all murderous human conflicts ("Tell Sammy's boy, he who flies, . . . to go to Stuttgart and see where Davy has no grave"). In a climactic passage, this vision gives rise to a series of associations in which the figure of stones pivotally connects the issues of Eva's life with the issues of global politics:

> Of stones (repeating Richard) there are three kinds: earth's fire jetting; rock of layered centuries; crucibled new out of the old (*igneous, sedimentary, metamorphic*). But there was that other—frozen to black glass, never to transform or hold the fossil memory . . . (let not my seed fall on stone). There was an ancient man who fought to heights a great rock that crashed back down eternally— eternal labor, freedom, labor (stone will perish but the word remain). And you, David, who with a stone slew, screaming: Lord, take my heart of stone and give me flesh.
>
> *Who* was screaming? why was she back in the common room of the prison. . . ? Screaming and screaming. No, it is the children screaming.

This crucial passage telescopes the story of Olsen's protagonists with that of the human race, conjoining child's play with the tragic riddles of history— "rock of layered centuries." Simultaneously an image of oppression and death and a figure of potential "metamorphic" transformation, stones are also, like the myth of Sisyphus and Olsen's own narrative, monuments to human endurance and transcendence in the face of overwhelming suffering. Thus they become reflexive figures for storytelling itself, "words" that endure to "hold the fossil memory" and testify to the mystery of regeneration, life "crucibled new out of old."

Like the text it names, the title of "Tell Me a Riddle" is also a provocative, unsettling conundrum. Prefiguring the grandchild's plea to Eva, it may be read also as a petition from author to reader—a possibility that puts us, quite literally, in Eva's place. Yet as spinner of the web of words in which the reader is caught, the author is also the riddling oracle, inviting us to decipher *her* meanings, placing us in the child's position. Poised on the margins of the narrative, between history and fiction, the phrase defies simple interpretation. Its very openness to many constructions forces us to "read" and reread our own shifting relations to the "riddle" the text unfolds. As Olsen elsewhere remarked, one of her aims in writing is to involve the reader in an active process of making and interpretation ("Tillie Olsen" in Yalom, 64). The root meaning of *riddling* is, after all, Old English *raedan*—to read. In posing her text as a kind of riddle, Olsen reminds us that the act of reading forms the core of the story's meanings. It is no accident that Eva equates books with revolution.

Olsen also induces us to ponder the status of riddling in the cultural history of the Western world, which the story continually evokes. In that context riddles inhabit a peculiarly liminal, unstable space, linking high and low, oracle and jest, religious mystery and children's game. In representing the riddle as both a form of play and a life-or-death proposition, the story recalls an earlier "child's" encounter with an enigmatic female riddler: Oedipus's confrontation with the sphinx, that complex emblem of diseased parent-child relationships, of a state grounded on familial violence and violation, of spreading contamination that imperils an entire society. And like the Oedipal story, Olsen's too pivots on a riddle whose answer is "humanity."

That answer finds its most complex and eloquent expression in the final movements of the narrative. On the one hand Eva's mortal agony is starkly realistic, a raw revelation of the effects of terminal cancer—unremitting pain that dehumanizes, ruptures the boundaries of meaning, and drives to the limits of abjection. In its remarkable blend of compassion and unblinking honesty, Olsen's depiction of dying is among the most powerful and moving in the language. But Eva's body also becomes an eloquent signifier that reflects, even as she herself reflects on, the breakdown and decadence of those very systems her frail voice mercilessly attacks. As a phenomenon of unbridled cellular proliferation, cancer is a grotesque figure of the relentless reproduction that has consumed Eva's life. And like the plague in *Oedipus*, her illness also marks the continuum between the diseased body and the corrupt body politic: "Your sickness is in you, how you live." Both bodies devour

themselves in an ecstasy of pain that restages simultaneously the cannibaliza-
tion of the mother and the proliferating global corruptions Eva repudiates.
Those bodies, in turn, are placed in relation to the corpus of literature within
which, via multiple quotations and allusions, Olsen situates her own story.

As Eva's body progressively breaks down, so too does the text that embodies her. In a radical mimetic gesture, Olsen progressively dis-integrates
her own narrative to replicate Eva's disintegrating life and consciousness as
her illness intensifies. The fragmentary, associative, discontinuous narrative
mode, present from the outset but initially subordinated to a more conventional telling, becomes increasingly pronounced as Eva moves into the final
harrowing stages of her illness, reaching a climax in her rambling, broken
monologues. Eva's words are cathartic, like "earth's fire jetting"—an overflow
of pent-up creativity and critique expressed in cryptic, incoherent utterances,
gasps, and gaps which we, like David, must decipher. Into this great prose
poem Olsen weaves multiple voices, "spilling memories," visionary speculations, and broken snatches of song, creating a profound meditation on the
stony "riddle" of the human condition. As with the "savage zest" of the
group sing, where voices "roar" together in a polyphonic carnival of sound—
"children-chants, mother-croons, singing of the chained love serenades, Beethoven storms, mad Lucia's scream, drunken joy-songs, keens for the dead,
work-singing"—and are "imprinted on her," so too in Eva's monologues her
voice becomes the voices of multitudes, unraveling itself plurally, progressively, as if "she had hidden a tape recorder, infinitely microscopic, within
her, . . . trapping every song, every melody, every word read, heard, and
spoken."

Paradoxically, only when confined to her deathbed does she enter at last
a place beyond censorship. Her words embody precisely that playful, subversive "heteroglossia" Bakhtin celebrated as a means to "free consciousness
from the tyranny" of the dominant discourse and the forms of repression it
would enforce (1981, 61, 68). At once decaying body and source of regeneration, figure of both death and life, Eva resembles the grotesque, paradoxical
terra cotta figures of old women that Bakhtin sees as the embodiment of the
carnival spirit, joining "a senile, decaying and deformed flesh with the flesh
of new life, conceived but as yet unformed" (1984, 25–26).

This outpouring of grotesque, liberatory discourse finds a counterpart
in the battering dialogue between Eva and David. Though he tries "not
to listen," his elaborately constructed, ironic defenses and willed blindness
gradually break down in the face of her eloquent, impassioned challenges
to alienation, conflict, and dogma. In a last gesture of resistance, he takes
up "his solitaire deck," a figure of the escapist games with which, for all his
superficial gregariousness, he has isolated himself from real human connec-

tion. But in her "tatter of an orator's voice" he hears the irresistible song of regeneration, "a girl's voice of eloquence that spoke their holiest dreams."

Though Eva's intravenous "solution bottle" is "empty," Olsen implies that her overflowing words evoke another sort of "solution"—a key to the riddles the text has propounded. That answer emerges in the final recognition scene in which, wounded by "the bright, betrayed, . . . stained words, that on her working lips became stainless," David at last acknowledges "the bereavement and betrayal he had sheltered . . . , and with it the monstrous shapes of what had actually happened in the century." His defenses crumble in the climactic moment of reconciliation, when he finally reaches out to her in "compassion," calling her not by one of the distancing ironic epithets by which they have addressed each other for years, but by her own name. And in these gestures of reconciliation he begins to break free of the alienating prisons of consciousness he has built around himself. It is a transformation in which Eva too is symbolically regenerated: "Instantly he left the mute old woman poring over the Book of Martyrs, went past the mother treading at the sewing machine, singing with the children; past the girl in her wrinkled prison dress, hiding her hair with scarred hands, . . . and took her in his arms, dear, personal, fleshed, in all the heavy passion he had loved to rouse from her."

In this narrative, which like Grekova's underscores the continuum between oppressive personal politics and broader global systems of oppression, Olsen suggests that David's renewal is more than a personal transformation, an individual "solution" to the riddle of human blindness. The connections he here acknowledges, the insight that turns conflict to compassion, are also symbolic signs of the possibility of larger social transformations.

As Eva's words "work in him," so Olsen's words work in the reader. In the intense reflexivity of the final paragraph, reader, characters, and author are joined in a festival of community, reconciliation, and renewal—"and they dance." That moment merges, immediately, with Olsen's own last words, a dedicatory inscription *"For two of that generation."* Seevya and Genya, friends who like Olsen's parents were Russian-Jewish revolutionaries and later emigrés, were among her models for David and Eva.[5] In rewriting their lives, Olsen explicitly places herself in the regenerative female genealogy she had evoked in the relationship of Lisa, Eva, and Jeannie, joining history with fiction through the act of redemptive storytelling.

"In spite of all the differences in our political systems, ways of life, and values, the people of the United States and the Soviet Union share much in common," writes Grekova in a recent introduction to an English anthology of Soviet women's fiction. Her words might stand as a commentary on the commonalities of "Ladies' Hairdresser" and "Tell Me a Riddle." For all their apparent differences, both historical and literary, in these stories Olsen and Grekova create for their female protagonists a free discursive space in which categories historically construed by both Western and Russian traditions to be mutually exclusive—*woman* and *artist*—are destabilized, redefined, and brought into fruitful relation. In so doing, both writers also contest the larger political forces of repression that divide people from themselves and each other. "Comprehensions possible out of motherhood," writes Olsen, "have never had the circumstances to come to powerful, undeniable . . . expression—have had instead to remain inchoate, fragmentary, unformulated, . . . unvalidated" (1965, 202). As each narrative's point of focus, the psyches of Eva and Marya become stages where the comprehensions of the mother/artist are played out, places for the uprising of "wild" carnivalesque forces that each author connects, whether directly or indirectly, to the power of women as agents of dissent and potential re-creation.

Notes

1. On the dangers of a simplistic reading of carnival as purely liberatory, see Stallybrass and White 12–19. On the import of this issue for women, see Russo. On the implications of the contemporary "Bakhtinskii boom" in post-Soviet Russia, see chapter 1, n. 5, in this volume.

2. Grekova 1967, 11. On the former dearth of literary experimentation among Soviet women writers, see Goscilo 1989, xxvi–xxvii.

3. The idea of the "private" is not the same in a society based on theories of the collective as it is in America. But to observe, as some do, that there is no word in Russian comparable to the English word "privacy" is not to prove the nonexistence of the concept in a Russian worldview. One of the meanings of *byt,* for example, recalls the American notion of the "private" sphere: the domestic realm of home, family, and intimate interpersonal relationships which, in Russia as in the U.S., is primarily associated with women. Grekova analyzes this aspect of *byt* in her "Introduction" (1990, 11).

4. Gray argues that Soviet women's "pathological obsession with fashion" is designed to impress not men but other women (159). But this idea of pathology, while compelling, overlooks the complexity of self-fashioning. As vehicles of both women's playful self-creation and of relationship to other women—not merely in competition, but in potential solidarity—costuming and cosmetics may serve not merely as signs of women's capitulation to an oppressive order but as resistance to it. Making herself up, both literally and figuratively, may place a woman not only in creative relation to other women but in a particular relation to herself: as Grekova implies, imaginative self-expression of any sort is potentially subversive in the neutralizing world of the collective, where monotony and uniformity amount to official doctrine.

5. Personal communication from Olsen to my graduate student Susan Sample.

Revolutions from Within

EKATERINA STETSENKO

Tillie Olsen and I. Grekova are infinitely distant from each other, yet at the same time closely connected by those invisible threads which in every epoch link different societies and cultures. Both belong to the generation that witnessed and participated in some of the most tumultuous events of this century, with its wars and revolutions. Both were raised on socialist ideals, Grekova as a citizen of a country dominated by communist ideology, Olsen as the daughter of revolutionary Russian emigrés and a participant in the radical left movement in America during the "Red" thirties. Both came rather late to literature: in her early years Grekova (working under her real name, E. S. Ventsel) devoted herself to a scientific career, while Olsen combined political activism with life as a factory worker, housewife, and mother. Having raised several children, both were fully aware of the joys of motherhood and the burdens of domesticity. However, the similarities of their lives only underscore the difference in their world views and their approaches to artistic representation. Both authors deal with similar themes and problems but do so within different historical, social, and cultural contexts.

Olsen and Grekova both began to write actively in the late fifties and early sixties, a period of political and spiritual upheaval in both the USSR and the U.S.A. This period in both countries can be characterized as an era of liberalization, which in one country replaced the oppressive obscurantism of the Stalinist dictatorship and in the other the intolerance of the McCarthy era. Thus occurred an inevitable reassessment of values, a rejection of the dogmatic, one-sided thinking of both conservatives and the radical left. In America, as anticommunism became less extreme, proponents of socialism also became more moderate, engaging in a critical examination of the convictions of their youth. In the Soviet Union this period, termed "the thaw" (*Ottepel'*), was marked by a warming of the political climate and by more courageous attempts to seek the truth, directed at humanizing the existing order. In both countries, it was necessary for people of Olsen's and Grekova's generation to reexamine their former beliefs and confront the fact that the younger generation had a different perception of the world and a different value system.

One of the reasons it was so painful and difficult to part with the illusions of the past in the Soviet Union was that reigning social, political, and economic ideas had a clear-cut ethical dimension and determined not only intellectual views but moral and behavioral patterns. All social phenomena were neatly polarized: capitalism, private property, economic inequality, individualism, and elitism were considered absolutely evil; socialism, public property, egalitarianism, collectivism, and the sovereignty of the people were considered as absolute good. Between these polarities there were no gradations; they were not viewed as components of complex and contradictory processes. They could be linked only through the conjunctions "either/or," never "both/and."

The worship of an idealized "simple people," belief in abstract "equality" and "justice," in absolute historical necessity, and in the purifying function of the revolution, the contempt for material well-being, and the supremacy of public over personal interests were sacrosanct to the Soviet way of thinking. The existence of absolute and eternally true ideas and ideals was never called into question. Society, the personality, and art had no right to deviate from fixed norms for the sake of individuality, spontaneity, and independence. In this atmosphere of universal regimentation, a person could count on the good will of others only by submitting to the ideology of the collective. Through such submission, he could guarantee self-respect and inner satisfaction by automatically, without any intellectual or spiritual effort, joining the "vanguard of humanity." Thus socialist ideals were considered unchangeable, needing only to be cleansed of the distortions during the time of the so-called personality cult of Stalinism. Elements of this worldview permeated the thinking of most of the sixties generation in the USSR. But even as they preserved many dogmas of the past, they simultaneously undermined those same dogmas, intentionally or unintentionally, by their eager acceptance of Western culture and their penchant for independent thinking.

These new tendencies in Soviet society had a considerable influence on literature which, given weakened censorship, broadened its horizons, turning to new themes and greater formal diversity, undoubtedly under the influence of previously banned Russian and foreign models. In prose works by young authors such as Vasilii Aksenov, Anatolii Gladilin, Anatolii Kuznetsov, Anatolii Pristavkin, and Vladimir Amlinskii, stock heroes of Socialist Realism were replaced by characters who did not fit into canonical schema. If previously young people were depicted exclusively as the heirs of their fathers and the guardians of received ideals, a stance that permitted only insignificant and superficial deviations from Soviet standards, now the images of the young stressed a hitherto unknown independence of thought and reflectiveness. In life as well as in art, generational change was accompanied by profound shifts in social and aesthetic consciousness.

In light of these processes, the works of I. Grekova are particularly interesting. Though part of the older generation, she came to literature along with the writers of the sixties—a fact that may explain why we sense a certain ambivalence, an inner conflict, in her fictions, which deal with events difficult to explain within the traditional Soviet system of values. The author is, as it were, laying bare the painful process of change taking place within her consciousness; she shares her doubts with her readers despite the risk of revealing her own lack of understanding of the world she describes.

Grekova adopts this position deliberately. She has frequently stated in interviews that her goal was never to force ideas on her readers; instead, she wished to convey impressions that had excited her, inducing the reader to reflect on them. "For me personally, in my stories there has never been a desire to teach somebody something, to reveal a certain truth or to expound on a system of beliefs. I think one of the feelings an author can convey to a reader—that an author has the right to convey—is a feeling of puzzlement or uncertainty. An author has a right to show his reader a situation that he himself does not understand" (1982).

This enigmatic situation is found in one of Grekova's most remarkable and popular works, "Ladies' Hairdresser." Its hero, Vitaly Plavnikov, is a representative of the strange new generation that the author, together with her heroine, Marya Vladimirovna Kovaleva, the director of a scientific research institute, strives to understand. For Grekova, to be able to understand people like Vitaly means, in many respects, to be able to understand herself. Thus she chooses for her heroine a character close to her own age, social status, and perspective, and tells the story from the first-person point of view. But Grekova preserves her own separate and distinct perspective by maintaining a certain distance between herself and the heroine—the distance of irony, which underscores the differences in their analytic understanding of self and world. These distinctive points of view become apparent in the heroine's comments on various subjects, her reactions to events, her attitudes toward other people, and the very manner of her narration.

Marya Vladimirovna is typical of liberal intellectuals at the time of the thaw: her social behavior is governed by firm moral principles. For Kovaleva there exists a hierarchy of values according to which working for the benefit of others is the main standard of human dignity; the public takes precedence over the personal, work over private life.

Kovaleva, of course, has her share of failures and difficulties, but all of these are, so to say, normal, typical, and justified by her way of life. Like most

Soviet women, she is torn between work and home, between business and public obligations on the one hand and the duties of motherhood on the other. For her, however, this conflict is more external than internal. Her disdain for "feminine" duties is reflected in her chaotic daily life and in her neglected home where no one cooks dinner, a situation that causes Kovaleva neither to lose her peace of mind nor to question her way of life. Disagreements with her family resemble a game, a home theatrical in which parts are defined in advance and a happy ending assured. In Marya Vladimirovna's relationship with her children, the problem of "fathers and sons" is solved according to a familiar stereotype of Soviet mythology: the continuity of the generations. Though Kostya and Kolya are entirely modern, inclined to free thinking and defiance, it is assumed that they will be devoted to their mother. They are, moreover, good students who have chosen engineering, a profession in vogue in the late sixties.

For Grekova and her heroine, a distinctive feminine psychology and a special role for women simply do not exist, though Grekova acknowledges that they may for women of lower social status and intellectual level. Women who have achieved high social and cultural status do not feel that their sex is an important factor. Grekova deliberately introduces into her story other female characters who are completely absorbed in their lives as women; they are incomprehensible to Marya Vladimirovna, who looks down on them and treats them with irony, irritation, or condescending sympathy. Among such characters are the old lady "in socks" in the salon, who wants a permanent so that her husband won't leave her for a young mistress; or Galya, the secretary with whom Marya Vladimirovna has "orthogonal relations" because she is unable to understand how one can be interested solely in trifles such as clothes and boyfriends.

Grekova emphasizes the equality or, more precisely, the equivalency between Marya Vladimirovna and men, not only because Kovaleva has assumed a traditionally masculine position but also because of her own self-perceptions. The author surrounds Kovaleva with characters next to whom she seems to be the only "man," and among whom she can display her manly qualities. Thus, compared with his female boss, Lebedev, the assistant director of the institute, is weak and chatty like a woman; he even dyes his gray hair.

Playing the masculine role of the boss at work, Marya Vladimirovna continues to play the same role at home. She comes into the apartment in the evening "dog tired." She is annoyed at her sons when she discovers that there is no dinner and that the house is a mess. In other words, she behaves exactly like an irritable husband who arrives home to confront a remiss wife.

But Grekova does not advocate a simple reversal of roles between men and women; instead, she wants to show that both men and women can play the same roles and have the same qualities. Yet although Grekova tries to indicate the essential equality of the sexes by means of her heroine, she nevertheless unconsciously accepts the pervading, primarily masculine point of view regarding the division of social roles, and in this respect remains at the level of cliches. This is evident in Marya Vladimirovna's condescending attitude toward Galya, whom she views as only a beautiful trinket: "A man would probably like to pick up a little thing like that by the waist with two fingers and move it around from place to place." Further, she is displeased by Lebedev because of the "ladylike" qualities in his character.

The heroine herself is constantly pressured by an environment in which her own actions may be viewed by others in the stereotypical manner: "Well, what do you expect? A broad is a broad." Thus, no matter how hard she tries to bring her sons up "properly," cigarette butts, beer bottles, and chess pieces—testimony to the "masculine" interests of Kostya and Kolya—are strewn all over the apartment. Marya Vladimirovna considers her role as a director, her scientific pursuits, her lectures, and her worries about her car and her garage unfeminine, depriving her of womanly attractiveness. She is elated when she succeeds in solving a science problem but at the same time perturbed when she notices a "pale, old face with circles under the eyes," a bad hair style, and mud-splashed stockings. Unable to reject the stereotypes imposed upon her by society, Kovaleva finds herself obligated to play a double role and carry on her shoulders a double burden. Faithful to the dogma of the priority of public over private interests, she finds only her "feminine" duties burdensome and thinks that if it were possible to eliminate them, society could solve the problem of sexual inequality.

Nevertheless, Grekova does not delve deeply into the historical, social, biological, or psychological roots of this problem, and the solutions she offers are rather simple. Fully accepting the emancipation of the workplace—which, in fact, was achieved in a country that badly needed manpower—she believes it necessary to extend this emancipation to family life by involving men in housework (Grekova 1981, 13). However, as a penetrating writer and psychologist, Grekova cannot shut her eyes to the contradictions and complexities of both life and human nature. Marya Vladimirovna does not doubt that she has made the correct choices in her life, but at the same time she is inwardly unsure that her point of view is the only one possible. While thinking with surprise about the narrowness of Galya's interests, she cuts short these thoughts with a rhetorical question to herself: "And so what if it is? That's also living."

Kovaleva's manner of speaking is indicative of the changes occurring in her mind. Her speech reflects two kinds of thinking that can be roughly described as the mentality of the old and that of the new generation. Adopting the uninhibited, deliberately vulgarized language common in liberal intellectual circles, she uses words like "pigs" (*svin'i*), "tavern" (*kabak*), "stupid chess game" (*duratskie shakhmaty*)—locutions that suggest her desire for affiliation with a younger generation. At the same time her thoughts frequently bear a lofty intonation that was more typical of her own contemporaries: "Two lowered heads, one yellow as straw, the other black as coal. My little fools, my sons." Marya Vladimirovna's verbal vulgarity is largely artificial, and her exaggerated complaints—"My whole life's shot to hell! Down the drain for nothing!"—are caused by the irritation of a moment, behind which we feel her satisfaction with herself and her life. In general her inner world is orderly and whole, her ideas of good and evil definite and unchanging.

Similarly, Grekova suggests that Kovaleva also sees the outside world as regulated by ethical norms. Inclined to view reality in abstract terms, she frequently projects her world view onto actual life. Thus, when encountering conflicts at work, squabbles, bureaucracy, unsettled everyday life, and dishonesty, she perceives them as unavoidable, although as a believer in ideal human and business relationships, she also feels that difficulties can be overcome or eliminated. She sees Akademgorodok near Novosibirsk as a center of science and culture, the city of the future. Similarly, she also imagines the possibility of personal happiness, embodied in the image of an "old friend" who "loved me his whole life, loves me to this very day, I know it."

For Marya Vladimirovna, the ideals of her youth are deeply rooted. She grew up during the period when the official image of the Soviet citizen was formed: eternally young in spirit, optimistic, full of faith in high ideals, and ready to bear any hardship for the sake of the common good. She tries to preserve this spirit despite difficulties and painful experiences, an attitude embodied in her response to Moscow in the springtime as she walks down the street eating an ice cream as in her student days. Kovaleva has the ability to soar in spirit above the prosaic aspects of everyday life, to resist the engulfing swamp by moving it to the periphery of her life, regarding it from a moral distance.

In a sense there is a contradiction between Grekova's strong interest in the minute details of life and her heroine's perspective, but Grekova resolves this apparent inconsistency through her methods of description. In Soviet literature writers who described scenes of everyday life were generally criticized for choosing an insignificant subject matter, for avoiding global problems by diverting attention to private life, which was considered to be of secondary importance. Grekova always objected to this oversimplified approach, emphasizing instead the necessity of including details which reflected the spirit of the time and thus had historical value. Portraying the common man with his everyday concerns was crucial for her. Placing a typical character in typical circumstances—one of the unalterable laws of Socialist Realism—became for her a way of reflecting the broader conditions of Soviet life and ideology.

The scenes of everyday life in "Ladies' Hairdresser" are written precisely in this key. For example, the episode of Marya Vladimirovna at the hairdresser's salon is constructed out of standard situations, images, and details. In the line no one responds to the question 'Who's last?' responding only to 'Who's behind you?'" The situation depicted here is typical: in the former Soviet Union, where universal equality presumably prevailed, no one could be "last." Among those waiting is the obligatory "simple woman": "her hands were red, worn, and lay heavily on her knees." There is the obligatory quarrel caused by someone who crashed the line.

Marya Vladimirovna is uncomfortable in this harsh world, which has its own values. She is afraid that the clients at the salon will criticize her. She is afraid of women who measure feminine dignity only on the scale of "young-old," "overweight-thin." For her the very thought that she could turn into a housewife who raised chickens and did laundry is "raving nonsense." She tries to reestablish order in the line according to her ideals of justice; she demands the complaint book and looks for sympathy, but finds only misunderstanding and hostility. Although this world of "lower" reality is alien to her, she seeks to subject it to her own clearly defined categories, to assimilate it into the "higher" world by making it normative and intelligible within her existing system of ideas. One might say that the "disorder" at the salon is, for her, not a form of chaos but rather a kind of negative order—anti-order, as it were—which does not destroy her polarized construction of reality and consequently cannot threaten the founding principles of her ordered existence, even though the anti-order has its own laws based on selfish interests. Thus the heroine, her point of view, the context of everyday life, and the form of the narrative all exist in a state of relative harmony and unity that fits within the framework of traditional Soviet thinking.

This harmony is destroyed by the appearance of the "ladies' hairdresser," Vitaly Plavnikov. He corresponds to no norm, and there is something strange, almost wild, in his appearance. Although the unpleasant atmosphere in the storage room, where Vitaly takes Marya Vladimirovna for her haircut and where scarce goods are sold on the black market, can be interpreted as deceptively simple, we are aware that it is precisely Vitaly who makes Kovaleva see the world in infernal, mystic terms. She notices that "there was a different smell here, something musty and stuffy," and that the hairdressers wear black instead of white uniforms. This symbolism grows out of real-life facts, as if against the will of the narrator, who begins here to lose control over her life and the distribution of roles in the family. In American radical literature, the theme of the disenfranchisement of women, part of the broader theme of social oppression, gradually began to develop along separate lines, becoming a specifically feminist issue. Olsen's book of essays *Silences*, in this respect, is characteristic of its generation. The author writes about specific aspects of the nature of women, asserting their equality with men and placing equal value on their respective world views. In addition, she argues for women's liberation from male domination and discusses the need for women's creativity, self-realization, and activism, exploring how women's experiences and consciousness are reflected in literature.

In her own fiction women's issues are viewed from a sociopolitical perspective. Although changing conditions in the world, as Olsen herself states, are more important than the quest for personal identity, in most of her works the characters are, in fact, in the process of discovering themselves, searching for their identities, trying to resist the pressures of the outside world, as Eva does in "Tell Me a Riddle."

Through the character of Eva, Olsen seeks to solve one of the preeminent moral problems: in achieving the full development of personality, what is the correct balance between life for oneself and life for others? Life for others is divided into two traditional categories: the "man's way," caring for the public good, and the "woman's way," devotion of oneself to family and children.

Eva, who in her youth had been a revolutionary but later abandoned her chosen path to become a housewife, feels that this choice has deprived her of the higher meaning of life. Olsen attributes Eva's fate to the unfavorable circumstances of her life: poverty, insecurity, and the struggle for survival. Gender is also represented as a crucial determinant in forcing Eva to assume her role in life. It is no coincidence that the target of her irritation and criticism is her husband David, who has lived with her, side by side, all these years, subjected to the same social circumstances. But David does not see his life as having been wasted. Even though he, as a man, carried the burden of financial responsibility, and had to limit himself in many ways, his spiritual interests and needs were somehow satisfied. He found time and energy for public life and for meeting friends. Because his heart was attached to the outside world, in his old age he dreams of freeing himself from the house and leading a carefree life in a retirement home with other elderly people. Eva, on the other hand, does not want to leave the house where she has spent her life and where, until now, she never enjoyed peace and quiet. Only when she grows old—when the children have left and the burden of household chores has lightened—does she begin to feel that it is her home. To leave it now means to be deprived of the last hope of living for herself. If she had suffered earlier from her husband's neglect and isolation from the outside world, she now longs to be alone with herself and her thoughts—a need her family fails to understand.

Eva rejects the traditional roles of wife, mother, and grandmother, desiring only one thing: "being able at last to live within and not move to the rhythms of others." Eva tries to distance herself from those around her; she fears being submerged once again in the lives of others and of losing control of her own life.

Eva strives to free herself from roles imposed on her, which stifle her personality and deprive her of individuality. She drives the rabbi from her deathbed and protests against religion as one of the superstitions of the past, a means of oppressing women. The radicalism of her youth, with its contempt and hostility toward tradition and its belief in the oppressiveness of all existing social institutions, reawakens in her. Applying the dogmas of socialist ideology, she links women's oppression with social injustice in general, to the point that David ironically asks, "You think you are still an orator of the 1905 revolution?"

Absorbed in reminiscences of her youth, of Russia and of her Siberian exile, and returning to long-forgotten emotions, Eva begins to feel that her life was a gap in time, devoid of meaning. Certain that real life had ended for her many years before, she dreams of stopping the stream of time, of plunging into nonbeing. Eva pushes aside everything that connects her with the past, even overcoming her natural feelings as a mother, and deliberately breaks contact with her children and grandchildren. David complains: "A lifetime you tended and loved, and now not a word of us, for us. Left us indeed. Left me."

Eva's estrangement is symbolized by her deafness, her ability to turn off her hearing aid and have no contact with the world. Olsen, like Grekova, conveys the various psychological states of her characters in the numerous dialogues and monologues that form the main body of the narrative. Eva's constantly changing manner of speech reflects her attitude to different people, events, and periods of her life. Her words take on a different coloring when she quarrels with her husband, reminisces about the hardships of a life spent in poverty, or romanticizes her youth.

It is precisely through words that Olsen reveals the illusory nature of Eva's notions of revolutionary ideals and her inability to base her life on them. When, before her death, Eva becomes delirious, her consciousness extracts from her memory lofty slogans, poetic phrases, and literary quotations that contain pathos, elevated feelings, rhetoric, and dogma, but no concrete truths of reality: "*Lift high banner of reason* (tatter of an orator's voice) *jus-*

of the grandchildren: 'Commercial's on; any Coke left? Gee, you've missed a real hair-raiser.'"

Young Americans of the second half of the century have lost the romantic dreams of the older generation. Pragmatic and hedonistic, they are absorbed not in public but in private, primarily materialistic concerns. The paradox is that people who lived in poverty were more spiritual than their carefree and blasé grandchildren. David remembers how he and Eva, in the midst of a world of hate and disease, had nevertheless managed to believe in so much. David wants to bequeath that sense of mattering to the new generation, but he understands that this is merely a new illusion, that human consciousness is formed under the influence of objective processes and cannot be handed down "in cereal boxes." For Olsen, ideas of a violent, preplanned transformation of society recede into the distant past and are perceived as nothing more than wishful thinking.

Yet through human kindness there remains a spiritual connection and continuity between the older generation and the best representatives of the younger. Jeannie, who devotedly cares for her dying grandmother, reminds Eva of Lisa, a follower of Tolstoy. People appear indissolubly linked as part of the general stream of life, which "may be hated or wearied of, but never despised." During her last days, Eva begins to see her entire life as an indivisible whole with a hidden meaning, a mystery that can be lived but not solved.

In this manner, both Olsen and Grekova come to regard the notion that life's extraordinary diversity and complexity cannot be reduced to abstract formulae. But Olsen, coming out of a different historical and national experience, a different cultural and literary milieu, moves further than Grekova from ideological and aesthetic clichés. The logic of her characters' development indicates that a person can achieve selfhood only by listening to her inner voice instead of blindly accepting societal roles. The misfortune of Grekova's and Olsen's heroines is that both, whether out of their own convictions or out of circumstances, fail to pay heed to their own deepest selves. Marya Vladimirovna has chosen a traditionally "masculine" option—public activity and scientific research—while Eva has chosen a "feminine" course: family. As a result, Marya Vladimirovna suppresses her "feminine" and Eva her "masculine" qualities. Thus neither is able to develop fully human qualities in which both principles are united.

For Grekova, men and women are not only spiritually equal, they are the same; for Olsen, they have equal value and significance but are different. As a result, the women's sphere of everyday life which, for Grekova, is a burdensome obstacle to be relegated to the periphery of life is, for Olsen, one of life's main components. Grekova, together with her heroine, stands still before the mystery of existence, unable to fit all its phenomena into a familiar schema; she tries to control narrative in all its elements by the presence of the author's point of view and persistently employs a traditional prose style. Olsen, on the other hand, is not afraid of stylistic spontaneity; she lets her text roam free via dialogue, inner monologue, and stream of consciousness.

Olsen portrays the inner dynamics of her heroine by showing her psychological development in historical time. Grekova's Marya Vladimirovna, however, remains static because her thinking is not formed by the events of her life but determined a priori by the ideological and ethical norms of Soviet society. It is not coincidental that when the author wants to portray an enigmatic character who does not fit into the normal framework—that is, Vitaly—she feels compelled to introduce his biography and the narrative of his personality formation. Almost unconsciously, Grekova is at the threshold of the crisis in traditional thinking which neglected the contradictions within human nature and tended to ignore the spontaneous element of life. The new directions in spiritual life, which in the sixties appeared primarily in generational conflict, demanded that great attention be paid to human individuality. Olsen's break from the ideas of a deliberate transformation of society, a concept that fascinated her during one period of her life, is seen most clearly in her focus on the inner life of the individual. In summary, the very different worlds created by these writers demonstrate not merely the obvious dissimilarity between the two literatures but also the common problems the two countries face—problems of generations, genders, and the relationship between the individual and society.

Translated by Irina Katz

Dialogue

ON GREKOVA AND OLSEN

Katya: Grekova's story reveals an ambiguous ideology. Kovaleva thinks that everything should correspond to a certain model. She's sure she should ignore the womanly part of her, yet it's there. This is our doublethink. We consider our deeds not as they are but as they should be. Often this inner ambiguity isn't caught by the conscious mind.

Maya: Yes. The correspondence between what is and what should be—this "should be" perspective—doesn't allow a person to see the realities of daily life.

Susan: Katya, what do you mean by "the womanly part of her"?

Katya: I think that women see things more elementally than men.

Susan: Some might say that's just a stereotype.

Katya: But women *are* more intuitive than men—not that we aren't all both rational and emotional, but women are more intuitive, and to me that's a higher order of thinking.

Maya: *I* think it has to do with individual personality much more than differences between men and women. For example, some men, especially artists, are intuitive. I think it's dangerous to make large generalizations about personalities relative to sex. The question of intuition, for example, points to a difference between Marya and Galya. Grekova's depiction of Galya suggests that she lives by intuition because of a lower level of awareness, education, and consciousness. She's just following the stream, reducing herself to a sort of instinctual being, making no more demands on herself than are necessary.

There's also a class analysis here that's very important. Among the common people (*narod*) marriage is regarded as the highest achievement, but not among the intelligentsia. Women of the intelligentsia would rather stay single than compromise values of what constitutes a happy union.

Adele: In Gorbachev's book on perestroika, he says that women should return to their "womanly place." Is it possible that he's being strategic, because he knows that this rhetoric will appeal to the masses?

Maya: Yes, but the attitude he expresses is also reflected in official policy. Only after I'd studied American literature for thirty years was I allowed to come to the United

States. One of the things that went against me was that I was divorced and a woman. The assumption was, if I'd "betrayed" my husband, why wouldn't I betray my country?

Susan: How would you relate Marya's dismissal of Vitaly at the end of the story to these questions of class difference?

Maya: Ultimately, people like Vitaly are inaccessible to Kovaleva. When she scolds Vitaly for not marrying Galya, for instance—in a way she's right because she thinks that common life should be based on mutual love. But she also neglects the fact that this union needs literal shelter—that material conditions aren't adequate to support spiritual needs. Her superior position leads to her complete absence of understanding of his human situation. She doesn't see all the necessary complexities.

Susan: Yet don't you feel that Grekova's sympathies are more with Kovaleva? Doesn't Grekova too dismiss Vitaly at the end for abandoning his art?

Katya: I don't think it's clear that Vitaly capitulates in the end.

Adele: Then this brings up the question, whose point of view does the ending support? Is this a typical working-class story with a happy ending where the protagonist becomes a useful member of society?

Maya: I don't think it's so simple. For instance, this insistence on the happy ending— I'm not sure Grekova is deliberately using Socialist Realism as irony. This was a time full of hope. The intelligentsia in 1962 were very hopeful.

Adele: So in a way, this kind of ending, which seems to reflect Socialist Realism, may in fact reflect the expectations of the class to which Grekova belonged?

Susan: Perhaps Grekova is aware that she has internalized certain ideologies, so the ending is a kind of self-ironizing moment. As an artist and as a woman, Grekova identifies with both Vitaly and Marya. I think Maya is right: Grekova refuses to simplify the contradictions of their respective situations.

2

❖

Toni Cade Bambara and

❖ ❖ ❖ ❖

Liudmila Petrushevskaia

© *Jill Krementz, by permission*

TONI CADE BAMBARA ❖ "What I enjoy most in my work is the laughter and the outrage and the attention to language," writes Toni Cade Bambara. "I come from a family of very gifted laughers." Born Toni Cade in New York in 1939, Bambara grew up in the ghettos of Harlem, Bedford Stuyvesant, and Jersey City. She began writing as a child, encouraged by her parents, who taught her "the power of the word, the importance of the resistance tradition, and the high standards our community has regarding verbal performance." She honed her own voice, pitch, and pace by listening to those performances and to the black music of the forties and fifties in what she has called "the bebop heaven of New York City" (all quotations from "Salvation is the Issue," 1984).

Bambara received her B.A. in theater arts and English literature from Queens College in 1959 and her M.A. in American literature from City College of New York in 1963. Along with her freelance writing, she has worked as a welfare investigator, an occupational therapist, a drug rehabilitation counselor and community organizer, and an instructor of English. She has taught at several universities, including Rutgers, City University of New York, Duke, and Emory, and has been writer-in-residence at Spelman College.

Widely anthologized, Bambara is the author of *Gorilla, My Love* (1972); *The Sea Birds Are Still Alive* (1977); *The Salt Eaters* (1980), for which she won the American Book Award; and *If Blessing Comes* (1987). She has edited two collections: *The Black Woman: An Anthology* (1970) and *Tales and Stories for Black Folks* (1971). She is also a playwright, scriptwriter, painter, filmmaker, and the mother of a daughter, Karma. She called herself Bambara, the name of an African tribe from the Niger river region, after a signature she found among her great-grandmother's papers.

Witchbird

TONI CADE BAMBARA

1

Curtains blew in and wrecked my whole dressing-table arrangement. Then in he came, eight kinds of darkness round his shoulders, this nutty bird scree-chin on his arm, on a nine-speed model, hand brakes and all. Said, "Come on, we goin ride right out of here just like you been wantin to for long time now." Patting the blanket lassoed to the carrier, leaning way back to do it, straddling the bike and thrusting his johnson out in front, patting, thrusting, insinuating. Bird doing a two-step on the handle bars.

Damn if I'm riding nowhere on some bike. I like trains. Am partial to fresh-smelling club cars with clear windows and cushy seats with white linen at the top for my cheek to snooze against. Not like the hulking, oil-leaking, smoke-belching monstrosity I came home on when the play closed. Lean-ing my cheek against the rattling windowpane, like to shook my teeth loose. Cigar stench, orange peels curling on the window sills, balls of wax paper greasy underfoot, the linen rank from umpteen different hair pomades. Want the trains like before, when I was little and the porter hauled me up by my wrists and joked with me about my new hat, earning the five my mama slipped him, leisurely. Watching out for my person, saving a sunny seat in the dining car, clearing the aisle of perverts from round my berth, making sure I was in the no-drama section of the train once we crossed the Potomac.

"Well, we can cross over to the other side," he saying, "you in a rut, girl, let's go." Leaning over the edge of the boat, trailing a hand in the blue-green Caribbean. No way. I like trains. Then uncorking the champagne, the bottle lodged between his thighs. Then the pop of the cork, froth cascading all over his lap. I tell you I'm partial to trains. "Well, all right," he sayin, stepping out his pants. "We go the way you want, any way you want. Cause you need a change," he saying, chuggin over my carpet in this bubble-top train he sud-denly got. Bird shouting at me from the perch of eye-stinging white linen. And I know something gotta be wrong. Cause whenever I've asked for what

I want in life, I never get it. So he got to be the devil or some kind of other ugly no-good thing.

"Get on out my room," I'm trying to say, jaws stuck. Whole right side and left paralyzed like I'm jammed in a cage. "You tromping on my house shoes and I don't play that. Them's the house shoes Heywood gave me for Mother's Day." Some joke. Heywood come up empty-handed every rent day, but that don't stop him from boarding all his ex ole ladies with me freebee. But yellow satin Hollywood slippers with pompoms on Mother's Day, figuring that's what I'm here for. Shit, I ain't nobody's mother. I'm a singer. I'm an actress. I'm a landlady look like. Hear me. Applaud me. Pay me.

"But look here," he saying, holding up a pair of house shoes even finer than mine. Holding em up around his ears like whatshisname, not the Sambo kid, the other little fellah. "Come on and take this ride with me."

All this talk about crossing over somewhere in dem golden slippers doing something to my arms. They jiggling loose from me like they through the bars of the cage, cept I know I'm under the covers in a bed, not a box. Just a jiggling. You'd think I was holding a hazel switch or a willow rod out in the woods witching for water. Peach twig better actually for locating subterranean springs. And I try to keep my mind on water, cause water is always a good thing. Creeks, falls, foundations, artesian wells. Baptism, candlelight ablutions, skinny-dipping in the lake, C&C with water on the side. The root of all worthy civilizations, water. Can heal you. Scrunched up under the quilts, the sick tray pushed to the side, the heal of rain washing against the window can heal you or make you pee the bed one, which'll wake you from fever, from sleep, will save you. Save me. Cause damn if this character ain't trying to climb into my berth. And if there's one thing I can do without, it's phantom fucking.

"Honey? You told me to wake you at dark. It's dark." Gayle, the brown-skin college girl my sometime piano player–sometime manager–mosttime friend Heywood dumped on me last time through here, jiggling my arms. Looking sorrowful about waking me up, she knows how sacred sleep can be, though not how scary.

"Here," she says, sliding my house shoes closer to the bed. "You know Heywood was all set to get you some tired old navy-blue numbers. I kept telling him you ain't nobody's grandma," she says, backing up to give me room to stretch, looking me over like she always does, comparing us I guess to flatter her own vanity, or wondering maybe if it's possible Heywood sees beyond friend, colleague, to maybe woman. All the time trying to pry me open and check out is there some long ago Heywood-me history. The truth is there's nothing to tell. Heywood spot him a large, singing, easygoing type woman, so he dumps his girl friends on me is all. I slide into the cold slippers. They're too soft now and give no support. Cheap-ass shoes. Here it is only Halloween, and they falling apart already. I'm sucking my teeth but can't even hear myself good for the caterwauling that damn bird's already set up in the woods, tearing up the bushes, splitting twigs with the high notes. Bird make me think some singer locked up inside, hostage. Cept that bird ain't enchanting, just annoying.

"Laney's fixing a plate of supper for Miz Mary," Gayle is saying, sliding a hand across my dressing-table scarf like she dying to set her buns down and mess in my stuff. My make-up kit ain't even unpacked, I'm noticing, and the play been closed for over a month. I ain't even taken the time to review what that role's done to my sense of balance, my sense of self. But who's got time, what with all of Heywood's women cluttering up my house, my life? Prancing around in shorty nightgowns so I don't dare have company in. A prisoner in my own house.

"Laney say come on, she'll walk to the shop with you, Honey. Me too. I think my number hit today. Maybe I can help out with the bills."

Right. I'd settle for some privacy. Had such other plans for my time right in through here. Bunch of books my nephew sent untouched. Stacks of *Variety* unread under the kitchen table. The new sheet music gathering dust on the piano. Been wanting to go over the old songs, the ole Bessie numbers, Ma Rainey, Trixie Smith, early Lena. So many women in them songs waiting to be released into the air again, freed to roam. Good time to be getting my new repertoire together too instead of rushing into my clothes and slapping my face together just because Laney can't bear walking the streets alone after dark, and Gayle too scared to stay in the place by herself. Not that Heywood puts a gun to my head, but it's hard to say no to a sister with no place to go. So they wind up here, expecting me to absorb their blues and transform them maybe into songs. Been over a year since I've written any new songs. Absorbing, absorbing, bout to turn to mush rather than crystallize, sparkling.

2

Magazine lady on the phone this morning asked if I was boarding any new up-and-coming stars. Very funny. Vera, an early Heywood ex, had left here once her demo record was cut, went to New York and made the big time. Got me a part in the play according to the phone voice contracted to do a four-page spread on Vera Willis, Star. But that ain't how the deal went down at all.

"I understand you used to room together" was how the phone interview started off. Me arranging the bottles and jars on my table, untangling the junk in my jewelry boxes. Remembering how Vera considered herself more guest than roommate, no problem whatsoever about leaving all the work to me, was saving herself for Broadway or Hollywood one. Like nothing I could be about was all that important so hey, Honey, pick up the mop. Me sitting on the piano bench waiting for Heywood to bring in a batch of cheat sheets, watching Vera in the yard with my nieces turning double dudge. Then Vera gets it in her mind to snatch away the rope and sing into the wooded handle, strolling, sassy, slinky between the dogwoods, taking poses, kicking at the tail of the rope and making teethy faces like Heywood taught her. The little girls stunned by this performance so like their own, only this one done brazenly, dead serious, and by a grown-up lady slithering about the yard.

Staring out the window, I felt bad. I thought it was because Vera was just not pretty. Not pretty and not nice. Obnoxious in fact, selfish, vain, lazy. But yeah she could put a song over, though she didn't have what you'd call musicianship. Like she'd glide into a song, it all sounding quite dull normal at first. Then a leg would shoot out as though from a split in some juicy material kicking the mike cord out the way, then the song would move somewhere. As though the spirit of music had hovered cautious around her chin thinking it over, looking her over, then liking that leg, swept into her mouth and took hold of her throat and the song possessed her, electrified the leg, sparked her into pretty. Later realizing I was staring at her, feeling bad because of course she'd make it, have what she wanted, go everywhere, meet everybody, be everything but self-deserving.

First-class bitch was my two cents with the producers, just to make it crystal clear I didn't intend riding in on her dress tails but wanted to be judged by my own work, my reputation, my audition. Don't nobody do me no favors, please, cause I'm the baddest singer out here and one of the best character actresses around. And just keeping warmed up till a Black script comes my way.

Wasn't much of a part, but a good bit at the end. My daddy used to instruct, if you can't be the star of the show, aim for a good bit at the end. People remember that one good line or that one striking piece of business by the bit player in the third act. Well, just before the end, I come on for my longest bit in the play. I'm carrying this veil, Vera's mama's veil. The woman's so grief-stricken and whatnot, she ain't even buttoned up right and forgot to put on her veil. So here I come with the veil, and the mourners part the waves to give me a path right to the grave site. But once I see the coffin, my brown-sugar honey chile darlin dead and boxed, I forget all about the blood mama waiting for her veil. Forget all about maintaining my servant place in the bourgy household. I snatch off my apron and slowly lift that veil, for I am her true mother who cared for her and carried her through. I raise the hell outta that veil, transforming myself into Mother with a capital M. I let it drape slowly, slowly round my corn rolls, slowly lower it around my brow, my nose, mouth opening and the song bursting my jaws asunder as the curtain—well, not curtain, but the lights, cause we played it in the round, dim. Tore the play up with the song.

Course we did have a set-to about the costume. The designer saw my point—her talents were being squandered copying the pancake box. Playwright saw my point too, why distort a perfectly fine character just cause the director has mammy fantasies. An African patchwork apron was the only concession I'd make. Got to be firm about shit like that, cause if you ain't some bronze Barbie doll type or the big fro murder-mouth militant sister, you Aunt Jemima. Not this lady. No way. Got to fight hard and all the time with the scripts and the people. Cause they'll trap you in a fiction. Breath drained, heart stopped, vibrancy fixed, under arrest. Whole being entrapped, all possibility impaled, locked in some stereotype. And how you look trying to call from the box and be heard much less be understood long enough to get out and mean something useful and for real?

Sometimes I think I do a better job of it with the bogus scripts than with the life script. Fight harder with directors than with friends who trap me in their scenarios, put a drama on my ass. That's the problem with friends sometimes, they invest in who you were or seem to have been, capture you and you're through. Forget what you had in mind about changing, growing, developing. Got you typecasted. That's why I want some time off to think, to work up a new repertoire of songs, of life. So many women in them songs, in them streets, in me, waiting to be freed up.

Dozing, drifting into sleep sometime, the script sliding off the quilts into a heap, I hear folks calling to me. Calling from the box. Mammy Pleasant, was it? Tubman, slave women bundlers, voodoo queens, maroon guerrillas, combatant ladies in the Seminole nation, calls from the swamps, the tunnels, the classrooms, the studios, the factories, the roofs, from the doorway hushed or brassy in a dress way too short but it don't mean nuthin heavy enough to have to explain, just like Bad Bitch in the Sanchez play was saying. But then the wagon comes and they all rounded up and caged in the Bitch-Whore-Mouth mannequin with the dead eyes and the mothball breath, never to be heard from again. But want to sing a Harriet song and play a Pleasant role and bring them all center stage.

Wives weeping from the pillow not waking him cause he got his own weight to tote, wife in the empty road with one slipper on and the train not stopping, mother anxious with the needle and thread or clothespin as the children grow either much too fast to escape the attention of the posse or not fast enough to take hold. Women calling from the lock-up of the Matriarch cage. I want to put some of these new mother poems in those books the nephew sends to music. They got to be sung, hummed, shouted, chanted, swung.

Too many damn ransom notes fluttering in the window, or pitched in through the glass. Too much bail to post. Too many tunnels to dig and too much dynamite to set. I read the crazy scripts just to keep my hand in, cause I knew these newbreed Bloods going to do it, do it, do it. But meanwhile, I gotta work . . . and hell. Then read one of them books my nephew always sending and hearing the voices speaking free not calling from these new Black poems. Speaking free. So I know I ain't crazy. But fast as we bust one, two loose, here come some crazy cracker throwing a croaker sack over Nat Turner's head, or white folks taking Malcolm hostage. And one time in Florida, dreaming in the hotel room about the Mary McLeod Bethune exhibit, I heard the woman calling from some diary entry they had under glass, a voice calling, muffled under the gas mask they clamped on hard and turned her on till she didn't know what was what. But calling for Black pages.

Then waking and trying to resume the reading, cept I can't remember just whom I'm supposed to try to animate in those dead, white pages I got to deal with till a Blood writes me my own. And catch myself calling to the white pages as I ripple them fast, listening to the pages for the entrapped voices calling, calling as the pages flutter.

Shit. It's enough to make you crazy. Where is my play, I wanna ask these new Bloods at the very next conference I hear about. Where the hell is my script? When I get to work my show?

"A number of scandalous rumors followed the run of the play, taking up an inordinate amount of space in the reviews," the lady on the phone was saying, me caught up in my own dialogue. "I understand most of the men connected with the play and Vera Willis had occasion to . . ."

There was Heywood, of course. Hadn't realized they'd gotten back together till that weekend we were packing the play off to New York. Me packing ahead of schedule and anxious to get out of D.C. fast, cause Bradwell, who used to manage the club where I been working for years, had invited me to his home for the weekend. For old times' sake, he'd said. Right. He'd married somebody else, a singer we used to crack on as I recall, not a true note in her, her tits getting her over. And now she'd left him rolling around lonely in the brownstone on Edgecombe Avenue she'd once thought she just had to have. I went out and bought two hussy nightgowns. I was gonna break out in a whole new number. But never did work up the nerve.

Never did have the occasion, ole Bradwell crying the blues about his wife. So what am I there for—to absorb, absorb, and transform if you can, ole girl. Absorb, absorb and try to convert it all to something other than fat.

Heywood calling to ask me to trade my suite near the theater for his room clear cross town.

"You can have both," I said, chuckling. "I'm off for the weekend."

"How come? Where you going?"

"Rendezvous. Remember the guy that used to own—"

"Cut the comedy. Where you going?"

"I'm telling you. I got a rendezvous with this gorgeous man I—"

"Look here," he cut in, "I'd invited Laney up to spend the weekend. That was before me and Vera got together again. I was wondering if you'd bail me out, maybe hang out with Laney till I can—"

"Heywood, you deaf? I just now told you I'm off to spend the—"

"Seriously?"

Made me so mad, I just hung up. Hung up and called me a fast cab.

3

Laney, Gayle, and me turn into Austin and run smack into a bunch of ghosts. Skeletons, pirates, and little devils with great flapping shopping bags set up a whirlwind around us. Laney spins around like in a speeded-up movie, holding Mary's dinner plate away from her dress and moaning, comically. Comically at first. But then our bird friend in the woods starts shrieking and Laney moaning for real. Gayle empties her bag into one of the opened sacks, then leans in to retrieve her wallet, though I can't see why. All I got for the kids is a short roll of crumbly Lifesavers, hair with tobacco and lint from my trench coat lining. Screaming and wooo-wooooing, they jack-rabbit on down Austin. Then we heading past the fish truck, my mind on some gumbo, when suddenly Gayle stops. She heard it soon's I did. Laney still walking on till I guess some remark didn't get a uh-hunh and she turns around to see us way behind, Gayle's head cocked to the side.

"What it is?" Laney looking up and down the street for a clue. Other than the brother dumping the last of the ice from the fish truck and a few cats hysterical at the curb, too self-absorbed to launch a concerted attack on the truck, there ain't much to keep the eyes alive. "What?" Laney whispers.

From back of the houses we hear some mother calling her son, the voice edgy on the last syllable, getting frantic. Probably Miz Baker, whose six-foot twelve-year-old got a way of scooting up and down that resembles too much the actions of a runaway bandit to the pigs around here. Mainly, he got the outlaw hue, and running too? Shit, Miz Baker stay frantic. The boy answers from the woods, which starts the bird up again, screeching, ripping through the trees, like she trying to find a way out of them woods and heaven help us if she do, cause she dangerous with rage.

"That him?" Gayle asks, knowing I'm on silence this time of night.

"Who?" Laney don't even bother looking at me, cause she knows I got a whole night of singing and running off at the mouth to get through once Mary lets me out from under the dryer and I get to the club. "Witchbird?" Laney takes a couple steps closer to us. "Yawl better tell me what's up," she says, "cause this here gettin spoooo-keeee!"

It's mostly getting dark and Laney don't wanna have to take the shortcut through the woods. Witchbird gotta way of screaming on you sudden, scare the shit outta you. Laney trying to balance that plate of dinner and not lose the juice. She is worried you can tell, and not just about Mary's mouth over cold supper. Laney's face easy to read, everything surfaces to the skin. Dug that the day Heywood brought her by. She knew she was being cut loose, steered safely to cove, the boat shoving off and bye, baby, bye. Sad crinkling round the eyes, purples under the chin, throat pulsating. Gayle harder to read, a Scorpio, she plays it close to the chest unless she can play it for drama.

"Tell me, Gayle. What it is?"

"Heywood back in town."

"Ohhh, girl, don't tell me that." Laney takes a coupla sideways steps, juggling the plate onto one hand so she can tug down the jersey she barmaids in. "You better come on."

"You know one thing," Gayle crooning it, composing a monologue, sound like. "There was a time when that laugh could turn me clear around in the street and make me forget just where I thought I was going." On cue, Heywood laughs one of his laughs and Gayle's head tips, locating his whereabouts. She hands me her suede bag heavy with the pic comb and the schoolbooks. It's clear she fixin to take off. "I really loved that dude," she saying, theatrics gone. Laney moves on, cause she don't want to hear nuthin about Heywood and especially from Gayle. "He gets his thing off," Laney had said to Gayle the night she was dumped, "behind the idea of his harem sprawled all over Honey's house gassing about him. I refuse," she had said and stuck to it.

"I really, really did," Gayle saying, something leaking in her voice.

Laney hears it and steps back. It's spilling on her shoes, her dress, soaking into her skin. She moves back again cause Gayle's zone is spreading. Gayle so filling up and brimming over, she gotta take over more and more room to accommodate the swell. Her leaking splashes up against me too— Heywood taking a solo, teeth biting out a rhythm on the back of his lower lip, Heywood at the wheel leaning over for a kiss fore he cranks up, Heywood wound up in rumpled sheets with his cap pulled down, sweat beading on his nose, waiting on breakfast, Heywood doing the dance of the hot hands and Gayle scrambling for a potholder to catch the coffeepot he'd reached for with his fool self, Heywood falling off the porch and Gayle's daddy right on him. Gayle's waves wash right up on me and I don't want no parts of it. Let it all wash right through me, can't use it, am to the brim with my own stuff waiting to be transformed. Washes through me so fast the pictures blur and all I feel is heat and sparks. And then I hear the laugh again.

"Oh, shit," Laney says, watching the hem of Gayle's dress turning into the alley. "That girl is craaaaa-zeee, ya heah?" Her legs jiggling to put her in the alley in more ways than one, but that plate leaking pot likker and demanding its due.

Bright's strung up lights in the alley and you can make him out clear, hunched over the bathtub swishing barbeque sauce with a sheet-wrapped broom. Cora visible too, doing a shonuff flower arrangement on the crushed ice with the watermelon slices. And there's Heywood, ole lanky Heywood in his cap he says Babs Gonzales stole from Kenny Clarke and he in turn swiped from Babs. One arm lazy draped around Gayle's shoulders, the other crooked in the fence he lounges against, sipping some of Bright's bad brandy brew, speakeasy style. Other folks around the card table sipping from jelly jars or tin cups. But Heywood would have one of Cora's fine china numbers. He's looking good.

"What's goin on?" Laney asks in spite of herself, but refuses to move where she can see into the yard. All she got to do is listen, cause Heywood is the baritone lead of the eight-part card game opus.

"Ho!"

"Nigger, just play the card."

"Gonna. Gonna do that direckly. Right on yawl's ass."

"Do it to em, Porter."

"Don't tell him nuthin. He don't wanna know nuthin. He ain't never been nuthin but a fool."

Porter spits on the card and slaps it on his forehead.

"Got the bitch right here"—he's pointing—"the bitch that's gonna set ya."

"Nigger, you nasty, you know that? You a nasty-ass nigger and that's why don't nobody never wanna play with yo nasty-ass self."

"Just play the card, Porter."

"Ho!" He bangs the card down with a pop and the table too.

"Iz you crazy?"

"If Porter had any sense, he'd be dangerous."

"Sense enough to send these blowhards right out the back door. Ho!"

"You broke the table and the ashtray, fool."

"And that was my last cigarette too. Gimme a dollar."

"Dollar! I look like a fool? If you paying Bright a dollar for cigarettes, you the fool."

"I want the dollar for some barbeque."

"What! What!" Porter sputtering and dancing round the yard. "How come I gotta replace one cigarette with a meal?"

"Okay then, buy some watermelon and some of the fire juice."

"You don't logic, man. You sheer don't logic. All I owe you is a cigarette."

"What about the table?"

"It ain't your table, nigger."

Laney is click-clicking up the street, giving wide berth to the path that leads through the woods. "Why Gayle want to put herself through them changes all over again," she is mumbling, grinding her heels in the broken pavement, squashing the dandelions. "I wouldn't put myself through none of that mess again for all the money." She picking up speed and I gotta trot to catch up. "I don't know how you can stay friends with a man like that, Honey."

"He don't do me no harm," I say, then mad to break my silence.

"Oh, no?" She trying to provoke me into debating it, so she says it again, "Oh, no?"

I don't want to get into this, all I want is to get into Mary's shampoo chair, to laze under Mary's hands and have her massage all the hurt up out of my body, tension emulsified in the coconut-oil suds, all fight sprayed away. My body been so long on chronic red alert messin with them theater folks, messing with stock types, real types, messing with me, I need release, not hassles.

"You think it's no harm the way he uses you, Honey? What are you, his mother, his dumping grounds? Why you put up with it? Why you put up with us, with me? Oh, Honey, I—"

I walk right along, just like she ain't talking to me. I can't take in another thing.

4

"Well, all right! Here she come, Broadway star," someone bellows at me as the bell over the door jangles.

"Come on out from under that death, Honey," Mary says soon's we get halfway in the door. "Look like you sportin a whole new look in cosmetics. Clown white, ain't it? Or is it Griffin All White applied with a putty knife?" Mary leaves her customer in the chair to come rip the wig off my head. "And got some dead white woman on your head too. Why you wanna do this to yourself, Honey? You auditioning for some zombie movie?"

"Protective covering," Bertha says, slinging the magazine she'd been reading onto the pile. "You know how Honey likes to put herself out of circulation, Mary. Honey, you look like one of them creatures Nanna Mae raised from the dead. What they do to you in New York, girl? We thought you'd come back tired, but not embalmed."

"Heard tell a duppy busted up some posh do on the hill last Saturday," Mary's customer saying. "Lotta zombies round here."

"Some say it was the ghost of Willie Best come back to kill him somebody."

"Long's it's some white somebody, okay by me."

"Well, you know colored folks weren't exactly kind to the man when he was alive. Could be—"

"Heard Heywood's back on the scene," Bertha comes over to say to me. She lifts my hand off the armrest and checks my manicure and pats my hand to make up for, I guess, her not-so-warm greeting. "Be interesting to see just what kinda bundle he gonna deposit on your doorstep this time." Laney cuts her eye at Bertha, surrenders up the juiceless meal and splits. "Like you ain't got nuthin better to do with ya tits but wet-nurse his girls."

I shove Bertha's hand off mine and stretch out in my favorite chair. Mary's got a young sister now to do the scratchin and hot oil. She parts hair with her fingers, real gentle-like. Feels good. I'm whipped. I think on all I want to do with the new music and I'm feelin crowded, full up, rushed.

"No use you trying to ig me, Honey," Bertha says real loud. "Cause I'm Mary's last customer. We got all night."

"Saw Frieda coming out the drugstore," somebody is saying. "Package looked mighty interesting."

Everybody cracking up, Bertha too. I ease my head back and close my eyes under the comb scratching up dandruff.

"Obviously Ted is going on the road again and Frieda gonna pack one of her famous box snacks."

"Got the recipe for the oatmeal cookies richeah," someone saying. "One part rolled oats, one long drip of sorghum, fistful of raisins, and a laaaarge dose of saltpeter."

"Salt pete-er salt pete-er," somebody singing through the nose, outdoing Dizzy.

"Whatchu say!"

"Betcha there'll be plenty straaange mashed potatoes on the table tonight."

The young girl's rubbin is too hard in the part and the oil too hot. But she so busy cracking up, she don't notice my ouchin.

"Saltpetertaters, what better dish to serve a man going on the road for three days. Beats calling him every hour on the half-hour telling him to take a cold shower."

"Best serve him with a summons for being so downright ugly. Can't no woman be really serious about messin with Ted, he too ugly."

"Some that looks ugly. . . ." Couldn't catch the rest of it, but followed the giggling well enough after what sounded like a second of silence.

"Mary"—someone was breathless with laughter—"when you and the sisters gonna give another one of them balls?"

"Giiirl," howls Bertha, "Wasn't that ball a natural ball?"

5

Bertha and Mary and me organized this Aquarian Ball. We so busy making out the lists, hooking people up, calling in some new dudes from the Islands just to jazz it up, hiring musicians and all, we clean forgot to get me an escort. I'd just made Marshall the trumpet player give me back my key cause all he ever wanted to do was bring by a passle of fish that needed cleaning and frying, and I was sick of being cook and confidante. I bet if I lost weight, people'd view me different. Other than Marshall, wasn't no man on the horizon, much less the scene. Mary, me and Bertha playing bid whist and I feel a Boston in my bones, so ain't paying too much attention to the fact that this no escort status of mine is serious business as far as Bertha's concerned.

"What about Heywood?" she says, scooping up the kitty.

Right on cue as always, in comes ole lanky Heywood with his cap yanked down around his brow and umpteen scarves around his mouth looking like Jesse James. He's got a folio of arrangements to deliver to me, but likes to make a big production first of saying hello to sisters. So while he's doing his rhyming couplets and waxing lyric and whatnot, I'm looking him over, trying to unravel my feelings about this man I've known, worked with, befriended for so long. Good manager, never booked me in no dumps. Always sees to it that the money ain't funny. A good looker and all, but always makes me feel more mother or older sister, though he four months to the day older than me. Naaw, I conclude, Heywood just my buddy. But I'm thinking too that I need a new buddy, cause he's got me bagged somehow. Put me in a bag when I wasn't looking. Folks be sneaky with their scenarios and secret casting.

"Say, handsome," Bertha say, jumping right on it, "ain't you taking Honey here to the ball?"

"Why somebody got to take her? I thought yawl was giving it."

"That ain't no answer. Can't have Honey waltzin in without—"

"Hold on," he saying, unwrapping the scarves cause we got the oven up high doing the meat patties.

"Never mind all that," says Mary. "Who you know can do it? Someone nice now."

"Well, I'll tell you," he says, stretching his arm around me. "I don't know no men good enough for the queen here."

"You a drag and a half," says Bertha.

"And I don't want to block traffic either," he says. "I mean if Honey comes in with my fine self on her arm, no man there is—"

"Never mind that," says Mary, slapping down an ace. "What about your friends, I'm askin you?"

"Like I said, I don't know anybody suitable."

"What you mean is, you only knows the ladies," says Bertha, disgusted. "You the type dude that would probably come up with a basket case for escort anyway. Club foot, hunchback, palsied moron or something. Just to make sure Honey is still available for you to mammify."

"Now wait a minute," he says, rising from the chair and pushing palms against the air like he fending us off. "How I get involved in yawl's arrangements?"

"You a friend, ain't ya? You a drag, that's for sure." Bertha lays down her hand, we thought to hit Heywood, come to find she trump tight.

Heywood puts the folio in my lap and rewraps the scarves for take-off, and we spend the afternoon being sullen, and damn near burnt up the meat patties.

"I'm getting tired of men like that," grumbles Bertha after while. "Either it's 'Hey, Mama, hold my head,' or 'Hey, Sister,' at three in the morning. When it get to be 'Sugar Darling'? I'm tired of it. And you, Honey, should be the tiredest of all."

"So I just took my buns right to her house, cause she my friend and what else a friend for?" one of the women is saying. Mary's easing my head back on the shampoo tray, so I can't see who's talking.

"So did you tell her?"

"I surely did. I held her by the shoulders and said, 'Helen, you do know that Amos is on the dope now, don't you?' And she kinda went limp in my arms like she was gonna just crumble and not deal with it."

"A myth all that stuff about our strength and strength and then some," Bertha saying.

"'If Amos blow his mind now, who gonna take care of you in old age, Helen?' I try to tell her."

"So what she say?"

"She don't say nuthin. She just cry."

"It's a hellafyin thing. No jobs, nary a fit house in sight, famine on the way, but the dope just keep comin and comin."

I don't know Helen or Amos. Can't tell whether Amos is the son or the husband. Ain't that a bitch. But I feel bad inside. I crumple up too hearing it. Picturing a Helen seeing her Amos in a heap by the bathtub, gagging, shivering, defeated, not like he should be. Getting the blankets to wrap him up, holding him round, hugging him tight, rocking, rocking, rocking.

"You need a towel?" Mary whispers, bending under the dryer. No amount of towel's gonna stop the flood, I'm thinking. I don't even try to stop. Let it pour, let it get on out so I can travel light. I'm thinking maybe I'll do Billie's number tonight. Biting my lip and trying to think on the order of songs I'm going to get through this evening and where I can slip Billie in.

"What's with you, Honey?"

"Mary got this damn dryer on KILL," I say, and know I am about to talk myself hoarse and won't be fit for singing.

1974

LIUDMILA PETRUSHEVSKAIA ❖ Born in Moscow in 1938, Liudmila Stefa-
novna Petrushevskaia spent much of her childhood in the city of Kuybyshev, where her
mother and other family members had been exiled because of the purges of the late thirties.
When her mother returned to Moscow in 1943, she left her daughter behind. Liudmila and
her remaining relatives suffered the hardships of famine until 1947, when she and her
mother were reunited, but because her mother was unable to care for her, she was placed
in an orphanage for undernourished children. Later, mother and daughter lived in Moscow
with Petrushevskaia's grandfather, a mathematician and specialist on Eastern languages,
whose library provided her with her first exposure to Russian and Western literature.

Petrushevskaia went on to study journalism at Moscow State University and after
graduation worked for eleven years as a radio reporter, taping interviews and dialogues
that would later provide material for her stories and plays. Although she began writing in
1963, initial critical response to her in her own country was uniformly negative because
her characters and situations violated the official tenets of the Soviet literary and political
establishment. By the early 1970s, however, her stories began to be published and she
began to receive the critical recognition she deserved. Although her first plays were often
barred from performance at the last minute, by the 1980s she began to enjoy a certain degree of official acceptance as a playwright, and is now regarded as one of the most talented
voices in contemporary Russian drama. Among her works are the plays *Liubov'* (*Love*), *Uroki
musiki* (*Music Lessons*), *Tri devushki v golubom* (*Three Girls in Blue*), and *Komnata kolum-
biny* (*Columbine's Apartment*), as well as numerous stories and monologues, many of which
are contained in her collection *Bessmertnaia liubov'* (*Immortal Love*, 1988). Petrushevskaia
currently lives in Moscow with her husband and three children.

That Kind of Girl

LIUDMILA PETRUSHEVSKAIA

Now she might as well be dead for me, or maybe she really is dead, although there hasn't been a funeral in our building in the past month. We live in an ordinary building—five floors, no elevator, four entrances, one just like it across the street, and so on. If she had died, everybody would have known right away. So she must still be living, one way or another.

Here: I have a photo taped to my blank forms drawer. That's her, Raisa, Ravilia, with the stress on the last syllable—she's Tatar. You can't see anything in this picture, her hair curtains her face, just two legs and two arms in the pose of Rodin's "Thinker."

She always sits that way, she even sat that way not long ago at my birthday party. That was the first time I watched her in a group of people: before that we always socialized just the four of us—she with her Seva and me with my Petrov.

It turned out she couldn't even dance, and she sat quiet as a mouse. My Petrov pulled her up for one dance, but right afterwards she went home.

Yes, she can't dance, but she's a real professional prostitute. Where did her Sevka get her, what cesspool did he drag her out of? No sooner had she gotten out of the penal colonies than she started sleeping around again, and he went and married her. He told me about this himself, when the mood took him, but asked me to take a solemn oath not to tell anybody. He told me about her father, too. He said that when Raisa was five she started gluing pill-boxes: she and her mother glued them for her father, he had gotten himself that job because he was an invalid. Then her mother died in the hospital from heart trouble, and Raisa's father began openly bringing women into their one room. All in all, horrible things. And how Raisa ran away from home, ended up with some guys in an empty apartment, and they didn't let her out for several months, and how later, after some time, that apartment was exposed. But that's all history, that doesn't concern anybody now, the important thing is that Raisa still practices.

Sevka goes to work, she stays home; she doesn't have a job. Sevka leaves dinner for her. He comes home, and she hasn't even heated it up, didn't even go to the kitchen. She lies in bed for days at a time and smokes, or hangs around in stores. Or she cries. She'll start to cry for no particular reason and cry for four hours straight. And, of course, the neighbor comes running to me, all white: "Run, save Rayechka, she's crying." And I fly off with Validol and valerian. Although I have plenty of times myself—and not just like that, for no reason—when I could just lay down and die. But what goes on inside me, what I have to endure, nobody knows. I don't shout, I don't roll around on the unmade bed. Only when my Petrov was leaving me for the first time, when he wanted to marry that Stanislava, and they were already trying to borrow money for a divorce and an apartment in a cooperative, and they wanted to adopt my Sasha—then for the only time in my life did I break down. True, Raisa defended me then like her own child, and lit into Petrov with her very nails.

This happens with my Petrov three or four times a year, eternal, undying love like that. Now I know that. But at the beginning, when he left me for the first time, I almost threw myself from our third-floor window. I was shaking all over I was so impatient to end it all, because the day before he had told me that he was going to bring Stanislava to meet Sasha. I took Sasha away early in the morning to my mother's on Nagornaia Street, then went home and waited for them all day. Then I climbed onto the windowsill and began tying a piece of cord left over from when Petrov had strung it across the kitchen in several rows for Sasha's diapers. The wire was strong, vinyl coated. And I tied it to a spike which Petrov had long ago driven into the cement wall to strengthen the ledge. That was when we had just gotten the room, and before we had Sasha, and I remembered that Petrov had pounded the wall for almost an hour. I tied the end of the cord onto the spike, but it was slippery and refused to stay. But I managed to wind it on, and made a noose at the other end—somehow I figured out how to do that. And at that moment someone turned the key in the apartment door.

And I forgot everything in the world—I even forgot about Sasha, and I remembered only that they wanted to adopt him, so it was as if he was defiled for me, as if it was not I who had given birth to him, nursed him. And I got scared that Petrov and Stanislava were already coming into the apartment, and I gave the window such a jerk that the adhesive cracked. We sealed the window with tape for winter.

It was already dark in the room, you could see the house across the street through the window, empty, without lights—nobody had been moved into it yet—only below, not too far, a street light burned. And I jerked the window again, so that even the frame gave way. And at that moment Raisa came into the room and threw herself down, hugging my knees. She's weak, and I was strong and furious at that moment, but she attached herself to my legs like a dog and kept insisting: "Let's do it together, together, wait for me." And I thought something to the effect of: "What are you butting into this for, what kind of hardships do you have," and I was even insulted somehow. "My life, you might say, has crumbled: my husband has left me, with a child, he wants to take that child away—what do you have to complain about?" But Raisa kept trying to get her knee on the windowsill, although to throw yourself from our third floor into deep snow without a noose around your neck would be just plain ridiculous. And I pushed her away with all my strength and hit her in the face by accident, and her face was wet, slippery, icy. And I jumped down from the window and closed it, but the tape was completely crumpled, and it was impossible to pull it tight, and also my hands wouldn't obey me.

I had only one feeling after that incident: coldness in my head. I don't know, maybe Raisa played a part in this, but I realized that all these senseless runnings around and actions at the first cry of the heart are just not my way. Why should I compete with Raisa?

And it turned out that everything just had to be done with brains after all. I got rid of that Stanislava for good. It was very easy, because Petrov foolishly told me where she worked and what her job was, and she had an unusual name. After that Petrov had others, and there were many whose names I didn't even know, and I couldn't have cared less about them, much less run and hang myself. And when he would begin talking to me about divorce I would just wave it off. His tears didn't affect me, nor did his telling me that he hated me. I would just tell him with a little grin: "You can't run away from yourself, my dear. If you're schizophrenic, then go get cured."

But to tell the truth, he was in a no-win situation: he knew I wouldn't give up the apartment. I had nowhere to go. We would never be able to exchange our sixteen-meter room for two. And another thing: when Sasha was born, Petrov's work promised him a two-room apartment. Because of this I knew every time that he would go have his fun and then return, because when a building went up, and they began to consider applicants, he would never get anything alone, what's more divorced. But when we get two rooms, then we can exchange them and get a divorce. So Petrov remained with me every time, to wait for a two-room apartment. Or maybe that wasn't it, and he came back to me for some other reason. Because I always felt: if Petrov ever really had the urge, he wouldn't think about the apartment or about anything else, he'd be gone without a trace.

But when an affair was winding down he would begin to stay home in the evenings. He'd watch me flying from the kitchen to our room, help me with Sasha—he'd even pick him up from day care and put him to bed when I was on the late shift. Then, finally, he'd bring a bottle of semisweet sparkling wine, which he knew I liked. I have to say that I always foresaw that moment and prepared for it myself, too. He'd say to me with a sigh: "Drink with me?" and I would get the Czechoslovakian wine glasses from the cupboard in the kitchen. It was always thrilling, like our first date; the only difference was that we both knew how it would end tonight. Those zigzags gave our life an edge. And Petrov would whisper to me that I was the hottest, most tender, most excitable.

But Raisa was a cold fish in such matters. Guys we knew who had done business with her—I can't say "slept" because it usually took place during the day when Sevka was out, and you only had to find her alone to get everything very easily—they said it was dull with her, and that she acted, not as if she didn't care, but as if it was all revolting to her. And she didn't want to talk to anybody afterwards, like people usually do—after all, people aren't just animals, but thinking beings, they want to know how the person next to them lives, who that person is. Petrov and I would sometimes talk all night long, especially after one of his zigzags, and we could never say enough. He would tell me about his women, compare them with me, and I could never know enough—I'd pry more and more new details out of him. And we would laugh together, in a friendly way of course, at Raisa. Because all of our friends, literally all, even those who came to visit from Petrov's home town, had gone to Raisa. And they all told us about her.

For instance, there was a boy named Grant, from Petrov's town. We had written to him that if he came and we weren't home, Raisa in the next apartment had a key, and she's almost always there. We had given the key to Raisa a long time ago, for convenience. And we had her key. So we wouldn't have to call each other's apartment too often and get the neighbors involved.

When we both got home from work Grant was already sitting on the sofa that served as Sasha's bed, red, sad, looking at an art book of Sisley. On the child's desk were Raisa's keys to our apartment. We saw right away what had happened and started laughing. I asked him, "What happened, did Raisa lose it?" And he gives us a look full of fear, all shaken up. Later, when we explained it all to him, he sobered up and calmed down and told us all the details. He said that when she opened the door for him he had said, "Why are you so scared of me? I don't bite." And she had jumped back into the corner. She was wearing just her robe; she always dresses that way at home. And he added that he had the impression that she herself gets herself into everything, because she's afraid of something—she just loses her head in terror. And because of that you're left with a horrible aftertaste, as if you had disgraced someone, although she said nothing, and didn't resist.

But we reassured him, told him not to get upset. She gives that impression to everyone. At first glance she looks like a little, dark, quiet girl, and she can't even dance, and when we have people over she sits stiller than water on Sasha's sofa-bed, and you can only get her to dance with great difficulty because she's afraid of crowds. And all the guys who are our friends fall for this, their hunter's instinct is aroused, they all pull her out of the corner by the hand, and she just shakes all over. And goes home.

From the very beginning of our acquaintance she made a sort of stinging impression on me, like a newborn animal, not a small one, but a real new-born, that doesn't touch you by being cute, but stings you right in the heart. No love troubles that desire, that pure pity that catches your breath.

It began with her ringing our doorbell one night after three A.M., not stopping to think that we were strangers and it was the middle of the night. I opened the door and she stands there in her robe, her cheeks wet, tears streaming from her chin, her hands in her pockets, trembling all over—and asks for a cigarette. I took her into the kitchen, turned on the light, and found an open pack of cigarettes in Petrov's coat pocket. We smoked together a little, and I asked her: "Where's your Seva?" And with swollen lips she an-swers, "On a business trip." We sat together a long time, and I made her coffee, until she stopped trembling. Then I sensed that Sasha had uncovered himself in his sleep; I went to our room, covered him up, come back—and she's hunched up on the stool again, crying. "What is it?" I ask. "You must miss your husband?" She raised her head and said, "I'm afraid of the atom bomb." She's not afraid of death, but of the bomb, imagine! And you can see that she's not acting in the least—that's one thing she never had in her. She did everything she had to, and never made any pretense. That's what was strange about her—like she had absolutely no resistance. Something was damaged in her, some instinct for self-preservation. And you could sense it right away.

As she was going out the door she started crying again and went home that way. I didn't try to keep her—it was already beginning to be morning, and I had to be at work at nine. And then, at work, I told all the girls about my neighbor, that girl, the conscience of the world. I even began to feel proud of her.

And we couldn't live a day without each other. Either she and Sevka would be hanging out at our place, or we'd be at theirs. I go to ask for a cigarette, she'd invite me in: Sit down, let's smoke one together. And I'd stay two hours. And I told her everything, just like I'm telling you now. I'm that kind of person, I feel better when I tell things. So we'd sit for two hours, dis-cuss world problems—life, people. I sit there unworried, talking. I'm a good housekeeper, I get everything done in the morning, even dinner is prepared, and right after dinner I rush off to the institute when I'm on the second shift. And she doesn't work, and never has anything done, as if she wasn't even

Sevka's wife. He works, and goes to the stores, and flies home like a mad-man as if he had a crying baby waiting. He comes and cleans everything up, although Raisa leaves nothing to clean, other than a full ashtray. She doesn't dirty the dishes. Sevka leaves her soup in a pot and dinner in a pan; she doesn't even glance at it, doesn't stick a spoon in it.

Sevka even took her to the doctor, got off from work to take her. The doctor found her completely emaciated, dystrophic even. Like somebody in a siege. He prescribed shots of aloe.

She bought a needle—and here's an idea of a good time—she gives herself injections in her thigh. She has everything in order, pads, alcohol, container for cotton balls; she boils the needle herself. Somehow she knows all that. Then she sits by the window, says, "Look the other way," and there's this quiet oozing sound, this little wheeze. I shudder inside, and look at Sevka—he stands there white, leaning on the doorjamb. And she says, "It's over, you fools," and hasn't even pulled the needle out yet, she's still watching the last drop go out of the syringe.

We were good friends, a lot of times she battled with my Petrov on my behalf. She wasn't good at cursing, and would only say: "You're a real bitch, you understand?" That must be how she cursed in the penal colony.

Not long ago Petrov took up with one girl, she works in our institute, in Antonova's lab. You know her, heavy, dumpy, nobody. And my Petrov keeps coming for me at work, even though he knows, for instance, that I'm on the late shift and can't come home. And he asks anyway: "Are you coming home?" I answer no. "Then I won't wait for you," and goes straight to her in the lab. And she, strangely enough, started coming to me in Records. And suddenly there's Petrov. General conversation, and before I know it, he's in-viting her to our house. He loves having guests anyway, he can't live without it. If we have an empty evening he'll sit there gloomy, then suddenly get up and go out.

And it just happened that the time came when that emptiness had to be filled with something. I physically felt it coming on. I looked around and took note of all the girls we knew and asked: Is it this one or that one? At that time we always had a lot of people at our house. I had nearly moved Sasha in with my mother on Nagornaia Street, even though she had a granddaughter there too. Every evening we had guests. Petrov and I lived feverishly; it was like an inn—groups of people would come with guitars, they'd bring wine. I'd make my house specials—sausage cookies with nuts in cellophane, and fried onions with egg yolk and rye croutons. And I had the impression that it was all going down the drain, everything was crumbling, everything was going to shatter any minute now, because despite the guitar-accompanied songs, and the dancing, despite the transistor tape recorder and the attractive guys and girls, everything was forced those evenings in our home, dull.

And I looked at all those young girls, who were ripening in clusters when I was having Sasha, raising him, going to stores, feeding Petrov and washing his clothes, when we were buying the transistor tape recorder and child's furniture for Sasha. The girls advanced in whole regiments, beautiful, with fashionable haircuts, managing smartly on their meager stipends and salaries, ready for everything, aggressive. But I knew it was not them I had to fear. I did know my Petrov, after all. And I looked at all of them and knew that he needed Raisa, and not just like that, but for life.

But, strangely enough, things between them didn't settle down, they got even worse. She couldn't even stand to be around him, and came to visit more and more rarely when he was there. She couldn't forgive him for the fact that I was worn down by uncertainty—I told her everything, of course, except my main suspicion.

And then he invited over this big, dumpy, Nadezhda from the third lab. He has this strange custom: he brings every one of his girls to our house. I can't understand what makes him do that. Sometimes I think he does it because of me, against me, to make me suffer even more, and so make the zigzag even sweeter for himself. But then I'll suddenly think that I have nothing to do with it, that Petrov is bringing the girl of the day home for his own peace of mind, so everything will be above board, so she'll know exactly what she's getting into, what she's challenging—and Petrov himself can then step aside, leave the field of death lying between me and that second woman, and let us carry on the fight between ourselves, and not with him. But maybe Petrov isn't capable of such subtle psychology, and is simply, in the beginning— before anything's gone as far as bed—luring that second girl in with the ambiguous, titillating role of family friend. After all, Petrov himself is pretty gray in appearance, and I don't know what all those women find in him.

To make it short, amidst all this bedlam in our home, this girl Nadezhda appeared. It even seemed to me that Petrov wasn't all that interested in her, that she was just my weak equivalent for the bed, and that this zigzag would be a short one. She was too submissive and undemanding. There was none of the wild animal in her, that would make you worry about scaring her off. She was a domestic creature, that you could herd with a stick. So I felt sorry for her. We became somewhat friendly. We'd leave the institute together when I worked the first shift. And it gradually became clear to me that she didn't understand anything in life, she didn't know from anything—good underwear, books, food. She just blindly sensed, with her whole skin, any warmth or kindness, and then, without changing her expression or saying a word, she'd go toward that warmth. She had several affairs to her account in the institute, all of which had ended in nothing, and even a pregnancy, which had resulted in stillbirth. I remembered that event, and remembered the women saying that it was better for Nadezhda that way.

Our three-way friendship lasted a fairly long time and would have continued even longer if it hadn't been for one incident. Going out of the room one day for the coffeepot, I glanced at myself in the mirror in the entranceway. Part of the room was reflected in it, and the table, with Petrov and Nadezhda sitting at it. And I saw Petrov carefully, like with a child, stroke Nadezhda's chin with his curved palm, and Nadezhda take Petrov's hand and lay it on her chest.

I controlled myself, though one thing only tormented me: how could I have missed it? Why had I been worrying about Raisa, when the real danger is right here, swelling up in front of me, and what makes it all the worse is that Nadezhda is nothing special. Raisa, after all, is the "conscience of the world, that girl," but this one is blank space.

Petrov walked Nadezhda home and returned at 1:00 A.M., exhausted and weak, broken down. I didn't bother him, didn't say anything because I knew: in that condition Petrov strives for only one thing—to sleep. If I said anything to him or kicked him out, he could sleep in the kitchen, on the stairs, on the windowsill. He could go off to Nadezhda's and stay there. For some reason he had come home. That meant all was not lost. That meant it hadn't yet reached the last stage, it's just the beginning of a new zigzag, which was nothing other than Petrov's protest against the monotony of married life. Nothing else made Petrov run around like that. One fine day he simply got bored. Sometimes he would bring home some illiterately typed and recopied lectures, medical advice, that he had gotten hold of somewhere—purest pornography. We read it aloud to Sevka and Raisa, but I have to say it didn't have the right effect on them. They listened politely, but it made no difference to them, we might as well have suddenly decided to read aloud advice for people suffering from arteriosclerosis. Although Petrov and I found those lectures hilariously funny and laughed ourselves sick. And we would begin a sort of zigzag of our own, but it was short lived, and lacked entirely that heartfelt reconciliation that would occur on those evenings when Petrov returned to the bosom of the family.

So, counting on Petrov to come home of his own accord this time as well, I didn't pay attention to anything—to his returning late at night, to the fact that he had completely abandoned Sasha and stopped teaching him to read. But after a while a neighbor in our apartment told me that all that week, when I had been working the late shift, Petrov had been bringing home some heavy girl, and taking her out right before I got home. Those evenings Sasha hadn't been home either—my mother had been picking him up at day care and taking him home with her to Nagornaia Street, so the room was available.

I called Mama right away, and asked her, just this once, to sit with Sasha that evening at our home, put him to bed, and wait for me. Mama didn't want to, because she had a lot of work at home; my older brother had virtually dumped his daughter, Ninochka, on her hands. But I talked her into helping me—let my brother manage this one evening by himself. I don't remember what all I said about my brother, just to soften Mama and get her to come over. Mama didn't know anything about Petrov's zigzags, and if she had found out, she would have divorced us in a minute. For that reason I never told her anything, and she got along pretty well with Petrov.

As I had expected, Petrov brought Nadezhda home again that night, and they stumbled into my mother. Something happened between them, Mama and Nadezhda. Because, I repeat, the war was not between me and Petrov, but between me and Nadezhda. And I was counting on Nadezhda being weak, and retreating at the sight of Petrov's enraged mother-in-law and crying child.

Maybe she did retreat. But not Petrov. He didn't come home at all that night, and it began to look as though he finally wasn't going to return at all. He came a few times—for his razor, for socks and shirts, then for the tape recorder. He became wild, taller, and suddenly looked like that sweet boy who once loved me madly.

I didn't say a word to him, gave him the tape recorder and everything he wanted without a sound, and he acted defiant, as if answering in his mind my unasked questions. But I kept silent, even though it was already clear that no noble behavior was going to get him back.

Then I realized that I was losing everything, the whole world. Only Raisa remained on my side, the whole world was on the other. Mama, frightened by the unexpected outcome of her interference, was angry at me for the contrived meeting. Sasha? I'm a sober woman. I realize that a child's affection and love are not given to the parents as specific individuals. He would have loved any other configuration of face, figure, hair color, personality, and mind, just as much. He would have loved me if I was a murderer, a great violinist, a clerk in a store, a prostitute, a saint. But that's only temporary, until he's sucked his life out of me. Then he'll leave, still indifferent to me as a person. This knowledge of his soon-to-come betrayal always disheartened me when I bent down to hug him, all fresh from his bath and lying on his sofa in the half darkness. Perhaps I had Petrov to thank for that feeling, for teaching me to expect unfaithfulness.

Mama didn't like me anymore either. But then, she never liked me as a person, only as her offspring, her flesh and blood. Now, in her old age, she was morbidly attached to Sasha and to her granddaughter, Ninochka. And I, Petrov, my older brother, and his wife were all the same to her—just relatives.

I went to Raisa and told her everything. As you see, I already have experience in storytelling. I tell the girls at the institute, I even tell chance acquaintances, like the women you hang around with for three days in the maternity hospital after an abortion. But I didn't tell Raisa like that. Raisa really understood that she was all I had in the world. That this wasn't a matter of a zigzag but the loss of a place for me and Sasha to live, of hope for that two-room apartment I had wanted so passionately, and even seen in dreams. How many times, in our nighttime conversations, had Petrov and I furnished it! Petrov wanted to paint the kitchen wall himself, like Siqueros, with one big fresco. He even wanted to paint the white enamel surface of the gas stove, and the refrigerator. It was all dreams, although my Petrov draws pretty well in ink, he copies portraits of famous jazz musicians from magazines, puts them in black frames, and hangs them on the wall. Petrov can play jazz piano; he did amateur performances for several years at the Victory Club, until he decided he was too old for all those talent shows, for required bus trips to kolkhozes and compulsory accompanying of the solo singing class. Petrov mastered percussion and a little bass. And several times he sang with his quartet—piano, guitar, bass, and drums—the English song "Shakeohem," I think that's how it was pronounced. But nobody appreciated his simple voice, without hoarseness or nuance, his flawless English pronunciation. He didn't sing the way he talked—that's artificial too. His singing was simple, loud, wooden, monotonous, but so straightforward, with so much masculine sincerity, vulnerability. He stood tensely when he sang, like a string, and quivered a little to the rhythm of the music. I only heard him once, when Sasha was two months old. I couldn't think about Petrov that evening, milk was just crushing my breast, standing in every passage, and my chest felt wooden, faceted. I was nervous, maddened, I could sense that Sasha was hungry and, as always, Petrov's number was at the very end of the program. Finally he and his group came out on stage, and they rolled out the piano. He carried a little microphone, a novelty. The drummer took a long time setting up, then they played Chamberlain, a soft little waltz, then, finally, "Shakeohem."

Petrov sang, his whole long body trembling to the rhythm, and I was even a little spellbound, but the milk was rising in my breast, and I knew I had to run to Sasha right away, that he was crying, right now, and demanding his own. And I got up, even though the song wasn't over, turned my back on Petrov, and ran out of the hall. I had no time for Petrov, just like right now

I have no time for him, because Sasha has taken up all of me, just like then milk took up my whole chest, leaving only the partitions. And to this day I don't know how Petrov made it through my escape, or whether he got the applause he deserved—I didn't ask, and he didn't tell me. I didn't explain anything to him—at that time we didn't discuss much.

I don't know why, but I told all this to Raisa. I cried in front of her, as though she alone could save me. I didn't know how to get Petrov back. Not only was the apartment—my dream—crumbling, but the terrible spectre of Sasha's fatherlessness rose before me, and that was my worst wound, and maybe it was for that reason that I always clung like that to Petrov. I would become a single mother, Sasha will long for a man's hand and leave me as soon as the first buddy he comes across calls him over. He'll follow after any pants, starved for men's words and company, he'll go into a gang and into a penal colony.

I cried to Raisa, and she sat like stone, in her pose on the edge of the sofa. She didn't even flinch at the word *colony*.

But by morning I dried up. It suddenly began to seem to me that this was just another of Petrov's zigzags, because it wasn't Nadezhda he loved, and there was nothing bad between us, no fights, no conversations—after all, it was only my mother who had fought with him, and my mother isn't me. And on my way to work, I suddenly had the crazy idea of going to talk to Nadezhda. But then I abandoned that idea. She could be moved only by what's good for her, by concern for her and kindness, and what could I propose that would be good for her? She had only just set her sights on Petrov—and would she leave him of her own free will? She wouldn't even understand me.

But that wasn't the most important thing. The main thing was to convince Petrov to return to us, if only fictitiously. Let him go where he wants, but just so Sasha would see him. But how to suggest that to Petrov—he wouldn't do it of his own accord, and not at my request either.

I went to Raisa and asked her to talk to Petrov on the phone. As if for no particular reason, just to say hi, haven't seen you for a long time, you should stop in, we could talk—that's the kind of conversation I suggested, simple and undemanding. She agreed. But she agreed frightened, somehow. I didn't actually pay attention to that.

In the evening I went to Raisa. She was lying on the sofa and smoking. She told me she had spoken to Petrov. That he would be back tomorrow. That was all she told me, and then suddenly, in her usual way, started to cry. I brought her a glass of water from the kitchen and ran to get Sasha at day care.

The next day Petrov returned with his briefcase and the tape recorder.

In his briefcase were socks and two shirts, balled up in newspaper. It felt clean and cozy in our home, the three of us ate breakfast together. Sasha reached for Petrov's newspaper and asked which letter was which.

It's true, I couldn't see an end to the zigzag. Petrov didn't notice me, was never home. But it was better than his complete absence.

Because I was busy, I somehow never got around to going to Raisa. And I didn't have any great need to. Home swallowed up everything. The question of Petrov's apartment was about to be decided. I was running around, getting onto the list to receive furniture, standing in line.

Petrov had already begun to look questioningly at me, watching with obvious pleasure as I flew from the kitchen to the room, as I talked with Sasha. Before supper he went out without a word, and returned with a bottle of semisweet sparkling wine.

He said:

"Drink with me?"

And I ran to the kitchen for the Czechoslovakian crystal.

We clinked glasses. I said jokingly:

"To Raisa. To our good genius."

But Petrov smirked, and said, somehow nastily, that the guys were right, she really was a cold fish.

Only then did I guess everything, and regretted that Raisa had betrayed me like that.

And she ceased to exist for me, as if she had died.

1968

Translated by Lise Brody

Children of the Sixties

MAYA KORENEVA

Though Liudmila Petrushevskaia and Toni Cade Bambara have lived on opposite sides of the globe unaware of one another, their artistic careers have
several important parallels. Both started writing in the late 1950s and early
1960s, and in their separate worlds, divided by more than just an ocean,
both belonged to literary generations powerfully affected by social changes
that resulted from the exposure of repressive methods and systems sanctioned by government power: in the Soviet Union, Stalinist despotism, and in
the United States, McCarthyism. While Stalinism and McCarthyism differed
drastically in scale and historical significance—a point I cannot pursue here
because of space limitations—paradoxically, their consequences were similar in certain ways. In both countries, the public denunciation of repression
brought about an emancipation of consciousness as people once again aspired
to create a more just society based on humanistic values. This phenomenon
is of primary importance for understanding the subsequent development of
literature in both the USSR and the United States.

In the United States, this aspiration produced a powerful resurgence
of democratic ideals, exemplified by the civil rights movement and, subsequently, the feminist movement. In the USSR, after decades of harsh oppression, the "thaw" (*ottepel'*) began; a vision of freedom arose throughout the
country, awakened by a renaissance of creativity. For literature and art, this
transformation signified a hope for the reorganization of social structures and
the spiritual revival of both man and society. The belief in the possibility of
beneficial changes engendered many of the significant works of the 1960s:
the prose of Alexander Solzhenitsyn, Andrei Bitov, and Vasilii Shukshin; the
songs of Bulat Okudzhava; and the films of Grigorii Chukhrai and Andrei
Tarkovskii.

This new freedom had broad implications for Soviet authors, manifested
in their choices of subject matter, the scope of their presentations, and their
methods of artistic expression, all of which had previously been harshly regi-
mented by the dogmas of Socialist Realism. While most of the officially sanc-

tioned literature of the previous decade, following the norms and postulates of the Soviet literary catechism, had presented reality in monstrously distorted form, disfigured beyond recognition, the writers of the sixties shared the idea of "the new word" (*novoe slovo*), based on the desire to convey the truth about life. But as the term "thaw" implies, this "seduction by hope" (*obol'shchenie nadezhdoi*), as it was generally known, did not last long; it was, rather, a temporary warming between spells of severe winter cold (Lakshin 91).

Even while the thaw lasted, however, it became increasingly clear that there was little to be elated about, that it was futile to pin hopes on a favorable course of events. The initial (and unreliable) benevolence of the authorities, who could be credited with neither education nor open-mindedness, was soon replaced by abrupt anger, which crashed down on those who had dared to believe in the promises of artistic freedom inspired by social liberalization. Two events that demonstrated this process unequivocally were the sadly memorable meetings of Khrushchev with writers, artists, and musicians, and the subsequent bulldozing of painting exhibits that portrayed the "new word" born out of social changes; now the very initiator of those changes was unexpectedly and inexplicably rejecting what he had initiated.[1]

Just as it was gaining momentum, then, the movement toward liberalization was halted in midair. The brief thaw came to a complete standstill, giving way to seemingly endless stagnation (*zastoi*), as impassable, muddy, and engulfing as a swamp. As in the famous fairy tale, everything was plunged into a deep sleep; all this frozen moment lacked was beauty. Once again society was subjected to the ugly resurgence of violence inflicted in an attempt to lock life back inside a stockade.

This brutal suppression of free thought in any form affected literature not only in terms of the socially significant aspects of works—ideas, themes, and critical attitudes—but also in terms of such personal and individual features as style, mood, and tone. Once again it was forbidden to write about the tragedies that abound in life, about the bleeding wounds of history, about the vices and abuses of a system that had resulted in incalculable suffering; all these were labeled distortions of reality. It was forbidden to give free rein to imagination, to paint fantastic worlds, or to use any of the devices of modernism: stream-of-consciousness narration, theoretical jargon, free verse, or black humor. It was forbidden to write in a sorrowful or even morose tone; pessimism was regarded as contrary to the Soviet way of life. The taboos were innumerable.

It is not surprising that many of the artists who had begun their careers in the sixties now disappeared from the cultural horizon. Works were left unpublished; paintings and sculptures were not exhibited; completed films were sent off to gather dust on the shelf; and rehearsed performances were banned, sometimes even on the day of their openings. These prohibitions were based on the suspicion that at the heart of works by "dubious" authors lay something unseen and unresolved but capable of undermining the official foundations, some suppressed thought concealed until it could be extracted by the vigilant guardians of the establishment—which would be admirable— or by the no less vigilant public—which would be intolerable. As theater critic Igor Shagin writes:

> Everything fell under suspicion: Russian classics, children's plays, dramas, comedies. The only reason tragedy was spared was that it did not exist. Not reckoning with the losses, authorities also banned one thing after another from the galley proofs of magazines: first whatever had not been approved by "GlavLIT" [the official organ of censorship] then even material that had been approved.
>
> In the theaters, the authorities prohibited the performance of plays that already had been printed by the thousands. The inconsistencies of the system are indicated by the fact that authorities might ban a play they considered harmful and then for no reason also ban an article in which that same play had been criticized. At first they explained why they issued prohibitions, but then even explanations ceased. Finally, as if at the end of a lost war, they themselves did not even know why. Anyone would participate in the process of suppression: central and local committees, institutions, departments, groups of spectators, individual politicians of various rank. They banned, and banned, and banned. (Shagin 72–73)

But as our own time indisputably demonstrates, the efforts of the system's faithful guards were essentially futile. It was possible to prohibit a publication or a performance, but it was not possible to stop the ongoing literary process, to force a hand, flying above a piece of paper, to throw down its pen, or to force an awakened conscience to be silent. Like a powerful river, literature threw its refuse out onto the surface, from Vsevolod Kochetov to Georgii Markov and Anatolii Ivanov, to be gratefully snatched up and glorified by the literary sycophants of those in power. But literature did not capitulate. Instead it sank into an unreachable underground stream, laying a new channel. The works created in these dark depths were dispersed from apartment to apartment, passed from hand to hand, retold and discussed, read in kitchens in one sitting or at meetings in various scientific research institutes or design offices. Information and legends gradually accumulated around these texts, and with increasing frequency they began to surface abroad. Very rarely, perhaps one in a thousand would make its way into print at home.

Only in the years of perestroika did the doors of the literary prison open, and for the first time the prisoners saw the light. This transformation created a distinctive effect, which perhaps can be defined most precisely as resembling illumination from a faraway star—one that no longer exists but whose light still streams down on the earth. The point is not simply that many authors did not live to see the publication of their own works; generally, all literature and art of the past make up a sphere that unfailingly widens, hence the image of light from a distant star. The key point is rather that the works produced during this period are now for the first time fully part of the current literary process, while simultaneously retaining the flavor of another era, whose values they have maintained and whose voice they transport into our days.

Liudmila Petrushevskaia was among those seized by the movement for a new word. Her stories and plays reveal an independent vision and a distinctive voice. Her works have been consistently distinguished by her abiding interest in every form of reality, even the "lowest"—reality not adjusted to fit certain standards, not ennobled in the name of any lofty goal. Petrushevskaia's realistic sketches are the opposite of the familiar, flattering pictures presented in the official press when she first began writing. Her main protagonist is not any particular character but rather everyday life—unattractive, depressing, even repulsive—with its total degradation and hopelessness.

When Petrushevskaia began writing, such works could hardly satisfy the taste of those who determined the fate of literature. As a result she was banished—not from literature, but from the reader. Petrushevskaia's first book appeared only in 1988, almost thirty years after she embarked on her creative career. In the collection *Immortal Love* (*Bessmertnaia liubov'*), she presented stories written in the sixties and seventies. When read together, not clandestinely or in newspaper minipublications, these narratives provide an overall impression of her artistic world, her distinctive style, and her understanding of the interrelation of art and life.

The texts in the collection fall into two categories: stories and monologues. "That Kind of Girl" ("Takaia devochka") belongs to the second type. The story is absolutely ordinary, trite, even banal, but that quality is precisely calculated to reveal the incalculable ugliness and inhumanity of contemporary life and the resulting moral degradation of the individual.

In the afterword to the collection, Inna Borisova defines the key image in Petrushevskaia's work as that of "the crowd of the large contemporary city with newly built suburbs sprawling on and on, with a multitude of small offices and large organizations in the center. This crowd is spread out over the apartments, over the floors of institutions, over the streets. . . . The individual continually feels the pressure of the crowd, continually senses the presence of multitudes" (219). Some clarification is necessary here. Petrushevskaia's subject is the contemporary city environment, but she does not describe it directly; rather, she focuses on the déclassé layers of humanity that have flooded all urban conglomerations.[2] The characters of Petrushevskaia's stories are people in an interim situation: recently moved to the city, flung out of the country by various social processes, they have lost their rural culture together with its way of life but have not yet adjusted to urban culture. Hence they have assimilated only its simplest structures, acquiring only the most primitive survival tactics. Under such conditions, the individual lacks ground for development and finds himself stifled, accepting the community's life style and mentality. Only if he is lucky may he preserve some trace of individuality.

All these elements can be seen in the heroine of "That Kind of Girl." Several details suggest that she has risen slightly above her environment: she works in a scientific research institute, she has art books at home, and her reference to Rodin's "Thinker" implies at least a minimal acquaintance with European art. But these are all external characteristics. In the depths of her soul, she shares fully the views, values, mundane traditions, and philosophy of her déclassé environment.

With perfect pitch, Petrushevskaia reveals the background of her heroine in everything she says. It is significant, for example, that in describing her reconciliation with her husband, she refers to Petrov only by his last name, conveying both their absence of genuine intimacy and the attempt to overcome this estrangement through irony and a bravado typical of semi-intellectual circles of the sixties. A similarly fine detail occurs when, as a gesture of ending his routine love affairs, Petrov brings home a bottle of "semisweet sparkling wine, which he knew [his wife] liked," and the injured wife, exultant from her triumph over her rival, ostentatiously mentions "the Czechoslovakian wine glasses from the cupboard in the kitchen." If the reconciliation were important to her, it would be sufficient to say simply "wine glasses." But the champagne, the "Czechoslovakian" crystal, their marital arrangement, their family life—repaired despite the many breaches of the past and the future—are all proof that the couple is no worse off than anyone else, confirming their conformity to conventional standards. Because the Czech wine glasses become a symbol of prestige in a world governed by external values, it is not surprising that both the champagne and the crystal appear again at the end of the story, when the heroine complacently celebrates her final victory.

The very process through which the heroine gradually acknowledges the possibility of an irrevocable break with her husband reveals the conventionality of her thoughts and values. Her thought processes are literally permeated by the mundane wisdom that derives its authority from the anonymous norm of how "everyone else" presumably acts and thinks.

Certainly, the heroine has not created her circumstances. They are the result of a cruel system which, instead of following its proclaimed slogans about emancipating man from all forms of oppression, placed him in a degrading position that made survival dependent on adapting oneself to circumstances. Petrushevskaia masterfully turns a minor study in family disorder into a portrait of a whole society. She does so seemingly unintentionally, without edifying declarations or a single direct authorial comment, conveying everything through the words, relations, and destinies she creates for the characters. This apparent absence of the author is the reason for that impassiveness and coldness critics attribute to her work.[3]

Only one question remains: why this coldness, and what does it mean? Does Petrushevskaia accept the world that appears in the pages of her works? Hardly. Rather, the coldness of her presentation might be read as only a means of achieving her goals, not an end—might be seen as one strategy the author adopts to enhance the impression of objectivity, so that descriptions in the work appear consistent with reality. As Borisova formulates the effect, Petrushevskaia "writes what she sees and sees things as they are" (220). But Borisova omits the main element—the creative act. Taking this into consideration, one might rewrite the formulation as follows: "She makes us believe that she writes what she sees and sees things as they are."

Petrushevskaia's striving for maximum descriptive authenticity inevitably leads to self-effacement of the author. Her choice of the monologue form for "That Kind of Girl" and the other stories in the same category finds its source in this erasure. Yet even the stories contained in the section entitled "Histories" are monologues. Strongly marked socially and psychologically, they never allow the narrator's voice to be confused with the author's. Their introduction of a second voice also emphasizes the distance between the author and the narrator, which is particularly important since the latter speaks for the great and amorphous human mass, deprived of moral grounding or cultivation. Out of cruel necessity, these people are forced to adapt to inhumane circumstances and in so doing help to perpetuate and reinforce them.

Though Petrushevskaia rejects the ugly circumstances she reproduces with such ruthless accuracy, she is not inclined to preach. Her works offer neither moral sermons nor advice about how to change society. This does not mean, however, that her artistic world represents a moral vacuum, as is sometimes argued. Rather, the absence of didacticism is testimony to Petrushevskaia's particular trust in the reader. Exposing the cruelty of the world, the moral degradation of both man and society, and arousing our disgust and horror at them, she offers us the opportunity to recall lost or profaned values. She does so, however, without condemning her characters, who are obviously victims of inhumane conditions. Her intent is rather to grasp the tragic lessons of our common existence.

It is difficult to say to what extent Petrushevskaia achieves this goal. Proponents of the methods of Socialist Realism would not consider resorting to strategies like hers—another reason for their refusal to publish her works. They believed only in the virtue of instruction and direct appeal, but they used these devices so crudely and neglected artistic considerations so thoroughly that now any literary attempts at edification in literature only arouse most readers' disgust.

In essence, this conflict reflects the long-standing argument about the way art can most effectively establish the laws of truth and beauty in the world, an argument that has taken different forms throughout history. One recent instance is the idea, well known in the West, that inasmuch as art has been unable to prevent the atrocities of fascism, its existence has lost all meaning. But the thinking of Soviet critics did not stretch even that far. They argued instead over the right to ban, which, as we have seen, they willingly employed, as they had with Anna Akhmatova, Osip Mandelshtam, and Andrei Platonov.

In fact, the reader's opportunity to achieve a profound understanding of existence is also open to Petrushevskaia's characters. Thus the heroine of "That Kind of Girl" might have been able to break the vicious circle into which circumstances had thrown her, had she not created those circumstances herself. But she does not break the circle. Not only does she adjust to the circumstances; she even manages to turn them to her advantage. She builds her own happiness not by overcoming the evil and viciousness of existence, but by incorporating them into her calculations. Everything is possible; everything is permissible. She finds questions about the morality of her own actions irrelevant. Thus, for example, the impossibility of solving her problem with the apartment turns the agonizing need to live with her philandering husband into a means of retaining him. No mention is made of feelings; the word "love" appears only once, and then only ironically: "This happens with my Petrov three or four times a year, eternal, undying love like that."

When abandonment by her husband threatens to become a reality, she still fails to speak of her own feelings, even while she searches for support from Raisa. Instead, she speaks of "the loss of a place for me and Sasha to live, of hope for that two-room apartment I wanted so passionately." Later, she represents her relationship with her son as the main motive for her actions. It is possible that her concern for the child really does overshadow all other impulses, but her description of her own mother suggests that the narrator herself may have a similar relationship to her son: "Mama didn't like me anymore either. But then, she never liked me as a person, only as her offspring, her flesh and blood."

Perhaps this deprivation of maternal love, even if only in the heroine's imagination, played a fatal role in her development, making her forever incapable of strong, deep feeling. Her mother's rejection, like Petrov's, offends and hurts her. Yet she does not love her mother for herself; she only uses her in fights with Petrov, the same way she uses both him and even her young child to ward off the regular contenders for her husband's heart and hand.

The heroine's consumer logic, permeating all her relationships, reveals itself most cruelly in her relationship with Raisa, "that kind of girl" who gives the story its title. This character is another testimony to Petrushevskaia's keen social vision: through Raisa she addressed a social phenomenon before it had become widely recognized. Absolutely helpless and defenseless, Raisa Ravilia is the definitive victim of circumstances. Events in her life have made her a prostitute, the toy of other people's passions, which she is incapable of sharing. Downtrodden, tormented, she trembles before destructive power, whether embodied in men or in nuclear disaster. The men who use her body feel no need to try to win it; instead they simply take it without a second thought. Pondering Raisa's unusually keen sense of wrong, the heroine is full of the self-righteous pride of the discoverer, dubbing Raisa the "conscience of the world" (sovest' mira).

Yet even though she is feeble, continually weeping from fear and help-lessness, Raisa is capable of profound feelings of gratitude, attachment, and faithfulness. Having once received help from her neighbor, Raisa becomes her defender, fearlessly standing up for her in arguments with Petrov, pro-tecting her home. The same cannot be said of the heroine, who makes vulgar entertainment out of Raisa's unhappiness and, even worse, willingly takes part in allowing her closest friends to visit Raisa and listens callously to their subsequent reports. In "That Kind of Girl" the prostitute is actually presented as the only person worthy of sympathy.

But the story is not dedicated to Raisa; she remains on the periphery of the action, serving primarily to illuminate the character of Petrushevskaia's heroine, who, feeling that her world has finally collapsed, puts her trump card into play. After guessing her husband's secret—"that he needed Raisa, and not just like that, but for life"—she asks her girlfriend to persuade him to return home, understanding what the price of the agreement will be for him. Yet when everything works out, she strikes a pose of insulted innocence and, with a feeling of superiority and self-righteousness, banishes Raisa from her life forever.

Her monologue, beginning with the words "Now she might as well be dead for me" and ending with the sentence "And she ceased to exist for me, as if she had died," is nothing but an accusation of Raisa and an attempt at self-justification. The attempt ends in failure because Petrushevskaia's artistic logic differs from the intentions of the narrator and leads to her self-exposure:

in her short-sighted craving for self-justification she loses the possibility of attaining the great mystery of life.

The characters in other stories and plays by Petrushevskaia share this trait. They all turn out to be grotesque, in Sherwood Anderson's sense of the term; victims of circumstance who suffer to a greater or lesser degree from the imperfections of the world, they are incapable of self-realization and thus deprived of the possibility of individuation. Only the appearance of a character who might be capable of realizing his or her own involvement with the evil triumphing around him could break the chain of hopelessness that pervades Petrushevskaia's artistic world. Only with the appearance of genuine individuality could this world acquire the treasure of the spirit, the absence of which resounds throughout Petrushevskaia's published works.

The problems of the individual are also at the center of Toni Cade Bambara's "Witchbird," but given her own particular background, her emphasis is more explicitly political than Petrushevskaia's. Characterizing the development of Afro-American literature in the seventies, Bambara emphasizes the resurgence of interest in the individual as a distinguishing characteristic:

> The energy of the seventies is very different from that of the previous decade. There's a different agenda and a different mode of struggle. The demystification of the American-style "democracy" and the bold analytical and passionate attention to our condition, status and process—the whole experience of that era led us to a peculiar spot in time, the seventies. Some say it's been a period of retreat, of amnesia, of withdrawal into narcissism. I'm not so sure. I'd say the seventies is characterized by a refocusing on the self, which is, after all, the main instrument for self, group, and social transformation. (Tate 13)

Aside from Bambara's disagreement with other critics over the value of the seventies, another point is worth noting: her rejection of an authoritarian approach to reality, of the regulation of actions or views according to some universal law. For her the highest value lies in the organic manifestation of life. Given its inexhaustible diversity, it is perhaps fully comprehensible only if the perception of it is not forced into a narrowly dogmatic framework. As *Sea Birds* repeatedly shows, Bambara herself seeks to overcome and surmount such confines.

Honey, the heroine of "Witchbird," is a singer who performs in local nightclubs and in other venues as well, but no one would call her a star. Bambara never makes clear whether "Honey" is her heroine's true name, a stage name, or just a term of endearment. Honey's emphatic stress on the full name of her friend Vera Willis, who is more successful on stage than she, introduces a formality of reference that strengthens the negative context in which Vera is presented. The people around Honey, on the other hand, call her by a name that emphasizes the intimacy of her ties with the community. At the same time, it is precisely this closeness that reflects the heroine's captivity, which is presented on several levels: her everyday life, her personal life, her artistic life, and her inner world.

Those around Honey, and especially her manager Heywood, understand her captivity perfectly. When his current infatuation ends and he feels a surge toward a new love, he brings the former beloved to Honey's house, "dumping" her with all the others. There are always several of these women, and thus, even in her own house, Honey is forced constantly to bear the burden of caring, assumed not through her own choice, but at someone else's will.

But this imposition, this necessary submission to circumstances created by others, arouses in her soul no bitterness or angry protest, which could turn her existence into hell. Bambara paints Honey not only as sensitive, sympathetic, and kind, but as perhaps the only spiritually mature person in her environment. She understands that the girls who have come to live with her are at a dead end and justifies her own motivation and behavior by observing that "it's hard to say no to a sister with no place to go."

Heywood is another matter. He is the reason Honey feels like "a prisoner in [her] own house." His actions arouse her protest, but it is listless and halfhearted. Honey's lack of vigor in this regard seems not to be tied to her indecisiveness or feelings of dependency on Heywood as her manager. Rather, she accepts him as part of the community, and thus for her he becomes part of the general stream of life, so powerful that fighting it is useless.

Now two of Heywood's ex-girlfriends, Laney and Gayle, are living with Honey. They not only make her uncomfortable with their presence, with their mundane habits so different from her own, but they also encroach on much more in her, demanding care and sympathy, not understanding how groundless their demands are and not considering Honey's own obligations. In short, they act like children, not independent adults ready to face life's misfortunes. This dependency is immediately apparent in the episode in which Gayle tells Honey that Laney is packing a dinner for them to take together to "Miz Mary." The actual reason for this plan is that one of the girls is afraid of the dark and the other fears staying home alone. Honey has long since seen through their games and childish fears, but because she possesses the wisdom of maturity, she does not expose their ploy, making it possible for them to preserve appearances in a situation in which their dignity has already been hurt by Heywood's betrayal and by their subsequent humiliating dependence on Honey's hospitality.

Honey has another advantage over the girls. Their existence is confined to everyday life, hardly the most important sphere to her. Perhaps this is why she lets things run their own course at home. In the theater everything happens differently. Using stream of consciousness in the scene where Honey is preparing to leave home, Bambara leads the reader into the inner world of the heroine and reveals an unknown side of her character. Honey remembers a call from New York informing her that, at the request of Vera, the current Broadway star, they will give Honey a small part in the play.

The ensuing situation reveals that despite her seemingly easy acceptance of the girls with whom she is stuck and of the way of life imposed on her, Honey can also be unyielding. Her inflexibility is not a random whim, a mere gesture of hurt pride; rather, she refuses to accept humbly what her more fortunate rival has handed her. She recalls how many times she fought with the director, the lighting technicians, and the set designer over the interpretation of her tiny role, trying to convince them of her point of view by enlisting one person's support, inspiring another with her ideals.

Yet Honey is not presented as a proud egoist, dreaming only of personal success, of rising to the heights of the stage. Certainly, like any artist, she has some of these feelings, but they are not what drive her in the moment of creation. Creativity gives her freedom, liberating her on the one hand from the burdens and confusions of everyday life and on the other from her own egoistical "I" by opening a sphere of higher intentions and higher truth to her. More than anywhere else in the story, Honey's identity appears in this burst: her understanding of art's great task, which she plans to achieve in her work, and of her vital feeling of ties to her people. Both these elements are joined in her insurmountable desire to allow the voices she carries in her soul to be heard—the voices of black women who have endured countless sufferings, have dreamed of and fought for freedom: "Dozing, drifting into sleep sometimes, the script sliding off the quilts into a heap, I hear folks calling to me. Calling from the box. Mammy Pleasant, was it? Tubman, slave women bundlers, voodoo queens, maroon guerrillas, combatant ladies in the Seminole nation, calls from the swamps, the tunnels, the classrooms, the studios, the factories, the roofs."

This desire becomes more urgent the better Honey understands that in American society, where strong prejudices still exist, reality is displaced by stereotypes that are both instilled by art and govern it: "But then the wagon comes and they all rounded up and caged in the Bitch-Whore-Mouth mannequin with the dead eyes and the mothball breath, never to be heard from again." Freeing the images swarming in her soul means not only freeing history from the grasp of death, getting rid of the artificiality and lies in which the past is enveloped; it also means restoring the historical justice that has been violated for centuries. Honey does not use these words, nor, in accordance with the narrative's logic, should she. But Bambara still draws a historical perspective, uniting the past with the present by invoking black women, from slaves to teachers, artists, and workers in contemporary factories. We can assume that in this common choir Honey also hears the voices of Heywood's cast-off girls, and that this is why she is reconciled to their presence in her home.

It is also in art that Honey finds the means for emancipating herself and her people: the rich legacy left behind by the great Negro singers. Pondering the need to embody that vision in her own art, the testimony of which is in the voices that urgently want to be released from her soul, Honey appeals directly to "the old songs"—to "old Bessie, Ma Rainey, Trixie Smith, early Lena . . . waiting to be released into the air again, free to roam." It is characteristic that when she recalls these women, what matters is not *how* the songs were sung but their spiritual content, the place they held in her people's culture, giving them language. Mary Helen Washington correctly remarks in her review of *Sea Birds* that "the use of these blues singers to symbolize creativity, the captivity and the freedom of the black woman, sets off many reverberations. Their raunchy, gutsy spirit, their flashy clothes and reckless lifestyles set them apart as much as their titles of 'Empress,' 'Queen,' and 'Lady Day.' They are a profound myth through which to view the lives of Toni Cade Bambara's contemporary blues women" (1977, 38).

But as we have seen, for Honey this myth is not only a means of discovering her own individuality. The emancipation she dreams of finding involves the spiritual emancipation of all black women, whom she sees in the tragic perspective of history. Elliot Butler-Evans points to the political aspect of this myth.

> The Blues Woman, while seemingly less directly engaged in the broad politics of the community, signifies rebellion on the personal level. Her primary action involves a movement away from the socially determined role of a "lady" and toward the full acceptance of her womanhood. She celebrates earthiness and eroticism, fashioning out of these a song that proclaims her rebellion. Her consciousness, as well as her social status, is distinctly working class, and her representation in the text assumes the form of a proto-feminist consciousness. (113)

To deny the meaning of the blues singers for the consciousness of contemporary black women would be pointless. Yet it is equally unfounded to remove the singers from the general framework of Afro-American culture and from American culture at large. The call to freedom, truth, and beauty that lay at the heart of the great art of Bessie Smith and Billie Holiday, Ma Rainey and Ella Fitzgerald, is a message to the entire world. In terms of Afro-American art, which attained its highest creative potential in the songs of these women, for all their originality and particular feminine charm, each, separately and together, gave it the spiritual impulse and the national character that defines it.

When the goal has been defined and the means to its attainment found, as in Honey's case, everything, it seems, should be already decided: what remains is only to act upon that knowledge. But in Bambara's story everything turns out to be much more complicated. As in the other stories in the collection, she is interested not so much in the actions of a person who has already chosen as in the path leading to that choice. The artistic problem that Bambara addresses in "Witchbird" is immeasurably complex, since she shows that the heroine's consciousness consists of several contradictory levels. What Honey accepts and values on one level she rejects on another. For example, the voices of the black women about whom she speaks prepare the reader to treat Honey as a person who has recognized the intolerance that lies in the stereotypes society continues to impose on black Americans. The reader expects that Honey will carry a proud awareness of the dignity of being a member of the black race not only on the stage, but also in life. But the moment the author takes the heroine from the world of dreams, artistic fantasies, and plans into a real world, the picture changes. When Honey goes to her hairdresser, the reaction from the people around her leaves no doubt about this difference: "'Come on out from under that death, Honey,' Mary says soon's as we get halfway in the door. 'Look like you sportin a whole new look in cosmetics. Clown white, ain't it? Or is it Griffin All White applied with a putty knife?' Mary leaves her customer in the chair to come rip the wig off my head. 'And got some dead white woman on your head too. Why you wanna do this to yourself, Honey?'" Mary's question goes precisely to the point: the entire meaning of the story lies in the reasons why Honey "does this to herself," even while realizing the full horror of such behavior. In these sentences the image of whiteness is examined in different variations. Given Honey's own earlier thoughts, we might expect that she would perceive whiteness as a mark of shame, yet she voluntarily brands herself with the hated stamp by putting on the wig and the make-up. The image of trying out whiteness in combination with the image of the buffoon is especially expressive and has several implications. It is, first, the white clown of the traditional circus role, the sad jester forever subjected to beatings, forever crying. But it also implies "the white race's buffoon," a black person whose art is meant for the pleasure of whites, or even worse, who places himself in the position of being a clown for whites. The combination of these readings vividly renders the extremity of Honey's humiliation and dependence on others.

In this context, the whole meaning of the episode with the voices appears in a different light. After all, they are so importunate to break out of her soul because they are imprisoned there. She herself is so imprisoned by stereotypes that she cannot break their power over her. Thus neither can she provide a voice to those who have been denied one in history. Contemplating her own relationship with Heywood and his ex-girlfriends, Honey calls herself a prisoner in her own house. This definition is just, but only in the deeper sense. Her captivity is not dependent on circumstances, since every living person is dependent in this sense. Rather, it is an inner obedience to the very norms she internally protests against yet remains incapable of throwing aside.

Thus the dominating image in the story is the cage, which is introduced on the first page and which, with modifications, permeates the entire narrative fabric. It is present in the heroine's dreams when she feels herself behind bars, in some kind of box. Even though she realizes through her sleep that she is lying in her own bed, Honey still cannot escape this feeling. It is intensified by the screams of a bird, which like her beats itself against the walls of its cage, trying to break away to freedom. A symbol of freedom and aspiration over the centuries, the bird becomes in Bambara's story as well the personification of the heroine's soul, suffering spiritual captivity. Thus it is that when Honey ponders her own art, she feels that there is a singer "locked away" inside her; Bessie and Ma Rainey "expect emancipation." Those habitual impulses to which Honey is prone also become a kind of cage: "They'll *trap* you in a fiction," "*locked* in some stereotype," "trying to call from the *box* and be heard much less understood long enough to *get out*" (emphasis added). The image of the cage arises again in connection with the episode of the calling voices.

Yet if Honey feels trapped, she is also frightened of freedom. She does not, of course, admit this to herself, but when one of the neighborhood boys, having run into the woods, scares the bird away, the possibility that the bird could break out to freedom frightens her as if it were a direct threat to herself.

The same fear and evasiveness can be felt at the end of the story. Until then, Honey has remained silent, outside the conversation; preparing for the evening's performance, she has saved her voice. She carries her silence through the entire narrative, as if it were a cup filled to the brim that she feared spilling. After all, each drop, as the reader knows, is the voice of suffering carried over through history. But at the very last moment, Honey suddenly breaks her vow of silence. There are several possible reasons. Perhaps it is complete capitulation to circumstances, the recognition of her own defeat in a battle in which she turns out to be weak. But another explanation is also possible. Having walked that inner path, which the reader has completed along with her, Honey can move on to what is most important: the realization of her own dependency. She can understand that while today she is not yet ready to say that new word pushing its way into her soul, nothing, in the future, can prevent her from saying it.

This ambiguous ending, which presents the heroine with a choice, projects the situation onto the reader, forcing him to think about his own attitude toward life. Having presented the most complex picture in the entire collection of contradictions in the heroine's consciousness, the author builds a kind of bridge between the story's world, locked into the printed page, and the real world. Bambara does not declare the necessity for some definitive solution that might be most desirable to her, but as an artist she does seem to believe in the possibility of a spiritual awakening.

Translated by Kristine Shmakov

Notes

1. Khrushchev's most brutal clampdown on artistic freedom was initiated by a speech during the Manezh exhibit in Moscow in 1963, in which he harshly rebuked the abstract work of such artists as Ernst Neivestny who produced art that thwarted the principles of Socialist Realism.—Aiken and Barker

2. The term *déclassé* here does not carry precisely the same connotations in Russian as it does in English. It refers to those strata of society that are sometimes called "the lost people"—that is, those who do not fit into any of the officially identifiable classes as the USSR constituted them when Petrushevskaia first began writing in the late sixties. "Déclassé" characters are, in effect, displaced persons, those who fall through the cracks of official categories (hence "déclassé" in the English sense as well). Yet ironically, by their very numbers they represent one of the largest groups in Soviet and post-Soviet urban society.—Aiken and Barker

3. In my opinion, this apparent absence is the main difference between Petrushevskaia and the contemporary Vasilii Shukshin, with whom, more than anyone else, she is connected by her sincere interest in the "lowest" forms of life, which she views without condescension or distancing.

Telling the Other('s) Story, or, the Blues in Two Languages

SUSAN HARDY AIKEN

There has to be a simultaneous other focus: not merely who am I? But who is the other woman? How am I naming her?—Gayatri Spivak, *In Other Worlds*

Writing on an issue much discussed among African American critics, Audre Lorde laments the fact that "black women are programmed to define ourselves within . . . male attention . . . rather than to recognize and move upon our common interests. . . . For so long, we have been encouraged to view each other with suspicion, as eternal competitors, or as the visible face of our own self rejection." Yet historically, she continues, "black women have always bonded together in support of each other, however uneasily and in the face of whatever other allegiances which militated against that bonding" (48–49). In view of the compounded oppressions African American women have endured as a result of their distinctive racial and sexual history, any comparisons between their situations and those of other women are inevitably problematic. Yet Lorde's observations are clearly applicable not only to Bambara's narrative but to Petrushevskaia's as well. The juxtaposition of "Witchbird" and "That Kind of Girl" reveals that despite the crucial disparities in their historical and cultural circumstances, Russian women and African-American women have shared certain common dilemmas. Both stories suggest that the rivalry and bonding Lorde describes are not merely oppositional impulses in women's lives but rather paradoxically congruent: both arise from a complex sense of identity with the other woman.

This suggestion is not so contradictory as it might at first appear. For like affinity, with which it often ambiguously intermingles, rivalry too begins in the perception of likeness: the awareness that "I" and "she" are somehow potentially synonymous, mutually interchangeable elements in masculine exchanges. As we shall see, the convolutions of consciousness both Bambara and Petrushevskaia trace in their narrators, like the shapes of their stories, emerge as a dynamic of recognition and resistance that challenges oppositional definitions of self and other and calls into question the sexual ideology that makes masculine validation the prime criterion for women's sense of identity and worth. What gives this dynamic its distinctive shape in each narrative is the particular cultural context through which it operates.

Trans/muted Voices, Bewitching Blues

We are the founders of civilization, the keepers of culture, the matrix. We sisters have endured. Through the dispersion of our people, the carving up of the Motherland, through the Middle Passage and slavery. Through the denigration of our bodies, our beauty, our culture. We have survived. We are here.—Susan Taylor, editor-in-chief, *Essence*

i wanna ask billie to teach us how to use our voices like she used hers.—hattie gossett, "billie lives! billie lives!"

In her foreword to *This Bridge Called My Back*, Bambara deplores the potentially crippling pressures women of color sustain in a society that marks them both racially and sexually as outcasts: the "power perversities engaged in under the guise of 'personal relationships,'" the "divide and conquer tactics" designed to separate women from each other, and the "accommodation to and collaboration with self-ambush" to which they are tempted. As a curative resource and strategy for survival, she urges them to cultivate "the habit of listening to each other and learning each other's ways of seeing and being," thereby reclaiming "ancient powers lying dormant with neglect." Like many black writers and critics, she associates these powers especially with African-American musical traditions, particularly jazz and blues. But where (as with the majority of black literary histories) most discussions of those forms have tended to focus primarily on the contributions of male artists, Bambara invokes a specifically female tradition.[1] Conjoining music and storytelling, she cites Billie Holiday as a figure of what it means for women of color to "use our voices" as forces of resistance and reclamation. For Bambara, song becomes a major means of black women's self-delivery, in several senses of that term: a formative and performative source of inspiration, imitation, and liberation that can create "new powers where they never before existed" (1981, vii).

The passage might serve as a gloss on "Witchbird," for Bambara's narrator also invokes Billie Holiday and other great female vocalists as models whose example might enable her to raise her own voice against the conventional plots of subordination constructed for black women. As a sometime actress, a blues singer, and a reluctant, unpaid landlady-cum-mother to her manager's cast-off girlfriends, Honey struggles against the conditions that entrap her as against "bars of the cage" she sees herself inhabiting, yearning for the recognition and rewards she all too rarely receives: "Hear me. Applaud me. Pay me."

Bambara suggests that not the least of those "bars" is Honey's internalization of the cultural codes she deplores, a process mimetically reproduced through the ambiguous rhetorical oscillations of her monologue. Caught up in Honey's subjectivity as a condition for reading the story, the reader too is kept off balance, forced to negotiate a series of seemingly irreconcilable positions and disjunctive perceptions. For paradoxically, even as Honey protests her manipulation by members of the black community like Heywood who imprison her in stereotypes of black maternity ("Shit, I ain't nobody's mother"), even as she acknowledges her own needs and insistently asserts her own integrity, even as she celebrates the creative originality of black women, she also capitulates repeatedly to alienating values and assumptions. Powerfully erotic, furious at the desexualized roles she is expected to play, she still remains fearful of both her anger and her sexuality, which she associates with disorder, rebellion, and (a particularly loaded word in racialized discourses) "darkness."[2] Drawn to powerful, self-assertive female figures, she nevertheless acquiesces to an aesthetics of the body which, linking female beauty with youth, slenderness, and light skin, virtually assures her own negation. Inwardly seething, outwardly obliging, she exhausts herself in the attempt to negotiate these conflicts, remaining a convenient object for those who use her.

The contradictions of Honey's life and subjectivity emerge full blown in the scenes with which Bambara brackets the narrative: the afternoon dream that opens the story and the visit to the beauty salon that concludes it. Between these two events lie a series of encounters with other women, ties that bind in several senses, at once entangling Honey in meshes not of her making and drawing together the loose ends of her life and of her story.

In the extraordinary opening dream sequence, a tour de force that so completely merges the reader's perspective with the dreamer's that we, like Honey, are momentarily unmoored, Bambara evokes the caprices of the unconscious in swift imagistic shifts, wordplay, and symbolic displacements. At once wish-fulfilling fantasy and object of horror, the uncanny, "insinuating" male figure, elaborately sexualized with his high-powered motorcycle, his phallic "thrusting," and the orgasmic "froth cascading all over his lap" from the "champagne bottle lodged between his thighs," offers Honey a seductive vision of flight in rapid double entendres that simultaneously evoke her stalled life and her sexual yearnings: "You in a rut, girl, let's go." Her terror of yielding to her own desires is also a fear of yielding to the male domination the dream lover embodies: release—both liberation and sexual ecstasy—becomes for her symbolically equivalent to destruction. The dream-lover's offer to "cross over to the other side" and the oneiric image of Honey's own yellow house shoes, which he appropriates like one of the tigers in "Little

Black Sambo," carry an ominous two-edged implication, for in the context of the black spirituals they echo, golden slippers and fording the Jordan—here a figure of both the promised land of sexual bliss and the escape from the confining wilderness of Honey's life—are also images of dying.

It is no wonder, then, that "all this talk about crossing over somewhere in dem golden slippers" literally makes Honey tremble. That "jiggling" merges with the cleansing, restorative imagery of water on which she fixes as a re-demptive antidote to her overheated vision: "You'd think I was holding a hazel switch or a willow rod out in the woods witching for water." But the aquatic quickly flows into the erotic: the water images—"skinny dipping in the lake," "falls," and "artesian wells"—so far from remaining "pure," become uneasily conflated with the river of sexual release and self-relinquishment Honey seeks to evade. This ambiguity reaches a climax in her telling description of "rain washing," which "can heal you or make you pee the bed one, which'll wake you from fever, from sleep, will save you. Save me. Cause damn if this char-acter ain't trying to climb into my berth. And if there's one thing I can do without, it's phantom fucking."

That the arousing "jiggling" is produced not by the phantom lover or even by her own trembling body but by another woman, Gayle, underscores the paradoxes of relationship Bambara elaborates throughout the narrative. Discarded by Heywood, dropped into Honey's life and home, Gayle and other would-be singers inhabit a female communal space that seems a cross between a "harem" (177), a sorority, and a mother-daughter household. It is a space no less nurturing for all the reluctance with which Honey accepts her ambiguous position as madame/mentor/mother: "A prisoner in my own house. . . . [But] it's hard to say no to a sister with no place to go. So they wind up here, expecting me to absorb their blues and transform them maybe into songs."

Longing for release and salvation, Honey becomes the saving center of other women's lives. Even as she focuses on male affiliations, disparages the "girl friends" Heywood "dumps" on her, and laments their rivalry with her for his attentions, she recognizes almost unconsciously their kinship, like her own, with the women she celebrates as creative ideals: "Bessie . . . , Ma Rainey, Trixie Smith, early Lena. So many women in them songs waiting to be released into the air again, freed to roam."

In constructing Honey's wry self-scrutinies, Bambara explores a phe-nomenon widely debated among African American writers and critics. While much of her fiction allies itself with the traditions of black nationalism that flourished during the sixties and early seventies, founded on a pervasive political critique of the effects of racism and white supremacy, her primary object in "Witchbird" is the gender politics of a black community.[3] Like other

black feminist critics, she suggests that the dynamics of oppression and subordination often exclusively attributed to white supremacist society can also
bleed over into African Americans' relationships with each other, especially
in black women's manipulation by black men and rivalry with each other. By
dwelling exclusively within a black woman's subjectivity—one of her most
frequent fictional devices—Bambara can examine the price African American
women may pay for their ambiguous position at once within and outside the
black male community, and can unravel the intimate weave of complicity and
resistance such a position entails.[4]

As members of an oppressed group whose male members have been historically disempowered and symbolically emasculated by the racial codes of a
white hegemonic society, black women have often been expected to redress
the balance, restoring male self-esteem, the assurance of phallic potency,
by providing unquestioning loyalty, admiration, and support. But in a tradition that has tended to conflate supporting the race with supporting its men,
many black women have faced a difficult double bind: too often, the exhorta-
tion to "get behind your man" has carried more than one meaning, equating
devotion with self-denial, sympathy with subordination. In this context black
women's assertions of agency and power risk being read as direct threats not
only to black men's pride and potency but to the racial cause with which
those attributes have often been identified.[5]

These gender conflicts can have potentially disastrous effects on black
women's relationships with each other, inspiring the rivalry for male attention
that Lorde and other black women have so cogently analyzed. Yet Bambara
also anticipates Lorde's observation that despite being "programmed" to self-
rejection and competition, black women have also "always bonded together."

As Bambara's title implies, the mysterious "witchbird" who appears at
the outset of the story becomes the major vehicle of these ambivalences.
Initially a figure of horror, confusion, and disorder ("Curtains blew in and
wrecked my whole dressing table arrangement. Then in he came, eight kinds
of darkness round his shoulders, this nutty bird screechin on his arm"), it
embodies the very essence of Honey's nightmare. Yet even as she shudders at
its destructive potential—"can't even hear myself good for the caterwauling
that damn bird's already set up in the woods, tearing up the bushes, splitting
twigs with the high notes"—she feels a peculiar affinity for it: "Bird make
me think of some singer locked up inside, hostage. 'Cept that bird's not enchanting, just annoying." Honey resists the witchbird's haunting songs just
as she resists breaking free of her own inhibitions, but Bambara, playing on
the etymology of "enchanting," which links singing with casting spells (en-
cantare), implies that the uncanny attraction the bird exerts lies precisely in
its oblique mimetic expression of Honey's own transgressive desires. Like the

conjure women whose chants and enchantments anticipated the spellbinding performances of the great blues singers, the bird provides a model of contestation to the invisible "cages" that entrap and stifle black women's creative powers.

Repeatedly, then, despite Honey's conscious repudiation of the witchbird and all it represents, her own language betrays a tacit perception of their connections. Like the bird calling from the darkness, seeking "to find her way out," Honey too is a misunderstood and undervalued singer, "locked . . . in stereotype," longing to break free. It is no accident that in her dream she explicitly imagines herself "witching" (168). As one of the multiple meanings of that term implies, her reveries dwell upon her female heritage, a lineage of heroic black women who devoted their lives to liberation. It is a legacy too readily coopted by a white society that demonizes, persecutes, and punishes self-assertive women of color: "I hear folks calling to me. Calling from the box. Mammy Pleasant, was it? Tubman, slave women bundlers, voodoo queens, maroon guerrillas, combatant ladies in the Seminole nation. . . . But then the wagon comes and they all rounded up and caged in the Bitch-Whore-Mouth mannequin with the dead eyes . . . never to be heard from again. But want to sing a Harriet song and play a Pleasant role and bring them all center stage." Recalling the "tearing" mouth and music of the bird, Honey's fondest memory is of that moment in her acting career when, breaking free of both stereotypical life scripts and theatrically scripted stereotypes of "the black woman," she "tore the play up with the song."

But like the witchbird, whom neither she nor we ever see except in the dream-eruptions of her unconscious, Honey remains figuratively invisible, her desires muted and unfulfilled. Yearning for "center stage," she is "typecasted" in the perpetually peripheral roles of "mammy" or "Aunt Jemima." Meditating on "changing, growing, developing," she feels imprisoned in the stout, aging body she herself has difficulty loving, caught in the "Matriarch cage." Her need for acknowledgment, fixated on attracting the admiring male gaze ("maybe it's possible Heywood sees beyond friend, colleague, to maybe woman"), leads only to frustration. Significantly, in the one minor role she recalls at length, her character carries a veil.

Only in the performance of her nightly songs, like the witchbird calling "in the dark," does she take the liberties she longs for. As Hortense Spillers observes in her analysis of blues, "To find another and truer sexual self-image the black woman must turn to the domain of music and America's black female vocalists, who suggest a composite figure of ironical grace."

In this instance of being-for-self, it does not matter that the vocalist is "entertaining" under Amerikkan skies because the woman, in her particular and vivid thereness, is an unalterable and discrete moment of self-knowledge. . . . We lay hold of a metaphor of commanding female sexuality with the singer who celebrates, chides, embraces, inquires into, controls her womanhood through the eloquence of form that she both makes use of and brings into being. (86–87)

Honey's grudging recognition of this transformative grace in Vera's performances implicitly applies to her own as well: "She could put a song over. . . . As though the spirit of music had . . . possessed her."

The questions of scripting, creativity, performance, and authority that Bambara raises here are inseparable from questions of authorship. In Honey's dilemma, Bambara obliquely comments on the position of black women writers as well. For as Deborah McDowell notes, the attempted suppression of African American women's literary productions derives not only from centuries of white oppression but also from social and ideological pressures within the black community. Thus, for example, many black male writers, threatened by unflattering representations of black men in the works of black women, have construed anything resembling a feminist assertion as a betrayal of the race. McDowell sees such critiques as especially problematic because "for all their questionable arguments" they "influence the masses of readers largely untutored in Afro-American literature." In attacks on black women's writings, "we see men telling *their* stories . . . , but seldom a counterresponse from a woman" (76). In "Witchbird" Bambara implicitly provides one such counterresponse, writing from the perspective of a black woman whose entire life has been shaped by the conflicting power dynamics deployed in debates about gender.

Lamenting the misrepresentations that render her peripheral or invisible —"Where the hell is my script?"—Honey recalls another dream, about "the Mary McLeod Bethune exhibit," which Bambara turns into a figure for all the lost voices, the undervalued texts, of black women throughout American history—an obliteration of such massive proportions as to be comparable to genocide: "I heard the woman calling from some diary entry they had under glass, a voice . . . muffled under the gas mask they clamped on hard and turned her on till she didn't know what was what. But calling for Black pages. . . . And catch myself calling to the white pages as I ripple them fast, listening to the pages for the entrapped voices, calling as the pages flutter." Those same entrapped voices echo in the witchbird's shrieks. In Honey's culminating fantasy, the bird explicitly emerges as her symbolic surrogate, a figure through whom she can ventriloquize her anguish, at once expressing and evading her own explosive emotions: "screeching, ripping through the trees, like she trying to find a way out of them woods and heaven help us if she do, cause she dangerous with rage."

Bambara suggests that the balm for this rage may come not from men but from the black female community. Paradoxically, it is the very women Honey initially repudiates who truly seek to see and hear her: "'Here,' [Gayle] says, sliding my house shoes closer to the bed. 'You know Heywood was all set to get you some tired old navy-blue numbers. I kept telling him you ain't nobody's grandmother,' she says, backing up to give me room to stretch, looking me over like she always does." Honey assumes that this look signifies jealousy, but the narrative implies otherwise, opening the possibility of genuine affection from the "girls" whose gratitude to Honey leads them, unlike the men in her life, to refuse to stereotype her, allowing her "room to stretch." This attitude emerges explicitly in Laney's plea that Honey reclaim herself, transcending the damage Heywood, the self-made man "on the make" in every sense, has wrought in their lives in the process, both literal and figurative, of "managing" them: "You think it's no harm the way he uses you, Honey? What are you, his mother, his dumping grounds? Why you put up with it? Why you put up with us, with me?"

A comparable expression of female solidarity occurs in the beauty salon, that longed-for site of solace towards which Honey's whole day and monologue move: "All I want is to get into Mary's shampoo chair, to laze under Mary's hands and have her massage all the hurts up out of my body. . . . I need release." So far from casting her in stereotypical roles or attaching "release" to the exercise of masculine power, as Honey has unconsciously done in her dream, Mary comically chides her for self-abnegation. Honey's awkward attempts to conceal herself beneath a cosmetic mask of whiteness ("Clown white, ain't it?") and "some dead white woman" wig suggest the fatality of the self-alienation and self-rejection that sap her spirit, turning her into a figure like the walking dead in "some zombie movie" or the fake Halloween "ghosts" who surround her on the way to the salon. In Mary's question— "Why you wanna do this to yourself, Honey?"—Bambara encapsulates the ongoing crisis of identity on which the story turns. And in the correlative injunction to "come out from under that death," she offers a potential salvation—a genuine "release"—from the self-repudiating patterns of Honey's life, as for the lives of all black women caught in similar "cages."

For it is in the salon, listening to stories of other women's lives, identifying with their sorrows, that Honey finally experiences the release she has been longing for. Both her own pent-up emotions and the narrative energies driving the story culminate in the tears that begin to flow as she sits under the dryer listening to Bertha's narrative of Helen: "A myth all that stuff about our strength and strength and then some." Recalling the salvational water imagery of the dream, Bambara represents this weeping as a kind of breakthrough, an unstoppable deluge that ruptures the carefully structured controls Honey maintains, encompasses the griefs of all black women, and openly acknowledges those women as sisters: "No amount of towel's gonna stop the flood. . . . Let it pour, let it get on out so I can travel light. I'm thinking maybe I'll do Billie's number tonight."

As this climactic scene implies, perhaps the most vital act women can perform for each other is "to absorb their blues and transform them . . . into songs." For in that creative process they also remake themselves—"crystallize, sparkling." Yet Bambara resists the reductiveness of the classic happy ending. "It's been a year," Honey had recalled earlier, since "I've written any new songs." The text suggests that she has absorbed so much sorrow that the transformative miracle may ultimately be beyond her. As the story ends we are left to conjecture whether her need to narrate her own blues, fusing them with the griefs of other women, has become so strong that she can literally no longer create: "I am about to talk myself hoarse and won't be fit for singing."

Yet that very talk, which returns us to the beginning of the story in its promise of an answer to Honey's insistent questions, is itself a kind of blues song, performed for a sympathetic audience of women. It embodies not only bondage but bonding, Honey's nurturing links to the community of women for whom and with whom she can go on speaking. Like Toni Morrison's Sethe, who finally learns, in *Beloved*, that she is "her own best thing," Honey needs to discover her own being as the best source of strength and magical sweetness. As the biblical allusions in her name imply, Honey herself, through her own creative energies, can transport herself and others to the "promised land" she longs for.[6]

Her story, in turn, becomes a figure for Bambara's own narrative art, whose swift modulations, repetitions, and diversions suggest a literary equivalent of the blues.[7] "Stories," Bambara has written, "keep us alive. In the ships, in the camps, in the quarters, fields, prisons, on the road, on the run, underground, under siege, in the throes, on the verge—the storyteller snatches us back from the edge to hear the next chapter. . . . That is what I work to do: to produce stories that save our lives" (1984, 41). In "Witchbird" Bambara implies that insofar as Honey experiences the breakthrough for which she has yearned and resists conventional plots of male domination and female rivalry, she does so precisely in the process of trying to speak for herself, to tell her own story, to sing her own song, which is also the song of others. And if her voice seems near exhaustion at last, "hoarse" and unfit "for singing," the story itself persists, merging Honey's voice with that of its author in a suggestive harmony that mimes the healing alliance of woman with woman unfolded in Honey's narrative.

In this context the witchbird, as Honey's figurative counterpart, becomes not an object of fear, chaos, and insanity but a potentially "enchanted" sign of release and restoration, a mimetic conjurer who, like Honey, Bambara, and their symbolic daughters/sisters, can sing in many voices. If not exactly a dream come true—Bambara refuses to sentimentalize, and the ending of the story is as ambiguous as Honey's own bedeviled relation to the witchbird and to the other women in her life—the bird at least suggests possibilities for resistance, redeeming self-irony, and even, occasionally, transcendence: a temporary escape from the cages society constructs for African American women. Though Honey herself may not consciously recognize the connections between her own "hoarse" voice and the "raucous shrieks" of the bird, Bambara's metaphors make them explicit. And in the modulated shifts and riffs of her own narrative, the cunning shaping of its themes and turns, Bambara herself becomes a kind of witchbird—the conjure woman who sings black women's blues.

Prostitutes, Property, and Propriety: Singing the Soviet Blues

Given the diminutions and disappointments of her life, Bambara's Honey might well reiterate the words of the Russian woman who, in a 1989 letter to the magazine *Woman Worker*, characterized her condition thus: "I am not complaining and I am not asking for anything. . . . But where is the justice in all of this?" (Melikhova 15). The question also encapsulates the issues Petrushevskaia explores in "That Kind of Girl." But with a difference. For in addition to issues of race and nationality, one of the crucial divergences between this narrative and Bambara's is the stress, in "Witchbird," on Honey's continued resistance to the manifold injustices she confronts—on her ability, however tenuous, to affirm her own creative, erotic energies, and on her ties with other women even in the face of all that would negate them. Alike in inhabiting sparse, overcrowded, working-class worlds where women are urged to view themselves as competitors for limited resources, both material and sexual, Honey and the significantly nameless narrator of "That Kind of Girl" respond to their circumstances in strikingly different ways. Where Honey's monologue vibrates with varied voices, explosions of the unconscious, humor, and song, Petrushevskaia's stripped, spare narrative exposes the devastating emotional impoverishment of a woman whose constricted living space becomes a figure for her limited understanding, narrowed sympathies, and psychological confinement.

Like Bambara's, the story is a monologue whose auditor remains undefined; but whereas Honey's world is continually inflected by images and voices of community, the world of Petrushevskaia's narrator, despite its location in the overcrowded apartment house, indistinguishable from all the others that typified Soviet urban life, is most notable for the sense of utter isolation it conveys. In light of Petrushevskaia's preeminence as a dramatist, it is no accident that this story, like so many of her short fictions, might easily be performed as a one-act play. The narrator's words, tumbling forth in nonstop, apparently random profusion, seem obviously driven by a desperate need to be heard; yet they appear to issue into the void. She makes no more connection with her nameless, faceless listener than would a player declaiming a solitary speech on an unpeopled stage, gazing outward into darkness and silence that might or might not conceal a living audience. That void, those silences, in turn configure the deathly alienation of her existence.

"That Kind of Girl": the very title projects the Other Woman as object of speech and speculation. In its judgmental overtones, the phrase aims to mark the distance between the "proper" narrator and the improper object of whom she speaks. Yet ironically, the eponymous "girl" (*devochka*) who forms the obsessive center of the narrator's consciousness and story is ultimately the one person with whom she has a genuinely intimate connection. In one of the climactic moments of her monologue, confronting the perpetual philandering of her narcissistic husband and the tenuous, "temporary," and contingent affection of her child, she concedes that "only Raisa remained on my side, the whole world was on the other." Yet it is that same "girl" whom, in the ritually reiterated dismissal that frames the monologue, the narrator consigns to oblivion: "Now she might as well be dead for me." As in "Witchbird," a kind of conjuring goes on here, but where the bird's bewitching utterances signify the ambiguous possibility of renewal, Petrushevskaia's text begins and ends in death.

In the narrator's world, both words and looks can kill. Reduced to an anatomical itinerary, the material inertness of a faceless body, Raisa first appears in the narrator's discourse as a kind of cipher, a rigid, hollowed-out icon: "I have a photo taped to my blank forms drawer. . . . You can't see anything in this picture, her hair curtains her face, just two legs and two arms in the pose of Rodin's 'Thinker.'" As the object of the narrator's baleful gaze, Raisa is figuratively turned to stone, a marmoreal monument set at the head of the narrative like a sepulchral sculpture above an epitaph. Significantly, as both Raisa's death sentence and her memorial, the story begins with its own last words, its dead-end quality intensified by the monotonous circularity Petrushevskaia introduces through this and other forms of repetition. Like Honey, the narrator and her object are "locked up in a fiction"; but from this deathly edifice, unlike the "ordinary building" with "four entrances" that Petrushevskaia's characters inhabit, there appears to be no exit.

Like Bambara's narrative, Petrushevskaia's turns on the paradoxical oscillation of companionship and competition between women. As the defensive wife whose husband's serial infidelities provide the "zigzag" emotional swerves that alone strike sparks in the lifeless marriage, the narrator smugly brands Raisa as the ultimate other woman, "a real professional prostitute" despite her official status as Seva's wife. The epithet, given its prominent position at the beginning of the narrative, is an extreme expression of the uneasiness, the literal and figurative dis-ease, Raisa seems to engender in everyone she encounters.

This disquiet is hardly surprising, and not merely because of the sexual inhibition of Soviet society. In Russia, as in other male-dominated social systems predicated on marriage and the preeminence of paternal genealogy, the prostitute has figured as a threat to the status quo because of her putative status as a free agent who assumes the right to control and market her own body—an anomaly intensified in a communist state that held private property of any sort to be suspect. Possessed by all men and yet owned by none, the prostitute emerges as a pivotal figure of transgression—roving, unstable, and destabilizing. Haunting the margins of culture, she remains an unsettling presence, at once attractive and repellent to the men she perpetually eludes even in the process of "yielding." For while deploying her body as object, she theoretically maintains the position of subject relative to the man to whom she temporarily contracts herself, thus undermining the official male-centered gender ideologies she appears to reinforce. If the prostitute is disturbing to men, it is at least in part because she is quintessentially the woman who will not stay in her "proper place." But she may be equally disturbing to "proper" women who do—that is, women legally attached, via marriage and motherhood, to men. As a free sexual and economic agent, the prostitute calls into question the ties that bind wives; and her very existence potentially devalues theirs in the sexual marketplace, where her apparent freedom at once marks and mocks the wife's confinement.[8]

That Raisa ultimately solicits the narrator's husband ("my Petrov"—a locution at once proprietary and, given its use of his surname only, oddly formal—) seems at first to be simply an ironic logical consequence of "that kind of girl's" symbolic potential as disruptive figure and an adequate explanation for the narrator's cold dismissal of her former friend. Yet a closer look suggests that so far from giving herself to Petrov in violation of the narrator's marital prerogatives, Raisa endures his sexual advances precisely to preserve those rights, in direct response to what she takes to be the narrator's request. And rather than rejecting Raisa simply because of the liaison with Petrov, as the narrator claims to have done, she herself appears to be driven as well by other, unexpressed desires and anxieties. Ultimately, Petrushevskaia implies that whatever the protagonist's marital insecurities, she is also fleeing the recognition that her bond with Raisa might be stronger than that with either her husband or her child.

Consider the ambiguous representation of Raisa herself. The text indicates repeatedly that despite her frequent liaisons, she is both frightened and repelled by heterosexual encounters. A "cold fish," as the narrator crudely puts it, Raisa listlessly accepts the advances of her various lovers "as if it was all revolting to her." From the narrator's dispassionate rehearsal of past events, an unmistakable pattern emerges: Raisa's wretched family history, her demanding and abusive father ("invalid" in both senses of the word), the gang rape she suffered as a young woman seeking to escape her debased circumstances, her stint in the penal colonies, the unspeakable "cesspool" that followed—all suggest sufficient rationale for her chronic depression, her anorexia ("the doctor found her completely emaciated, dystrophic even"), her sexual aversion to men, and her existential despair. "Something," as the narrator observes, "was damaged in her, some instinct for self-preservation." The narrator's willful obtuseness—"that's all history, that doesn't concern anybody now"—is a measure, most obviously, of her own decision to ignore the entanglement of past and present, her profound insensitivity to the import of Raisa's unassuageable grief and "coldness" to men, and her anger at what she regards as Raisa's betrayal. But her curious blindness also suggests how thoroughly she has repressed the more profound implications of Raisa's passionate appeals to her, which initially draw from her an equally intense response: "From the very beginning of our acquaintance she made a sort of stinging impression on me, like a newborn animal . . . that . . . stings you right in the heart. No love troubles that desire, that pure pity that catches your breath." Petrushevskaia implies that what drives the narrator's ultimate rejection of Raisa's love, and repression of her own reciprocal emotions, is not simply anger, but fear of that answering response in herself.

The intensity of their "good friendship" is disclosed not only in the narrator's acknowledgment of their inseparability ("we couldn't live a day without each other") or of Raisa's repeated fiery defenses ("she battled with my Petrov on my behalf"; "she defended me like her own child, and lit into Petrov with her very nails"), but most vividly in her passionate intervention in the narrator's attempted suicide: "Raisa came into the room and threw herself down, hugging my knees, . . . attached herself to my legs like a dog and kept insisting: 'Let's do it together, together, wait for me.'" Not surprisingly, given the barely concealed sexual double entendre in Raisa's words, the profundity of "attachment" this moment reveals provokes the narrator's most explicit enactment, both literally and linguistically, of the moment of repression: "I had only one feeling after that incident: coldness in my head. . . . I realized that all these senseless runnings around and actions at the first cry of the heart are just not my way. Why should I compete with Raisa?"

Ironically, Raisa's ultimate proof of love for the narrator is the event that destroys their relationship: Petrushevskaia implies that so far from seducing Petrov because of attraction for him, Raisa sacrifices herself to his attentions in order to fulfill the narrator's plea that she "convince Petrov to return to us, if only fictitiously": "She agreed. But she agreed frightened, somehow. I didn't actually pay any attention to that. . . . In the evening I went to Raisa. . . . She told me she had spoken to Petrov. That he would be back tomorrow . . . then suddenly [she] started to cry."

Petrushevskaia suggests that the real alliance Raisa seeks is not with Petrov, but with the narrator. Rather than merely objectifying herself in the carnal exchange, Raisa uses Petrov as a mediating object to sustain her relationship with his wife. And if the ostensible message of the wife's narrative is a sweeping condemnation of "that kind of girl," the interstices of her monologue echo with her own repressed desire. The male-centered social system, like Petrov himself, pits the narrator against the other woman on a "field of death" that demarcates the distance between them. But the tragic subtext of the story suggests that under different circumstances the narrator and the woman she regards as an enemy might have found, in each other, the solace and security each yearns for.

These issues, as Petrushevskaia implies, are intimately related not only to the body of the prostitute, but also to the body of her text—the story itself. Peter Brooks has remarked astutely that a potential link exists between the prostitute's circulation of her body, the circulation of property, and the production of narrative: "In the life of a prostitute at least, . . . accounting gives something to recount, money and story flow from the same nights of sexual exchange" (162–63). In her arch retelling and retailing of Raisa's relationships with "guys we knew who had done business with her," as in her active encouragement of those liaisons, the narrator herself becomes a kind of purveyor, extending the traffic in female bodies into the realm of story by turning Raisa to account, in both senses of the phrase. In thus doubly avenging herself for what she insists is the treachery of "that kind of girl," the narrator overlooks her own complicity in the system that trades in women's sexuality, the sources and effects of both her own and Raisa's relation to that system, and the unexpressed, inexpressible bond of love that draws the two women together and might ultimately have subverted the system that oppresses them.

In brilliantly unfolding the narrator's refusal or inability to acknowledge and preserve this bond, her repression of their mutual attraction, the total self-absorption that presses her to misconstrue Raisa's ultimate act of sacrifice, and her consequent rejection of the one person in the world who seems truly to love her, Petrushevskaia suggests that it is ultimately the narrator, not Raisa, who betrays both the friendship and herself. Ironically, though, even as she rejects Raisa, barbarizes her as both outcast and alien ("she's a Tatar"), and unwittingly supports the very system that abuses both of them, the narrator's monologue reveals their underlying identity. In defining "that kind of girl," the narrator also defines herself. Even as she speaks in order to confirm their distance and difference, to fix firm boundaries between them, her words disclose the intimate reciprocity of their relationship, its meshes of mutual displacement and desire, and the joint fabrications that compose their intricately interwoven stories.

For both the narrator and Raisa "have experience in storytelling"—in the double sense of narration and duplicity. Raisa's concealments and deceptions find their counterparts in the narrator's own distortions of reality. How conscious this process might be remains an open question. For all their destructive possibilities, the women's mutual misreadings and misstatements remain touched with a curious sort of naiveté. Their stories take on a life of their own, proliferate with their own internal energy, so that in this world made of words, the reader too remains uncertain of what is reality, what fiction.

And where is the storyteller herself, Liudmila Petrushevskaia, in this story of women's storytelling? At once nowhere and everywhere. Beyond the authorial presence implied by her signature, she might also be seen to occupy the places of both the narrator and "that . . . girl" whose story they both tell. For like Raisa, Petrushevskaia herself has been widely regarded as mystifying, provocative, controversial, even scandalous—an enigmatic figure whose fabulations elude ordinary understanding. "What's to be done with Petrushevskaia?" demands one recent critic, raising a question posed with repetitive insistence in Moscow circles. "They told me in advance," writes another, "that the meeting [the author had sought with Petrushevskaia] was hardly likely to take place. They told me about someone's unsuccessful attempts to interview her, about her difficult character." Similarly, Petrushevskaia's plays, for which she is better known than for her short fiction, produce "a feeling of unease" and "anxiety"; they "torment us," writes one critic, "with their questions and shame" (Svobodin; Vainer 1989b, 72, 77). The words might as aptly describe Raisa; and we might well read the narrative as Petrushevskaia's playful self-reflexive exploration of woman as text—"that kind of girl" as a mask of the author's own unsettling role.

But like the narrator, Petrushevskaia is author as well as object of narration. Both she and her protagonist express themselves through telling tales, constructing characters; in more than one sense, they live to plot. Petrushevskaia's own uneasy, multiple, and contradictory positions as a contemporary woman writer in Russia are played out, then, in the multiple positions she projects in the women of the story. At once seducer (of the reader) and seduced (by the desire to go on speaking, to tell the story), at once alien and familiar to Western women readers, she eludes stable placement in conventional interpretive schemes and plots.

Naming the Other

These reflections bring us back to the question with which we began: "Who is the other woman? How am I naming her?" Such interrogation of self and other leads the critic inevitably to the disquieting sense of complicity in the processes she seeks to disentangle. For if, as Petrushevskaia and Bambara suggest, narration has a way of becoming analysis, so analysis also implies an untold narrative: the story of one's own reading. As a white, middle-class, American academic analyzing Bambara and Petrushevskaia, I enter into a relationship with them and their texts uncomfortably comparable to that of Petrushevskaia's narrator with the "girl" who becomes, in more than one sense, her objectified other. As Petrushevskaia makes clear—and as critics have often observed about white women reading texts by women of color—to analyze is also, potentially, to appropriate. It is now a critical commonplace that in presuming to name, to speak about, to speak *for* the other woman, one risks engaging in a kind of literary colonization. We ignore at our peril the implications of what Barbara Christian has called the "distanced and false stance of objectivity" (67).

Yet I am equally uneasy about the formulaic quality of such apologias, which have by now become virtually de rigueur for white bourgeois critics seeking to engage the texts of those who to them are Other. So firmly installed, even institutionalized, are these self-deprecating gestures among literary critics in the United States that they have approached the status of generic inevitability. Taken to its logical conclusion, the respectful hesitation we feel in attempting to analyze another can lead only to silence. The attempt to speak about any other, even those closest to us, is after all an act of hubris; how much more so when a white woman speaks of women of color in a society still pervaded by racist assumptions, or an American critic speaks of an (ex)Soviet writer whose works she reads in translation? Those limitations acknowledged, however, I would nevertheless argue that with reference to women who have been systematically excluded from dominant symbolic orders, our silence is at least as dangerous as our speech. For the refusal to speak, to attempt the act of empathy from which any effort at understanding ultimately proceeds, perpetuates alienation and reinforces a continued ghettoization of the very works we might seek, by our silence, to honor.

In any case, of course, the dialogue works both ways. The texts themselves are sturdier and more canny than we sometimes think, and like the women they represent, they always speak back to us, reminding us of our own limitations. By the very nature of their narrative forms, Petrushevskaia and Bambara encourage us to engage in skeptical self-reflections, prompt us to recognize that critical presumptions—in either sense of that word—lead inexorably to misreadings. Petrushevskaia's narrator ultimately finds her own view of reality disrupted and demolished by the other woman('s), and Honey's monologue reveals that the witchbird, like the black vocalists "she" recalls, always sings in unexpected registers, her disquieting riffs and rhythms constructing a different song from what the listeners, fixed by conventional definitions of musical propriety, can fully comprehend.

So in my own analytic project, listening to the voices of these women so differently situated by race, class, nationality, and a whole host of specific personal circumstances unamenable to those tidy classifications, I am reminded of how fragile are all our efforts, no matter how well intended, to speak of the other woman. In the silences, the blind spots, the missed connections of my own attempts at capturing her meaning, there are always the haunting echoes of another story, fading into distance like the witchbird's elusive, mocking song.

Notes

1. See Washington 1977, 38; Baker 1987, 92–96, and 1984; Wallace 1990, 54; Gossett 109–12.

2. On the problematics of representing black women's sexuality, see Spillers.

3. For an illuminating study of Bambara's short fiction as a feminist intervention into the politics of black nationalism, see Butler-Evans 91–122.

4. For a useful analysis of Bambara's use of black female narrators, see Butler-Evans. Bambara's groundbreaking collection *The Black Woman* played a vital role in establishing the distinctive differences in the circumstances and perceptions of black male and black female writers. Bambara comments on her own work in the context of Black liberation movements in "What It Is I Think I'm Doing Anyhow" in Sternburg 153–68.

5. On this much-discussed topic, which was catalyzed by Michele Wallace's *Black Macho and the Myth of the Superwoman*, see McDowell.

6. In her narrator's name Bambara recalls the formulaic representation of the promised land as a place flowing with milk and honey. See also Old Testament ref-

erences to the magical empowering qualities of honey, which was ritually imbibed before a battle to endow warriors with strength and courage (I Sam. 14:23). See also the narratives of the celebrated Hebrew judge Deborah, whose name, "Honey Bee," connotes not only her maternal role as nurturer ("a mother in Israel") but her empowering role as singer, whose chanted stories, like Honey's, lead to the salvation of her people (Judges 4–5).

7. Several critics have fruitfully analyzed Bambara's incorporation of jazz and blues into her own narrative structures, e.g., Traylor; Washington 1977, 36, and 1975, 6; Byerman 115–70. Burks compares the stories in *Gorilla, My Love* with "Negro spirituals" (49).

8. On prostitution in the USSR, see Waters 1989, 3–19, and Heldt 1992, 160–75. For a fuller discussion of the cultural semiotics of prostitution, see Aiken 1990, 120–22. Petrushevskaia herself has been fascinated with the cultural role of prostitutes. In "Ksenia's Daughter" ("Doch' Kseni") she writes that "literature has always [sought] to describe the prostitute's justification. Actually, it is funny to imagine someone daring to describe a prostitute with the purpose of blackening her. The task of literature . . . consists in showing all those who are typically scorned as people deserving respect and pity" (*Bessmertnaia liubov'* 81–82).

Dialogue

ON BAMBARA AND PETRUSHEVSKAIA

Katya: I feel uncomfortable including a story about prostitution because it has for our public some connotations I don't like. All of our magazines right now are full of stories about prostitutes. I think if we publish a story about it in our country, it won't be in good taste, because everybody is deeply ashamed of this subject.

Susan: But don't you think Petrushevskaia's story makes a useful comparison with "Witchbird"? In the West, a provocative critical discourse on prostitution has developed over the past couple of decades. These stories offer some intriguing insights, especially regarding the various ways women's bodies are used as a form of property, available for men to exchange.

Maya: It seems that the prostitution theme in Petrushevskaia has an ironic twist. It's an age-old story of the prostitute with the golden heart. And Petrushevskaia uses it cleverly, in an original way, because the prostitute is not the one who has a magnanimous heart. She just charms this man by her indifference in the sexual act—makes him feel bad.

Susan: I disagree somewhat; Raisa certainly doesn't fit the cliché of the golden-hearted whore, but she does have, as you put it, a "magnanimous heart." What I find striking is that her magnanimity is not directed to a man, but to another woman: she uses her body as a gift to entice her friend's strayed husband home again, as an act of self-sacrificing generosity.

Adele: In Bambara the subject of women's bodies is also related to race. How do you think American blacks are perceived in the USSR?

Maya: Even before the revolution, the general feeling among educated classes was compassionate and understanding—and there were protests against slavery, beginning with Pushkin. Russian writers of the nineteenth century saw a similarity between slavery and serfdom. "Don't criticize us," we said to America. "You still have slavery." During the revolution this mentality found its way into political propaganda and the situation was oversimplified, without any awareness that changes might have occurred in America.

Adele: When the Soviets began finding out about American culture, even during times of repression, one of the things they loved most was American jazz, which comes from America's black heritage. The culture of American blacks was embraced as that of an oppressed people.

Susan: Many black writers and critics here—Bambara, Houston Baker, and others—have explored the vitality of the jazz tradition. Jazz is both a literal embodiment of black art and self-expression and a figure for the importance of black influence on American cultural life—ultimately a major shaping force in our society.

Maya: But jazz for us didn't necessarily mean black people—it meant America. Our attitude toward blacks was greatly influenced by *Uncle Tom's Cabin*. For many generations, it inspired so much compassion for blacks in our country. Even now, I hesitate when I hear criticism of Uncle Tom attitudes, for this man had a great capacity for love that shouldn't be denigrated. Our reception of this character continues to be different, I guess, than yours. We see him as a great figure. Despite his suffering, he continued to love the child, Little Eva. That love makes him great. Even now, when I read criticism of how submissive he was, I say "Yes, he was, but he had other qualities too."

Adele: Do you think your attitude toward his submissiveness has anything to do with how highly valued that quality has been in Russian cultural tradition?

Maya: It's not submissiveness, but loyalty. This quality is very highly regarded in our tradition. In Pushkin, there is the character of Pugachev, who stays loyal to his young master in *The Captain's Daughter*. Pushkin doesn't dismiss him.

Susan: But here, as black critics have suggested, Uncle Tom's attitude is seen as having less to do with his capacity for love than with his capacity for servitude—in other words, his attitude helps reinforce a grossly unjust system. Here's the irony: even as Stowe attacks that system, she seems to exalt the kind of character it can produce; her idealization of Uncle Tom anticipated one of the primary popular responses to her novel—especially by whites, for whom *Uncle Tom's Cabin* was one of the most influential texts of the nineteenth century. The character of Uncle Tom was extolled for the very qualities that made blacks the most useful, the least threatening, to whites.

Maya: Discrimination against blacks is still pervasive in our country too. I remember when some people came to a conference who were from Patrice Lumumba University in Moscow, where people from developing countries study. One of the girls complained to me that they were treated badly by Russian students. She said, "They regard us as monkeys. But if I'm a monkey, I'm a very desirable monkey"—the students had made sexual overtures to her. People in our country sometimes do refer to Negroes in such crude terms. Discrimination still persists.

Susan: That sounds like America. Black women here, since the time of slavery, have been repeatedly subjected to extremes of sexual harassment and violation, while at the same time being labelled with the stereotype of the hypersexed femme fatale that white society has used to justify treating them in the most heinous ways.

Adele: We also need to remember that American blacks have had a long and complex history in the Soviet Union. It seems ironic that so many black people, for example, Paul Robeson, believed in the so-called egalitarianism promised by Soviet ideology. The USSR became an emblem of the radiant future, a just society.

Susan: The black poet Langston Hughes is another example—he travelled in the USSR and had strong ties with that small group of American blacks who had emigrated to the Soviet Union in the twenties and thirties in quest of a better life.

Maya: I saw Paul Robeson once. He was invited to sing at the All-Union Society for Cultural Ties with Foreign Countries. It was expected that he would sing only to those inside, but he came into the building and opened the window out onto the square. And he sang to all of them. A huge crowd gathered. He was a great giant of a man, standing in a black suit, singing. He chose to sing for the people.

3

❖

Jayne Anne Phillips

Elena Makarova

© Jill Krementz, by permission

JAYNE ANNE PHILLIPS ❖ Born in Buckhannon, West Virginia, in 1952, Jayne
Anne Phillips began publishing while still a student at West Virginia University, where she
received her B.A. in 1974. She took the M.F.A. from the University of Iowa in 1978, two
years after the publication of her first collection, *Sweethearts,* which won the Pushcart
Prize and the Fels Award in Fiction. *Counting* appeared in 1978. But it was *Black Tickets*
(1979) that established her reputation as one of the finest contemporary writers of her
generation. In addition to the short story collections *How Mickey Made It* (1981) and *Fast
Lanes* (1984, rpt. 1987), she has published the novel *Machine Dreams* (1984), which won
a National Book Critics Circle Award nomination, an American Library Association Notable
Book citation, and the *New York Times* Best Books of 1984 citation.

Widely anthologized, Phillips has received many other awards for her fiction, including
fellowships from the National Endowment for the Arts, the Sue Kaufman Award for First
Fiction from the American Academy and Institute of Arts and Letters, and a fellowship from
the Bunting Institute. In 1985 she married Mark B. Stockman, a physician, with whom she
has one child and two stepchildren.

Home

JAYNE ANNE PHILLIPS

I'm afraid Walter Cronkite has had it, says Mom. Roger Mudd always does the news now—how would you like to have a name like that? Walter used to do the conventions and a football game now and then. I mean he would sort of appear, on the sidelines. Didn't he? But you never see him anymore. Lord. Something is going on.

Mom, I say. Maybe he's just resting. He must have made a lot of money by now. Maybe he's tired of talking about elections and mine disasters and the collapse of the franc. Maybe he's in love with a young girl.

He's not the type, says my mother. You can tell *that* much. No, she says, I'm afraid it's cancer.

My mother has her suspicions. She ponders. I have been home with her for two months. I ran out of money and I wasn't in love, so I have come home to my mother. She is an educational administrator. All winter long after work she watches television and knits afghans.

Come home, she said. Save money.

I can't possibly do it, I said. Jesus, I'm twenty-three years old.

Don't be silly, she said. And don't use profanity.

She arranged a job for me in the school system. All day, I tutor children in remedial reading. Sometimes I am so discouraged that I lie on the couch all evening and watch television with her. The shows are all alike. Their laugh tracks are conspicuously similar; I think I recognize a repetition of certain professional laughters. This laughter marks off the half hours.

Finally I make a rule: I won't watch television at night. I will watch only the news, which ends at 7:30. Then I will go to my room and do God knows what. But I feel sad that she sits there alone, knitting by the lamp. She seldom looks up.

Why don't you ever read anything? I ask.

I do, she says. I read books in my field. I read all day at work, writing those damn proposals. When I come home I want to relax.

Then let's go to the movies.

I don't want to go to the movies. Why should I pay money to be upset or frightened?

But feeling something can teach you. Don't you want to learn anything?

I'm learning all the time, she says.

She keeps knitting. She folds yarn the color of cream, the color of snow. She works it with her long blue needles, piercing, returning, winding. Yarn cascades from her hands in long panels. A pattern appears and disappears. She stops and counts; so many stitches across, so many down. Yes, she is on the right track.

Occasionally I offer to buy my mother a subscription to something mildly informative: *Ms., Rolling Stone, Scientific American.*

I don't want to read that stuff, she says. Just save your money. Did you hear Cronkite last night? Everyone's going to need all they can get.

Often, I need to look at my mother's old photographs. I see her sitting in knee-high grass with a white gardenia in her hair. I see her dressed up as the groom in a mock wedding at a sorority party, her black hair pulled back tight. I see her formally posed in her cadet nurse's uniform. The photographer has painted her lashes too lushly, too long; but her deep red mouth is correct.

The war ended too soon. She didn't finish her training. She came home to nurse only her mother and to meet my father at a dance. She married him in two weeks. It took twenty years to divorce him.

When we traveled to a neighboring town to buy my high school clothes, my mother and I would pass a certain road that turned off the highway and wound to a place I never saw.

There it is, my mother would say. The road to Wonder Bar. That's where I met my Waterloo. I walked in and he said, 'There she is. I'm going to marry that girl.' Ha. He sure saw me coming.

Well, I asked, Why did you marry him?

He was older, she said. He had a job and a car. And Mother was so sick.

My mother doesn't forget her mother.

Never one bedsore, she says. I turned her every fifteen minutes. I kept her skin soft and kept her clean, even to the end.

I imagine my mother at twenty-three; her black hair, her dark eyes, her olive skin and that red lipstick. She is growing lines of tension in her mouth. Her teeth press into her lower lip as she lifts the woman in the bed. The woman weighs no more than a child. She has a smell. My mother fights it continually; bathing her, changing her sheets, carrying her to the bathroom so the smell can be contained and flushed away. My mother will try to protect them both. At night she sleeps in the room on a cot. She struggles awake feeling something press down on her and suck her breath: the smell. When my grandmother can no longer move, my mother fights it alone.

I did all I could, she sighs. And I was glad to do it. I'm glad I don't have to feel guilty.

No one has to feel guilty, I tell her.

And why not? says my mother. There's nothing wrong with guilt. If you are guilty, you should feel guilty.

My mother has often told me that I will be sorry when she is gone.

I think. And read alone at night in my room. I read those books I never read, the old classics, and detective stories. I can get them in the library here. There is only one bookstore; it sells mostly newspapers and *True Confessions* oracles. At Kroger's by the checkout counter I buy a few paperbacks, best sellers, but they are usually bad.

The television drones on downstairs.

I wonder about Walter Cronkite.

When was the last time I saw him? It's true his face was pouchy, his hair thinning. Perhaps he is only cutting it shorter. But he had that look about the eyes—

He was there when they stepped on the moon. He forgot he was on the air and he shouted, 'There . . . there . . . now—We have Contact!' Contact. For those who tuned in late, for the periodic watchers, he repeated: 'One small step. . . .'

I was in high school and he was there with the body count. But he said it in such a way that you knew he wanted the war to end. He looked directly at you and said the numbers quietly. Shame, yes, but sorrowful patience, as if all things had passed before his eyes. And he understood that here at home, as well as in starving India, we would pass our next lives as meager cows.

My mother gets *Reader's Digest*. I come home from work, have a cup of coffee, and read it. I keep it beside my bed. I read it when I am too tired to read anything else. I read about Joe's kidney and Humor in Uniform. Always, there are human interest stories in which someone survives an ordeal of primal terror. Tonight it is Grizzly! Two teen-agers camping in the mountains are attacked by a bear. Sharon is dragged over a mile, unconscious. She is a good student loved by her parents, an honest girl loved by her boyfriend. Perhaps she is not a virgin; but in her heart, she is virginal. And she lies now in the furred arms of a beast. The grizzly drags her quietly, quietly. He will care for her all the days of his life . . . Sharon, his rose.

But alas. Already, rescuers have organized. Mercifully, her boyfriend is not among them. He is sleeping en route to the nearest hospital; his broken legs have excused him. In a few days, Sharon will bring him his food on a tray. She is spared. She is not demure. He gazes on her face, untouched but for a long thin scar near her mouth. Sharon says she remembers nothing of the bear. She only knows the tent was ripped open, that its heavy canvas fell across her face.

I turn out my light when I know my mother is sleeping. By then my eyes hurt and the streets of the town are deserted.

My father comes to me in a dream. He kneels beside me, touches my mouth. He turns my face gently toward him.

Let me see, he says. Let me see it.

He is looking for a scar, a sign. He wears only a towel around his waist. He presses himself against my thigh, pretending solicitude. But I know what he is doing; I turn my head in repulsion and stiffen. He smells of a sour musk and his forearms are black with hair. I think to myself, It's been years since he's had an erection—

Finally he stands. Cover yourself, I tell him.

I can't, he says, I'm hard.

On Saturdays I go to the Veterans of Foreign Wars rummage sales. They are held in the drafty basement of a church, rows of collapsible tables piled with objects. Sometimes I think I recognize the possessions of old friends: a class ring, yearbooks, football sweaters with our high school insignia. Would this one have fit Jason?

He used to spread it on the seat of the car on winter nights when we parked by country churches and graveyards. There seemed to be no ground, just water, a rolling, turning, building to a dull pain between my legs.

What's wrong? he said, What is it?

Jason, I can't. . . . This pain—

It's only because you're afraid. If you'd let me go ahead—

I'm not afraid of you, I'd do anything for you. But Jason, why does it hurt like this?

We would try. But I couldn't. We made love with our hands. Our bodies were white. Out the window of the car, snow rose up in mounds across the fields. Afterward, he looked at me peacefully, sadly.

I held him and whispered, Soon, soon . . . we'll go away to school.

His sweater. He wore it that night we drove back from the football awards banquet. Jason made All-State but he hated football.

I hate it, he said. So what? he said, that I'm out there puking in the heat? Screaming 'Kill' at a sandbag?

I held his award in my lap, a gold man frozen in midleap. Don't play in college, I said. Refuse the money.

He was driving very slowly.

I can't see, he said, I can't see the edges of the road. . . . Tell me if I start to fall off.

Jason, what do you mean?

He insisted I roll down the window and watch the edge. The banks of the road were gradual, sloping off into brush and trees on either side. White lines at the edge glowed up in dips and turns.

We're going to crash, he said.

No, Jason. You've driven this road before. We won't crash.

We're crashing, I know it, he said. Tell me, tell me I'm OK—

Here on the rummage sale table, there are three football sweaters. I see they are all too small to have belonged to Jason. So I buy an old soundtrack, *The Sound of Music*. Air, Austrian mountains. And an old robe to wear in the mornings. It upsets my mother to see me naked; she looks at me so curiously, as though she didn't recognize my body.

I pay for my purchases at the cash register. Behind the desk I glimpse stacks of *Reader's Digests*. The Ladies Auxiliary turns them inside out, stiffens and shellacs them. They make wastebaskets out of them.

I give my mother the record. She is pleased. She hugs me.

Oh, she says, I used to love the musicals. They made me happy. Then she stops and looks at me.

Didn't you do this? she says. Didn't you do this in high school?

Do what?

Your class, she says. You did *The Sound of Music*.

Yes, I guess we did.

What a joke. I was the beautiful countess meant to marry Captain von Trapp before innocent Maria stole his heart. Jason was a threatening Nazi colonel with a bit part. He should have sung the lead but sports practices interfered with rehearsals. Tall, blond, aged in makeup under the lights, he encouraged sympathy for the bad guys and overshadowed the star. He appeared just often enough to make the play ridiculous.

My mother sits in the blue chair my father used for years.

Come quick, she says. Look—

She points to the television. Flickerings of Senate chambers, men in conservative suits. A commentator drones on about tax rebates.

There, says my mother. Hubert Humphrey. Look at him.

It's true. Humphrey is different, changed from his former toady self to a desiccated old man, not unlike the discarded shell of a locust. Now he rasps into the microphone about the people of these great states.

Old Hubert's had it, says my mother. He's a death mask.

That's what he gets for sucking blood for thirty years.

No, she says. No, he's got it too. Look at him! Cancer. Oh.

For God's sake, will you think of something else for once?

I don't know what you mean, she says. She goes on knitting.

All Hubert needs, I tell her, is a good roll in the hay.

You think that's what everyone needs.

Everyone does need it.

They do not. People aren't dogs. I seem to manage perfectly well without it, don't I?

No, I wouldn't say that you do.

Well, I do. I know your mumbo jumbo about sexuality. Sex is for those who are married, and I wouldn't marry again if it was the Lord himself.

Now she is silent. I know what's coming.

Your attitude will make you miserable, she says. One man after another. I just want you to be happy.

I do my best.

That's right, she says. Be sarcastic.

I refuse to answer. I think about my growing bank account. Graduate school, maybe in California. Hawaii. Somewhere beautiful and warm. I will wear few clothes and my skin will feel the air.

What about Jason, says my mother. I was thinking of him the other day.

Our telepathy always frightens me. Telepathy and beyond. Before her hysterectomy, our periods often came on the same day.

If he hadn't had that nervous breakdown, she says softly, do you suppose—

No, I don't suppose.

I wasn't surprised that it happened. When his brother was killed, that was hard. But Jason was so self-centered. You're lucky the two of you split up. He thought everyone was out to get him. Still, poor thing.

Silence. Then she refers in low tones to the few months Jason and I lived together before he was hospitalized.

You shouldn't have done what you did when you went off to college. He lost respect for you.

It wasn't respect for me he lost—He lost his fucking mind if you remember—

I realize I'm shouting. And shaking. What is happening to me?

My mother stares.

We'll not discuss it, she says.

She gets up. I hear her in the bathroom. Water running into the tub. Hydrotherapy. I close my eyes and listen. Soon, this weekend. I'll get a ride to the university a few hours away and look up an old lover. I'm lucky. They always want to sleep with me. For old time's sake.

I turn down the sound of the television and watch its silent pictures. Jason's brother was a musician; he taught Jason to play the pedal steel. A sergeant in uniform delivered the message two weeks before the State Play-Off games. Jason appeared at my mother's kitchen door with the telegram. He looked at me, opened his mouth, backed off wordless in the dark. I pretend I hear his pedal steel; its sweet country whine might make me cry. And I recognize this silent movie—I've seen it four times. Gregory Peck and his submarine crew escape fallout in Australia, but not for long. The cloud is coming. And so they run rampant in auto races and love affairs. But in the end, they close the hatch and put out to sea. They want to go home to die.

Sweetheart? my mother calls from the bathroom. Could you bring me a towel?

Her voice is quavering slightly. She is sorry. But I never know what part of it she is sorry about. I get a towel from the linen closet and open the door of the steamy bathroom. My mother stands in the tub, dripping, shivering a little. She is so small and thin; she is smaller than I. She has two long scars on her belly, operations of the womb, and one breast is misshapen, sunken, indented near the nipple.

I put the towel around her shoulders and my eyes smart. She looks at her breast.

Not too pretty is it, she says. He took out too much when he removed that lump—

Mom, it doesn't look so bad.

I dry her back, her beautiful back which is firm and unblemished. Beautiful, her skin. Again, I feel the pain in my eyes.

But you should have sued the bastard, I tell her. He didn't give a shit about your body.

We have an awkward moment with the towel when I realize I can't touch her any longer. The towel slips down and she catches it as one end dips into the water.

Sweetheart, she says. I know your beliefs are different than mine. But have patience with me. You'll just be here a few more months. And I'll always stand behind you. We'll get along.

She has clutched the towel to her chest. She is so fragile, standing there, naked, with her small shoulders. Suddenly I am horribly frightened.

Sure, I say, I know we will.

I let myself out of the room.

Sunday my mother goes to church alone. Daniel calls me from D.C. He's been living with a lover in Oregon. Now he is back East; she will join him in a few weeks. He is happy, he says. I tell him I'm glad he's found someone who appreciates him.

Come on now, he says. You weren't that bad.

I love Daniel, his white and feminine hands, his thick chestnut hair, his intelligence. And he loves me, though I don't know why. The last few weeks we were together I lay beside him like a piece of wood. I couldn't bear his touch; the moisture his penis left on my hips as he rolled against me. I was cold, cold. I huddled in blankets away from him.

I'm sorry, I said. Daniel, I'm sorry please—what's wrong with me? Tell me you love me anyway . . .

Yes, he said, Of course I do. I always will. I do.

Daniel says he has no car, but he will come by bus. Is there a place for him to stay?

Oh yes, I say. There's a guest room. Bring some Trojans. I'm a hermit with no use for birth control. Daniel, you don't know what it's like here.

I don't care what it's like. I want to see you.

Yes, I say. Daniel, hurry.

When he arrives the next weekend, we sit around the table with my mother and discuss medicine. Daniel was a medic in Vietnam. He smiles at my mother. She is charmed though she has reservations; I see them in her face. But she enjoys having someone else in the house, a presence; a male. Daniel's laughter is low and modulated. He talks softly, smoothly: a dignified radio announcer, an accomplished anchorman.

But when I lived with him, he threw dishes against the wall. And jerked in his sleep, mumbling. And ran out of the house with his hands across his eyes.

After we first made love, he smiled and pulled gently away from me. He put on his shirt and went to the bathroom. I followed and stepped into the shower with him. He faced me, composed, friendly, and frozen. He stood as though guarding something behind him.

Daniel, turn around. I'll soap your back.

I already did.

Then move, I'll stand in the water with you.

He stepped carefully around me.

Daniel, what's wrong? Why won't you turn around?

Why should I?

I'd never seen him with his shirt off. He'd never gone swimming with us, only wading, alone, down Point Reyes Beach. He wore long-sleeved shirts all summer in the California heat.

Daniel, I said, You've been my best friend for months. We could have talked about it.

He stepped backwards, awkwardly, out of the tub and put his shirt on.

I was loading them on copters, he told me. The last one was dead anyway; he was already dead. But I went after him, dragged him in the wind of the blades. Shrapnel and napalm caught my arms, my back. Until I fell, I thought it was the other man's blood in my hands.

They removed most of the shrapnel, did skin grafts for the burns. In three years since, Daniel made love five times; always in the dark. In San Francisco he must take off his shirt for a doctor; tumors have grown in his scars. They bleed through his shirt, round rust-colored spots.

Face-to-face in bed, I tell him I can feel the scars with my fingers. They are small knots on his skin. Not large, not ugly. But he can't let me, he can't let anyone, look: he says he feels wild, like raging, and then he vomits. But maybe, after they remove the tumors—Each time they operate, they reduce the scars.

We spend hours at the veterans' hospital waiting for appointments. Finally they schedule the operation. I watch the black-ringed wall clock, the amputees gliding by in chairs that tick on the linoleum floor. Daniel's doctors curse about lack of supplies; they bandage him with gauze and layers of Band-Aids. But it is all right. I buy some real bandages. Every night I cleanse his back with a sponge and change them.

In my mother's house, Daniel seems different. He has shaved his beard and his face is too young for him. I can only grip his hands.

I show him the house, the antiques, the photographs on the walls. I tell him none of the objects move; they are all cemented in place. Now the bedrooms, my room.

This is it, I say. This is where I kept my Villager sweaters when I was seventeen, and my dried corsages. My cups from the Tastee Freeze labeled with dates and boys' names.

The room is large, blue. Baseboards and wood trim are painted a spotless white. Ruffled curtains, ruffled bedspread. The bed itself is so high one must climb into it. Daniel looks at the walls, their perfect blue and white.

It's a piece of candy, he says.

Yes, I say, hugging him, wanting him.

What about your mother?

She's gone to meet friends for dinner. I don't think she believes what she says, she's only being my mother. It's all right.

We take off our clothes and press close together. But something is wrong. We keep trying. Daniel stays soft in my hands. His mouth is nervous; he seems to gasp at my lips.

He says his lover's name. He says they aren't seeing other people.

But I'm not other people. And I want you to be happy with her.

I know. She knew . . . I'd want to see you.

Then what?

This room, he says. This house. I can't breathe in here.

I tell him we have tomorrow. He'll relax. And it is so good just to see him, a person from my life.

So we only hold each other, rocking.

Later, Daniel asks about my father.

I don't see him, I say. He told me to choose.

Choose what?

Between them.

My father. When he lived in this house, he stayed in the dark with his cigarette. He sat in his blue chair with the lights and television off, smoking. He made little money; he said he was self-employed. He was sick. He grew dizzy when he looked up suddenly. He slept in the basement. All night he sat reading in the bathroom. I'd hear him walking up and down the dark steps at night. I lay in the dark and listened. I believed he would strangle my mother, then walk upstairs and strangle me. I believed we were guilty; we had done something terrible to him.

Daniel wants me to talk.

How could she live with him, I ask. She came home from work and got supper. He ate it, got up and left to sit in his chair. He watched the news. We were always sitting there, looking at his dirty plates. And I wouldn't help her. She should wash them, not me. She should make the money we lived on. I didn't want her house and his ghost with its cigarette burning in the dark like a sore. I didn't want to be guilty. So she did it. She sent me to college; she paid for my safe escape.

Daniel and I go to the Rainbow, a bar and grill on Main Street. We hold hands, play country songs on the jukebox, drink a lot of salted beer. We talk to the barmaid and kiss in the overstuffed booth. Twinkle lights blink on and off above us. I wore my burgundy stretch pants in here when I was twelve. A senior pinched me, then moved his hand slowly across my thigh, mystified, as though erasing the pain.

What about tonight? Daniel asks. Would your mother go out with us? A movie? A bar? He sees me in her, he likes her. He wants to know her.

Then we will have to watch television.

We pop popcorn and watch the late movies. My mother stays up with us, mixing whiskey sours and laughing. She gets a high color in her cheeks and the light in her eyes glimmers up; she is slipping, slipping back and she is beautiful, oh, in her ankle socks, her red mouth and her armor of young girl's common sense. She has a beautiful laughter. She and Daniel end by mock arm wrestling; he pretends defeat and goes upstairs to bed.

My mother hears his door close. He's nice, she says. You've known some nice people, haven't you?

I want to make her back down.

Yes, he's nice, I say. And don't you think he respects me? Don't you think he truly cares for me, even though we've slept together?

He seems to, I don't know. But if you give them that, it costs them nothing to be friends with you.

Why should it cost? The only cost is what you give, and you can tell if someone is giving it back.

How? How can you tell? By going to bed with every man you take a fancy to?

I wish I took a fancy oftener, I tell her. I wish I wanted more. I can be good to a man, but I'm afraid—I can't be physical, not really . . .

You shouldn't.

I should. I want to, for myself as well. I don't think—I've ever had an orgasm.

What? she says, Never? Haven't you felt a sort of building up, and then a dropping off . . . a conclusion? like something's over?

No, I don't think so.

You probably have, she assures me. It's not necessarily an explosion. You were just thinking too hard, you think too much.

But she pauses.

Maybe I don't remember right, she says. It's been years, and in the last years of the marriage I would have died if your father had touched me. But before, I know I felt something. That's partly why I haven't . . . since . . . what if I started wanting it again? Then it would be hell.

But you have to try to get what you want—

No, she says. Not if what you want would ruin everything. And now, anyway. Who would want me?

I stand at Daniel's door. The fear is back; it has followed me upstairs from the dead dark bottom of the house. My hands are shaking. I'm whispering. . . . Daniel, don't leave me here.

I go to my room to wait. I must wait all night, or something will come in my sleep. I feel its hands on me now, dragging, pulling. I watch the lit face of the clock: three, four, five. At seven I go to Daniel. He sleeps with his pillow in his arms. The high bed creaks as I get in. Please now, yes . . . he is hard. He always woke with erections . . . inside me he feels good, real, and I tell him no, stop, wait . . . I hold the rubber, stretch its rim away from skin so it smooths on without hurting and fills with him . . . now again, here, yes but quiet, be quiet . . . oh Daniel . . . the bed is making noise . . . yes, no, but be careful, she. . . . We move and turn and I forget about the sounds. We push against each other hard, he is almost there and I am almost with him and just when it is over I think I hear my mother in the room directly under us—But I am half dreaming. I move to get out of bed and Daniel holds me. No, he says, stay.

We sleep and wake to hear the front door slam.

Daniel looks at me.

There's nothing to be done, I say. She's gone to church.

He looks at the clock. I'm going to miss that bus, he says. We put our clothes on fast and Daniel moves to dispose of the rubber—how? the toilet, no, the wastebasket—He drops it in, bends over, retrieves it. Finally he wraps it in a Kleenex and puts it in his pocket. Jesus, he swears. He looks at me and grins. When I start laughing, my eyes are wet.

I take Daniel to the bus station and watch him out of sight. I come back and strip the bed, bundle the sheets in my arms. This pressure in my chest. . . . I have to clutch the sheets tight, tighter—

A door clicks shut. I go downstairs to my mother. She refuses to speak or let me near her. She stands by the sink and holds her small square purse with both hands. The fear comes. I hug myself, press my hands against my arms to stop shaking. My mother runs hot water, soap, takes dishes from the drainer. She immerses them, pushes them down, rubbing with a rag in a circular motion.

Those dishes are clean, I tell her. I washed them last night.

She keeps washing. Hot water clouds her glasses, the window in front of us, our faces. We all disappear in steam. I watch the dishes bob and sink. My mother begins to sob. I move close to her and hold her. She smells as she used to smell when I was a child and slept with her.

I heard you, I heard it, she says. Here, in my own house. Please, how much can you expect me to take? I don't know what to do about anything . . .

She looks into the water, keeps looking. And we stand here just like this.

1978

ELENA MAKAROVA ❖ Elena Grigorievna Makarova, the daughter of the poet Inna Lisnianskaia, was born in 1951 in Baku, Azerbaijan, where she spent her childhood. She studied at the Surikov Art Institute and the Gorky Institute of World Literature in Moscow. Her position as a kindergarten art teacher and children's art therapist in Moscow led to her collection of essays *Osvobodite slona* (*Free the Elephant,* 1985). Makarova began writing fiction in the 1970s and has produced five volumes of short stories—*Katushka* (*The Spool,* 1978), *Perepolnennye dni* (*Overfilled Days,* 1982), *Leto na kryshe* (*Summer on the Roof,* 1987), *Otkrytyi final* (*The Open Final,* 1989), and *V Nachale bylo detstvo* (*In the Beginning was Childhood,* 1990). In 1990 she emigrated to Israel, where she now lives with her husband and children.

This move was, in her words, "less a decision to emigrate than to return to the land of my own history" and to recover an inner life denied her by the events of the past few years in Moscow. Since resettling in Israel, Makarova, in conjunction with the Prague Jewish Museum, has curated an exhibit of children's artwork from the Terezin concentration camp in commemoration of the artist Friedl Dicker-Brandeis. The exhibit has been shown in Jerusalem, Vienna, and Amsterdam. Makarova currently teaches art to children in Jerusalem and is editing an anthology of Hebrew literature.

Needlefish

ELENA MAKAROVA

On the dance floor, in its illuminated open-air cage, people jerked, shook, tossed loose hair, lay on the ground, yelped, whistled; the local band, all with round glasses, mustaches, and beards, cranked out a Raymond Pauls* tune.

Alka was outside the cage with her sketchbook. She wanted to throw away her pad and pencil, to ooze through the tightly woven netting; to go in there, where people don't observe, but act, where they meet and fall in love, where even her older sister, Inka, is clumsily shifting from one foot to the other with some glossy guy. She would show them what dancing is—how you have to spring lightly from your whole foot; she'd show them a dance like a dream, in which you fly up and fall backwards into an abyss. Inka is a clod, she feels nothing, she's dense; but she's grown up, she's allowed in, while Alka stands behind the netting, trembling feverishly. The pencil won't obey her, a smooth line, nauseating like algebra lessons, crawls out from under her hand like a viper. No, no sketches, no art, nothing can stop her thin legs, her scrawny body. So what if she doesn't wear a bra yet, like Inka, she knows: she's a woman, and it's not her sister, but her, Alka, that the students stare at; they search for her in the crowd, feel her figure with their glance, drown in her enormous eyes.

The line, brittle, broken, cuts the paper in a zigzag. No, she's not drawing Inka. However much she draws Inka it's always dull, dull, dull, and Inka doesn't like it, and Mama says, "It looks like an old lady, not Inka." But Inka is an old lady, a wretched old lady. Alka smudges the line with her finger. She would happily draw with her fingers if they left a mark on the page; she would draw with her palm, her lips, her feet; she would dance on the blank sheet, roll on it. Pencil and paint are intermediaries, she wants to do it without intermediaries, to draw with herself. Alka suddenly saw the world as an endless paper, on which you can draw with your body, your walk; she'll draw something yet, there's so much power in her, so much springing and

* Latvian composer of pop music. Briefly Minister of Culture in Latvia. Very popular among Soviet youth, particularly in the 1970s and 1980s.

running, smoothness and soaring! Alka hid behind her pad; that cow Inka couldn't find a better place to stamp with her guy. In a moment she'll notice her and yell out: "What are you doing here?!" Like a little child, Alka covered her face with the sketchbook, as if she wouldn't be seen that way.

"Snuck over again! What did you lose here?" came Inka's lazy, moist voice.

"You," snapped Alka. "Why did you take my chain?"

She's decked out enough. Her whole chest covered with chains, blouse so tight you can even see her nipples, floor-length flowered skirt. Gypsy! What kind of gypsy are you trying to be, stamping in one place! Puts me to sleep.

You're behind bars, but I'm free. Nobody's shoving me with their backside. I'll teach you how to dance.

Alka wound herself up on her Keds, spun like a top, flew like a cork from a bottle into the illuminated square, swooped like a stork over the drummer's shaggy head, galloped like a horse over trampled grass, shook her ash-colored hair like a mane, beat the grass with her hooves/Keds, twisted her hips and hollow stomach, wound like a snake on the white gravel of the path, choking on the ringing of the silver cymbals, flew up to the stars and fell, as in a dream, into the green abyss of earth.

Nostrils flaring like wings, huge, darkening the night-time expanse; nostrils, swallowing the music, the shouts, the air, the light . . . the edge of a cheek, pink, scarlet, brown . . .

"Home, march!"

"What about Inka?"

The music grows distant, life is over, everything is over.

"But Inka, make Inka go too . . ."

Holding Mama's hand she walks along the road, in the heat, into the stupefying warmth, to bed, into their shared bed, to sleep till morning, lie dully on the pillows, don't turn over, don't move suddenly, Mama sleeps badly, Mama works two jobs, Mama's alone, you should feel for her, feel for her.

"Mama, let's go swimming!"

"It's too late."

"We'll just swim a little . . ."

She runs. The spray flies out from her knees, her skinny knees cut the water like the prow of a ship, water streams past her thighs, rises to the bottom of her bathing suit . . .

"What are you standing there for, let's go!"

. . . tickles her protruding tailbone, then retreats, baring her knees like nail heads. Alka stands still, the path of the moon is silver on the still water,

solitary buoys bob; Alka jumps, pulling her legs high up under her, so that
the splash reaches her chest, her wishbone-like collarbone, her long neck,
goosebumped from cold; and falls flat in the water. She lies on her back, looking at the star filled sky, listens to the music from the dance floor; she dances
in the water, dives and resurfaces. ("Again you got your hair wet, how many
times do you have to be told—either don't dive or wear a bathing cap," that
detested prison to Alka's protruding ears, to those deep shells that catch the
flow of water and the quiet singing of the sand . . .)

"Let's go, let's go!"

. . . Alka swims to the buoy, clasps it in her arms, shoves it under her
chest, and kicks her legs with all her strength. She's a fish, a real needlefish,
with fins and a tail; she cuts the water with her nose, she cuts into everyone
who crosses her path; she's a mermaid, her unbound hair floats out under
the water like seaweed, she's a jellyfish, she envelops the space, she is everything: the stars, the sky, the moon's path, she draws fantastic designs with
her body, she beats the pillow, falls naked on her back, thick lips stir, following some general melody from the dance floor, an arithmetical average of
sound, stamping, crashing of silver cymbals; Mama's nostrils, illuminated by
the moon, dilate evenly like a perch's gills, Mama's cool body pushes Alka to
the edge of the bed, she will not, she will not close her eyes, not until Inka
comes, steals over to the table on tiptoe and starts gobbling bread, smacking
her lips in the darkness. Then Inka's zipper will whistle, her fat legs will step
over her skirt, her synthetic blouse will rustle, sparks will fly when it touches
her slip. Her bra clasp will snap, and two huge pink orbs will roll out shame-
lessly, her panties will fall on the floor, exposing her bulging stomach with its
thick growth at the bottom; she'll slap herself on the hips, making sure that
everything's in place, but everything's always in place on her; she'll lick her
lips—she and that sticky guy were kissing, French kissing. They bit into each
other at the gate of the summerhouse and swooned; she'll wipe her eyelashes
with cream, and two black-stained cotton balls will remain on the oilcloth
on the table. Such vileness, something dishonest about those two tufts of
cotton, Alka hates them, it's as if Inka were peeling off someone else's skin.
The green smell of cucumber lotion will filter out from under the unscrewed
cover, she wants so badly to jump up, grab the bottle from Inka's hands,
and throw it out the window. She'll draw Inka that way—naked, shameless,
and she'll show it in school, at the viewing: here's my summer work—no
stinking fishery, no fishnets, no fishermen with weathered red faces, here's
flesh, the fat, unbridled flesh of her demure sister. What's she like, there in
her drafting office?! Inochka, kitten, sweetie, dearie, so soft, but that Inka of
yours is a slut, only quiet—she lowers her eyes, but she has one thing on her
mind, to squeeze with somebody on the dance floor, no, she doesn't sleep

with anyone, that's what's disgusting: if you're going to love, love with your whole self, not your heels, not your navel, not your teeth, all of you.

What will happen to Alka?! She is disturbed by dreams. She dreams of a skating rink: she glides naked on the ice before the eyes of the senior class, they want to catch her, but she dives from their hands like a fish. Take that, haughty seniors, why did you invite us to your party, then dance with your beautiful ladies while we clung to the wall like orphans. She glides over the ice, drawing white circles with her skates, draws the sun, flowers and trees, draws the art teacher and everybody gasps: oh, it looks just like her! Alka gets down from the edge of the bed and Mama turns on her side. Mama's a seal, streamlined, smooth; Alka shivers when she thinks of how Mama slept with Inka's father, then with Alka's, how it was all sweaty, slippery, in the pictures Mama is beautiful—fine curls, small teeth with ridged edges, smiling with Inka's father, then with Alka's, how can that be? Two times, identically happy, one's enough to choke on. It's base, somehow—first she undresses in front of Inka's father, that smile, so even, natural, as if she were just going to brush her teeth, or go to the bathroom, pliantly belonging to one person, and then just the same way to another. And then this circus trainer, Pyotr Pompelov, damn him, Alka stayed awake on purpose, eavesdropped on their murmuring behind the screen, it's all vulgarity, lies! Mama lets Inka do everything, she thinks it'll make it easier for her to get married in a hurry, and then she and Alka will live in clover in their little pencil-box room. Alka is Mama's joy, talent, star; the artists' academy; Alka is taken to local celebrities: look, here is a still life from 1976, and this one is new, from 1977, a noticeable leap, don't you think?

But Alka would like to fly, swim, dance, what can you put on paper, even with triple talent, what can you tell it, if you have such hands, and a soft chin, and your face is half eyes?

Alka presses on her pedals. Faster, faster, away from the overpopulated summerhouse with the black currants that you can't pick, from the dull thud, like a clock ticking, of the ping-pong ball on the table, from the noise of the commuter train (hooray, Mama and Inka have gone to work!), from the crowding in the communal kitchen; Vaivara; Kauguri;* sand, pines, campground; Tukumsky region. The sea emerged from behind a hill, the nets are golden, they really are beautiful, how many times she's drawn them, hung out on their sticks, dully, without feeling, because she had to, and she's only just now seen them, felt them, mended and mended again, smelling of the sea and fish, tender, like a spider's web, salt sparkles on them like crystal.

* Summer resorts on the Riga coast.

Alka whistled, it's cheerful, the sea is in a haze, has merged with the sky, a huge half-circle with no horizon—that straight line hurts the eye, this way it's smooth, the loving confluence of sea and sky, she forgot her pastels, idiot. Bigaunciems.* Alka jumped off her bike and caught her breath; last night's nightmare of waiting for Inka dissolved in the steamy sky, melted like the dirty smoke spewn into the sky by the fishery chimneys. Alka knows where she's going: to the cozy cafe in Ragaciems. She picked it out long ago, rather, not it, but the deaf-mute. She's going to draw him, and he'll come, he must sense that she's coming, he senses everything, like Alka's beloved Julia, whom they took to the animal hospital in spring, and she howled and struggled in the doctor's hands, old lady, beloved, what did they do to her there? How she had whimpered when they took her away from Alka forever, how she had looked at Mama with inflamed red eyes! Alka had rushed up, screamed, give her back, my mother lied, she said they'd give her a shot for distemper and we'd take her home, my love, Julia, how she had put her tail between her legs, lain down on her paws, sprawled out, and quietly whimpered, meekly, piercingly. She sensed, she sensed, she sensed . . .

The smell of smoked lutsishi tantalized Alka; the coffee machine forced out thick brown liquid in jolts.

"E-o-u!" Trembling fingers (he's already drunk) danced out words of greeting, his fist pressed into his chest, his fingers uncurled like fish, splashed in the air, a happy smile, an animal's mute grin, his finger in the bottle, the edge of his hand to his neck, it's clear, he's drunk. Alka pointed at a seat, and he sat on the edge of the chair like a naughty schoolboy, fell silent, and laid his hands on his round knees in their greasy canvas pants; his suit jacket (last time he had worn a fisherman's jacket, he must have lost it to drink), obviously not his own, puffed out at his chest. No, he's not the same today, she shouldn't have come, he has a defeated look, he must have gone to her. Exactly—he draws a silhouette in the air, smooths full hips with his fingers like a sculptor with a chisel, carves out round breasts, giggles, pressing his pictured silhouette to his chest, and purses his lips in a kiss. Nausea rose to Alka's throat. Damn imaginings. His wife took up with another man, kicked him out—she's kicked him out a hundred times, but still he goes back to her, demeans himself. Alka wants to hit him with her fists, no, it's not him, it's not him she came to draw, it's someone else, her faithful friend, who feels everything like Julia; he told her himself with his hands: you're special, extraordinary, wonderful, we are solitary friends. . . . No, not for anything, you're a stranger, a stranger!

* Summer resort on the Riga coast.

But he just wants his own; he points at the paper: draw, draw. Alka grabbed her pad and pencil box. He ran after her, talking the whole time, cutting the air with his hands, but she had stopped paying attention, stopped understanding, it had all turned into empty gesticulation, nothing.

He ran after her bike, but Alka worked her legs furiously, she panted from hurt and jealousy, as if she were his wife and he had cheated on her, sold out, betrayed her; after all, he had promised he wouldn't go to her any more, why did he beat his chest like that if he was only going to go there, to snivel, to receive a crumb from that bitch. He went to her, he waves his hands, "E-O-U," she answers him, their hands fight, make a racket, then they tangle themselves up in false animal embraces, they fall on the floor or on the dirty bed with broken springs, and everything is forgotten—the insults, the fights. There was no point, no point imagining, trying to be so smart and fancy. Look, all around: regular vacationers with towels over their shoulders, plenty to draw, practice, everybody practices, but she needs the deaf-mute, she has to show off, fool, idiot, get what's coming to you!

The bank is covered with sedge, the low tide has revealed a thick mass of brown silt, the sand is warm and dry. Alka fell down flat in the light brown softness, jumped up and stared at her long, awkward impression, swimming away before her eyes; sand flowed into the imprints of her arms and legs, leaving dents from her head and backside. Alka ran to the water; sand squeaked in her teeth, fell from her hair onto her shoulders; she squeamishly plunged her feet into the warm, heavy silt, stiffened at the slimy touch of the brown slush as it surrounded her ankles. The water was clean, untouched. Alka mournfully imagined how the sand would be stirred up from her step, and the water would become cloudy by the shore as it took in her thin body. She lay in the warm, shallow water, rolled like a wounded fish, beat her fins, gasped at the air with her mouth. Mama is a seal, Mama will leave a seal's silhouette in space; Inka leaves nothing. Inka is a one-celled animal, an amoeba; she leaves dots, dots where her lustful body has touched the space, and what do I leave, what picture do I make? A fish, a bird, a restless animal, Julia, Julia printed herself entirely, from the ends of her turned-up ears to her warm black nose, velvety and tender, from her lean, barren belly to her narrow red paws with their soft pink cushions, all, all, all of her, look, there's my Julia!

Alka ran out of the water, her legs jerking, her teeth chattering; she dried herself with her undershirt, drops fell from under her arms onto the white sheet of paper, the paper puckered, the pencil got stuck in damp yellow holes, ripped it. Alka took another sheet, here, Julia, jump, here's some sugar, she smudged the pencil with her finger, the lean belly cut the page, Julia scrambled out, whimpered, no, she will never forgive that hospital, never; Julia left a sad, mournful picture, and all because of me and Mama, Inka couldn't care less, Inka never once even took her for a walk!

Alka threw off the bottom of her bathing suit, put her jeans on over her bare body, ran to an upside-down boat and clambered onto it, sang, danced, jumped to the sky, where did everybody go, where are all the people, oh, she would have given a free performance for those interested.

But there was nobody interested, there was nobody at all. She jumped down from the boat, raising the sand with her hoof-feet, ran to her bike, dragged it to the level road, and pedaled; her wet hair pressed down on her shoulders like a weight. She pushed on the pedals with all her might, away from the deserted beach, away from herself, her empty, pointless self, needed by nobody.

She braked at the campground. The sun bounced off cars, shining with cold enamel paint. A man in a white cap and ripped jeans was spraying a red Moskvich with a hose.

"Hi."

The hose faltered in the man's hands, jerked, and a cold stream drenched Alka from head to foot.

"I'm sorry."

Small black pupils wandered in immense blue whites of his eyes; thin lips parted, a mouth like a garage, out of which drove white cars of laughter which sped up, gathering momentum. Alka's mouth surrendered, her lower lip dropped to her chin, and they roared with laughter, rolled, and simultaneously fell silent.

"There's nothing funny." Alka turned her headlights on the man. They lit up, illuminated the already bright noon, with a child's despair; water ran from her jeans, there was something indecent about the puddle forming beneath her; childhood shame pierced her. ("What have you done, you'll have to change your pants again, shame on you!")

"I'll take you home."

The man put her bike on top of his car, it shrank under the tight straps. Alka sat in front; it was wet under her feet, in the cold swamp frogs croaked, ducks quacked, and reeds grew.

Alka introduced herself formally, giving her name and patronymic. The man had a funny name: Erast. She had never heard that name in her life.

"Can I draw a picture to remember you by?"

"An artist!" hemmed Erast, and began talking about drawing, and about graphic artists he knew.

Alka didn't listen to him; she was looking at his chiseled profile, his cleft chin; she fell in love with him completely, with her entire self, with her wet jeans, with the swamp under her feet, with her braless chest. And he loved her, she knew that, otherwise he would simply have apologized, he wouldn't have bothered with her bike, wouldn't have bothered driving her home, and going on about artists.

"This is my Julia. I love her more than anybody."

"You love everyone!" sighed Erast, and stopped the car at her house. "Change your clothes and drink some hot tea."

He clapped her on her wet shoulder; her shoulder burst into flame, blazed. Alka leaped up the steps, hurried to throw off her wet, burning shirt, pressed her wound with her hand, licked it, like Julia when the boxer bit her.

"You're not afraid of me?"

"Of you? I'm afraid of myself, everything's in me."

They lay on the hot sand, the pressed chintz squeezed Alka's chest, whispered to her that she was a woman, a small, skinny woman; it seemed to her that he was staring at that piece of cloth, under which was nothing, all the girls in her class had something there, and she had nothing, a flat plain with two buttons.

Alka was silent. Something indistinct filled her to the brim; the fresh milk sky, the sun beating on her closed lids, under which it seemed as if a fire burned; one moment she was enraptured with her own unimaginable nerve, and would fly, light, weightless, over the beach—the next moment that nerve of hers would throw her from a high springboard, she would fall into the sea, choking on salt water.

"You're a strange girl."

"I'm extraordinary. Something's definitely going to happen to me."

"Nonsense. I thought the same thing, then nothing ever happened. Precisely nothing."

Alka turned on her side and looked at Erast; for the first time she looked him all over calmly, impartially, as if he were a stranger; she wouldn't have dared if his eyes hadn't been closed. A person like any other; he's lived this long, and nothing's ever happened to him.

"I'm going."

Alka pulled her sweater on as she went, jumped into her jeans; she ran from him as she had run from the deaf-mute. She squeezed herself into the bus as it left, got into the back door grabbing on to some vacationer; some loathsome knob stuck into her chest, the pressed chintz bit into her body, and she thought she would suffocate from the sweaty air in the bus.

At the gate to the summerhouse was a red Moskvich.

Alka softened as if the bones had been taken out of her legs, fell on the grass, and began sobbing loudly. He put her in the car (what would she get from Mama—all the neighbors saw), she grew into the seat, she was becoming absent, immersed in the rocking motion, in sleep.

"Look, I drew you first."

Alka came to and looked at the paper. A broken line, like the one that had leapt out in a zigzag from under her hand the day before yesterday, described Alka's silhouette, her swooping over the drummer, her kicking like an untamed steed, a smooth picture of a snake.

"Did you see me or something? You drew with my line!"

They got out of the car and went down into a ditch. Alka's feet drowned in velvet moss; thickets of raspberries glowed red among sparse aspen trees; they stuffed their mouths with raspberries, pink juice trickled down her chin, neck, and chest, she rubbed raspberries on her stomach, pieces of raspberries rolled down her legs, the green depth of the woods absorbed Alka, sucked her in like quicksand. She's a wood spirit, that's who she is, she lives in the forest and plays a reed pipe, the squirrels love her, she's a tree, slender, fragile, she's everything.

As if in slow motion they swam into the moss, Alka lost her mind, went mad, their raspberry bodies beat against each other like moths on a window-pane; a needlefish entered her body, tore through her, the scorching sun flooded her with raspberry heat, she's a fish, a bird, she has revived him from the dead, she has breathed all of herself into him, into sleep, into nonbeing. Now she is not her own, not herself; that bitter and happy thought crawled in goosebumps over her body.

Alka drew and drew, she didn't hear her mother, didn't see Inka, there it is, a weak reflection appears on the paper, pieces of chalk crumble in her hand, raspberries, green, a needlefish goes into her, the velvet paper drinks in the soft pastel shades . . .

"Who do you go riding in a car with!"

"Mama, stop it," Inka's conciliatory voice. "She just went for a ride."

"And what's that?!" Mama's fingernail bites into the velvet smooth paper.

With her finger Alka rubs out the pink chalk chest, the brown button nipples. She spins, dances before the easel, here, for you, sleepy seals with your even smiles!

Nostrils flare, cheek turns pink, red, brown, hand gives her a ringing slap on the face.

"Idiot, you're gonna bring home a kid in your skirt!"

The words bounce off Alka like ping-pong balls from the table. They relate to her like πr_2 relates to a circle, alien, abstract algebra, the dullness of theorems, it is given, therefore it must be proved. Everything has been given to Alka, she doesn't need to prove anything. She's a woman, happy, wonderful, she has learned everything, entirely, Mama's secret is nothing now, empty nonsense, she slides down the banister, runs across the road, she's a butterfly, a one-day butterfly, she will leave behind a flapping of wings, she has received everything, completely, the rest is tedium, dreary habit, "nothing ever happened all my life," she chokes, water flows into her open mouth, suffocates her, takes her in, she's a fish, a needlefish, she leaps from the sea, her fins, like wings, raise her above the water, she soars, she's stronger than anybody on earth, because she's stronger than herself, hair like seaweed, like a jellyfish's tentacles, like wings, she flies over the water, she pours into it, grows heavy, and becomes emptiness, herself, nothing and everything.

1982

Translated by Lise Brody

The World of Our Mothers

ADELE MARIE BARKER

Someplace not far from Charleston in the southwest part of West Virginia, deep in coal-mining country, roads thread through towns with names like Corinne and Jean, Dorothy and Ethel. Named for the women who were born and died there, they are company towns, distinguished by the same used sofas abandoned on porches and the oversized televisions in the living rooms where someone like Corinne or Jean, Dorothy or Ethel might have sat watching their soaps. I never knew these women, but I have had my share of driving their roads on the way to nowhere, and I always suspected that whoever they were, they had no more chance of getting out than did the dust from the mines that encircled their towns, only to be trapped by the surrounding hills. Somewhere in this state, maybe over roads like the ones I've described, Jayne Anne Phillips's protagonist comes home to her mother.

In a town somewhat more prosperous than those in which Corinne or Dorothy lived, desperation cloaks itself in acts of charity regularly doled out by the Ladies' Auxiliary or the Veterans of Foreign Wars, or in the endless knitting of afghans before the television at night. It is a town like this that becomes a metaphor for the central relationship of the mother and daughter in Phillips's story. Like the town it depicts, "Home" is a tightly interwoven texture of affection and entrapment. The inescapable attachments it represents are all the stronger because they are unnamed and because the cycle of love and bondage is played out under the guise of anything other than what it is.

Narrated by the twenty-three-year-old protagonist who returns to the home she has never really left, Phillips's complex, compelling story explores the dynamics of the mother-daughter relationship as part of an invisible triangle created by the lingering, unresolved presence of the father. Married to the one, pursuing the other, he implicitly forced the daughter to "choose," as if in a courtship, between him and the mother. Even before he left for good he repeatedly wandered out of bounds, straying into his daughter's room and "pressing himself against [her] thigh, pretending solicitude." And despite his departure his presence lingers, at once dividing and drawing the two women together in an unspoken closeness.

Both mother and daughter have internalized the wounds from this family romance. The mother has sanitized her world into a sex-free environment where she sits counting her stitches night after night as if to keep herself on the "right track," where her own desires and hurt can be safely contained. In her various obsessive ablutions she seeks to wash away all that frightens her. Her own suppressed desire for a man around the house finds its safest expression in a nonthreatening paternal figure, the avuncular person of Walter Cronkite, who dispenses wisdom to America's heartland every night, setting the topic to be discussed, mixing morality with meat and potatoes over America's dinner tables. Unlike the father, Cronkite knows his place, remaining safely ensconced inside the television set. No midnight wanderings for him.

If the mother has dealt with her own hurt by seeming to recede from all that smacks of sexuality, the daughter initially flaunts what she fears most, "going to bed with every man [she] take[s] a fancy to," as the mother complains. Yet despite the daughter's seeming openness on the subject of sex, she comes to admit that she has never truly been able to "be physical" with any man. Hence the mother's suppression of her own desire ironically finds its closest corollary in the daughter's unfulfilled sex life, a bond Phillips's heroine does her best to deny. Further, as if deliberately refuting Cronkite's desexualized and therefore acceptable presence in the house, the young woman flagrantly resexualizes him in her mother's presence, explaining his recent absence from the evening news as the result of sexual dalliance: "Maybe he's in love with a young girl."

The daughter's own sexual life has become both the manifestation of her frigidity and the means by which she has concealed it. At the heart of her fear of being "physical" is the probability that she herself was seduced, in childhood, by her own father, an event made more troubling by her incomplete repression of it and her vulnerability before all that it represents. The ghost of the father is omnipresent, hovering just beneath the surface of the protagonist's consciousness. His haunting presence informs her comment to her mother about Walter Cronkite's supposed affair with the "young girl," for it is precisely the figure of the older man and the young girl that has most deeply scarred the daughter. The ghost of the father also haunts her relationship with her ex-lover Daniel. Significantly, of all her old lovers, she chooses to see and to sleep with Daniel, whose shrapnel-scarred back makes him as afraid as she of physical closeness and thus becomes at once the sign of safety and the visible external manifestation of her own hidden scars.

Phillips gives shape to the young woman's unresolved relations with the father through the dream, which merges indecipherably with the *Reader's Digest* story about the girl who barely escapes the terrors of the grizzly's maw. Couched within the story of how two teenagers elude a scene of primal terror are all the configurations of sexual and domestic relations that are ordered and suppressed within the protagonist's life and perhaps within society in general. Happily rescued from the arms of the grizzly, the young woman, Sharon, a fallen contemporary incarnation of the virginal Victorian hearth angel, lives to serve her boyfriend food on a tray in the hospital. According to the story she has managed to suppress all memory of her abduction by the grizzly except, tellingly, for the canvas of the tent that fell across her face like a veil.

Though the story sparks the daughter's dream about the father, it is not merely a causative prefiguration of the dream. Rather, Phillips reverses the predictable pattern, suggesting that the protagonist's own memories of the father intrude upon her reading of the story even before the dream begins. At the point at which "the grizzly drags [the girl] quietly, quietly . . . ," the protagonist in Phillips's own larger story of seduction and entrapment drags her own fantasies and recollections into the act of interpretation, transforming the text from a simple adventure yarn to an account of sexual rivalry between the boyfriend and the bear, who in abducting the girl also becomes her solicitous seducer.

The ambiguous role of the young "virginal" woman and the choices she must make are highlighted in this story by the two male figures who vie for her. As the story makes explicit, her future is with the teenage boy whom she will compliantly serve in the hospital, reenacting the role to which women have traditionally been enjoined as part of the tacit agreement that underwrites sex and marriage. The archetypal image of the bear suggests that should she renege on this unspoken social contract, her alternative is a retreat into the arms of the father, at once protector and voracious seducer.

That the bear's seduction of the girl is also, by implication, the father's seduction of the daughter is underlined by the origin of the name Sharon. Taken from the Song of Songs (II:1–2), the line "Sharon, his rose" imagistically recalls the biblical line "I am the rose of Sharon, and the lily of the valley," imparting to the girl's seduction both poetic nuance and biblical validation. The passage from the Song of Songs continues with the line "as the lily among thorns, so is my love among the daughters," implicitly linking the bear's appropriation of Sharon as his beloved to the father's appropriation of her as daughter. It is here that we come to feel most intensely the intrusion of Phillips's protagonist into the text. Suddenly the tale departs from its own stated aims and seems to ascribe thoughts to the bear as Sharon lies in his "furred arms." Phillips's protagonist gives free rein to her own repressed imagination and allows herself to enter the text by projecting onto the bear human feelings that reflect her thoughts about her own seduction years before. The bear's promise to care for Sharon "all the days of his life" suggests not only abduction masquerading as solicitude but the enormous seductive power of the world he represents.

That power derives from other associations as well. The image of the bear also has roots in Native American traditions. In many tribal narratives the bear is identified not only with the seducer but with the wild, uncivilized, untrammeled forces in both the natural world and the self, forces that call us back both to nature and to what is natural and unconstrained within us.[1] Drawing on these ancient traditions, Phillips cuts at the heart of the values of "decency" and propriety with which middle-class American society has invested itself. To be part of those values in the world of Phillips's characters is to marry a boy like Jason, whose football letter suggests his bourgeois legitimacy, or the teenage boy in the tent whose values, like those represented by Walter Cronkite, are predictable and safe. The bear thus becomes the force that threatens that value system and awakens in the young girl desires long dormant. In that sense the grizzly comes to represent not merely the father, whose greater power is in itself a form of incestuous seduction, but the bear within the girl, who chafes at the world commissioned for her by those who would read of her adventures on the pages of *Reader's Digest*.

The poetic license the bear takes by desiring "to care for her all the days of her life . . ." and the thinly concealed biblical element creates a disturbing parallel between seduction/abduction and paternal solicitude as the latter is used to legitimize the former. Thus when the father appears to Phillips's protagonist in the actual dream sequence, his own apparent seduction of the daughter simply makes explicit what was already implied in the earlier story. For whatever else the story is about, through the narrative intervention of the young woman as reader into the text we are made to see the complexities of the daughter's seduction, feared yet desired, paralyzing yet in some indecipherable way also liberating.[2]

What emerges in this dream is the repressed life of Phillips's protagonist who, for all her bravado about sex, is unable to step outside what both frightens and tantalizes her. Her fear and repression find their most explicit outlet in the relationship with the mother, who becomes both the daughter's natural rival and her double as she acts out what her daughter can only repress. The mother-daughter rivalry is most apparent in the scene in which Daniel comes for a visit. Sensing their similarity, he brings the rivalry to the surface by asking, "Would your mother go out with us?" That rivalry unfolds during the course of the evening as the mother "stays up with us, mixing whiskey sours and laughing," and finally plays the role more appropriate to the daughter as she and Daniel mock arm wrestle, with Daniel pretending defeat. The scene is a prelude to a seduction. Vying for power, the male lets the female win, giving her a false sensation of control, only to retreat to the bedroom, where the real power relations will unfold. But Phillips, having turned the seduction scene around once, comes full circle as the daughter, not the mother, follows Daniel upstairs. The daughter, however, falls victim to a different kind of seduction, that by the father, embodied in the same forces that "will come in [her]sleep . . . dragging, pulling." This seduction began earlier in the evening through her own gradual withdrawal as she allowed her mother to take over her role in the relationship with Daniel.

If the father's unarticulated presence has set up an unacknowledged but divisive rivalry between mother and daughter, that rivalry paradoxically strengthens the bond between them. It is not simply the collusion between mother and daughter which is at issue here but a Dostoyevskian kind of doubling in which each reflects forces that the other has deeply suppressed within herself. Significantly, the young woman's most sensual moments are those in which she describes the body of her own mother, transferring the sensuality repressed within her to the one person who will not injure, scar, or reject her: "I dry her back, her beautiful back which is firm and unblemished. Beautiful, her skin." This doubling often takes the form of role reversal as Phillips attributes to one character traits or ideas that might seem more appropriate to the other. "I don't think I've ever had an orgasm," says the protagonist. "'What?' [the mother] says, "Never? haven't you felt a sort of building up, and then a dropping off . . . a conclusion? like something's over?' 'No, I don't think so.'" Ironically, it is the mother here who reveals her own superior knowledge of the world to which the daughter presumably has the key. The daughter can talk about the mechanics of sex, but only the mother has experienced its delights.

Through these complex webs of bondings, rivalries, and doublings, Phillips comes to suggest the real nature of "home" as it is understood in this story. So far from the bourgeois American ideal celebrated on the television commercials that punctuate the Cronkite news, it is a world in which the father becomes a figure of both fear and attraction, both protector and seducer, just as the mother becomes the force that undermines the very values she seemingly upholds.

In the final moments of the narrative, the male having once more departed from their lives, mother and daughter face each other alone over the kitchen sink. In this last scene all familial positions seem as steamy and obscure as the scene itself. Comforting the mother as a mother would a sobbing child, the daughter once more exchanges roles with her. In this exchange the mother once again retreats into the sanitized Victorian world whose values she had espoused in the opening moments of the story. Similarly, Phillips's young protagonist again figures as the threat to that morality, upon which she has intruded by bringing sex into the house. On one level, their relations are resolved once more into a reflection of conventional social mores, according to which home is the place domesticated and protected by those who rule over it, and the child acts as the force of rebellion, challenging those deeply instilled official codes. What distinguishes Phillips's narrative from the values of the environment it depicts is her suggestion that this conventional middle-class morality and the configuration of safe relationships on which this world is predicated contain the seeds of their own rupture. In the final moments Phillips's narrative reveals its own insights about both the fluidity and the complexity of the "home"-grown relationships the daughter must negotiate.

"Home" is finally a story of retreat, the mother's from her own sexuality and desires, a daughter's from her seeming emancipation. That the two chronicles are woven so closely together that the one becomes almost a mirror reflection of the other suggests not only the depth of the bonding between the two women but the degree to which this young woman's identity ultimately becomes indistinguishable from that of the mother. Perhaps because that selfhood was never fully formed, Phillips was reluctant to give her protagonist a name. Wounded by what she cannot even articulate, the daughter withdraws into the mother's safe haven, into a world in which images of the two women resolve themselves into each other. And that, for Phillips, is what it means to come home.

If Phillips's story is that of an incomplete initiation in which the ties of hurt and love bind her protagonist to all that home represents long after she has seemingly distanced herself from it, Elena Makarova's story "Needlefish" is ironically the story of a young girl's weaning of herself from that same place, from that source of sexuality and power, long before she ever, in fact, leaves her home. Written in 1978, Makarova's story sensitively explores through the person of Alka, a young girl poised on the verge of pubescence, that unarticulated region where art, power, and sexuality all coalesce.

Makarova's story traces the prehistory of the artist and the woman. Waiting nervously to enter that secret world of adulthood which both attracts and repels her, Alka sees the world in terms of line and form, reflecting on the "silhouettes" those closest to her leave "in space": "Mama leaves a seal's silhouette." Inka, the clod, will leave nothing. Alka herself thinks not so much of what she will become as of what form she will leave once she is gone.

Much of Alka's world is also shaped by feelings. She responds to her own approaching womanhood with a rush of emotion that cascades over itself as she heads from boat to beach to bicycle, transforming herself, shaman-like, into other worlds and other bodies. She swoops "like a stork over the drummer's shaggy head, gallop[s] like a horse over trampled grass, [shakes] her ash-colored hair like a mane . . . [flies] up to the stars and [falls], as in a dream, into the green abyss of earth." Fearing her approaching womanhood even as she accedes to it, she revels one moment in her own uniqueness and power, only to be overcome by her own emptiness and nothingness the next. Through these rich descriptions of Alka's emotional life Makarova creates an underlying tension between Alka's own passions and the sexuality and power with which she is grappling but which she is unable to name.

The world of adulthood Alka is soon to enter is also the world of sexuality and thus implicitly a world of power and subordination. Recalling her mother's past loves, Alka begins to sense the dialectic of domination and submission that lay at the heart of her relationship with the men whom she had loved. Remembering that her mother had been two times identically happy, "belonging to one person and then just the same way to another," Alka is concerned not so much that her mother has loved several men as that she has "pliantly" given herself to each.

It is this same notion of compliancy and possession that subconsciously infuriates Alka as she witnesses her older sister's participation in the rite of courtship. Alka watches at night at the seashore as Inka dances with her "glossy guy" (*s losniashchimsia tipom*) inside the *voliere*, where Alka is not allowed. For Alka the netting of the *voliere* becomes a cage which locks her out of the world of adulthood and sexuality. But it is also the place which, as Alka intuitively senses, locks Inka in as well. What Alka witnesses is the underside of this adult world the entrance into which she so craves, the side where women pay a price for their own coming of age. Inka gets to be courted and gets to be unattainable, but the price she must pay for the state she now enjoys, if her mother's example is any guide, is her own eventual subordination in the marriage unit.

If Alka is confused and thus put off by her sister's participation in this secret rite of courtship, she is similarly repelled by the giving and withholding of one's sexuality in the courtship process. Alka is disgusted both by the physical manifestations of her sister's sexuality and by its commodification, which she intuitively senses. She is vaguely aware of her mother's own complicity in Inka's commodification: "Mama lets Inka do everything, she thinks it'll make it easier for her to get married in a hurry, and then she and Alka will live in clover in their little pencil-box room." But what she cannot fully articulate is Inka's complicity in her own commodification, as she leads the "glossy guys" on, going far but never too far. Not yet familiar with the rules or the semiotics of courtship, Alka remains for the moment an idealist: "If you're going to love, love with your whole self, not your heels, not your navel, not your teeth, all of you."

Secretly fascinated by this world from which she is thus far excluded, Alka also strives to distance herself from it. What in her view saves her from the cycle of power, complicity, and commodification into which her mother and her sister have been lured is her art. This is what makes her fly, makes her live differently, makes her capable of leaving an imprint upon the world that Inka never will. But what Alka fails to understand as she strains to break free is her own emerging vulnerability to that world. Makarova suggests that ultimately the same dialectics of power that govern the world of sexuality likewise lie at the heart of the artist's relationship to her own art. Alka draws out of her need to impose an image of her morality on the world around her. She goes back to draw her faithful friend, the deaf-mute, so long as he conforms to her image of how she believes he ought to lead his life and ratifies her idealized image of herself as "special." It is she, the artist, who is able to give him shape with her pad and pencils. And as long as he remains symbolically as well as literally mute—that is, as long as he conforms to the image she has created of him—Alka can draw him and thus effect an illusory control over her artistic materials, her subjects, and her life.

But even as she strains as an artist to imprint her will upon the canvas, the other artist standing behind her, Makarova herself, suggests through the image of the deaf-mute that finally the ability of Alka or any artist to shape and control her material is finite at best, for in art as in life both will and morality ultimately yield to the stronger force of sexuality. It is the deaf-mute's defiance of Alka's sexual codes, the fact that he has demeaned himself and gone back to the wife who had "kicked him out a hundred times," that turns him in Alka's imagination into an object of revulsion. Once again it is that unarticulated element of power and bondage inherent within sexual relations that repels Alka. Sex is power. The deaf-mute's wife lures the husband back through that power. By imagining herself as the true wife whom the deaf-mute betrays, Alka, panting "from hurt and jealousy," gets to flirt with the idea of adulthood and sex without actually having to cross over into the world it encompasses. Thus, in ways that Alka can only vaguely begin to sense, the two worlds of art and sexuality are closely conflated in her relationship with the deaf-mute. In returning to the wife and having sex with her, the deaf-mute simultaneously not only engages in the act that Alka most fears but in doing so transgresses her artistic credo, which demands that the artist control her material by molding its morality.

If the themes of art and sexuality in the scene with the deaf-mute seemingly skirt each other unresolved as Alka flees from what she cannot control, in her encounter with Erast Makarova attempts to resolve these notions of power for Alka and implicitly for herself as both woman and artist. The scene is laden with sexual imagery from that first moment when Erast sprays her with the hose to the final moment in which the culmination of desire is symbolically reenacted as the two go raspberry picking in the "green depth of the woods."

In choosing the name Erast, Makarova suggests the complexity of the world Alka is about to enter, where desire and power mingle for both the artist and the woman. Alka has not heard Erast's name before, but Makarova's Russian readers have. Who can forget the name of the spoiled aristocratic cad in Karamzin's eighteenth-century tale of seduction and abandonment *Poor Liza* (*Bednaia Liza*), in which Erast loses his heart to a poor peasant girl, only to abandon her and become the cause of her eventual suicide? Here is the modern incarnation of the old story of the innocent young girl first encountering her own desires for a bewitching young man who may or may not attempt to seduce her. Alka falls for him "completely, with her entire self, with her wet jeans, with the swamp under her feet, with her braless chest," and thus begins to enter that adult world whose dialectics of power and desire she had so feared. But it is not just Alka the prepubescent girl to whom this is happening but Alka the artist as well. As such she strives to give permanence to what is happening (can I draw a picture to remember you by?), thereby effecting a kind of elusive control over both body and canvas by giving form to both her desire and her vulnerability.

If in the scene with the deaf-mute Alka flees from a morality she cannot control, in her encounter with Erast flight is no longer possible because the sexuality she is up against this time is her own. Her own desire races through her like a needlefish (*ryba-igla*) while she strives somehow elliptically to control it through her canvas. Art and sex become intertwined as Alka attempts through the one to harness the other. But the awful moment for her arrives when Erast, throwing her into the car in a gesture suggestive of coercion, says, "Look, I drew you first." It is the moment in which Alka intuitively grasps that the fate of one's body and one's canvas are not so different after all, that desire in sex as in art is ultimately resolved into relations of power. Her art, which she perceives as the thing that frees her from Mama's, Inka's, and the deaf-mute's pliant subordination, becomes sadly an instrument of her own subordination as Erast claims his right over her by having been the first to draw—literally to represent and possess—her.

These issues come together in the final scene. As Alka and Erast descend into the moss, Makarova intricately explores both the potential and the impotence of the artist to control her own world. Here the moment of the young girl's sexual initiation takes symbolic form through the image of the needlefish entering her body as the "raspberry bodies beat against each other like moths on a windowpane." The moment of initiation is described in such a way that as readers we are persuaded both of its actual occurrence and of its function as a by-product of Alka's imagination. Makarova deliberately leaves the moment vague. What is important is that Alka—perhaps physically but most certainly imaginatively—has experienced that rite of initiation she had both sought and feared: "She's a woman, happy, wonderful, she has learned everything, entirely."

Makarova suggests in this complex and moving conclusion the duality of Alka's entry into the world of womanhood that simultaneously liberates and oppresses her. Something flickers disturbingly at the end as Alka both "soars over the sea" and then "grows heavy, and becomes emptiness, herself, nothing and everything." Commingling images of heaviness and flight, Makarova suggests the complexity of the world Alka has entered. In metaphors reminiscent of Inka's ponderous "cow"-footed plodding around the dance floor, Alka too grows heavy as she "pours herself into the sea . . . becoming nothing and everything." In this image Makarova subtly suggests the persistence of the world which Alka had most feared. For to become part of its dimensions is to be caught up in the corollaries of power and subordination, complicity and compliance which are the oil that make the machinery run.

What lifts this ending out of the pedestrian world to which Alka's mother and sister belong are the images of flight with which Makarova figures the moment of initiation and its aftermath. If she enters a world predicated on relations of power and submission, Alka also manages to free herself of that world and to demythologize it ("Mama's secret is nothing now, empty nonsense") as she leaps from the sea and rises above its waters, transforming the experience shamanistically even as she gives in to it. It is Alka's imaginative world, her power as an artist, that enables her to liberate herself from all that shackles her. The fact that the images of her freedom come out of her own imaginative experience suggests that ultimately she fashions her own pleasure as an artist, makes her own world, is responsible for her own liberation.

Like Stephen Dedalus in Joyce's *Portrait of the Artist as a Young Man*, Alka sees her art as a means of flight from a world to which she cannot conform. Alka's and Stephen's worlds are both self-engendered, created from within. Thus it is that Alka's physical joy at her sexual initiation becomes at the same time a metaphor for the artist's own release as she comes to derive her greatest pleasure from engendering her own world.

It is important that Makarova has Alka depict the moment of real or imagined sexual penetration through the image of the same needlefish with which she had earlier described herself and her own power as she swam strongly and effortlessly in the water. Toward her mother's warning that she's going to end up pregnant, Alka remains detached. For whatever else may have transpired in the woods, her pleasure ultimately has its source in her own creativity. As such her initiation into womanhood is raised and transformed from the awkward confines of the dance cage and the bedroom into a world of flight as "she leaps from the sea, her fins, like wings, [raising] her above the water."

As with Joyce's portrait of the artist as a young man, so with Makarova's portrait of the artist as a young woman there is something affectionately ironic. For like the still immature but self-aggrandizing Stephen, Alka imagines herself having found the secrets to everything, while remaining to the reader decidedly young—unfinished, immature, and blinded by her very insights.

But Makarova's greatest irony is perhaps reserved for the implicit self-portrait of herself, through Alka, as both woman and artist. Given the recent events in Makarova's own life, the story assumes a double irony. Though her narrative focuses on the world of an adolescent girl and though she herself was still a young woman when she wrote it, it reveals no naiveté about the harsh realities that the artist confronted in her country in the 1970s. Makarova sees all too well—and how could she not?—the duality of art as both oppressor and suppressor in the Soviet Union. It is Erast's comment, "I drew you first," that jolts us as it does Alka into the realization that art does not merely give us wings to fly but can be used to clip those wings as well. Like the world of sexuality with which it shares its lot, it both liberates and subordinates as it mingles pleasure with pain.

This reflexivity has yet another dimension. In 1990 Makarova emigrated to Israel, where at this writing she continues to live. Seen in the light of her decision to leave the country where she had been born and raised, "Needle-fish" seems to prefigure Makarova's own artistic sojourns. Alka's internal emigration as an artist anticipates the author's own eventual departure from the Soviet Union. Makarova's self-reflexive portrait is not merely that of an artist in retreat from what she cannot condone and control but also that of one who perceives her own artistic freedom to be dependent on the degree of her own estrangement from the institutions and mores that stifle authentic creative expression. If it is Makarova the creator who draws for us the portrait of Alka and gives her the wings to become an artist, it is then Alka the artist who shares those wings with her creator. In taking artistic flight, both she and her author had already accomplished the most important work of emigration.

It is not surprising that both Phillips and Makarova have chosen to deal with images of flight in "Home" and "Needlefish," for both stories implicitly reflect how that notion resolved itself in the personal lives of the two young women who wrote them. Phillips fled the world she describes on the pages of "Home"—first to Iowa and then later to New York. Significantly enough, however, her internal geography as a writer so far is the world of Appalachia. While remaining apart from the values and the people she depicts, she nevertheless returns to them both as the subjects of her own art and as part of her past to which, as a writer, she strives to give permanence in her fiction. Thus in some important way, even while physically distant from the world of her childhood, she has retained her bonds to it.

For Makarova the notion of the writer's escape may be even more complex, for her internal exile from Russian society began before she ever started writing: by both birth and cultural positioning she experienced numerous forms of displacement from a society which she never felt was hers to begin with. As a Jew she was born an outsider to Russian society. As an artist, by virtue of the canons laid down by the official literary establishment, she necessarily walked the thin line between acceptance and rejection. Finally, as a woman writer she violated canons of what was deemed proper and appropriate: "Needlefish" is only one of the many examples of her insistence on treating subject matter, especially explicit sexuality, which the guardians of the socialist canon traditionally deemed unfit for literary texts.

Makarova's answer to the Soviet world that stifled her was, like Phillips's, flight. But like many artists in the Soviet Union in the seventies and early eighties she chose her own internal emigration before physical flight had actually become a possibility for her. Makarova's escape from "home" may have been more permanent than Phillips's—perhaps because the stakes were so much higher. If Phillips writes about those who never effect a true separation from the world she describes, Makarova creates portraits of young women who find ways to transcend their surroundings and indeed take flight before they are totally aware of the world that constricts them. But what they lack in maturity they more than make up for in their own keen intuition that in a world that represses from the outside, one's only liberation is to be found through emigration within.

The Russian poet Joseph Brodsky, himself living in exile in the United States, once observed that his childhood spent in the Russian city he called "Peter" (Leningrad/St. Petersburg), built on foreign models antithetical to the rest of Russia, prepared him for his exile in the West. To that Makarova might add that being born, like Brodsky, a Jew in the Soviet Union was in itself enough to prepare her for emigration, forcing her to pack her intellectual and imaginative bags early on in life. It is a pattern with which all Soviet Jews were familiar, but perhaps their poets and writers knew it best of all.

Notes

1. The image of the bear has deep roots in Native American folklore as it does in the folklore of Russia. The bear as symbolic of both internal and external forces of seduction is conveyed powerfully by Pushkin in Tatiana's dream in *Eugene Onegin*. Silko's "Story from Bear Country" (*Storyteller*, 204–9) draws upon traditional notions of the bear as that which seduces us away from the civilizing forces within us:

> The problem is
> you will never want to return
> Their beauty will overcome your memory
> like winter sun
> melting ice shadows from snow
> And you will remain with them
> locked forever inside yourself
>> your eyes will see you
>> dark shaggy and thick. (Silko 204–5)

2. See Gallop; Sadoff; and Zwinger. All note that although the oedipal story has conditioned Western thinking on sexual taboos and incest, the daughter is equally bound by these same taboos, yet her desire and seduction have been veiled by psychoanalysts and critics alike.

Hopes and Nightmares of the Young

MAYA KORENEVA

Both Jayne Anne Phillips and Elena Makarova started writing in the 1970s, a decade which, unlike the previous ones, aroused little hope in either the Soviet Union or the United States. Yet it was not a period of great social tensions or catastrophes. In the USSR, after a short-lived "thaw," a time began which later came to be known as "the period of stagnation." In the United States, the end of the infamous Vietnam war was followed by the Watergate revelations and ensuing scandal. Both countries witnessed the political manipulation of ideals and spiritual values by members of the establishment who exploited their positions to advance their own immediate interests. These circumstances aggravated the general atmosphere of disappointment and disillusionment: in both countries, individuals felt ever more acute alienation from societies that had chosen unrighteous ways to achieve unrighteous goals. Earlier concern with social issues gave way to a desire to shut oneself up in one's own individual world, to guard it against society's aggression, and to turn it into a shelter where one could hide from social storms.

This fatigue in public consciousness was manifest not only in the pervasive desire for withdrawal into a private world but also in notions about the nature of that world. Where spiritual values were distorted, disgraced, or discredited, the whole sphere of the mind and spirit fell under suspicion, coming to be regarded as totally unreliable, deceptive as quicksand. The only thing one apparently could still trust was one's own senses, which seemed to restore the lost connection with the world from which man had been severed in all other respects. Reliance on the senses let one believe in the reality of one's own existence. Hence the search for moral and spiritual values gave way to a search for personal satisfaction, which became a sort of motto of a whole generation during the seventies. The odyssey to achieve self-knowledge through sexual intercourse or drugs became the individual equivalent of the space odyssey to conquer the unexplored expanses of the universe. Where spiritual bonds do not exist, people remain atoms moving haphazardly in space, their contacts momentary and inconsequential. Rootless emotions, receiving insufficient sustenance, cannot develop into genuine feelings, and the physical sensations that dominate existence continually demand greater and greater stimuli. Sex and drugs, the strongest of these, seem attractive if only because they allow one momentarily to forget one's loneliness. But the forgetfulness is an illusion, the pursuit of which ultimately drives people further apart rather than building human ties.

This escapist reliance on sex and drugs seems to govern the world created in *Black Tickets*, the short story collection that brought Phillips wide literary recognition. But her depiction of this sordid world aims not simply to shock her readers into the recognition of grim reality. Rather, by combining the disinterestedness and objectivity of a scientist with the imagination of a poet, she seeks to explore the malaise of a society that had disintegrated into what sociologist David Riesman called "the lonely crowd."

Like many other characters in the book, the protagonist of "Home" suffers from extremes of loneliness. "Out of money" and feeling like a misfit in a world where she finds neither love nor comfort, she takes her mother's advice and comes home to heal her wounds. Because she is young, her defeat seems temporary. But she does not find what she seeks in the familiar situation in which she immerses herself. This time it is home, traditionally man's last refuge from the encroachments of society, that fails her. What it once represented no longer exists. Its former foundation, the family, is irreparably broken. Her parents are divorced and still harbor feelings of mutual ill will, and the absence of inner, spiritual ties that characterized the world the young woman has left behind is now replicated in her relationship with her mother.

Phillips symbolizes this emptiness through the mother's favorite pastimes—watching television, knitting afghans—both stupefyingly monotonous, meaningless occupations. Since the story never even hints at how the afghans will be used, they merely suggest an endlessly repetitive action, a woman's version of Sisyphean labors. The daughter notices the same qualities in the TV programs, so artistically weak that the primitive devices employed to manipulate the audience—especially the "repetition of certain professional laughters"—are glaringly obvious.

Phillips presents the invasion of home by television as something dangerous, even sinister. This symbol of the omnipotence of modern technology violates the sacred privacy of the domestic world, destroying all human ties. It tears the mother away from those around her, locking her into a one-dimensional electronic space. The young woman's attempts to rescue her mother from this McLuhanesque desert are futile. Ironically, the means of salvation the daughter chooses are representative of earlier, traditional family activities—reading and going together to the movies—that once were aimed at cementing the ties of kinship through the collective involvement of the family unit. That the mother rejects her daughter's proposals to subscribe to informative magazines or to replace television with books signifies the surrender of the older generation to the new technology, the loss of both traditional ways of life and the moral values inherent in them.

Obviously, the conflict between mother and daughter can be attributed to the generation gap: each is a product of her own era, sharing all its truths and delusions. The mother grew up during World War II, her ideas of the future shaped by global events. Like millions of others, she survived the difficulties of wartime, but also endured other, more personal burdens, nursing her sick, bedridden mother for years. She uses her claim that she had done her duty as a form of didactic reproach, justifying her superior, moralistic attitude toward her daughter, whose integrity she constantly questions. But her moral stance contains irritating overtones of self-satisfaction, pride, and complacency. She assumes that in a similar situation, which is more than just a possibility, *her* daughter would neglect to do "everything she could" for her.

Nonetheless, the mother's absolute conviction of her own righteousness, though it accords with the circumstances described in the story, appears less well founded when examined in detail. If her hasty marriage, just two weeks after first meeting her fiancé, does not refute her words, it nevertheless throws a shadow of doubt on past events. Was the wedding an unconscious attempt to flee a difficult situation, an irreproachable kind of psychological, as well as literal, escape from that duty of which she is so proud? Seeking to explain her action to her daughter, she can say nothing but that "he was older. . . . He had a job and a car. And mother was so sick." No word of feelings—no hint of the romantic infatuation or sudden blaze of passion commonly associated with elopements. Though she is reluctant to recognize the fact, it seems clear that circumstances rather than feeling precipitated her decision. Her unwillingness or inability to face the truth about herself makes her once again insist on "doing her duty," which becomes for her a kind of psychological mask for all occasions.

For the characters in this story the truth is too painful to bear. It must be concealed because it makes them vulnerable in their relations with the outside world. What began in one generation continues in the next, growing in proportion. The most dramatic symbol of this pervasive flight from reality is Daniel's refusal to take off his shirt, even during his most intimate moments. The daughter's lost true love, Daniel trusts neither her nor his own feelings. Fearing that a view of his napalm-seared back will shock love literally to death, he chooses concealment. Thus the generations, estranged from and averse to each other, become ironically united through their similar approaches to life's dilemmas.

Phillips's portrayal of the old and young generations is remarkably precise, though her characters act and speak as individuals. The daughter feels the mother's implied reproach but does not rush to justify herself in her mother's eyes. She bursts with indignation, but in the spirit of her generation she refuses altogether to acknowledge an a priori power of moral obligation over herself or anyone else, and she dismisses the guilt required by her mother's ethical code: "No one has to be guilty." But her words are bravado, aimed not to reveal but to conceal her true impulses, her true self.

One of the fundamental principles of Phillips's poetics manifests itself in such delineations of character. Phillips conceives the individual as a multi-faceted, even multidimensional entity, composed of many unrelated elements. She constructs her characters by revealing the interaction of these elements—words, actions, a general orientation to life, subconscious impulses, involuntary emotional bursts—with large gaps between them, which become an essential part of the modern fragmented consciousness.

One of these gaps is evident in the relation of mother and daughter. The unyielding stubbornness of the daughter springs from the authoritarian stubbornness of the mother, whom the daughter feels bound to defy. Yet beneath defiance and confrontation lurks their mutual love. They seem almost ashamed of it, for they never speak of their feelings, assuming that to mention them would be a tactless display, demeaning for both of them—a kind of emotional nakedness, like the physical nakedness that embarrasses the mother, prompting the daughter to buy a stranger's old bathrobe at a sale in order to avoid an uncomfortable situation. Here, as everywhere else in the story, the truth—particularly the truth concerning one's own feelings—remains concealed and thus works to further separate and isolate the characters.

Only once does Phillips make the reader aware of the true nature of the daughter's feelings for her mother. Characteristically, they are revealed not through words or descriptions, but through a simple physical action: helping her mother take a shower. Yet even here Phillips, bringing together all the lines of the stories, presents the daughter's tenderness, care, and affection for her mother in conjunction with her sense of nakedness as embarrassing and nauseating. Even the most innocent touch becomes unbearable for modern man, threatening his (or her) very existence.

As a result, life comes to mean exclusion, not inclusion, loss rather than enrichment through a meeting with the other. Intolerance turns the mother and daughter into irreconcilable opponents. This is obvious in the young woman's attitude toward her parents' relations, her outrage that her mother could not separate from her father for so long, and perhaps even that she married him in the first place. In a series of flashbacks Phillips reveals the heroine's consciousness as that of a damaged child who grew up in a house without love and understanding. In the narrative, presented from the daughter's point of view, the father appears as a coarse and unfeeling person who withdraws into himself, caring not at all what happens to his wife and daughter. He has lost all emotional ties with his family, with whom his relations are reduced to primitive demands for service.

Yet the young woman's memory includes something besides this crude, depressing picture which for her overshadows everything that precedes it. Although inclined to see her father as a villain, she describes him in terms that create rather a portrait of a luckless man, unhealthy and unsuccessful in business. Significantly, Phillips uses illness, which marks all three generations presented in the story, as the central motif of "Home," both an indication of the sickness of the modern psyche and a metaphor for the illness of a society past its prime.

The atmosphere in the house is poisoned by the mutual hostility resulting from a lack of understanding on all sides. So strong was the evil feeling pervading the family that the girl recalls staying awake for hours, fearing that her father "would strangle her mother, then walk upstairs and strangle her." However, next to this picture of the father as monster Phillips places the daughter's unexpected confession, which allows us to see the family drama in a new light, suggesting that all three of its players were in fact also its victims: "I believed we were guilty: we had done something terrible to him."

As in other stories from *Black Tickets*, Phillips does not explicitly point out the reasons behind the drama in "Home," leaving them entirely to the reader's imagination. This refusal to comment is part of the author's strategy, aimed at engaging the reader by presenting a cluster of emotionally charged images as ambiguous as life itself. Imperceptibly, though, she dissuades the reader from believing that there is only one solution, implying not so much a multitude of answers as a multitude of circumstances, each contributing to the sorrowful outcome of the story.

The girl's immature consciousness has reacted defensively to a painful situation. Forced to choose between her parents, she condemns her father, oversimplifying a set of extremely complicated relationships. Yet the young woman does not feel that her mother, with whom she has sided, is completely right either. The daughter's consciousness is torn by contradictions that underscore the ambivalence inherent in the situation. As if in retaliation for her unhappy childhood, she sentences her mother to carry the burden of family chores alone.

It appears, however, that her condemnation of her mother has another explanation of which the young woman is unaware. Phillips's portrayal of the protagonist's relations with her parents has obvious Freudian implications. These appear most obviously in the young woman's retelling of the dream, itself a reflection of subconscious drives, in which her father comes to her bed, half naked and sexually aroused, urging her to engage in sex. The dream shows that the threat she felt from him as a child is still present, with sexual assault substituting for her former fear of strangulation. But we can also interpret her animosity toward her father as an expression of suppressed desire, thwarted by the prevailing cultural code of her society, whose moral authority she unconsciously recognizes while revolting against it on the level of consciousness and behavior.

The latter interpretation is supported by her erotic fantasies, inspired by the story she reads before going to sleep, which in turn inspires the dream of her father. With the use of the story-within-the-story device, Phillips touches upon important moral and cultural issues directly related to sexual behavior. In her imagination the young woman transforms the simple, even simplistic and didactic story from *Reader's Digest,* with its cheap dramatic effects, into a humorously obscene anecdote. There is a marked parallelism between dream and story—both deal with violations of ancient taboos—but while the rendering of the dream treats the theme seriously, the story-within-a-story provides an ironic commentary on its subject. Its central episode, the abduction of a teenage girl by a bear, is a travesty of ancient plots such as the rape of Europa or the tale of "Beauty and the Beast," enhanced by biblical allusions ("Sharon, his rose"). This juxtaposition of diverse elements from classical Western traditions helps draw the cultural boundaries of a modern civilization, vacillating between remnants of veneration for traditional values on the one hand and parody and ridicule on the other.

At the same time, by introducing an irony not present in the original into the heroine's musings over the "love story of a bear," Phillips indirectly exposes the mechanism by which sanctimonious conventional morality exercises its controls. As the description of the girl in the love story shows ("a good student loved by her parents, an honest girl loved by her boyfriend"), by making some superficial concessions to changing public mores, the story evades more profound transformations.

The norms of traditional morality have lost all spiritual meaning for the heroine of "Home"; they are nothing but standards of conformity society imposes on the individual. Rejecting them as false and restrictive, yet equally distrustful of the whole sphere of the spirit, she seems to find solace only in the physical side of love. Even her mother deems her a lighthearted seeker of amorous adventures and an advocate of free sex. But though her behavior and manner of speaking do indeed give the impression that the young woman is uninterested in anything but sex, Phillips delineates her inner drama as a function less of sexual dissatisfaction than of the historical traumas inflicted upon the social consciousness of the era which continue to victimize the younger generation.

The major instance of these traumatic events is Vietnam. In introducing this theme, still painful for America in 1979, Phillips carefully avoids inflated rhetoric about the atrocities and consequences of the war, instead using her heroine to convey how damaging the experience was for the nation. It is obvious that both the young woman's lovers are war victims: Jason, her first teenage love, goes insane from fear after his brother is killed in Vietnam; Daniel, wounded and badly burned in combat, has for years gone from one hospital to the next, a living embodiment of the physical and spiritual suffering the war caused. Though the young woman never speaks, like her mother, about "doing her duty," mentioning only in passing how she took care of Daniel in the hospital, she too has every right to be proud. Yet unlike her mother, she has gained neither satisfaction nor peace of mind from the experience—another mark of the difference between the generations. The sight of Daniel's suffering does not destroy her love for him, but it does paralyze her physically, making impossible the healthy and joyful relations of which she dreams, the harmony of the physical and the spiritual. Sharing the fragmentation to which modern man is doomed, she comes to believe that in the contemporary world there are on the one hand love and spiritual communion and on the other physical intimacy, and that the two are now irreconcilable. She settles for the latter, hoping to find in it oblivion, although she fully realizes that she actually needs something quite different; as she admits to her mother, "I can't be physical, not really" (22).

The picture that unfolds in "Home," as in others of Phillips's stories, is grim and hopeless. Here is a world of endless evil and vice, dominated by dark desires and vile passions, a world beyond redemption, stretching from the infinite past into the infinite future, from the fall to complete disintegration. Here, virtually everyone is doomed. If there are exceptions, they are rare, and the hope is not so much to escape the common lot as perhaps to retard its process and, if only for a moment, to experience the closeness of the other.

"Home" ends with one of these rare moments. The women stand close together, the daughter holding her mother. The image could serve as a metaphor for Phillips's understanding of modern man's predicament. The words the women say, born of anger and frustration, continue to hurt, suggesting the failure of language as a means of communication. But the estranging effect of words is countered by a gesture, bringing through touch the saving grace of love.

It should be emphasized that Phillips's style is characterized by the absence of even the slightest trace of didacticism. She does not make judgments or preach but rather delves into the essence of the phenomena she chooses to represent in her artistic world. She strives for an emotional, psychological effect, founded on a combination of narrative objectivity and a remarkable ability to immerse herself in her subject. This paradoxical effect accounts for the unique double focus of her writings. The characters are drawn from both within and without, with an immediacy and spontaneity marked by the whimsical interplay of fleeting impulses, unexpected bursts, and sharp swings of emotion.

The closing scene of "Home" may serve as an example. This episode brings together in counterpoint words, actions, and emotions. The kitchen where the mother and daughter find themselves is literally full of "the sound and the fury"—the steam, the noise of hot water, the clatter of dishes, and above all the bitter words the two exchange. By contrast, when the theme of love is introduced, it is characterized by silence. Through understatement, Phillips makes her characters and the situation as a whole absolutely convincing, achieving artistic mastery rare in a writer of her age.

Artistic principles similar in many ways to Phillips's form the basis of Elena Makarova's fiction. Makarova too tries to achieve maximum effect by combining narrative objectivity with an accurate recreation of the internal states of her characters. "Needlefish," which appeared in her collection of stories and novellas *Overfilled Days* (*Perepolnennye dni*, 1982), is a striking example. Although the story is told in the third person, unlike the first-person narration of "Home," it is written from the point of view of the teenage protagonist, Alka. This device allows Makarova to narrow her focus, concentrating on the emotions and insights of an adolescent, without necessarily feeling compelled to narrow the range of issues the story deals with.

Alka's views are permeated with typical adolescent extremism, and as a result she is merciless. There is no denying her powers of observation, yet she is incapable of understanding much of what she sees around her. Nevertheless, she condemns everything and everybody, separating herself from them. This attitude is felt in the intonation of the opening sentence. The action of the scene unfolds on a dance floor, where, forbidden by her mother to appear, Alka can watch the dancers only in secret. Hurt by being treated as a child, she observes them with scorn; the dance floor becomes an "open-air cage" where dancers did not dance but only "jerked, shook, tossed loose hair."

As the opening passage makes clear, Alka feels powerless and dependent, estranged from the world and the people around her. Yet though adults deprive her of freedom, she believes that she alone is really free. Her bondage is that of the body, her freedom that of the spirit. With the people around her, on the contrary, the body is free but the spirit is in bondage. Taking her revenge on them, she mentally encloses them in a cage.

Her only means of doing so is through language. Alka is not interested in words as a means of communication. Like the characters in Phillips's stories, she feels the failure of language to effect communion with others. Rather, as the episode with the deaf-mute later in the story shows, Alka trusts the nonverbal communication of eyes and gestures—the movements and poses, colors, lines, and sounds that her imagination has revealed to her. What attracts her is the invocatory power of the word, and her greatest joy comes in using language in this way.

One of the most striking instances of this tendency is her use of imagery. Just as the dichotomy of body and spirit is basic for the story, so the imagery of the body is essential for conveying narrative meaning. In relating to those she regards as antagonists, Alka verbally exaggerates the physical aspects of their appearances and behaviors, representing them as grotesquely deformed. Like the young woman of "Home," she is least lenient with her own relatives. Watching the dancers, she looks critically on her sister Inka. Paired with "some glossy guy," Inka becomes a "clod," a "cow," "clumsily shifting from one foot to another." A wave of nausea sweeps over Alka when, lying in bed, she imagines her sister returning home, preparing for bed, her "fat, unbridled flesh" fully exposed.

Alka has similar feelings toward her mother, whom she condemns, like her sister, for maintaining artificial relationships with men—first with Inka's father, then with her own, whose place has now been taken by a new lover. Neither woman, Alka believes, follows her genuine feelings—the sister because, accepting philistine morality, she exchanges real emotion for the "titillation" of the flesh while awaiting marriage; the mother because her change of partners is, from her adolescent daughter's point of view, proof of "false" feelings.

Like the central character in "Home," Alka has grown up in a family where traditional ties based on love, care, and understanding have been broken. The family itself no longer exists, and an anonymous lover has usurped the father's position. The girl easily reconstructs the course of events in her life as she observes her sister's daily ritual of returning from the dance as well as the changes in the family situation. But what gives these events meaning and color are Alka's hurt feelings, envy, and resentment. From her surroundings she perceives only hostile signals, to which she reacts with a concomitant hostility, regarding whatever adults do as an encroachment on her rights and freedoms—on her very identity. Trying to defend herself from the aggressive world she rejects, Alka escapes from reality into an imaginary world. There she feels not only safe, but superior to those who in real life, she believes, force her into submission. Thus, in her imagination she dances better than her sister, better even than all the adults on the dance floor. She alone understands the secret meaning of events invisible to others, burdened as they are by petty daily worries. She sees and hears what others do not. With all her being she feels the invisible pulse of life, while they, it seems to her, have long ago grown internally paralyzed.

In her childish egoism Alka places herself in the center of the world, omnipotent. There she observes from a distance the actions of adults, which seem to her no more than trivial bustle. But in fact, this egoism, together with inexperience, prevents her from penetrating below the surface of reality. Her wild imagination helps her to fill the vacuum of understanding in accordance with her own moods and emotions. But this pattern only intensifies her feeling of alienation from those around her.

Estrangement, then, dominates Alka's relations to her mother and sister, but perhaps most revealing in this regard are her relations with the deaf-mute whom she sets out to draw. She is attracted by his picturesqueness, the very coarseness and primitivism that seem to her a sign of an authenticity which her mother and sister lack. This perception in a way establishes some kind of inner connection between her and the deaf-mute, allowing him to enter her ordinarily closed-off world. But in becoming part of this private world, he seemingly takes upon himself, in Alka's mind, the obligation to break his ties with the ordinary world. When she goes to see him for the second time to capture his authenticity on paper, she realizes that he has seen his wife, who now has a lover. She takes this event quite literally as a betrayal, regarding his feelings towards his wife as a breach of the secret agreement that has tacitly existed between him and Alka since their first meeting. From this instant she banishes the deaf-mute from her world of chosen people. He returns to the contemptible world of everyday life, and she loses all interest in him.

If Alka's imagination only aggravates her feeling of alienation from others, it helps her overcome that estrangement in the world of nature. Makarova endows her heroine with the imagination of an artist. The natural world is no longer simply an environment for her; it comes to life, gaining the authenticity people irreparably lack. Entering this world, she feels herself transformed, changed first into a tree, then into a needlefish cutting through the resistant water, then into a line in the air that has caught the fleeting movement. Makarova is remarkably expressive when, with masterful impressionistic touches, she depicts Alka's immersion in the world of elements which makes the girl feel herself a part of infinite, immortal nature. In some of the most powerful descriptions in the story, Alka dissolves into the world of color and sound, which break out of their earthly shell and become something unknown and fantastic, like a three-dimensional abstract painting, its fourth dimension a symphony of sounds. All these effects—sounds, colors, and lines, conglomerations of life's overflowing energy—stir the girl to rapture.

The creative energy so strongly awakened in Alka is the symbol as well of the awakening woman in her. But her new feelings leave her confused and fearful. She reacts so enviously to the "feminine" nature in her mother and sister precisely because she herself is, for the first time, discovering and displaying her own. Her desire for self-affirmation leads her to a kind of annihilation of the feminine in other women—sister, mother, deaf-mute's wife. Frustrated at her inequality with the grown women who continue to treat her as a child, she takes imaginative revenge on them, thereby, as she believes, restoring justice. In her mind they exchange places: Alka is the only true woman, who has grasped the mystery of love. All the rest become grotesque figures, governed by repulsive, "inauthentic" feelings: Inka with her lusty movements on the dance floor and her philistine calculations about getting married; her mother, smiling in the same way, taking in the different men who come to possess her body, which, lacking the redemptive grace of love, is dehumanized, leaving "a seal's silhouette in space."

As all these events make clear, "Needlefish" is an initiation story. On the brink of discovering the world, Alka confronts her feminine nature, her artistic nature, and the possibility of self-affirmation in an adult world in which she will be an equal member. Because of the alienation governing this world, however, self-affirmation proves impossible. And her experience of her feminine and artistic identities only increases her feelings of estrangement, widening the abyss between her and her family.

In this context the concluding episode in the forest acquires a special meaning. Erast, who is also an artist, has already "captured" Alka, not only because she has fallen in love with him but, more importantly, because in drawing her he has grasped that inner self the secret of which she believes she alone possesses. The image of the forest symbolically reinforces the theme of initiation. At first everything appears rather innocent: Alka and Erast pick berries, walking through velvety moss. But even here the imagery prefigures sexual consummation, particularly the stains of red berry juice on their bodies, with its evocation of the bloodshed inevitably associated with the initiation process. The further they go into the woods, the more sensual the description becomes. Sexual images come to the foreground, occupying an important place in the story's structure: Alka and Erast "swam into moss," and the references to scarlet juices occur repeatedly. Finally, the needlefish which Alka has earlier imagined herself to be, and which gives its name to the story, "entered her body," "tore through her." But its meaning has changed. Moving away from a representation of Alka's freedom and power, imaginary though they may be, it now signifies the sexual power of the other over her. In a broader sense, the association of sexual initiation with pain ("tore through her") turns the event into a symbol for any traumatic transition experience.

Makarova's associative style corresponds to the perceptions of the heroine whose point of view the story adopts, allowing the author to present accurately and with a certain delicacy the inner world of a teenage girl whose lack of sexual knowledge necessarily makes her transform sexual experience into metaphor. The style of narration also accords with Makarova's presentation of Alka as an artist for whom metaphoric, associative thinking is a natural element. Not least important, the indirection of metaphor allows Makarova to avoid an explicitly naturalistic description of Alka's and Erast's relationship, especially in the scene in the wood—description that at the time would have made publishing the story difficult. The literary mores in the former Soviet Union did not condone an interest in private matters, to say nothing of sex, even in the most liberal times. Moreover, the episode in the forest contains one of the most delicate moments in the story. Erast is much older than Alka; she thinks of him as "a man." Thus, according to Soviet mores, a realistic description of the scene would have required of the author a more direct expression of moral indignation than Makarova, who did her best to avoid didacticism, desired to provide.

The narrative style based on implication rather than on direct statement and straightforward description permits Makarova once again to separate Alka from the world around her. For the heroine, her own imagination and the world of others are juxtaposed as high and low, and any transition from one to the other seems impossible. At the end she becomes even more convinced of her superiority to those around her. They are ordinary, she is "extraordinary." She dismisses the remarks of her mother, who has noticed a change in her, as insignificant and annoying, something that could issue only from small-mindedness. Alka feels no need to be near any of her family; she no more seeks to be understood by them than she seeks to understand them, for she is sure that she can reach heights of which ordinary people dare not even dream. Her notions are confirmed by the image of flight with which the story ends, a symbol which also signifies her transcendence of the fear and confusion caused by sexual awakening.

In effect, the introduction of the flight image makes the story's conclusion resonate with optimism. Flight represents the young girl's soaring hopes, but it reflects the author's views as well. In fact, there is here virtually no distance between Makarova and her heroine. Since Makarova fails, or does not wish, to maintain the distance between them, she tends to romanticize and glamorize sex as a liberating force. As a result, her portrayal of the heroine and the situation is, in both substance and tone, opposite to that in the stories of Phillips, with whom Makarova has otherwise much in common. Her optimistic, affirmative ending, like her use of the sexual theme, challenges the prevailing modes of Soviet literary expression.

"Needlefish" does not contain explicit social overtones; its impact depends entirely on the accuracy of psychological nuances. But what in one cultural situation may be taken as a given can in another stand for artistic innovation or political comment. Indeed, Makarova's very failure to introduce a social context had in itself a certain political resonance at the time the story was written. She openly challenges the conventional notions associated with the dogmas of Socialist Realism. This doctrine, prescriptive by its very nature, claimed that there could be only one ideologically correct interpretation of reality, conveyable by ideologically correct artistic devices. Everything outside these prescriptions was labeled subversive, and those found guilty of violation could suffer the most serious consequences.

As her subject matter and artistic form suggest, Makarova chose artistic freedom. She was not, of course, the first to do so. But each period dictates its own conditions and finds its own ways of establishing the independence of artistic individuality. Perhaps it was her understanding of the significance of the artist's task that made Makarova represent the protagonist of her story as an artist. In any case, the concentration on the psychological, intimate, erotic experiences of her characters, which she shares with Phillips, was the form of rebellion Makarova chose in order to affirm her creative freedom. In this sense, both women have been able to disclose certain crucial truths about human experience.

Translated by Maya Koreneva
Edited by Susan Hardy Aiken

Dialogue

ON MAKAROVA AND PHILLIPS

Katya: The difference between Adele's and Maya's approaches seems to result from the fact that they belong to different schools of literary criticism, as well as from a difference between Russian and American mentalities. Adele analyzes the personal traits and behaviors of the characters primarily as projections of their inner worlds, while Maya emphasizes that even the most intimate aspects of human life are socially conditioned.

Maya: You're right about the difference of our approaches. A strong anti-Puritanical bias in twentieth-century American literature turns sex into an absolute value. For the Russian cultural consciousness, sex has always been a part of the whole concept of love—and the lowest and most subordinate one, too. It was most often represented in Russian classical tradition in a comical, grotesque form. Even twentieth-century Russia, with all its experiments (actually, comparatively few), hasn't produced so far a radical change in this system of values.

Katya: Since the great interest in sex in contemporary American culture is largely a re-action to Puritan asceticism and bigotry, it's possible that in Russia we shall confront sex with the same splash of fascination in the future.

Susan: I'd disagree somewhat—I mean about the fascination with sex being largely a reaction to Puritan asceticism. Granted, that's had an important effect—this country *was* strongly influenced by bourgeois moral codes and concomitant forms of repres-sion—but I think the issue of sexuality is shaped by much more than that one factor. Psychoanalytic theories, which also might be seen as reactive to nineteenth-century mores, have had a striking effect on contemporary American thinking, even for those who disdain psychoanalysis. But the history of psychoanalysis is part of a larger cul-tural history. My point is that the very idea of what constitutes sexuality—how it's constructed, culturally reproduced, interpreted, policed, or suppressed—comes from a complex interplay of social formations and individual perceptions.

Adele: Can we turn to another question of cultural interpretation—the implications of Makarova's Jewish heritage?

Katya: In your essay, the general problem of the artist's alienation is connected to Makarova's personal fate. In your view, Makarova has always been an exile in Russia because she was born a Jew.

Maya: I think the alienation Adele speaks about is a more complex phenomenon, where the dominating factor is ideological rather than national or ethnic. There were Jews who unquestioningly shared the Soviet ideology and served the system, on the one hand, and those who were persecuted for their convictions on the other.

Katya: The complexity is increased by the fact that all these writers, being born Jews, were formed as artists within the Russian culture, absorbing its traditions, its values, its world view. That's true of Makarova as well. It seems to me that the ambiguity of the metaphoric treatment of Alka's and Erast's relationship is to a large extent due to Makarova's acceptance of Russian literary tradition rather than only to the former impossibility of publishing a frank treatment of sex in the Soviet Union. More than that, the portrayal of her characters' private lives was for her, as for many other Soviet writers, a form of escape from the dominant ideology.

Maya: Nowadays, people still look for psychological relief from politics and the burden of life in erotic films and "romances."

Susan: In the United States we see similar patterns. Several feminist studies have looked at how gender inflects popular culture—films, television, best-sellers. There's been some really interesting analysis, for example, of Harlequin romances and similar popular "bodice rippers," which attract millions of readers, almost all women. It's a huge economic industry in this country and tells us a good deal about the psychological needs and fantasies women develop through the process of acculturation.

Katya: In Russia this pattern is even more conspicuous on television. Most spectators watch endless Mexican and American soap operas, which are now on prime-time TV. The love Russians, especially women, feel for the heroes of these serials is sometimes expressed rather oddly. Many mothers have named their newborn daughters after the heroine of a popular Mexican soap opera. While it's on the screen, all domestic chores are put aside; husbands and children are completely forgotten. One of these husbands, after trying in vain to get his wife to cook dinner while she was carried away by the TV program, wrote obscenities all over her arms and shoulders. Another one, who happened to say something critical about the heroine, was stabbed by his wife with a kitchen knife. In Moldova, where the Moscow TV channel was disconnected for political reasons, Moldovan women led a protest demonstration because they couldn't watch this soap opera.

Maya: Apparently these naive, sentimental plots attract our women precisely because within the paternalistic culture certain aspects of a specifically feminine approach to life haven't been satisfied. Yet the very showing of these films can also be regarded as a means of control on the part of those who want to maintain power over the "tender sex."

Susan: And thus, in effect, such romances exist on a cultural continuum with misogynistic pornography.

4

Anna Nerkagi

Leslie Marmon Silko

ANNA NERKAGI ❖ Anna Pavlovna Nerkagi, a Nenka, was born in 1952 on the Yamal Peninsula near the Kara Sea coast. From the age of six she lived in a boarding school, returning to her father's reindeer camp at the Laborovaia Trading Station only during holidays. In 1974 she graduated from the Tiumen Industrial Institute and in 1978 became known to the literary world for her short novel *Aniko of the Nogo Tribe,* which gained her entrance into the Writer's Union. In 1980 Nerkagi returned to the nomadic life of her ancestors in Siberia, where she now lives with her husband, a hunter, on the Yamal Peninsula. In addition to *Aniko,* she has written a short novel, *Ilir* (1983), about events in the tundra during the revolution, and most recently a sequel to *Aniko,* entitled *White Arctic Moss,* which she wrote while living in a choom.

Aniko of the Nogo Tribe

ANNA NERKAGI

The wolf laid its muzzle on its paws and listened intently to the howl of the snowstorm. Here in the den, covered with snow, it was warm and calm, but the animal sometimes trembled, and its eyes screwed up tightly. The wolf wanted to fall asleep in order to gather strength since its stomach had been empty for several days. The Nentsy* had nicknamed this wolf the "Lame Devil" for his cunning and evil deeds. He would sleep a little and then get up and stalk a deer on the winter road.**

Animals too exhausted to make it to camp were often abandoned on the road until morning. Alongside a weakened reindeer people would put a scarecrow. They would dress up a stick or little tree with a hide giving off a human scent. They would attach a branch—as if someone were standing there with a rifle.

Lame Devil did not fear these "guards." But he would approach the reindeer with caution. Long ago he had learned a cruel, unjust law: a beast with two paws would always kill a beast with four. This was a special world with its own laws and reckonings. Lame Devil knew this. Because of man he had lost his back paw. . . . Formerly, he had held no malice or spite towards man. He had been content. He had his underground lair, four cubs with broad foreheads, and a she-wolf mate. Once, however, returning from the hunt, he had gotten caught in a trap. This one was big, not like the kind men usually set for the stupid polar fox, but obviously intended for a large beast.

All night the wolf had tried to break free of it. Toward morning, when the scent of man was everywhere, he chewed off his own paw. Afterward, Lame Devil left the pack. With years of solitude came both intelligence and cunning.

. . . A sudden sound resembling a human cry interrupted the wolf's

---

* Nentsy is the plural of Nenets.

** In the tundra most of the roads are impassable in the summer because of the swampy conditions. When the tundra freezes over, the ground is more solid, allowing sleighs to pass over.

watchful sleep. He pricked up his ears. As the wolf turned his head, listening cautiously, pockmarks and scars were visible on his neck. The cry, muffled by the moans of the storm, was repeated. "The two-legged beast!" The wolf felt hot burning anger. Giving a hollow growl, he flinched and sucked in his sides. Going from a warm place into the cold is not very pleasant. Lame Devil almost fell from the biting wind. He had three paws, not four. When he had stood for a bit he hobbled off after the scent.

The camp settled down for the evening. At night a storm always seemed more dangerous than during the day. It sometimes happened that the poles that make up the framework of a choom* would not hold out—and the wind would break up people's homes and carry off their belongings and sledges.

Here in the quiet canyon the snowstorm was not as severe—high above the wind was howling, leaving a snowy white tail behind. There were three chooms in the canyon. One belonged to Seberui of the Nogo tribe. Next to it stood the home of his friend Passa Ledkov, and a little farther on lived Aleshka Laptander with his mother and younger brothers.

The chooms were surrounded by sledges tightly packed with household goods. There were also empty sledges filled with snow. In front of each choom was a big pile of dry branches. It was difficult to obtain fuel in the tundra.

The wind, though it was not very fierce, still penetrated the canyon. It made the sledges creak and seemed to beat angrily against the walls of the chooms which only moaned, refusing to give way to the snow or the wind.

The tundra was harsh not only in its climate but in its life. It seemed as if time stood still, as if a huge mammoth might appear out of the white whirlwind of the blizzard.

Toward morning the storm died down, but the heavy leaden sky hung so low that it was murky and hostile. In such bad weather no one wanted to stir, and no bluish smoke curled up from the chooms standing in the canyon.

The reindeer had banded together into a herd. Not far from the natural snow-covered boundary of the camp, a forest of mighty horns was swaying in the wind as the animals warmed themselves by huddling together.

On the previous morning Passa had noticed the overcast brow of the Saurei range and herded the reindeer into the deepest part of the canyon, closer to the people. Not much could go wrong there. . . . And he wasn't mistaken.

Passa and Aleshka had been guarding the herd all night, and now Passa was sitting on his sledge looking in the direction of the chooms and wondering if any smoke could be seen there. He really wanted some tea. He

*A tent made from animal skins used by the nomadic tribes of the Far North.

felt frozen through and through, even though his savak* was new and warm, and its fur was still quite thick. Icicles tinkled on Passa's brow and mustache, and he carefully peeled them off. Next to him Aleshka was trying to light a cigarette, but snow had gotten into the matches and they wouldn't catch fire.

"That's the last snowstorm for this year," said Passa, offering Aleshka his matches.

"Why?"

"This one had spite. A mean one!"

The sky now looked down almost innocently; here and there through the dishevelled clouds a timid blue light shone through, promising something springlike, and only above the Saurei ridge a shaggy black cloud still hung as before.

Seberui had hardly slept at all the whole night, listening to the heartrending howling of the snowstorm. In such blizzards, even the ten skins covering the choom seemed like a spider web. In addition, his big old hound, Buro, tossed and turned at his feet, continually pulling off the yagushka** that Seberui had thrown over himself. The dog hadn't slept either. Today the two of them stayed alone in the choom.

Two days earlier Seberui's wife had taken their little daughter and gone after supplies. She had also wanted to stop by and see a friend whose choom, according to rumor, was not far from the village. The storm had come up suddenly, and Seberui, of course, had begun to worry that it might have caught them on the road.

The dream came just before morning and had not lasted long. He dreamed that his wife and daughter had returned, and that they were already drinking tea; the little girl asked her father to pick her up, and Seberui, smiling joyfully and tenderly, was reaching out to her.

He woke up suddenly and immediately realized that the wind had already died down. The wall of the choom was not shuddering so violently, and snow was no longer sifting down through the smoke outlet.

Buro stood and pricked up his ears, listening to the sounds coming from outside.

"Passa and Aleshka are here," Seberui thought, and he immediately heard Passa's voice: "Hey friend, come on, get up! The choom is almost completely snowed in."

"It's not so bad. I've seen worse."

Seberui threw back the curtain covering the doorway and heard the scraping of a shovel. Passa was digging out the entrance. So as to avoid sitting

---

*A winter coat with fur on the outside.
**A fur coat without a hood.

there and doing nothing, Seberui shook the snow from his bed and dishes and then lit the stove. Before leaving, his wife had got some dry firewood ready, and it didn't take Seberui long to get the fire going. Usually after a snowstorm only the women had the strength to light a fire.

Coming out of the choom, Seberui squinted—the white snow was blinding. He sat down beside Passa on the front of the sledge and struck up a conversation about reindeer and the storm. Seberui was sixty-four years old. He was rather short, and his grey eyes were always attentive and kind.

Although they were the same age, Passa looked younger than Seberui. He too was short, but he had broader shoulders, and his walk—well, the way a Nenets walks reveals everything, both smoothness and resolve, pride and dignity. Around his waist Passa wore an embroidered red cloth belt with homemade bronze decorations. At the back five wolf teeth hung on little chains—the sign of a valiant hunter—and at his side a sheath, also decorated with copper plates, and an awl in a little bone case.

A man is judged according to how he ties his belt. If the skirt of his malitsa* hangs down below his knees and makes walking difficult, then he's a poor hunter and a poor workman. You couldn't say that about Passa. He was always well dressed, and when he left his choom even for a short time, Passa looked as if he were going hunting. He was respected both in camp and throughout the tundra. He was a wise hunter; he knew the places where there was plenty of moss for the reindeer. He could hunt anywhere, even where there were no roads. People were also attracted to him because of his persistence. When he heard that some people didn't want to send their child to school, he would race out to their camp. Sometimes he would harness a special team and ride many kilometers just to talk to the stubborn father.

At tea he would ask how the hunt for the polar fox was going, whether the wolves were disturbing anyone, and then he would request that everyone close their eyes. He would then ask, "Is it dark?" Receiving an answer, he would continue, "Now open your eyes. It's light. If you know what's on paper you can walk with your eyes, and if not you're almost blind. Nowadays in life you need to see more than just the tracks of the fox." The shepherds laughed at his explanations, but they sent their children to school.

Passa also distinguished himself through his ability to believe. When the Soviet power came, he was the first in the camp to embrace it and even to help. Then there was the war, and he believed in victory. For his faith and his labors he was decorated. Passa and Seberui both received medals: "For Valiant Labor in the Great Patriotic War, 1941–1945." Now he firmly believed that it was necessary to teach the children to read and write so that

*A fur coat made of two reindeer hides with fur on the inside and outside.

they would have clear heads on their shoulders and would be able to design a good warm choom where you could take off your malitsa even in the winter and not just when the stove was lit. It wouldn't be a bad idea to have a radio in the choom so that sometimes they could speak in Nenets about everything that was going on in the world. It would also be good to hang up a light bulb just like in the village.

For the time being Passa kept all of these thoughts to himself. He was waiting for the time when his son, who was now in the sixth grade, would grow up and begin to understand serious things.

Passa had invited Seberui over for tea, and Seberui, sitting next to his friend, was finishing up his fourth cup. As usual, they drank unhurriedly and in measured fashion. In the tundra tea is everything. It warms you in freezing weather; it relieves fatigue after the hunt or after long wanderings. Serving tea is both a ritual and a sign of respect for one's guest. Women know how to make tea from herbs which they call "bird tea."* It comes out greenish but tasty, and the old Nentsy say that it is good for you.

Although he didn't say so, Seberui was very happy. The storm had passed. Soon his wife and little daughter would return. It wasn't far to the village. They would get back quickly on their well-fed reindeer and should be home by dinnertime.

Having drunk his tea, Seberui set to cutting a new pole for driving reindeer. After all, a new bride was growing up. Seberui would not send her to school. No! Never! No matter how many times Passa would say "darkness," "light," he would never send her to school. She would leave for the city like his oldest daughter, and she would forget the choom and the reindeer. There would be no one to keep the family hearth, and then there would be neither "darkness" nor "light." The hearth fires would go out.

Seberui had another daughter, but no one in the camp, not even Seberui himself, knew where she was or how old she might be. Maybe she was nineteen, maybe twenty. The girl was not yet seven when a Russian came on horseback to Seberui's choom, spoke to him, and took Aniko away to school. And since that time Seberui had not seen his daughter, not even in his dreams.

That same winter Seberui had moved his camp to the mountains where there were fewer mosquitoes in the summer and where it wasn't so hot. His daughter had come home for the holidays, but her mama and papa were nowhere to be found. She had lived with some other people and had earned herself a little boiled fish. The next summer she didn't appear. Evidently things were better with the Russians.

* Tea made of blackberry leaves.

Seberui's situation was understandable. You don't trust just anyone with what you have gone to a lot of trouble to attain and what you have dreamed about all your life. He had to buy some starved-looking reindeer and give several barrels of perfectly good fish for each one. Then he had to take care of them. He had done all of this and made his life better and worked hard like an innocent doe, never cheating on anyone, but nevertheless, there kept flashing across his mind, "Old man, you may be guilty before Aniko."

At moments like this he would take his second daughter into his arms. She was still small, and he would silently caress her, having decided that his whole life was in this little girl. And the Idols would forgive him for Aniko.

By dinnertime the weather was much improved. It cleared on the ground and in the sky, and only the tired old ripples of snow crawled along the ground, slowly and pensively faltering over the snowdrifts and stones.

Seberui looked more frequently now in the direction of the forest from which his wife should appear. Knowing Nekochi's impatient character, he was uneasy. His wife always hurried home, believing that without her the choom would fall apart, or the fire within it would die out. Another woman would sit over at her neighbors' all the time drinking tea; you couldn't drag her away from company with a lasso. Nekochi, however, loved her choom and everything in it. She knew how to find joy in everything. She would brighten up at some little thing or other, and then the whole day she would communicate her joy to Seberui and their neighbors.

Seberui did not hear Passa come up and sit down next to him on the sledge. He put aside the stick which he had been working on and took out a yellowish-brown snuffbox made of mammoth bone. He poured out some tobacco onto his thumbnail.

"I just got your savak out from under the snow," said Passa.

"I thought that Nekochi took it with her." Seberui barely managed to get the pinch of snuff to his nose when he stopped in mid-sentence.

"She probably forgot."

His heart skipped a beat. Without a savak even in a normal frost you would freeze. Seberui was lost in thought. Buro came up. He looked at his master with intelligent eyes, and Seberui clearly saw anxiety, concern, and affection in his glance. He had lived many moons, many springs, on this earth, but he did not remember the dog's eyes ever expressing anything different.

"What do you think, Buro?" he asked. "Where's your mistress?"

Buro turned away, showing by his manner that he was unable to answer.

"Which one did you harness up front?" asked Passa. "Let me have the snuffbox."

"Temuiko. He's a smart one. You know yourself that he understands the road. . . ."

Seberui wanted to add something else, but he was silent. He suddenly thought that a good reindeer wouldn't always save its master in a bad blizzard. . . .

Aleshka was asleep after night duty, and his mother was walking around on tiptoe. She kindled a fire, put on the teapot and also a kettle with meat. She took Aleshka's two younger brothers outside. The storm had quieted down. Let them amuse themselves; they were just sitting there knocking stones together. Aleshka had bought them some toy rabbits, dogs, and some pistols. They didn't know anything. Give the boys some little stones and that's all they need. Pretty stones, some with a white streak in the middle, some with the design of a wise shaman, and then some that were simply black. Their mother collected the stones and carefully placed them into a bag which she then put into a dish drawer, a place the children couldn't get into. Let them search a little; otherwise they wouldn't let their older brother sleep.

The mother sat down near the fire with her sewing, listening to the voices of the children outside. The Idols had blessed her with four sons. One was in school, but he would return, and four mighty hunters would plow the tundra on stags as white as snow. Why shouldn't the heart of a mother be proud? The eldest was only twenty years old, but he was already a real man. The wise old hunters would talk to him as if he were an equal, and his mighty stags were in no way inferior to those of Seberui and Passa. And Aleshka knew the paper. He could read and write. He could speak just like a real Russian. And he could talk to the people who were looking for something in the ground just as easily as he could with the Nentsy. When their choom stood not far from Harasavei, Aleshka one time had gone over to see the Russians and had stayed the whole day. He had returned in the evening and had been thinking about something for a long time so that his face first glowed with joy and then turned to a frown. His mother didn't ask him anything. Let him think he is a man, a feeder of his mother and little brothers.

The mother's thoughts were interrupted by one of the little boys, who had stuck his head into the choom and shouted:

"Ma!"

"Quiet! What?"

"Passa says to wake up brother."

"What for?"

"I don't know. Have him come out."

"They don't let a boy sleep. It's as if Aleshka were the only one," muttered his mother, but remembering that Seberui's back had been aching that day and that Passa also hadn't slept, she began carefully though against her will to awaken her son.

It was difficult for Aleshka to wake up.

"What is it, Ma?"

"Passa is calling you for some reason."

"Has Nekochi come?"

"No."

Aleshka sat up with alarm. His face, which had been slightly swollen from sleep and fatigue, began to come into focus. His mother brought him his reindeer coat and lunch bag. Aleshka went out and, feeling sorry for her son, she again began muttering, and he could hear her dissatisfied voice even from outside.

Passa was waiting for Aleshka beside the choom.

"You can sleep later. Nekochi still hasn't returned."

"Mother told me."

"Use my sledge and check the road. Take your savak."

"Should I go by the village?"

"Yes. Ask around, find out when they saw her last. Don't tell our people that you are going. You can tell your mother that a reindeer got separated from the herd, and that you have to go look for it."

Aleshka nodded.

"Did you get some tea?"

"I'll have time."

"Drink up. Who knows how long you'll have to look."

At those words both felt uneasy.

Seberui couldn't wait any longer. After dinner he had asked Passa to round up the reindeer and harness the team. The latter shook his head silently. And suddenly . . . "Look!" the children were shouting, pointing to the road.

Someone was approaching the camp. The dogs began barking belatedly in order to justify themselves before their masters. It was only Buro who continued to hesitate, wondering if it was worth disgracing himself. Could the mistress have come home so suddenly?

Seberui stared at the team flying toward them until his eyes smarted. It was as if his heart were paralyzed with the cold.

"No, it's not Nekochi. It's Aleshka."

But then Passa got a good look at what was lying on the sled behind Aleshka's back, and he turned pale.

Aleshka brought the team to a sharp halt. The reindeer dropped on the spot. They were out of breath and wheezing. Aleshka, pale, with a horribly contorted face and wild eyes, silently passed by the people. He paused, as if about to turn toward Seberui, but, biting his trembling lips hard, he stopped short next to Passa. The latter was not looking at him.

"I've found them," Aleshka barely managed the words and slowly stepped up to Seberui. "Father, may your heart be greater than the heavens."

Seberui did not hear him. He was standing stooping awkwardly and look-ing fixedly at the sledge. The wind was rustling the edge of the skin which covered the load, attempting to rip it away, as if wishing to show the people what was lying underneath. Seberui straightened himself up with difficulty and did what the wind was either unable or reluctant to do.

Buro, who up until now had been following circumspectly, suddenly lunged toward his master and unexpectedly began to growl, gnashing his teeth.

"It's OK, boy," Passa called gently, but the dog bared its teeth at him also, then stood up on its haunches and gave a long mournful howl. The other dogs joined in.

Seberui just stood there, covering his face with his hands. Everything left him: the people around him, time, even he himself. There remained only a cry. A terrible, soul-shattering cry from the heart.

Aleshka and Passa carefully placed the cradle with the little girl onto some skins. Her swollen little arm stood out sharply against the background of the fur blanket. It was difficult to call the torn remains of Nekochi a body. Only her head, with bloody spots on the lips, and her cheeks remained untouched.

Buro continued his howling, and Seberui, as if he had just woken up, raised his head.

"Buro, lie down!" he whispered.

Hearing the voice of his master, Buro quieted down and lay at his master's feet, trembling and baring his teeth. Passa bent over the remains.

"It's him, Lame Devil!"

Passa knew the teeth marks of this wolf. Many times he had seen them on the carcasses of slain deer. And in the tundra he had often encountered the nervously tangled tracks of this three-pawed beast.

It seemed that their paths had just crossed once more.

.   .   .   .   .

The Nogo family cemetery was gloomy and foreboding. It was overgrown with rough stubbly larches, and the trees gave such shade that even dur-ing the day it seemed dark as night there. Sounds were muffled and would quickly fade away; in winter they would drown in the snow, and in summer they were buried in the succulent, damp moss.

It was an ancient cemetery. The Nogo tribe had been burying its kins-men there from time immemorial. The ground had been sanctified by the sacrifice of reindeer blood, by the flames of campfires, and by the thoughts and tears of generations.

People brought sacrifices to the ferocious, wise, and insatiable Idol of

Death, Nga, not only when they were in distress, but also when they were happy and at peace. Here lay Seberui's father, his mother, his grandfather, his grandmother, and his children whom the Idol had carried off to Nga. And now his wife and little daughter would be waiting here for him, the last remaining man of a once large, intelligent, and kind family.

The very first Nogo people had lived in the mountains. They had never crossed the Urals and did not know what was to be found on the far side. After all, there was really no need to know. The clan was large; there was something for everyone to do. Some fished; some hunted wild animals; others made knives and axes of stone.

They lived in peace and tried not to wage war against other tribes. They did not take offense at their neighbors, and if someone with a black thought gazed enviously at their rich pastures, the Nogo people silently broke camp and left.

"The land is large," said the elders. "Why quarrel?"

They would teach their young people wisely and calmly. They learned peace, love, ingenuity, and kindness. One could not say that the Nogo people were very rich and famous. You could not compare the Nogos with the Laptanders, people of the valley who even today are still strong, handsome, and proud.

People of the Nogo clan were not distinguished by their height like the shapely, dark-browed and black-eyed Laptander folk, nor were they as arrogant and maybe not even as inventive, but no one in the tundra would say that the Nogo people were inferior to anyone in strength of spirit, kindness, or dignity. They were strong with bright eyes the color of ripe Iceland moss. They loved the hunt, quiet games, and lengthy nomadic wanderings accompanied by a long song. They sacrificed generously to the earth, to the Idols, and in the evenings, after having partaken of some well-marbled meat, they loved to recount and sing the old legends. These were handed down from generation to generation, and new ones were also composed.

The clan was fortunate. Wars and quarrels passed them by. The Nogo felt no ill will toward anyone, nor did they offend anybody.

And then life itself turned against them. One hot summer the reindeer fell ill with hoof disease. They died by the hundreds. Many families were left without meat and hides.

The elders held a council. There were not enough healthy reindeer for the entire tribe. It was decided that part of the tribe would settle near large lakes so that they could sustain themselves on fish. The rest would tend the healthy reindeer.

The situation with the animals gradually righted itself. A new healthy herd was raised. The tribe labored long and hard. The elders went from campsite to campsite that had almost been forgotten and, straining their memories to capacity, managed to secure a fair amount of supplies which had been set aside in the eternal permafrost during more carefree days. These were the blue-fox furs, the rusty fox furs colored like the sun, the amber sables, and the squirrels. They traded them for reindeer with the wealthy tribes, and there came a time when the Nogo people were happy, when once more one could hear cheerful, bright-spirited songs about life and its joys.

Many years passed. The tribe grew strong. It was wealthy enough to stand up to the Laptanders. Offended members of all tribes came to visit the Nogo people: the poverty-stricken for aid, the rich for suitable brides, and friends for a good word.

Who knows what the good Nogo tribe might have done for the world!

A new misfortune came crashing down upon them. Whole camps were dying. Death spared neither the young nor the old. Those who were alive and healthy brought rich generous sacrifices to the good Idols. The elders and shamans implored the good spirits not to touch the children. But all was in vain. The Idols maintained stony silence. Nothing moved them, neither tears nor moans nor prayers.

At that time many perished in the tundra. The insatiable Idols drank much blood. Illness swallowed up the tribe. Of the entire Nogo clan there remained only a few people who happened to be in the camp of Yaga, a wealthy Nenets. It was there that the fathers of Seberui and Passa met. Each one left two sons. The younger brother of Seberui went off to war in 1941 and did not return.

.   .   .   .   .

. . . Seberui walks from tomb to tomb, each familiar and dear to him. Last year he had repaired a board on his father's coffin. He had changed the legs of many coffins.

Nenets and Russian cemeteries differ. The Nenets coffin is shaped like an ordinary box which, unlike the Russian coffin, is raised above ground. It stands on four one-meter legs and is roughly similar to an Egyptian sarcophagus.

There were no inscriptions on any of the boxes, but Seberui remembered each one. Each and every death had touched his heart.

They placed Nekochi and her daughter in one coffin. Now Passa's wife, his mother, and Aleshka's mother were fussing over them. They put Nekochi's things—her pots, skin bags, an old yagushka, and cups—into the coffin. All these things were broken or torn to pieces. Such was the custom.

The women were talking quietly:

"Don't forget to put in a needle."

"Where is her bag?"

"By her head."

"Put a thimble there too. She'll need everything there."

Nekochi was dressed in a new yagushka with brightly colored decorations. This was her last work. She did not want to wear it when she went to the village.

"I'll have the chance," she said, "my whole life is ahead."

The expression on her face was peaceful. It was as if at the moment of death she had not been thinking about anything very painful. It was as if she didn't believe that she would die. On the other hand, the girl's face was terrified. Her features were distorted, and her little mouth was all twisted.

Passa and Aleshka were already bringing up the reindeer. Now it was the custom to sacrifice two of the very best and most beloved reindeer to the deceased so as not to offend her, and so that she would have something to ride over there in the other world.

The people did not want to insult Nekochi. While the meat was cooking they generously sprinkled tobacco into the corners of the sarcophagus, into the fire and simply onto the ground.

They sat around the fire silently with their heads bowed. Each one wanted to do something for Seberui's wife and to ask her, there in the camp of the departed, to put in a good word for those who were left behind and to tell the departed ones in detail just how they were getting along. After all, this wasn't so much a funeral as the seeing off of a person who had decided to go to the other world.

Passa's mother was the eldest person present. She knew all of the customs best and therefore said, "Don't be silent! You have to talk about something. Right now many of the departed ones have come to her. And they are all listening to her stories. They must hear our voices too."

"Yes," Passa added. "They must know that we have come to see her off, that she lived well on earth."

The old Nenka continued, "Do not be offended, mother of Aniko.* We have dressed the girl well. She will not be cold. Look, see for yourself, you're wearing your new yagushka."

She touched the yagushka of the deceased with her small hand.

"I didn't make it painful for you?" she asked and answered herself with satisfaction, "No."

Then she took out of her sack a beautiful wool dress. Slowly she turned it

---

* Women rarely call each other by their first names, but more often they go by the name of the mother of a living child.

over and held it as if she were showing it to someone; not to the ones sitting by the fire but to someone seen only by her.

"Mother of Aniko, please give this dress to my mother. She never had one like this. See how nice it is. I bought it with my pension. Now we old women also get money like all people."

The old woman smiled radiantly.

"Let her take off the deerskin dress that we buried her in and put on this one," and she carefully put the present for her mother into one corner of the coffin. On her face was an expression of satisfaction and peace which remained as she took out her snuffbox and sprinkled some tobacco onto Nekochi's yagushka, carefully adjusting the little sack with the girl's toys.

Passa added some twigs and branches to the fire. The flame rose up brighter. For Nekochi it was burning for the last time, and the fire seemed to understand this. Tongues of flame caressed each other, forming strange flowers and leaves.

Passa took some meat and cut it into small pieces. His wife gave him two mugs of blood. He put the meat and mugs at the head and feet of Nekochi.

"Mother of Aniko, taste these yourself and give meat to everyone who has come to see you. Tell my father that I am getting along day by day, and that my sons are growing up. Two of them are in school. They are learning how to live another way, not at all like he and I lived. Tell him that this fall, when the deer hide is good, I'll slaughter some bulls, and he will find the hides at the sacred place near Khara-pe. He'll have enough for a malitsa."

Passa's father, who had only worked part-time, never even had a good malitsa, not to mention a good savak, and one night he had caught a terrible cold. Within half a year they buried him. His relatives could not even provide him with a new malitsa as a going-away present. Passa always remembered this, even though he had been only a child. They had put his father into the coffin in some shabby old clothes, and all the time it had seemed to the son that his father was freezing. Several times Passa had slaughtered bulls in various sacred places, leaving the hides for a malitsa for his father. In this way he attempted to atone for his own guilt and that of his kinfolk.

Having fallen silent, Passa added, "And don't fear for Aniko's father. You yourself know how well they lived. We shared the deer and tea, as we will now share his grief like food."

Aleshka, lowering his head, was sitting next to Seberui. Only a few months had passed since he too, like Passa, had been speaking with his deceased father. He had promised to take pity upon his mother and to help his younger brothers become real hunters.

"Mother of Aniko, you never had any sons," Aleshka said unexpectedly.

"I remember how you called me son when I was still little. I will be a son to grandfather Seberui. My father has come to visit you. May he hear this! And again, I have promised father that I will help my little brothers become hunters. I don't want to deceive him. He has probably started to think something different. I was with the geologists. They are guys just like me. They are looking for oil all over the world. They make kerosene from it. Sometimes you can't get it in the village. We'll find oil, and that will be our kerosene."

Aleshka said this about kerosene on purpose, although he knew that it was possible to make a lot of other necessary things from oil. But the deceased Nekochi and his father knew only about kerosene. Everyone listened attentively to Aleshka. Noticing this, he continued animatedly.

"We Nentsy know our land best of all. And if my brothers train to be geologists it will be easier for them. And they won't even be afraid of mosquitoes."

"That's true," confirmed Passa. He really liked the thought of kerosene.

The meat was cooked, and Aleshka's mother dished out some pieces onto plates and set them at Nekochi's head and feet. She gave each person sitting by the fire a bowl of bouillon. They all tried it and then poured the remainder onto the ground around the coffin.

Seberui provided for all those who came to visit the subterranean camp of the dead. Mechanically he sprinkled tobacco, took some meat, and his heart ached with sadness. The old man looked at the fire and at the smoldering embers. It seemed to him that they represented his life which had fallen out of the hands of the Good Idol and was now charring and sputtering.

Little daughter . . . wife . . . they are not here. The voices of the people brought him around, and for a long time he stared through sunken eyes at those who were sitting around the fire, trying to make some sense of their words. Passa was watching him carefully.

"You can't explain what happened with words. Yes, this day is truly one of the blackest. Idol of Life, give Seberui the strength to endure this day."

This is what Passa was thinking about as he cared for his friend. He was also thinking about Temuiko, Nekochi's favorite deer. Aleshka said that there weren't any deer, that they had run off at the scent of the wolf. But what had happened to Temuiko?

The sun was setting now. It was necessary to finish the rite while its rays still fell upon the earth. Later, after dark, people were not supposed to be here. That was the time for others, those who were not seeing off the deceased but were instead coming to meet them.

Passa and Aleshka chose a spot where they would put the coffin. The snow was still deep. For the time being it would be necessary to drive the legs into the snow and then in the spring they would do what had to be done.

Aleshka readied the nails in order to fasten the lid to the coffin, and suddenly he froze. Seberui was looking at him so strangely that Aleshka wanted to throw down his hammer and run away.

For a long time, Seberui retained his composure. He had conducted himself courageously both yesterday and today when he laid the bodies of his loved ones in that cold box, and when he had guarded their eternal sleep throughout the night. But now he clutched his head.

"Alone, all alone!"

A person understands this fully only when he really is left all alone. An orphan among people is like a stump in the middle of a dense forest.

"I'm alone," Seberui whispered, and what he had said resounded so clearly and deeply that it bared his terror and cut him to the quick. It was only now that his shudders began in earnest, as he finally grasped that what had happened was irrevocable.

His wife and daughter were dead. This meant that for him there was no past nor any future. If a person has no future he must rely on the past and live by it. And suddenly there was darkness both before and behind. How and for what to go on living?

The last ray of the sun was still taking leave of the earth when everything was finished. The people were putting out the fire, quietly repeating in unison, "Mother of Aniko, do not be offended. We are not the ones putting out the fire; it is the snowstorm."

Aleshka suddenly nudged Passa.

"Look!"

Passa shuddered. There was a deer walking along and holding its head proudly in the rays of the setting sun. Temuiko! Yes, it was Temuiko. During the night he had wandered into a strange herd and had remained there until morning. And now he was hurrying toward the people. Having approached, he surveyed all of them carefully. His gaze rested on Seberui. It seemed as if he were asking, "Where's mother? Where's the mistress?"

He then went up to the sarcophagus. He was happy, for he had found his mother. He rubbed his muzzle against the boards and, fatigued, lowered himself nearby. Seberui turned to the side, attempting to hide his tears from the people, and went up to the reindeer to say good-bye. Temuiko was Nekochi's very favorite reindeer. She must take him with her. Such was the custom.

The deer covered Seberui's palm with warmth and again lowered his muzzle. He was tired and wanted to sleep. His mother was nearby. Why not take a rest? Passa picked up the axe, made a lasso, and called to Aleshka.

"Let's go, you can help."

They took Seberui away silently. He wanted to say something but only waved his hand feebly. Temuiko did not move when they approached him.

Passa threw the lasso. Temuiko was not afraid, and just shook his head so that the noose would lie more comfortably and not chafe his neck.

The law of the tundra is harsh. The departed take their things with them. If you don't give them their things, they will come back for them. Thus it had happened that whole camps had been taken by the dead.

Pain gripped Temuiko's throat. He jumped up and staggered, trying to get a foothold on the ground which was slipping away from him. Seberui turned away, but suddenly, choking, shouted, "Stop! Don't! I'll take this sin on myself! Let him live! She suckled him."

It was as if Passa had been waiting for these words. He threw down the lasso and said to Aleshka, "Let him go."

Aniko jumped down from the sleigh. Turning in the direction of the chooms she caught sight of a small person. He was staggering and bustling toward her. The word "Father!" flashed into her head and was immediately followed by apprehension and uncertainty.

Was this totally unknown and awkward-looking old man really her father? She would have to embrace him, to sort out the grains of feeling which once were alive in her. She would have to come to love him all over again, to make him the person closest to her. Aniko was taken aback, and for some reason she quickly removed her briefcase from the sleigh and held it out in front of her as if attempting to defend herself or hold at bay the one who was rushing toward her. When her father had come up close she unwillingly took a step backward.

The old man smelled of smoke, tobacco, and unwashed flesh. Seberui didn't notice anything. Twice he passed the palm of his hand over his dirty malitsa as if he were wiping it off, then he extended it to her.

But Aniko did not respond to this greeting. She looked with fear at her father's black malitsa, at his matted, greasy hair, wrinkled face, and dirty hands. A feeling of nausea rose in her throat.

Seberui didn't notice his daughter's reaction. All of his paternal instincts, which had suffered in loneliness and grief, triumphed over him. He was overjoyed, and with all of these emotions he reached out to the grown daughter who had come to visit him. He was not embarrassed when Aniko failed to shake his hand. On the contrary, he was angry with himself for merely extending his hand and not greeting his daughter with a kiss.

Seberui awkwardly reached out to her, and Aniko caught sight of something black and wet on his mustache. "Tobacco," she realized. She did not succeed in stepping away and just managed to close her eyes when her father's lips touched her cheeks. The briefcase fell, painfully striking her knee.

The father turned away, ashamed of his agitation and joy. Aniko snatched a handkerchief from her pocket and wiped her cheek. Aleshka, who was standing nearby, could not believe his eyes. It was possible to put on a clean fancy coat and smell of perfume, but to wipe away a father's kiss as if it were spit! Desiring to see the girl's face, he came a little closer. Maybe his eyes were deceiving him and there was no handkerchief nor loathing expression. He approached and immediately felt depressed. Yes, her eyes were fidgety. That look of disgust had not left them.

Seberui managed to get himself under control. He turned to Aniko, took her by the hand, and joyfully looked at the people who were nearby, inviting them to admire his daughter. They were already coming closer, having decided that now they could greet the guest.

Seberui picked up the briefcase and for some reason passed it to Aleshka. The old man's hands were trembling. Oh, Aleshka knew very well what it meant when the hand of a Nenets shook.

The first to approach was an elderly woman.

"*Torova*, hello," she said in the Nenets language.

"Hello," Aniko said in Russian, at the same time understanding that it was not a good thing for her to greet these people in Russian, but her tongue could not seem to form the Nenets word for "hello." She had gotten out of the habit, and she was too embarrassed to speak. An old woman in a very worn and tattered yagushka scurried out from underfoot like a hen.

"*Torova*, do you recognize me?" she asked, extending a brown wizened hand.

"*Nyet*," Aniko quietly answered in Russian.

"*Kele! Kele!*" The old woman seemed to be scolding her, then shook her head and added in Russian, "You were little then."

It seemed to Aniko that the old crone was sorry that she had grown up.

Aleshka decided not to say hello. He moved away to a pile of twigs and angrily began to cut the cold branches. Thoughts crowded in his head like disobedient reindeer, and the offense he felt for the sake of the old man did not pass.

"It's a good thing that he didn't notice anything," Aleshka soothed himself while neatly piling up the branches. "Do we really disgust her that much?"

It was not yet dark; what a wonderful April night! It was as if the people had no intention of sleeping. They were bustling about preparing meat, cleaning up their chooms, or hurriedly changing into some clean clothes even though it was considered a great sin for the living to dress up for the night. Who could have known that such an unexpected joy would come this very evening!

Only Aleshka continued to cut wood. He knew that Seberui and Passa would send him after a reindeer if they got it into their heads to make a holiday. Who could entertain a guest without fresh meat? But this time he didn't really want a holiday, and it wasn't because he didn't respect Seberui and their customs. Aleshka was experiencing something else resembling a protest against their guest. He knew that this was not good, and he was ashamed, but he continued to be stubborn.

Passa came up carrying parts of a harness taken from the sleigh.

"How come you've taken to that firewood like a fox goes after bait?"

Aleshka waved the ax, threw it down, and glanced sullenly at the old man. His neighbor's eyes had a peaceful look, and his lips were curved in a smile.

"Go chase the reindeer where we were yesterday. It's a good spot. There's a lot of moss around there," he said. "You can take my dog. She's had a good rest."

"It's not necessary. My dog's also resting." Aleshka nodded at Ichka, who was sleeping under the sleigh.

Only now did Passa notice that the fellow was not quite himself. He was frowning. Whatever for? Wasn't he happy for Seberui? No. Something wasn't right here. With these thoughts he went to see Seberui and Aniko. Seberui was talking with his daughter, but so quietly that Passa even with his hood down did not hear a thing. But he did notice that his friend had an offended look, and he took another step.

Approaching, he asked with concern, "Neve, Aniko probably wants some tea?" And he suggested to her, "Come over to my choom. My wife will give you some tea to drink."

When the girl had left, the men were silent. Seberui was sitting all hunched over.

"You're sitting like you'd been hit on the back with a deer-harness pole."

Passa gave a little smile and took the snuffbox from Seberui's hands. The latter did not stir. It was as if he had not even seen Passa. He only gazed at the choom in which his daughter was hidden, and his head sank even lower.

"What's the matter with you?" Passa asked in a serious tone, and it was as if the quiet, muffled voice of his friend were also downcast.

"She doesn't remember our language."

Passa was dumbfounded. He had not expected this. Children left and came back and left once again, but for someone to forget her native language, that which had been given by the Idols as a treasure, as the eternal distinguishing characteristic of humanity—this had never happened before. He felt a certain spiritual chill, as if he had eaten too much cold meat. He was on the verge of uttering a terrible curse. He didn't even know to whom, but he only said aloud, "She will remember everything." But to himself he added, "If she wants to!"

Being next to her father was awkward for her because she knew that it was necessary to love him, but there was no love, just pity. Aniko trembled each time her father touched her with his hand or even if the flap of his malitsa would graze her coat. It was not any easier for her when she was with the women. They were bustling joyfully around the table, glancing at her briefcase as if expecting presents, and they treated her royally with humorous importance. They took meat in their hands and kept putting it closer to Aniko's cup. She again felt nauseous and wondered to herself if their dresses, their plates, and their hands were clean. And they also reeked of tobacco, dogs, rotten hides, and dampness. She felt like going outside. She had barely finished drinking one cup of tea, happy that the women were silent. How could she have known that laying the table was up to the host, but conversation was the responsibility of the guest?

Finding herself outside at last, Aniko took a breath of fresh air and, putting her briefcase into the sleigh, she sat down feeling weary and lonely. Her father and Passa were standing near the third choom, and talking quietly about something.

Aniko jumped up. Mother! . . . It was her choom. How could she have forgotten that her mother was gone. Everyone had forgotten. No one had said a word about her. Her poor mother was waiting for her daughter to remember that she had not come to see these women, nor had she come to visit her father, but to see her mother. Quickly she went up to the choom. Mother's home. Here she had lived.

Seberui was standing next to his daughter. It was necessary for them to enter the choom together so that his wife would see that all was well, and that they had come to see her. True, it seemed to him that he was not bringing his daughter into his home but a stranger, a completely different person. His daughter just had to look somewhat like the one whom he and his wife had loved and cared for until her sixteenth year, but this girl in no way resembled that little one in the threadbare malitsa. He felt like crying instead of rejoicing.

Aniko thought very hard and implored her memory to remind her just what it was necessary to do. She turned away slightly so that her father would not notice that her eyes had filled with tears. Seberui thought that his daughter had simply forgotten how it was necessary to enter the choom, and he hurriedly threw back the door flap.

"Go on in! Go on in!"

Mama's house . . . a world created for her with love by her weary but tireless hands. Aniko swallowed her tears. She should not upset her father.

"Come on in. Sit down," said Seberui. "Now I'll build a fire."

Aniko wanted to say that she would do everything herself, but her voice failed her. The father went out. Aniko stood for a little while and then sat down on a box in which, as she recalled, the tea service had been kept. From all the corners, from every little thing, childhood and her mama seemed to gaze at her. Aniko covered her face with her hands, but the past had already come back to her. It was standing before her very eyes. . . .

. . . Father who had returned from the hunt; the dogs lying by the fire with their heads facing the early morning light. The warmth of the choom, not only from the happiness around the fire but more so from their smiles. Mama was busying herself around the fire heating up a kettle of meat for the evening.

But then the very nicest thing happened. Neighbors came to see them, earnest folk with beautiful pipes and snuffboxes. Some carried small horns and handmade knife handles, spoons, or buttons. Father, having set his same old snuffbox by his side, began to sing old yarobtsy* legends. Aniko would sit down beside him. She could listen all night because the yarobtsy were very long.

"Why am I remembering all of this?" Aniko asked herself. Suddenly it seemed to her that through these recollections she wanted in some way to make things right with her childhood and her mother. And with her father too.

She stood up and went to the place where her mother always sat, busy with her sewing and with her simple thoughts. What had her mother been thinking about all of her life without her daughter? How had she managed?

Father appeared unexpectedly. He touched her shoulder lightly. "Let's go over and see the neighbors now."

Aniko silently nodded. Yes, it would be easier for her there.

After tea Aniko went to visit her mother. The cemetery wasn't very far away. She took a small vial of tobacco out of her pocket and put it into her briefcase so as not to lose it. Her father had asked her to give this to her mother.

She decided to carry the little wreath of bright flowers in her hand, fearing that she might crumple them. The bouquet was small and delicate. She had bought it at the market just before her flight left. In the camp she did

*Oral stories of the Nentsy people.

not wish to display it because she was shy, and she was afraid that they would not understand and might criticize her for this.

Getting there was not difficult. The snow path was as hard as asphalt. It was obvious that people had been traveling on it for several decades. Here and there last year's grass peeped out from under the wet snow. Aniko tried to imagine it green and luxuriant, but she could not.

Soon one could see the sacred place and behind it the cemetery.

She immediately found her mother's grave. Aniko stood for a little while in silence and then poured the tobacco over the coffin and onto the earth as her father had instructed. She sat down on a board left from the funeral and leaned her shoulder against the coffin.

"When she was alive, I didn't have the chance, but at least now even though she is dead I can caress her and beg forgiveness that I was not with her.

"Forgive me. I was guilty of separating us. I left you in order to study and better myself. But have I really become any better?"

She recalled that several times after her geological field work she could have come home. At least once a month she could have written or sent small packages. Her parents would have been happy to receive any news at all from her. But they were forgiving people. They never knew exactly where their daughter was living.

How terrible that one cannot change anything in the past. Aniko felt on the verge of tears. She straightened up the flowers on the wreath, placed it on the coffin, and weighed it down with a stone. She tried to imagine her mother's face . . . and could not.

"What was it like? Kind? Malevolent?" Aniko removed her mitten and stroked the cold boards. Her mother's face. . . . She just couldn't remember it. There was the severe face of Elizaveta Ivanovna, the teacher at the boarding school. When Aniko was in the fourth grade Elizaveta Ivanovna wanted to make a good gymnast of her. . . . Then there was the kind little smile of old Liza, the night nurse, whose face was disfigured by smallpox. Aniko often went over to her house to drink tea and listen to her stories and songs for hours at a time. . . . And then there were the eyes of Valentina Georgievna Starenko, her favorite teacher, gazing at her so brightly and sternly, which had replaced much if not all of her former life.

Aniko began to cry. It didn't make any difference that these were belated tears, tears of shame. How cozy, peaceful and nice it must be for people who have mothers . . . even if they are somewhat old and wrinkled. It wouldn't even make any difference if they were a little stupid and funny. At least they were alive!

We come to our mothers and bring them our hurts and our needs, and we forget about their own cares and concerns. We take our happiness to our mothers less often, although we know that they will not request even a little piece of it but will actually redouble it.

It is very difficult to visit the dead, to know that you have come too late, and to realize that it is all your own fault, your fault alone, that the hustle and bustle of everyday life, which you have become so accustomed to blaming for everything, has absolutely nothing to do with anything. Aniko did not cry any longer, for she understood that tears would not earn her mother's forgiveness.

Temuiko slowly moved away from the herd. He kept raising his head and looking at the dog. If only it wouldn't notice. Then he again lowered his muzzle, giving the appearance of nibbling diligently at the moss. Seeing that there would not be any chase, Temuiko moved on more boldly. At first he took the snow path and soon turned toward the cemetery. It was not every day that he came here, but he remembered very well the spot where his mother lay, and now he was approaching her with quick and confident strides.

Suddenly Temuiko stopped. His nostrils twitched—he had caught sight of Aniko. He stood there sniffing, accustoming himself to her scent, and then cautiously approached the grave, but from the other side. He touched the planks with his lips, and lowering his long eyelashes just a little, he remained absolutely still.

Aniko stood there unable to believe either her eyes or her heart. A reindeer at the grave?! Maybe it had accidently wandered away, become separated from the herd and, seeing a person, turned in here. It seemed like that proud-looking one she had seen yesterday. Yes, it was he!

Temuiko wasn't paying any attention to her. His large melancholy eyes gazed at the sarcophagus and at the thawed patches of earth near it. He seemed to be thinking of something sad which was not of the reindeer world. Aniko examined him silently. The reindeer's antlers had already fallen off, and in their place damp new shoots were sticking out, but this did not make him ugly. On the contrary, they gave his head a special elegance and youthfulness, and emphasized his broad, slightly prominent forehead.

"He hasn't come here for nothing or wandered here by chance. Then why?" she wondered, already guessing that the deer had "consciously" come to see its mother, but for some reason she was ashamed to admit this even to herself.

Aniko stood up, placed the bottle with the remaining tobacco onto the sarcophagus, adjusted her scarf and hat, and awkwardly bowed her head, mentally bidding her mother farewell.

The meeting with the deer had left a weight on her soul, but in addition a certain radiant feeling. She started to follow Temuiko's fresh tracks, thinking that she had left, and that he had remained. She turned around. Temuiko was not looking at her. He was standing with his beautiful head hanging low.

It suddenly seemed to Aniko that the reindeer was crying. Otherwise, why would he be standing like that? It must have been very difficult for him. She waited for Temuiko to raise his head, but the reindeer did not stir. Suddenly from somewhere a partridge began to give a boisterous laugh and was immediately answered by another. They were laughing just as one should in spring, easily and joyously.

.   .   .   .   .

Seberui was sitting with his face to the sunset. The warm rays of the sun ran along his deep wrinkles, and it seemed to the old Nenets, who was dozing, that his young daughter was stroking his face with her soft fingers.

Although the sun was huge and caressing, there was no warmth that could stir the lonely old man. Seberui understood that his daughter was leaving. After supper he glanced through the open door flap quite by accident and saw that she was packing her things without paying any attention to the gifts which the women of the camp had given her. The presents were lying on the bed in a forgotten heap.

Already on that first evening, even at the moment when they met, a certain fear had crept into his mind along with joy. But Seberui had attempted to deceive himself, and at times he actually believed that all would be well and that his daughter would not abandon him in his old age. But now he knew that Aniko was in a hurry to return. In that great land many kilometers away something waited for her that was closer and more akin to her than her father and his grief. He would have to live out his last days alone. After all, he couldn't even move to the big village. His wife and daughter were here. His happiness had been here.

Buro carefully approached his master, lay down, and also watched the sunset for a little while. Then he crawled up to Seberui and licked the toes of his boots. He always did it like this so that the master would not be angry at being bothered. Seberui bent down, passed his hand over the dog's neck, and again became lost in thought. . . .

Aniko awoke in fear. She had had a dream. Her mother was defending her from someone. Aniko didn't understand from just whom. Her mother was waving her arms and shouting something angrily, barring the way to her daughter. And she had no face.

Having hurriedly thrust aside the door flap, Aniko threw on her coat. She took a long drink of water, searching for her father with her eyes. He was nowhere to be seen. The yagushka that he always wore was lying on the bed just as Aniko had put it there on the day before. "Where is he? What is the matter with him?" A little more frightened, she ran outside, walked around the choom and saw her father in the sleigh.

After taking a few steps, Aniko heard her father's voice, quiet and unsuspecting. It was as if he were talking to his closest friend.

"Buro, we're going to be left alone again."

Aniko was a little taken aback. It seemed to her that her father had lost his senses. Opposite him sat his dog, attentively looking at its master. Neither one noticed Aniko.

"Don't cry," said Seberui in a quiet and affectionate whisper. "We'll live quietly. We won't bother anybody. You know, I've learned how to sew. I'll fix my own kisy* and malitsa. Just think ahead a little. Passa's mother will go into the other world, and there won't be anyone to fix our things. Just look."

Seberui bent over and pointed at his foot. There was a little hole with a piece of straw jutting out of one of his kisy. They usually put some straw behind their chizhi.**

"Tomorrow I'll sew up that little hole. Just don't say anything to anybody."

Buro sniffed the straw and gave a snort.

"Good, good! Don't look at me like that."

Seberui was silent for a little while and then continued in a calm tone.

"I have a perfectly good malitsa, and it's still new. The mistress herself sewed it for me. And you just track those deer well so that nobody looks down on us and says that Seberui and Buro don't work."

Aniko could not hold herself back.

"Papa!"

Seberui turned around sharply. Rushing up to him, she threw her arms around her father's head, choking back the tears.

"Don't talk, don't talk to the dog!"

Just as in his dream she stroked his arms, his hair, while all the while repeating, her voice breaking, "Don't talk. Look at me! I'll come back, papa, just let me go for a while! I can't stay. I need to figure it out."

She hid her face in her malitsa, speaking quickly.

"Wait for me. I'll get myself together, and I'll be with you, OK? Do you believe me? Do you believe?"

Seberui only nodded and wiped her tears away with his palm. Yes, he was ready to let her go even if forever because now he knew that he had a

---

* Reindeer-skin boots worn by the people of the Far North.

**Long fur stockings worn under the kisy.

daughter, a blood relative on earth, and that these roots would remain and not perish or wither away.

"Go, daughter, but be a good person. And if you return all this will be yours. I will die, but these places will always accept you as their own."

He kissed Aniko on the head, stood up, and said, "Wait for me here."

Returning, he put something wrapped up in a red piece of cloth into the sled. His eyes had a severe and strange look, as if there was not his daughter standing before him but a wise person who had lived a difficult life not unlike his own. He unraveled the cloth, sank to his knees, and remained in that position for some time with his head bowed. Then he stood up, called his daughter over with a nod, and pointed with his eyes at the sled. There sat a little tiny person in a snow-white malitsa. Holding her breath, Aniko looked into his bright eyes and seemed unable to remove her gaze.

"On your knees!" her father requested quietly and affectionately. Aniko obediently lowered herself, feeling the warmth of her father's hand on her shoulder.

"You alone are the last of the Nogo tribe. Look, this is its master. Talk with him."

"About what?" Aniko asked, a bit frightened, feeling that she was accomplishing something important, sacred, and wise.

"Ask him to be kind to you." The voice of her father was heard from somewhere in the distance, and it seemed that the bright eye sockets of the master of the tribe were becoming first larger, then smaller, as if he were gazing intently at the girl.

"I have already asked him. Now you don't be afraid. He will be with you and with the one who will become your husband. Just ask him. He is wise even if he wasn't able to protect your mother and little sister."

Aniko bowed her head and closed her eyes. At that moment she believed that her fate, the fate of her tribe and of her children, depended upon the Idol calmly looking at her. She believed, and was already requesting that he be kind to her, to her people, and especially to her lonely father.

Aniko's father touched her shoulder. She stood up. Her eyes now had that same severe look which her father had assumed just a minute ago. Her face turned pale. Seberui took the Idol and, approaching his daughter, stopped.

"Remember, he must always live. It isn't important where. In a choom or in a wooden house, but he must live."

Aniko said nothing, but with wide-open eyes and a heart filled with love for life, for her father, and for the land of her ancestors, she took the Idol, and for a few minutes stood motionless, understanding that she had now accepted the soul of her father, her mother, her grandfather and of all those who had lived on the land before her. It was not the Idol that her father had handed over to her, but a right, a sacred duty to live in one's native land and be a good person.

1978

Translated by Delbert Phillips

LESLIE MARMON SILKO ❖ "The stories are always bringing us together, keeping this whole together, keeping this family together, keeping this clan together." Thus Leslie Silko describes the role of storytelling among the Laguna Pueblo people in New Mexico. Silko was born in Albuquerque in 1948, of mixed Native American, Mexican, and Anglo heritage. She grew up at Laguna, attending the Bureau of Indian Affairs school there and, later, a Catholic school in Albuquerque. After receiving her B.A. in English at the University of New Mexico and studying briefly in law school, she decided to pursue fiction writing full-time. She has held teaching positions at several colleges and universities, including Navajo Community College, the University of New Mexico, and the University of Arizona, and has received fellowships from the National Endowment for the Arts and the MacArthur Foundation.

For Silko, the impetus to write grew out of hearing the old stories of her people, especially as told by her grandmother Lillie and her grandfather Hank Marmon's sister-in-law, "Aunt Susie," as well as from her conviction of the ceremonial function of storytelling: "You don't have anything," she says, "if you don't have the stories." She is concerned not only with her own self-definition in her complex relation to the Laguna and Anglo worlds but with looking after the communal stories she perpetuates through her short fiction, poems, novels, and films. She has authored several collections of poems and stories, including *Laguna Woman* (1974) and *Storyteller* (1981), and two novels, *Ceremony* (1977) and *Almanac of the Dead* (1991). The mother of two sons, Silko lives on a ranch outside Tucson.

Storyteller

LESLIE MARMON SILKO

Every day the sun came up a little lower on the horizon, moving more slowly until one day she got excited and started calling the jailer. She realized she had been sitting there for many hours, yet the sun had not moved from the center of the sky. The color of the sky had not been good lately; it had been pale blue, almost white, even when there were no clouds. She told herself it wasn't a good sign for the sky to be indistinguishable from the river ice, frozen solid and white against the earth. The tundra rose up behind the river but all the boundaries between the river and hills and sky were lost in the density of the pale ice.

She yelled again, this time some English words which came randomly into her mouth, probably swear words she'd heard from the oil drilling crews last winter. The jailer was an Eskimo, but he would not speak Yupik to her. She had watched people in other cells, when they spoke to him in Yupik he ignored them until they spoke English.

He came and stared at her. She didn't know if he understood what she was telling him until he glanced behind her at the small high window. He looked at the sun, and turned and walked away. She could hear the buckles on his heavy snowmobile boots jingle as he walked to the front of the building.

It was like the other buildings that white people, the Gussucks, brought with them: BIA and school buildings, portable buildings that arrived sliced in halves, on barges coming up the river. Squares of metal panelling bulged out with the layers of insulation stuffed inside. She had asked once what it was and someone told her it was to keep out the cold. She had not laughed then, but she did now. She walked over to the small double-pane window and she laughed out loud. They thought they could keep out the cold with stringy yellow wadding. Look at the sun. It wasn't moving; it was frozen, caught in the middle of the sky. Look at the sky, solid as the river with ice which had trapped the sun. It had not moved for a long time; in a few more hours it would be weak, and heavy frost would begin to appear on the edges and spread across the face of the sun like a mask. Its light was pale yellow, worn thin by the winter.

She could see people walking down the snow-packed roads, their breath steaming out from their parka hoods, faces hidden and protected by deep ruffs of fur. There were no cars or snowmobiles that day; the cold had silenced their machines. The metal froze; it split and shattered. Oil hardened and moving parts jammed solidly. She had seen it happen to their big yellow machines and the giant drill last winter when they came to drill their test holes. The cold stopped them, and they were helpless against it.

Her village was many miles upriver from this town, but in her mind she could see it clearly. Their house was not near the village houses. It stood alone on the bank upriver from the village. Snow had drifted to the eaves of the roof on the north side, but on the west side, by the door, the path was almost clear. She had nailed scraps of red tin over the logs last summer. She had done it for the bright red color, not for added warmth the way the village people had done. This final winter had been coming even then; there had been signs of its approach for many years.

She went because she was curious about the big school where the Government sent all the other girls and boys. She had not played much with the village children while she was growing up because they were afraid of the old man, and they ran when her grandmother came. She went because she was tired of being alone with the old woman whose body had been stiffening for as long as the girl could remember. Her knees and knuckles were swollen grotesquely, and the pain had squeezed the brown skin of her face tight against the bones; it left her eyes hard like river stone. The girl asked once what it was that did this to her body, and the old woman had raised up from sewing a sealskin boot, and stared at her.

"The joints," the old woman said in a low voice, whispering like wind across the roof, "the joints are swollen with anger."

Sometimes she did not answer and only stared at the girl. Each year she spoke less and less, but the old man talked more—all night sometimes, not to anyone but himself; in a soft deliberate voice, he told stories, moving his smooth brown hands above the blankets. He had not fished or hunted with the other men for many years, although he was not crippled or sick. He stayed in his bed, smelling like dry fish and urine, telling stories all winter; and when warm weather came, he went to his place on the river bank. He sat with a long willow stick, poking at the smoldering moss he burned against the insects while he continued with the stories.

The trouble was that she had not recognized the warnings in time. She did not see what the Gussuck school would do to her until she walked into the dormitory and realized that the old man had not been lying about the place. She thought he had been trying to scare her as he used to when she was very small and her grandmother was outside cutting up fish. She hadn't believed what he told her about the school because she knew he wanted to keep her there in the log house with him. She knew what he wanted.

The dormitory matron pulled down her underpants and whipped her with a leather belt because she refused to speak English.

"Those backwards village people," the matron said, because she was an Eskimo who had worked for the BIA a long time, "they kept this one until she was too big to learn." The other girls whispered in English. They knew how to work the showers, and they washed and curled their hair at night. They ate Gussuck food. She lay on her bed and imagined what her grandmother might be sewing, and what the old man was eating in his bed. When summer came, they sent her home.

The way her grandmother had hugged her before she left for school had been a warning too, because the old woman had not hugged or touched her for many years. Not like the old man, whose hands were always hunting, like ravens circling lazily in the sky, ready to touch her. She was not surprised when the priest and the old man met her at the landing strip, to say that the old lady was gone. The priest asked her where she would like to stay. He referred to the old man as her grandfather, but she did not bother to correct him. She had already been thinking about it; if she went with the priest, he would send her away to a school. But the old man was different. She knew he wouldn't send her back to school. She knew he wanted to keep her.

He told her one time, that she would get too old for him faster than he got too old for her; but again she had not believed him because sometimes he lied. He had lied about what he would do with her if she came into his bed. But as the years passed, she realized what he said was true. She was restless and strong. She had no patience with the old man who had never changed his slow smooth motions under the blankets.

The old man was in his bed for the winter; he did not leave it except to use the slop bucket in the corner. He was dozing with his mouth open slightly; his lips quivered and sometimes they moved like he was telling a story even while he dreamed. She pulled on the sealskin boots, the mukluks with the bright red flannel linings her grandmother had sewn for her, and she tied the braided red yarn tassels around her ankles over the gray wool pants. She zipped the wolfskin parka. Her grandmother had worn it for many years, but the old man said that before she died, she instructed him to bury her in an old black sweater, and to give the parka to the girl. The wolf pelts were creamy colored and silver, almost white in some places, and when the old lady had walked across the tundra in the winter, she was invisible in the snow.

She walked toward the village, breaking her own path through the deep snow. A team of sled dogs tied outside a house at the edge of the village leaped against their chains to bark at her. She kept walking, watching the dusky sky for the first evening stars. It was warm and the dogs were alert. When it got cold again, the dogs would lie curled and still, too drowsy from the cold to bark or pull at the chains. She laughed loudly because it made them howl and snarl. Once the old man had seen her tease the dogs and he shook his head. "So that's the kind of woman you are," he said, "in the wintertime the two of us are no different from those dogs. We wait in the cold for someone to bring us a few dry fish."

She laughed out loud again, and kept walking. She was thinking about the Gussuck oil drillers. They were strange; they watched her when she walked near their machines. She wondered what they looked like underneath their quilted goosedown trousers; she wanted to know how they moved. They would be something different from the old man.

The old man screamed at her. He shook her shoulders so violently that her head bumped against the log wall. "I smelled it!" he yelled, "as soon as I woke up! I am sure of it now. You can't fool me!" His thin legs were shaking inside the baggy wool trousers; he stumbled over her boots in his bare feet. His toenails were long and yellow like bird claws; she had seen a gray crane last summer fighting another in the shallow water on the edge of the river. She laughed out loud and pulled her shoulder out of his grip. He stood in front of her. He was breathing hard and shaking; he looked weak. He would probably die next winter.

"I'm warning you," he said, "I'm warning you." He crawled back into his bunk then, and reached under the old soiled feather pillow for a piece of dry fish. He lay back on the pillow, staring at the ceiling and chewed dry strips of salmon. "I don't know what the old woman told you," he said, "but there will be trouble." He looked over to see if she was listening. His face suddenly relaxed into a smile, his dark slanty eyes were lost in wrinkles of brown skin. "I could tell you, but you are too good for warnings now. I can smell what you did all night with the Gussucks."

She did not understand why they came there, because the village was small and so far upriver that even some Eskimos who had been away to school did not want to come back. They stayed downriver in the town. They said the village was too quiet. They were used to the town where the boarding school was located, with electric lights and running water. After all those years away at school, they had forgotten how to set nets in the river and where to hunt

seals in the fall. When she asked the old man why the Gussucks bothered to
come to the village, his narrow eyes got bright with excitement.

"They only come when there is something to steal. The fur animals are
too difficult for them to get now, and the seals and fish are hard to find.
Now they come for oil deep in the earth. But this is the last time for them."
His breathing was wheezy and fast; his hands gestured at the sky. "It is approaching. As it comes, ice will push across the sky." His eyes were open
wide and he stared at the low ceiling rafters for hours without blinking. She
remembered all this clearly because he began the story that day, the story
he told from that time on. It began with a giant bear which he described
muscle by muscle, from the curve of the ivory claws to the whorls of hair at
the top of the massive skull. And for eight days he did not sleep, but talked
continuously of the giant bear whose color was pale blue glacier ice.

The snow was dirty and worn down in a path to the door. On either side
of the path, the snow was higher than her head. In front of the door there
were jagged yellow stains melted into the snow where men had urinated.
She stopped in the entry way and kicked the snow off her boots. The room
was dim; a kerosene lantern by the cash register was burning low. The long
wooden shelves were jammed with cans of beans and potted meats. On the
bottom shelf a jar of mayonnaise was broken open, leaking oily white clots on
the floor. There was no one in the room except the yellowish dog sleeping
in the front of the long glass display case. A reflection made it appear to
be lying on the knives and ammunition inside the case. Gussucks kept dogs
inside their houses with them; they did not seem to mind the odors which
seeped out of the dogs. "They tell us we are dirty for the food we eat—raw
fish and fermented meat. But we do not live with dogs," the old man once
said. She heard voices in the back room, and the sound of bottles set down
hard on tables.

They were always confident. The first year they waited for the ice to
break up on the river, and then they brought their big yellow machines up
river on barges. They planned to drill their test holes during the summer to
avoid the freezing. But the imprints and graves of their machines were still
there, on the edge of the tundra above the river, where the summer mud had
swallowed them before they ever left sight of the river. The village people
had gathered to watch the white men, and to laugh as they drove the giant
machines, one by one, off the steel ramp into the bogs; as if sheer numbers
of vehicles would somehow make the tundra solid. But the old man said they
behaved like desperate people, and they would come back again. When the
tundra was frozen solid, they returned.

Village women did not even look through the door to the back room. The priest had warned them. The storeman was watching her because he didn't let Eskimos or Indians sit down at the tables in the back room. But she knew he couldn't throw her out if one of his Gussuck customers invited her to sit with him. She walked across the room. They stared at her, but she had the feeling she was walking for someone else, not herself, so their eyes did not matter. The red-haired man pulled out a chair and motioned for her to sit down. She looked back at the storeman while the red-haired man poured her a glass of red sweet wine. She wanted to laugh at the storeman the way she laughed at the dogs, straining against the chains, howling at her.

The red-haired man kept talking to the other Gussucks sitting around the table, but he slid one hand off the top of the table to her thigh. She looked over at the storeman to see if he was still watching her. She laughed out loud at him and the red-haired man stopped talking and turned to her. He asked if she wanted to go. She nodded and stood up.

Someone in the village had been telling him things about her, he said as they walked down the road to his trailer. She understood that much of what he was saying, but the rest she did not hear. The whine of the big generators at the construction camp sucked away the sound of his words. But English was of no concern to her anymore, and neither was anything the Christians in the village might say about her or the old man. She smiled at the effect of the subzero air on the electric lights around the trailers; they did not shine. They left only flat yellow holes in the darkness.

It took him a long time to get ready, even after she had undressed for him. She waited in the bed with the blankets pulled close, watching him. He adjusted the thermostat and lit candles in the room, turning out the electric lights. He searched through a stack of record albums until he found the right one. She was not sure about the last thing he did: he taped something on the wall behind the bed where he could see it while he lay on top of her. He was shriveled and white from the cold; he pushed against her body for warmth. He guided her hands to his thighs; he was shivering.

She had returned a last time because she wanted to know what it was he stuck on the wall above the bed. After he finished each time, he reached up and pulled it loose, folding it carefully so that she could not see it. But this time she was ready; she waited for his fast breathing and sudden collapse on top of her. She slid out from under him and stood up beside the bed. She looked at the picture while she got dressed. He did not raise his face from the pillow, and she thought she heard teeth rattling together as she left the room.

She heard the old man move when she came in. After the Gussuck's trailer, the log house felt cool. It smelled like dry fish and cured meat. The room was dark except for the blinking yellow flame in the mica window of the oil stove. She squatted in front of the stove and watched the flames for a long time before she walked to the bed where her grandmother had slept. The bed was covered with a mound of rags and fur scraps the old woman had saved. She reached into the mound until she felt something cold and solid wrapped in a wool blanket. She pushed her fingers around it until she felt smooth stone. Long ago, before the Gussucks came, they had burned whale oil in the big stone lamp which made light and heat as well. The old woman had saved everything they would need when the time came.

In the morning, the old man pulled a piece of dry caribou meat from under the blankets and offered it to her. While she was gone, men from the village had brought a bundle of dry meat. She chewed it slowly, thinking about the way they still came from the village to take care of the old man and his stories. But she had a story now, about the red-haired Gussuck. The old man knew what she was thinking, and his smile made his face seem more round than it was.

"Well," he said, "what was it?"

"A woman with a big dog on top of her."

He laughed softly to himself and walked over to the water barrel. He dipped the tin cup into the water.

"It doesn't surprise me," he said.

"Grandma," she said, "there was something red in the grass that morning. I remember." She had not asked about her parents before. The old woman stopped splitting the fish bellies open for the willow drying racks. Her jaw muscles pulled so tightly against her skull, the girl thought the old woman would not be able to speak.

"They bought a tin can full of it from the storeman. Late at night. He told them it was alcohol safe to drink. They traded a rifle for it." The old woman's voice sounded like each word stole strength from her. "It made no difference about the rifle. That year the Gussuck boats had come, firing big guns at the walrus and seals. There was nothing left to hunt after that anyway. So," the old lady said, in a low soft voice the girl had not heard for a long time, "I didn't say anything to them when they left that night."

"Right over there," she said, pointing at the fallen poles, half buried in the river sand and tall grass, "in the summer shelter. The sun was high half the night then. Early in the morning when it was still low, the policeman came around. I told the interpreter to tell him that the storeman had poisoned them." She made outlines in the air in front of her, showing how their bodies lay twisted on the sand; telling the story was like laboring to walk through deep snow; sweat shone in the white hair around her forehead. "I told the priest too, after he came. I told him the storeman lied." She turned away from the girl. She held her mouth even tighter, set solidly, not in sorrow or anger, but against the pain, which was all that remained. "I never believed," she said, "not much anyway. I wasn't surprised when the priest did nothing."

The wind came off the river and folded the tall grass into itself like river waves. She could feel the silence the story left, and she wanted to have the old woman go on.

"I heard sounds that night, grandma. Sounds like someone was singing. It was light outside. I could see something red on the ground." The old woman did not answer her; she moved to the tub full of fish on the ground beside the workbench. She stabbed her knife into the belly of a whitefish and lifted it onto the bench. "The Gussuck storeman left the village right after that," the old woman said as she pulled the entrails from the fish, "otherwise, I could tell you more." The old woman's voice flowed with the wind blowing off the river; they never spoke of it again.

When the willows got their leaves and the grass grew tall along the river banks and around the sloughs, she walked early in the morning. While the sun was still low on the horizon, she listened to the wind off the river; its sound was like the voice that day long ago. In the distance, she could hear the engines of the machinery the oil drillers had left the winter before, but she did not go near the village or the store. The sun never left the sky and the summer became the same long day, with only the winds to fan the sun into brightness or allow it to slip into twilight.

She sat beside the old man at his place on the river bank. She poked the smoky fire for him, and felt herself growing wide and thin in the sun as if she had been split from belly to throat and strung on the willow pole in preparation for the winter to come. The old man did not speak anymore. When men from the village brought him fresh fish he hid them deep in the river grass where it was cool. After he went inside, she split the fish open and spread them to dry on the willow frame the way the old woman had done. Inside, he dozed and talked to himself. He had talked all winter, softly and incessantly, about the giant polar bear stalking a lone hunter across Bering Sea ice. After all the months the old man had been telling the story, the bear was within a hundred feet of the man; but the ice fog had closed in on them now and the man could only smell the sharp ammonia odor of the bear, and hear the edge of the snow crust crack under the giant paws.

One night she listened to the old man tell the story all night in his sleep, describing each crystal of ice and the slightly different sounds they made under each paw; first the left and then the right paw, then the hind feet. Her grandmother was there suddenly, a shadow around the stove. She spoke in her low wind voice and the girl was afraid to sit up to hear more clearly.

Maybe what she said had been to the old man because he stopped telling the story and began to snore softly the way he had long ago when the old woman had scolded him for telling his stories while others in the house were trying to sleep. But the last words she heard clearly: "It will take a long time, but the story must be told. There must not be any lies." She pulled the blankets up around her chin, slowly, so that her movements would not be seen. She thought her grandmother was talking about the old man's bear story; she did not know about the other story then.

She left the old man wheezing and snoring in his bed. She walked through river grass glistening with frost; the bright green summer color was already fading. She watched the sun move across the sky, already lower on the horizon, already moving away from the village. She stopped by the fallen poles of the summer shelter where her parents had died. Frost glittered on the river sand too; in a few more weeks there would be snow. The predawn light would be the color of an old woman. An old woman sky full of snow. There had been something red lying on the ground the morning they died. She looked for it again, pushing aside the grass with her foot. She knelt in the sand and looked under the fallen structure for some trace of it. When she found it, she would know what the old woman had never told her. She squatted down close to the gray poles and leaned her back against them. The wind made her shiver.

The summer rain had washed the mud from between the logs; the sod blocks stacked as high as her belly next to the log walls had lost their square-cut shape and had grown into soft mounds of tundra moss and stiff-bladed grass bending with clusters of seed bristles. She looked at the northwest, in the direction of the Bering Sea. The cold would come down from there to find narrow slits in the mud, rainwater holes in the outer layer of sod which protected the log house. The dark green tundra stretched away flat and continuous. Somewhere the sea and the land met; she knew by their dark green colors there were no boundaries between them. That was how the cold would come: when the boundaries were gone the polar ice would range across the land into the sky. She watched the horizon for a long time. She would stand in that place on the north side of the house and she would keep watch on the northwest horizon, and eventually she would see it come. She would watch for its approach in the stars, and hear it come with the wind. These preparations were unfamiliar, but gradually she recognized them as she did her own footprints in the snow.

She emptied the slop jar beside his bed twice a day and kept the barrel full of water melted from river ice. He did not recognize her anymore, and when he spoke to her, he called her by her grandmother's name and talked about people and events from long ago, before he went back to telling the story. The giant bear was creeping across the new snow on its belly, close enough now that the man could hear the rasp of its breathing. On and on in a soft singing voice, the old man caressed the story, repeating the words again and again like gentle strokes.

The sky was gray like a river crane's egg; its density curved into the thin crust of frost already covering the land. She looked at the bright red color of the tin against the ground and the sky and she told the village men to bring the pieces for the old man and her. To drill the test holes in the tundra, the Gussucks had used hundreds of barrels of fuel. The village people split open the empty barrels that were abandoned on the river bank, and pounded the red tin into flat sheets. The village people were using the strips of tin to mend walls and roofs for winter. But she nailed it on the log walls for its color. When she finished, she walked away with the hammer in her hand, not turning around until she was far away, on the ridge above the river banks, and then she looked back. She felt a chill when she saw how the sky and the land were already losing their boundaries, already becoming lost in each other. But the red tin penetrated the thick white color of earth and sky; it defined the boundaries like a wound revealing the ribs and heart of a great caribou about to bolt and be lost to the hunter forever. That night the wind howled and when she scratched a hole through the heavy frost on the inside of the window, she could see nothing but the impenetrable white; whether it was blowing snow or snow that had drifted as high as the house, she did not know.

It had come down suddenly, and she stood with her back to the wind looking at the river, its smoky water clotted with ice. The wind had blown the snow over the frozen river, hiding thin blue streaks where fast water ran under ice translucent and fragile as memory. But she could see shadows of boundaries, outlines of paths which were slender branches of solidity reaching out from the earth. She spent days walking on the river, watching the colors of ice that would safely hold her, kicking the heel of her boot into the snow crust, listening for a solid sound. When she could feel the paths through the soles of her feet, she went to the middle of the river where the fast gray water churned under a thin pane of ice. She looked back. On the river bank in the distance she could see the red tin nailed to the log house, something not swallowed up by the heavy white belly of the sky or caught in the folds of the frozen earth. It was time.

The wolverine fur around the hood of her parka was white with the frost from her breathing. The warmth inside the store melted it, and she felt tiny drops of water on her face. The storeman came in from the back room. She unzipped the parka and stood by the oil stove. She didn't look at him, but stared instead at the yellowish dog, covered with scabs of matted hair, sleeping in front of the stove. She thought of the Gussuck's picture, taped on the wall above the bed and she laughed out loud. The sound of her laughter was piercing; the yellow dog jumped to its feet and the hair bristled down its back. The storeman was watching her. She wanted to laugh again because he didn't know about the ice. He did not know that it was prowling the earth, or that it had already pushed its way into the sky to seize the sun. She sat down in the chair by the stove and shook her long hair loose. He was like a dog tied up all winter, watching while the others got fed. He remembered how she had gone with the oil drillers, and his blue eyes moved like flies crawling over her body. He held his thin pale lips like he wanted to spit on her. He hated the people because they had something of value, the old man said, something which the Gussucks could never have. They thought they could take it, suck it out of the earth or cut it from the mountains; but they were fools.

There was a matted hunk of dog hair on the floor by her foot. She thought of the yellow insulation coming unstuffed: their defense against the freezing going to pieces as it advanced on them. The ice was crouching on the northwest horizon like the old man's bear. She laughed out loud again. The sun would be down now; it was time.

The first time he spoke to her, she did not hear what he said, so she did not answer or even look up at him. He spoke to her again but his words were only noises coming from his pale mouth, trembling now as his anger began to unravel. He jerked her up and the chair fell over behind her. His arms were shaking and she could feel his hands tense up, pulling the edges of the parka tighter. He raised his fist to hit her, his thin body quivering with rage; but the fist collapsed with the desire he had for the valuable things, which, the old man had rightly said, was the only reason they came. She could hear his heart pounding as he held her close and arched his hips against her, groaning and breathing in spasms. She twisted away from him and ducked under his arms.

She ran with a mitten over her mouth, breathing through the fur to protect her lungs from the freezing air. She could hear him running behind her, his heavy breathing, the occasional sound of metal jingling against metal. But he ran without his parka or mittens, breathing the frozen air; its fire squeezed the lungs against the ribs and it was enough that he could not catch her near his store. On the river bank he realized how far he was from his stove, and the wads of yellow stuffing that held off the cold. But the girl was not able to run very fast through the deep drifts at the edge of the river. The twilight was luminous and he could still see clearly for a long distance; he knew he could catch her so he kept running.

When she neared the middle of the river she looked over her shoulder. He was not following her tracks; he went straight across the ice, running the shortest distance to reach her. He was close then; his face was twisted and scarlet from the exertion and the cold. There was satisfaction in his eyes; he was sure he could outrun her.

She was familiar with the river, down to the instant ice flexed into hairline fractures, and the cracking bone-sliver sounds gathered momentum with the opening ice until the churning gray water was set free. She stopped and turned to the sound of the river and the rattle of swirling ice fragments where he fell through. She pulled off a mitten and zipped the parka to her throat. She was conscious then of her own rapid breathing.

She moved slowly, kicking the ice ahead with the heel of her boot, feeling for sinews of ice to hold her. She looked ahead and all around herself; in the twilight, the dense white sky had merged into the flat snow-covered tundra. In the frantic running she had lost her place on the river. She stood still. The east bank of the river was lost in the sky; the boundaries had been swallowed by the freezing white. But then, in the distance, she saw something red, and suddenly it was as she had remembered it all those years.

She sat on her bed and while she waited, she listened to the old man. The hunter had found a small jagged knoll on the ice. He pulled his beaver fur cap off his head; the fur inside it steamed with his body heat and sweat. He left it upside down on the ice for the great bear to stalk, and he waited downwind on top of the ice knoll; he was holding the jade knife.

She thought she could see the end of his story in the way he wheezed out the words; but still he reached into his cache of dry fish and dribbled water into his mouth from the tin cup. All night she listened to him describe each breath the man took, each motion of the bear's head as it tried to catch the sound of the man's breathing, and tested the wind for his scent.

The state trooper asked her questions, and the woman who cleaned house for the priest translated them into Yupik. They wanted to know what happened to the storeman, the Gussuck who had been seen running after her down the road onto the river late last evening. He had not come back, and the Gussuck boss in Anchorage was concerned about him. She did not answer for a long time because the old man suddenly sat up in his bed and began to talk excitedly, looking at all of them—the trooper in his dark glasses and the housekeeper in her corduroy parka. He kept saying, "The story! The story! Eh-ya! The great bear! The hunter!"

They asked her again, what happened to the man from the Northern Commercial store. "He lied to them. He told them it was safe to drink. But I will not lie." She stood up and put on the gray wolfskin parka. "I killed him," she said, "but I don't lie."

The attorney came back again, and the jailer slid open the steel doors and opened the cell to let him in. He motioned for the jailer to stay to translate for him. She laughed when she saw how the jailer would be forced by this Gussuck to speak Yupik to her. She liked the Gussuck attorney for that, and for the thinning hair on his head. He was very tall, and she liked to think about the exposure of his head to the freezing; she wondered if he would feel the ice descending from the sky before the others did. He wanted to know why she told the state trooper she had killed the storeman. Some village children had seen it happen, he said, and it was an accident. "That's all you have to say to the judge: it was an accident." He kept repeating it over and over again to her, slowly in a loud but gentle voice: "It was an accident. He was running after you and he fell through the ice. That's all you have to say in court. That's all. And they will let you go home. Back to your village." The jailer translated the words sullenly, staring down at the floor. She shook her head. "I will not change the story, not even to escape this place and go home. I intended that he die. The story must be told as it is." The attorney exhaled loudly; his eyes looked tired. "Tell her that she could not have killed him that way. He was a white man. He ran after her without a parka or mittens. She could not have planned that." He paused and turned toward the cell door. "Tell her I will do all I can for her. I will explain to the judge that her mind is confused." She laughed out loud when the jailer translated what the attorney said. The Gussucks did not understand the story; they could not see the way it must be told, year after year as the old man had done, without lapse or silence.

She looked out the window at the frozen white sky. The sun had finally broken loose from the ice but it moved like a wounded caribou running on strength which only dying animals find, leaping and running on bullet-shattered lungs. Its light was weak and pale; it pushed dimly through the clouds. She turned and faced the Gussuck attorney.

"It began a long time ago," she intoned steadily, "in the summertime. Early in the morning, I remember, something red in the tall river grass. . . ."

The day after the old man died, men from the village came. She was sitting on the edge of her bed, across from the woman the trooper hired to watch her. They came into the room slowly and listened to her. At the foot of her bed they left a king salmon that had been slit open wide and dried last summer. But she did not pause or hesitate; she went on with the story, and she never stopped, not even when the woman got up to close the door behind the village men.

The old man would not change the story even when he knew the end was approaching. Lies could not stop what was coming. He thrashed around on the bed, pulling the blankets loose, knocking bundles of dried fish and meat on the floor. The hunter had been on the ice for many hours. The freezing winds on the ice knoll had numbed his hands in the mittens, and the cold had exhausted him. He felt a single muscle tremor in his hand that he could not stop, and the jade knife fell; it shattered on the ice, and the blue glacier bear turned slowly to face him.

1981

Retelling the Legends

EKATERINA STETSENKO

The evolution of archaic cultures under the foreign influence of so-called civilized societies is slow and complex. Because the literature of Russia's northern peoples was predominantly oral until the Soviets introduced written forms of their languages after the 1917 revolution, the history of their written literature has been relatively short. Coming of age in an atmosphere of tight ideological control, this literature was forced to employ the methods of Socialist Realism. Professional poets and prose writers, who gradually replaced traditional storytellers, were expected to espouse the official view of their peoples' histories, promulgating as indisputable dogma a vision of their happy life under Soviet power and of the rebirth of their formerly suppressed cultures. A simplistic approach to past and present, folk beliefs and customs, and the interactions of indigenous peoples with industrial society and the new order became commonplace. Indisputably, this situation retarded the development of incipient indigenous literature by impeding the creation of works of high aesthetic quality that might profoundly explore the mentalities and lives of native peoples. While gradually appropriating alien forms of expression, peoples of the Far North have experienced significant losses within their own traditions. In spite of their ongoing efforts to preserve their unique cultures and ways of life, industrialization, collectivization, and socialist ideology have to a great extent Europeanized them.

Nevertheless, this nascent literature, despite its lack of an indigenous written tradition, has increasingly found the threads that could link it to the age-old culture of its ancestors. Writers employed traditional forms, imagery, and symbolism from the myths, legends, and folk tales preserved in their oral narratives and included ethnographic descriptions of local peoples, customs, and traditional beliefs. Thus, intentionally or unintentionally, these authors found themselves juxtaposing radically different ways of life, cultural traditions, and moral precepts. By counterbalancing prescribed ideological clichés of Socialist Realism with realistic descriptions of everyday life, they created a relatively truthful picture of reality, reflecting the essential contradiction in the lives of peoples who inhabited two worlds simultaneously: nature and "civilization" in its Soviet incarnation. By the middle of the century, with the growth of both ecological problems and environmental awareness in the broadest spiritual and humanistic sense, different cultures found themselves drawn into a mutual dialogue in which the roles were not rigidly defined and both sides could act as teachers and students.

Man's relationship with nature and civilization, his ties with ancestral traditions and contemporary life, are the themes of Anna Nerkagi's *Aniko of the Nogo Tribe*. From the first pages the reader is immersed in the world of the northern tundra, its inhabitants and its laws. Wild nature, beasts, and human beings appear to be indissolubly connected and, despite the harsh struggle for survival, have learned to exist in a peculiar kind of harmony. Nerkagi represents this life from the inside, from a pagan, mythological consciousness which endows animals with human qualities. The main characters of the animal kingdom—the wolf Lame Devil, the reindeer Temuiko, and the dog Buro—are the bearers of good and evil in their peculiarly "natural" sense. Lame Devil kills Aniko's mother and sister, attacks the reindeer herds, and causes great damage to the community, but the people do not respond with corresponding feelings of hatred and vengefulness, for the Nentsy, unlike their urbanized contemporaries, do not view themselves as masters of nature. They are willing to submit to its laws. Lame Devil himself in his youth suffered from man. He is motivated by the natural instincts of hunger and the desire to survive. His feelings are understandable, his actions justifiable.

In this opposition between humans and animals, the story suggests that there is no right or wrong: "This was a special world with its own laws and reckonings." If anyone is culpable, it is the human beings who invented specialized means of killing animals. Despite losing his wife and daughter, Seberui respects his enemy as having acted "by his own laws." Nerkagi implies that between animals and man there exist special relations, founded on both enmity and attachment, but based invariably on mutual respect. Spiritual ties between human beings and animals can occasionally be even closer than those between people. Thus the closest friend of the aging, lonely Seberui is his dog Buro, and the reindeer Temuiko was purportedly breast fed by Aniko's mother, Nekochi—an indication of the mythic qualities Nerkagi associates with him.

In the episodes devoted to traditional Nenets life, this mythological consciousness is imprinted on the narrative, filling it with its particular tonality, its particular notions of life and time. People living in rhythm with nature acquire an unchanging perception of the world and a stable daily life (*byt*) developed over the centuries. Thus, for example, the scene of Nekochi's funeral and burial feast, like the descriptions of Nentsy homes, clothing, and customs, contains elements of an ethnographic essay which fixes our attention on a stability of existence outside the realm of time. Every event has its own norm, its own rules, its own morals, which insure the continuity of generations and the eternal repetition of life in harmony with nature. In folkloric time the life of an individual is inscribed into the life of the entire tribe.

Women become particular vehicles for these perceptions. A woman, for instance, is most often addressed in terms of reproduction, as the mother of her living child. Thus Nekochi is referred to as "the mother of Aniko." But every phenomenon, whether it involves human beings, objects, or customs, is invested with its own rationale as part of the larger mythic scheme.

Nerkagi is frequently inclined to idealize life in the tundra. This tendency can be felt even in the tone with which she presents neutral ethnographic information, but it is particularly evident in the clearly legendary story about the fate of the Nogo tribe. The distant past is viewed as a kind of golden age when the Nentsy were benignly engaged in hunting and crafts. People living in harmony with nature and with themselves were clever, kind, handsome, and full of dignity. Their misfortunes and deaths were linked primarily not to social but to natural causes, such as reindeer plagues or epidemics. But in the face of death, they preserved their inner peace, for they believed in the continuity of their existence in nature. For them, parting with the dead was "not so much a funeral as the seeing off of a person who had decided to go to the other world."

This idyll is shattered with the advent of social laws. Yet Nerkagi indicates that the people suffered under social injustices even prior to the advent of Soviet power. In addition, following the ideological canons of Socialist Realism, Nerkagi endows the latter with mythic features, attempting to fuse the folkloric tradition with socialist ideology. The hunter Passa, for instance, believes in the new life as one would believe in the Idols. Soviet power, like a just God, repays good with good and rewards the poor man who is industrious and honest. But because the life of the Nenets did not change radically, Passa had to believe in something new—education. A curious mixture of mythological and primitively pragmatic features, Passa's thoughts on these issues reveal the changes in consciousness of the peoples of the North who were forced to assimilate themselves into new ways of being.

Nerkagi, however, illuminates Nenets life not only from within, but also from the position of someone who, though a Nenets by birth, has been urbanized. Aniko's perceptions are not those of her tribespeople. When she returns to her native camp after an absence of many years, she is stunned by the contrast between life in the tundra and that in the city. She fixates only on the outward and superficial features of the reality before her, seeing in the unchanging traditions of Nenets life only backwardness, ignorance, and lack of development. She is disgusted by the clothes, the dwellings, and the food of the reindeer herdsmen, and for her father she feels not love but revulsion and pity. She cannot respond to his welcome in daughterly fashion: "She looked with fear at her father's black malitsa, at his matted, greasy hair, wrinkled face, and dirty hands. A feeling of nausea rose in her throat."

Aniko has become a person from another world. Her behavior towards her countrymen reflects what happens in the encounters between people of different and disconnected cultures. Nerkagi does not directly criticize official Soviet nationality policy; such accusations would have been impossible in the 1970s. But in describing the everyday life of the Nentsy and by showing us her characters' fates, she offers a sufficiently objective picture of their situation. It is clear from the text that the life of the Northern peoples remained unsettled and difficult and that attempts to incorporate them into Soviet life had mixed results.

The history of Aniko exemplifies these problems. Taken away from her camp to a city boarding school at age seven, later studying at the institute, she gradually learned to love books, theater, and films and became accustomed to modern civilization. But because she was not taught to love her native language and people, to respect their laws and customs, she became completely alienated from her tribespeople, who in turn perceive her as an outsider. It is characteristic that when Aniko was taken away from her parents, they felt that their daughter was irrevocably lost to them and were no longer interested in her whereabouts. Thus, on her first return home on school vacation, the young girl couldn't find her parents and her sister because they had pulled up stakes for a new encampment.

Yet the drama is not so much in Aniko's separation from her family as in her falling away from her native culture, her break from traditional systems of thought. Passa, who had pinned his hopes for Nenets children on education, is completely shaken by the fact that Aniko has forgotten how to speak the language of her ancestors. For the Nentsy, becoming part of modern civilization means becoming excommunicated from their own roots. Thus Seberui has decided not to send his younger daughter to school: "She would leave for the city like his oldest daughter, and she would forget the choom and the reindeer. There would be no one to keep the family hearth, and then there would be neither 'darkness' nor 'light.' The hearth fires would go out."

In representing the interactions of the technological and tribal worlds, Nerkagi confronts one of the most pressing problems of the clash between tribal societies and Europeanized civilizations: the physical and moral degeneration of a people. She epitomizes this degeneration in the Russians' importation of vodka to the Nenets village and plans to extort expensive goods in exchange. Here Nerkagi's usual calm, often sentimental and lofty narrative tone gives way to expressions of horror: "In the evening, something incomprehensible and—to tell the truth—horrible started to happen. Drunken parties—wild, dark, and terrifying—began. Those of the Nentsy who could still stand on their feet, were wandering from one sledge to another; others were sitting or lying prostrate in the snow, mumbling, screaming, giggling, singing. Where was their calm, dignity and pride?"[1] This scene of moral degradation is made particularly poignant by the fact that the person bartering furs for alcohol is himself a Nenets, who thus embodies the decay of a people from within.

Nerkagi provides one of the most poignant elaborations of social problems in her descriptions of the kinds of Russians with whom the Nentsy had the most prolonged contact: not the teachers, doctors, or construction workers, but the geologists—that is, those interested not in enlightening or in improving the quality of Nenets life but merely in exploiting the mineral resources beneath the tundra. Pioneers of industrial civilization, the geologists destroyed the age-old relationship between man and northern nature and deprived the Nentsy of their traditional occupations. The older generation of Nentsy, who instinctively understood the difference between consuming the tundra and respecting it, saw the geologists as alien and exploitative, but the youth are seduced by the new possibilities they offer. Aniko's childhood friend Aleshka dreams that his younger brothers will become oil prospectors in order to improve their lot. But Aleshka also develops his own plan for the future, through which the Nentsy may improve their daily lives through the use of modern technology and methods without severing their ties to nature or the ethical basis of their culture.

Yet Nerkagi insists that neither the material benefits nor the educational acquisitions that come with civilization can automatically make a person happier or more complete than a life committed to preserving the traditions. The white people, by destroying the traditional Nenets way of life, have brought enormous damage to their spiritual world. Aniko begins to realize this after she returns to her father. At the story's climax, seeing even the reindeer Temuiko as more loyal and more attached to his dead mistress—her own mother—than she herself is, she experiences profound regret for the immorality of her pride.

But Nerkagi does not simply contrast the evils of urban, technological civilization with a sentimentalized vision of tribal life. For civilization is not only banal or corrupt but a source of imaginative and intellectual stimulation: "How can I abandon it all: the institute, theatre, movies, dancing, the discussions with friends about art and our interesting bright future. How can I forget the noise and heat of the city, my favorite places where I loved to think and dream. How can I voluntarily give myself to the frozen silence, be lost in the white expanses of snow, put on traditional yagushka, live with a kerosene lamp and . . . get old?"

For Nerkagi, it is not only reluctance to bear the difficulties of everyday life in the tundra and to abandon the comforts of civilization that makes Aniko reluctant to remain. Most importantly, perhaps, Aniko undergoes a psychological crisis because she is unable to assume the role she would have to play as a woman if she stays in the camp and marries a Nenets like Aleshka, as the story suggests she might. In Nenets society, women are viewed chiefly as a means of perpetuating the family. They are supposed to tend the fire, bring joy to the people around them, and obey their husbands absolutely. All important decisions are made by men. A woman's lot is silence.

Aniko rejects this assumption. Reproached by Aleshka, who asserts that she merely wants comfort and advises her to experience the harshness of tundra life in order to learn how she can help her people, like other Nenets women, Aniko resists; she simply cannot repeat her mother's fate. Her reluctance to return is not based on inconvenience or physical hardships: she is concerned, primarily, with how one can morally justify the everyday life of her people. Having left for the city, having been reared in the traditions of European culture, having ceased to live according to the rhythms of nature, having lost her tribal consciousness, Aniko can no longer feel an integral part of her people. She needs a personal goal and a personal meaning for her own life.

Nerkagi juxtaposes real life with the mythological folk motif of the prolonged absence of the hero by placing the myth within a historical framework. In folkloric time, the period between the hero's departure and return, though filled with different events, remains in some sense empty because the events have no effect on the hero's character (Likhachev 234–43). But with Aniko, in whom Nerkagi creates a feminine version of the folk myth, the world of historical time replaces that of mythic time. Aniko's years away from home have brought about profound change in both her character and perspective.

Seberui and his friends think that Aniko must continue the family; she is a link in the endless chain of generation, and it is her duty to take her mother's place by the fire. They do not understand that the formative years Aniko spent in the city cannot be erased without a trace, or that they have radically changed her consciousness. Thus her return is not simply symbolic but also, and primarily, a psychological problem which demands inner work: a thorough re-evaluation of her own feelings and desires. She must recover the lost ties with her early childhood, her father, her tribespeople. She must see the tundra differently and consciously connect it with the world of civilization. But we feel that Aniko is not as confident as Seberui that everything can be successfully resolved. Her psyche, then, becomes the ground on which the central conflicts of the story, between contemporary civilization and tribal custom, are played out in all their complexity.

Aniko's father bequeaths the Idol, the master of the Nogo tribe, to her in order that she may save the tribe from extinction. Having received this symbol of Nenets culture, she takes upon herself responsibility for the future of her entire people. Aniko intuitively grasps that another, quite different world view is possible than the one she has imbibed in the city, and that no system of rational and pragmatic thinking is adequate to evaluate the Nentsy. Gradually, Aniko feels that she is beginning to understand the great dignity and meaning of the expression on the faces of the tundra dwellers. They have achieved a higher knowledge, "something essential to life that she does not know," because they are at one with nature and feel themselves part of its laws, because they feel an equality and kinship with everything on earth, and because they have faith in the spirituality of the world. Aniko is able to return to her tribe only because a portion of this knowledge has been handed down to her genetically. A. Mischenko quotes a statement by Nerkagi that can be interpreted as her credo: "I want to go to my father in the tundra. I feel calm in my soul when I am with him. He knows something that I don't know. . . . There lives in everyone the sacred fire of one's ancestors, but one must realize that it exists, and then pass it on to others down the chain" (Mischenko 14).

The American author Leslie Marmon Silko, a Laguna Indian, is concerned with problems very similar to those that occupy Nerkagi. In "Storyteller," Silko describes the life of Alaskan Yupik—another nation of the Far North— and their relations with whites, raising the same complex questions about the conflicts of nature and civilization and the preservation of traditional cultures. In contrast to the official Soviet point of view—in which socialism brings rebirth, material well-being, and cultural renaissance, while capitalism brings degradation, decay, and assimilation—both authors persuade us that the confrontation between industrial civilization and a tribal society engenders identical phenomena under any economic or political system. In *Aniko* and "Storyteller" the authors describe settlements lost in the wilderness, decayed shelters, degenerating families, the ruthless exploitation of natural resources, and alcoholism. In both stories children are raised in boarding schools far from home, forgetting their native language and customs, and old people seek to preserve the traditions of their ancestors.

For Silko, as for Nerkagi, the whites (*Gussucks* in the native language) are primarily geologists, oil drillers, and merchants who are interested in the Yupiks' natural resources. Whereas Nerkagi seeks to be impartial and to preserve the balance of good and evil by populating her story with many positive characters who are white, Silko, writing entirely from an aboriginal point of view, represents the whites as a faceless dark force who "only come when there is something to steal." Silko's powerful imagery depicts the world of the whites as completely divorced from nature and, therefore, from the Yupik point of view, devoid of soul and sense. The whites want to subjugate the earth by tormenting it with harsh metal tools. The earth in turn avenges itself by demonstrating its power and might: "The metal froze; it split and shattered. Oil hardened and moving parts jammed solidly. . . . The cold stopped them, and they were helpless against it."

For the heroine, the English language itself is senseless and coarse; it is not a means of human communication, as Russian is to Aniko, but a symbol of mutual estrangement. The Yupik prison guard addresses the heroine in English precisely in order to create an insurmountable barrier between them. In the heroine's mind, English is associated with violence because the teacher had beaten the students who refused to speak it; and she does not want to listen to the Gussuck trader because for her his words are mere noise. Like Nerkagi, who deals with the disintegrating links between generations and the threat of the disappearance of the whole culture, Silko emphasizes that Yupik youth who switch to English are changed not only outwardly but inwardly as well.

Unlike others of her generation, Silko's heroine feels closely connected to her native culture and unable to betray it. But she is curious about the world of the whites, with which she is in frequent contact. She voluntarily lives in the boarding school; she wanders around the village and sleeps with the Gussuck oil drillers. In her pagan consciousness, which animates everything around her, physical union is one avenue to comprehension. Unfettered by biblical notions of morality, she does not perceive sexual intercourse with whites as a sin, for Yupik women do not perceive themselves as playthings for male amusement and see nothing shameful in sexuality. Silko underscores the difference between the heroine's freedom and the new sexual roles imposed by the whites, in which a woman falls into dependency on male whim. The attempt of native schoolgirls to invent different tricks to attract men— for example, by curling their hair—seems absurd and humiliating. As Kate Shanley Vangen remarks, "The girls at the mission school are genderized to see themselves as objects, rather than to see themselves as sexual persons who interact with men within their tribal communities according to traditions evolved over many hundreds of years" (118).

At first the heroine sees both worlds—tribal and white—as equally hostile and repulsive. She is disgusted both by young white men and by a decrepit old Yupik whose bed she is forced to share. But the sexual relations with the old man bring an unexpected sequel. When he dies and loses his physical power over her, she becomes his spiritual heir, taking over his role as the keeper of the tribal memory. With the white people, however, the barrier of mutual alienation is insurmountable.

The whites, as portrayed through the heroine's consciousness, are perverse in their relations with women and transgress the laws of nature, as the Gussuck's pornographic picture of the woman and the dog aptly illustrates. The whites are so alien to the girl that she stops seeing them as people or even as animate beings. Thus, when she breaks a ban imposed by a Christian priest on Yupik women entering a tavern where white men congregate, she is calm under the white men's gaze because she feels invincible. She is totally indifferent to what they think, feel, or say because she believes their system of thought is incapable of interpreting events in a true light.

Silko projects the perversity of the whites' way of life onto their attitude towards the environment they destroy, killing the animals and depriving the Yupik of their traditional occupations and finally of life itself. The only "gift of civilization" the natives receive—alcohol—has become for them a deadly poison, a point reinforced by the death of the heroine's parents, literally because they drink poison sold to them as whiskey.

The daughter takes revenge on the proprietor of the store—not, significantly, on the perpetrator of the tragedy, but on his successor, a substitution that underscores the native perception of all whites as faceless and undifferentiated. Having lured her enemy out onto the cracked river ice, the girl consummates her vengeance, which Silko represents as part of a global apocalypse for all whites unable to realize that their end is near: "He didn't know about the ice. He didn't know that it was prowling the earth or that it had already pushed its way into the sky to seize the sun."

The heroine lives in one rhythm with time and with nature, finely attuned to all its manifestations and changes, aware of the sun's movement at every instant, and distinguishing omens in the colors of the sky. The world for her is a system of signs, a kind of magical book. The frozen river, which seems to have caught the sun in a trap, illuminated by the pale, deadly light, becomes for her a presentiment of apocalypse. For her all phenomena are endowed with a secret meaning that draws them into the flow of life. For example, the color red appears constantly in the story: the tin which fortifies Yupik homes, the red canister containing the poison, the red lining of the girl's clothing, and the rust-colored hair of her Gussuck sexual partner. Gradually red becomes a mark of evil and death, the color of the coming retribution: "She felt a chill when she saw how the sky and the land were already losing their boundaries, already becoming lost in each other. But the red tin penetrated the thick white color of earth and sky; it defined the boundaries like a wound, revealing the ribs and heart of a great caribou about to bolt and be lost to the hunter forever."

As with Nerkagi's story, the whites see something disquietingly strange and mysterious in the natives' ability to distinguish the voices of nature. The Yupik live in a unique time frame, at once frozen and infinitely prolonged—a continuous present capable of absorbing both past and future into itself. One means of merging with this time is the oral tradition, the unending story passed down from person to person, from generation to generation, thereby guaranteeing the existence of the clan. The native language, for them, is the soul of the people, the living link between the surrounding world, one's ancestors, and one's descendants. Actions and events are real and meaningful only when they become the subject of story, imprinting themselves onto the series of other events which once occurred or are presently occurring.

So scrupulously and precisely does the narrative define each moment, each detail of reality, that the story itself becomes an organic part of that reality. A story such as the old man's about the hunter and the bear takes place over several months. Every movement, muscle, claw, and hair of the bear is described, every sound and smell, every motion. Even in the face of his own approaching death, the old man cannot accelerate or alter his narrative because death has no power to interrupt the eternal flow of life: "Lies could not stop what was coming." As with Seberui's responses to nature, the old man's story is full of love for the world which he, in contrast to the Gussucks, treats with respect and care. This relationship carries over onto his speech: "On and on in a soft singing voice, the old man caressed the story, repeating the words again and again like gentle strokes."

The heroine, tossed between the world of her tribe and the world of the whites, has lost her connection with time. She regains it only when she reconstructs the details of her parents' death and thus restores the continuity of the family history. Her revenge, the murder of the storekeeper, is an act of reincorporation into the tribe, realized through the word. Therefore, the version of this event presented by the white lawyer, which interprets the storekeeper's death as an accident—an event that occurs by chance rather than necessity—is completely unacceptable to her. From the perspective of the Gussucks, the world consists of a multiplicity of discrete phenomena and facts which can be separately defined and classified. Further, while the Christian religion interprets the present in relation to the future, mythological consciousness is oriented towards the past. For the Yupik, each fact is a link in a chain, a thread in the web of events, and therefore carries within itself a secret meaning that can be understood only in light of the whole tapestry of existence. According to these laws, the girl creates her own model out of building blocks from time immemorial. For her to accept the white man's interpretation of events would mean to break the chain of time, of reason, and of consequence, and to give birth to a lie. She is convinced that she must fulfill her grandmother's testament: "It will take a long time, but the story must be told. There must not be any lies." Thus she refuses to accept the version of events that would exonerate her.

The girl begins her tale with the moment engraved on her memory, her parents' death, placing it in an unending stream of speech and time. "'It began a long time ago,' she intoned steadily, 'in the summertime. Early in the morning, I remember, something red in the tall river grass. . . .'" Silko shows the change in her heroine's world view through the very composition of the story. The narrative, begun in a contemporary manner, with periodic transpositions and flashbacks, at the end loses its modern features as the continuity of time is restored and, in Silko's words, is woven into the "spider's web" of the story. Because in tribal consciousness a person exists chiefly as part of the tribe, the heroine becomes indifferent to her own individual fate, her own future, and devotes herself fully to restoring the past and serving her tribespeople, who come to listen and to feed her as earlier they had come to the old man. If Nerkagi's heroine attempts to reenter the tribal way of life while simultaneously preserving a sense of self common to modern perceptions, Silko's heroine finds herself by shedding her identity in the Western sense of the term and by dissolving herself into the history of her tribe and of her listeners.

Narrator and listeners need each other because, for the tribe, a tale is not only a custom or a ritual but a peculiar form of existence and self expression. In native cosmology, where one of the mythological personages is "Thought-Woman," consciousness and material reality, the collective and the individual memory, are indivisible. As Linda Danielson writes, "Silko's story, finally, is about a storyteller, the living embodiment of Thought-Woman, as in the writer herself, thinking personal and tribal memory into existence" (334). Danielson quotes Paula Gunn Allen, who considers that in principle mythological thinking is more typical of women, who are called by nature to preserve the tribe, than of men, who are generators of rational thought (Danielson 325).

Only through story, which restores the unity of existence and consciousness, is it possible to save an ancient culture which has experienced the pressure of alien forces. These forces are embodied, for Silko, in the white inhabitants of the village, the men whose own rough force and aggressiveness is applied equally to nature and to women. It stands to reason, then, that it is woman in particular who takes over the old man's position, becomes the guardian (*khranitel'nitsa* [f.]) of tribal traditions, and resists ruin and decay.

The works of Silko and Nerkagi demonstrate how an oral folk tradition which articulates a particular culture functions differently in different literary contexts. For Nerkagi, mythological thinking is something which can become an object of analysis and description, included in a narrative which approximates an ethnographic essay and directly suggests solutions for the problems raised in the story. Nerkagi's impulse toward a truthful reflection of reality is realized through the realistic depiction of the details, phenomena, and events of daily life. The story is narrated from the rationalist perspective, while other approaches to reality are either explained with reference to this world view or else appear mysterious and enigmatic. The image of the heroine, which is tied in to both types of consciousness, reveals not only their differences but their points of convergence, and the story ends with the heroine's hope for a happy resolution between the two.

In Silko, mythological consciousness is above all the subject of the narrative, and the heroine, who neither understands nor accepts modern civilization, evaluates outsiders exclusively from this position. As a result, in Silko's story only one of the two cultures, between which stands an insurmountable barrier, is given the opportunity for self-expression, while the other culture is distorted and demonized. Reality itself, as conveyed through the heroine's perception, becomes a reflection of her inner world.

Both authors search for the authentic essence of analogous phenomena, accentuating different sides of the complex processes they describe. The stress each gives to a particular mode of consciousness results in a certain one-sidedness in the depictions of both authors. Nerkagi frequently makes reality conform to a preconceived plan, while in Silko that same reality is submerged into the mythological flow of consciousness. Nerkagi's narrative poetics, even when representing the inner psyches of the characters, focus on the obvious, outward consequences of the confrontation between two cultures. Nevertheless she reveals the deep inner contradictions between rational and mythological consciousness. Silko, concerned mainly with their inner correlations, focuses primarily on the psychology of the heroine. She creates a modern story out of oral folkloric traditions, revealing similar tendencies between them: the seemingly spontaneous unfolding of the story, the apparent separation of the author from the narrative, and a belief in the magical force of language. Thus Silko is able to recreate elements of reality not apparent at first glance. Her heroine, drawing on mythological consciousness, creates a new story, reconstructing past and present as organic unities.

Nerkagi also treats mythological consciousness, but distances herself from it, always writing from the point of view of modern civilization. As a result, she does not achieve the same unity of oral and written literary traditions as does Silko. As Nerkagi's history of the Nogo tribe moves from earlier times to the modern period, her story sheds its legendary features and becomes a conventional piece of realistic prose. For her, the restoration of the link between different eras and generations occurs within the context of a rational world view which is essentially oriented toward the future. Mythic time draws itself up into linear time, bearing the Nenets tribe into new life. But for Silko, whose heroine rejects linear temporality for cyclical notions of time wherein each cycle may end in catastrophe, existence acquires an eschatological cast.

Silko and Nerkagi take different approaches to the problem of renewing the traditions of tribal peoples. For Silko the preservation of the world of the ancestors means a continuation of ancient ways of life. For Nerkagi, this renewal means the restoration of certain carefully selected elements of the old customs and modes of being within the context of modern civilization, even with the help of outsiders. Thus for Silko, the oral story is the very form of the heroine's existence, while for Nerkagi the *yarobtsy* are exotic artifacts, something to be written down by white enthusiasts.

Despite their differences, it is characteristic that both authors reject the use of ethical categories to distinguish between "natural" and "civilized" peoples. Nerkagi introduces into her text images of Nentsy, as well as Russians, who are both noble and corrupt. Silko, depicting the white oppressors as a faceless mass of aggression, at the same time does not idealize the Yupik, who are also portrayed as capable of lying, depravity, and even murder. Similarly, neither Silko nor Nerkagi associates male and female characters with ethical oppositions. Instead, the sympathies of both authors are always with those who share a common language with nature. For both authors, however, it is women who become the primary bearers of the mission to renew folk traditions and preserve the tribal memory. These two women writers see in the representatives of their own sex the primary force capable of overcoming the destructive element in contemporary civilization and of returning it to harmony with the surrounding world.

Translated by Irina Katz

Notes

1. This passage is one of several quoted by Stetsenko and Barker which are not part of the translated text.

Crossings

ADELE MARIE BARKER

By Way of a Preface

In early September 1992, my son Noah and I headed north from Tucson up
to the Pacific Northwest, our pickup loaded with a dog, fishing gear, toys,
and the notes and ruminations of a book four years in the making. The day
we stopped in Monument Valley the air was still, red with the dust from the
mesas and buttes whose silhouettes framed the pastureland below. We pulled
the truck over and headed up an embankment while the lizards scattered and
Noah watched for snakes lying in ambush. Coming round a bend, we saw
that the trail ended precipitously on a ledge where an old Navajo woman
was sitting with her back turned to us. I said a couple of words to her, but,
receiving no answer, I sat down on a rock and made circles in the dust with a
stick. A loud whirring sound punctured the air as Noah transformed himself
into a police mobile unit. I was tired from the drive and spent most of the
next half hour watching this woman from my perch on the rock. Driven to
interpret what I saw, I invented a story for her. First I imagined that she was
waiting for her husband and three sons to bring the sheep back from north
of the border. Then I imagined her divining a wind I could not hear. After
a while I retrieved Noah from the shelter of a jojoba bush and headed down
to the truck. Looking back, I saw the old woman's motionless figure sitting
as before, as seemingly unaware of our departure as she had been of our
presence. We settled in for the drive through the high desert, telling stories
to each other all the way to Montana. Mostly they were about ourselves.

In 1981 Leslie Silko, a member of the Laguna tribe from New Mexico,
and Anna Nerkagi, a Nenka from northern Siberia, were both at work on
the narratives that appear in this volume—Silko in the "frozen silence" of
Ketchikan, Alaska, Nerkagi in the Siberian city of Tiumen. Though Silko
hardly perceived herself as belonging to the literary mainstream, she had

been embraced by Anglo critics after the appearance of *Ceremony* in 1977.
But Nerkagi, despite the praise *Aniko* garnered, has remained relatively un-
known in her own country, never receiving the same literary attention among
Soviet readers as Silko has among readers in the United States.

The fact that critical response to these two writers has differed so dramatically may have something to do with the literary merit of their works.
A valid case can be made that of the two writers Silko is the more gifted, if
only because her writing has been considerably less burdened by ideological
baggage than Nerkagi's. Nerkagi wrote *Aniko* in the pre-glasnost era, and
despite her obvious sensitivity to tribal life, her vision of her own people was
partially impaired by the reigning ideological constraints of that era, which
dictated that writers pay the requisite homage to the Soviet state for bringing "civilization" to the peoples of the North. But even more than relative
aesthetic merit, the difference between the critical responses to Nerkagi and
Silko is probably related to the place occupied in their respective countries
by the literature of indigenous peoples.

In Russia that literature, like the people who author it, has since the
thirties been simultaneously touted and demeaned by the Soviet literary
establishment. Under Stalin the effort to homogenize the Soviet peoples into
one happy family produced a number of native sons—but few daughters—
from the non-Russian peoples of Siberia. Writers such as Grigorii Khodzher,
Yurii Rytkheu, and Yuvan Shestalov made literary careers of sorts by fulfilling
the mandate to extol the virtues of the Soviet state. Thus it was that while
"native" writing was encouraged within the Soviet Union for the better part
of this century, it was accepted only so long as it was not *too* native—that is,
so long as the writer understood that *his* allegiance was first and foremost to
the state and only secondarily to the tribe.

This conflicting pressure on Russia's indigenous Siberian writers to retain their ethnicity while writing prescriptive literature meant that they were
often estranged from both of the literary traditions they were attempting to
straddle. Most not only wrote in or translated their works into Russian, the
language of the dominant culture, in order to reach a broader, non-native
audience, but eventually moved away from their tribal roots to Moscow or St.
Petersburg, making only occasional trips back to their homelands. Thus Russia's native sons gradually lost their linguistic if not their psychological ties
to their own people without ever really becoming part of the Soviet literary
mainstream.

Ironically, the situation of indigenous Siberian writers today has been
complicated by the collapse of the Soviet Union. Though now for the first time
they are able to speak in their own voices, few are choosing to do so, having
long ago severed themselves from their tribal heritage as the price of assimilation into Soviet society. The collapse of the USSR has also deprived many

of the small peoples (*malyi narod*) of the protection they once enjoyed under the former government. Thus, for example, as the Writers' Union is carved up into smaller independent unions, each representing a former republic, the indigenous writers in Russia are increasingly fearful that their voices will be silenced by the vocal majority of Russian nationalists (Whitney 13).

While Soviet critics, reflecting party policy, have attempted for the better part of this century to deemphasize ethnicity in favor of homogeneity among indigenous peoples, white American critics have long sought to emphasize the otherness of Native Americans and their literature. If initially this tendency to look at the Indian as the Other was born out of our need to distance, demonize, and ultimately conquer what we didn't understand, literary critics beginning in the twenties turned that Other into a set of ideas to be emulated rather than anathematized. Writers and critics alike began to see in Native Americans a way of life that nourished our own critique of ourselves as a nation. As we began in the sixties to question the myths that had long sustained us, we saw in Native American philosophy a set of assumptions quite different from our own. With the subsequent explosion of technology in the seventies and eighties, our misuse of natural resources, and the ensuing environmental crisis, we began to take seriously the philosophy of the Other as offering a viable response to an environment we were systematically destroying and to a set of myths in which we could no longer believe (Castro 161).

Among literary critics the attraction to Native American experience has been fueled in recent years by the postmodernist obsession with the deconstruction of self and with new modes of narration that subvert long-hallowed concepts of personality. Native American literature has in many ways been the object of the postmodernist search for new ways of perceiving selfhood, and its nonmimetic forms have answered the need for new methods of literary representation (Sangari).

But even as we look to Native American literature to answer our own needs, it is also necessary that we ask ourselves to what extent our agenda has influenced the directions taken by native writers. Have we not displaced onto them our own desire that they be and remain substantially different from us? Has their art become more self-consciously "native" both in answer to and in retreat from our expectations? These are very difficult questions, not least because they are posited from a distinctly Anglo point of view, predicated on the notion that there is among Native American writers a kind of static tribal Ur-literature which implicitly must remain within certain prescribed limits defined for them by us.

In one way or another, however, most native writers these days, whether from the Americas or from Eurasia, are engaged in an ongoing and often complex dialogue with the dominant cultures in their respective countries. That dialogue is present on multiple levels, from the languages in which these writers tell their tales to the configurations of their respective plots. For Nerkagi and Silko that dialogue takes shape through their exploration of the boundaries and the crossings that shape and inform their worlds. No less than the literary traditions out of which they come, the works by Nerkagi and Silko deal with what happens when that invisible and sacred circle called tribe is broken, rendering unclear the sets of allegiances and identities that formerly lay at the heart of the relationship between oneself and one's people.

It is ironic that both works are concerned with problems of alienation and fragmentation, for the literary traditions out of which both grew gave voice to a sense of belonging. The traditional tales and legends passed down by both northern Siberian and Native American peoples fostered in their audiences a sense of place within their tribal cultures. Among the most pervasive themes in Native American lore are those which recount the process by which a lost member of a tribe is gradually restored to his or her rightful place by the end of the narrative (Allen 1986, 127ff). For centuries the Nentsy similarly listened to their native legends and stories (*yarobtsy*), which recounted the deeds of gods and heroes from whom they were descended.[1] The assumption, then, within both cultures was that the function of the storyteller was not only to preserve the old legends but to bring out the story that the listeners already had within them. The stories grounded them, enjoined them to see themselves as part of a continuum, and cemented for them the unity between tribal and individual identity.

If the older tales were concerned with reaffirming that fundamental relationship with tribe, the contemporary literary traditions focus on the dissolution of these ties. This dissolution is manifest, on its most obvious level, through linguistic displacement: Silko and Nerkagi both write in the language of the dominant culture. The relative importance which each attaches to this fact suggests not only the fluidity of the boundaries between tribal and nontribal cultures in their two countries but the subtle sense of displacement that informs the work of both writers. Silko does not speak Laguna and has stated that what is crucial to the survival of a people is not what language the stories are told in but the remembering and the passing down of the stories themselves: "I came from a family which has been doing something that isn't quite English for a while. I come from a family which is basically intent on getting the stories told; and we *will* get those stories told, and language *will* work for us. It is imperative to tell and not to worry over a specific language. The imperative is the telling" (1979, 61).

For Nerkagi the issue of language is more central. Though she writes in

Russian, she does so in the knowledge that this act estranges her from her own people. She recalls being unable to speak to the Nentsy when she first returned to them after years of living in a Russianized environment, a dilemma replicated in *Aniko*, where the protagonist has forgotten the language of her own people after living for almost fifteen years among Russians (Omelchuk 126). Through Aniko, Nerkagi gives voice to her own deep conviction that if you lose your language, you lose the keys to your own culture as well.

Despite the seemingly diverse roles language plays for these two writers, there is nevertheless a tension in the prose of both between the language in which they are writing and that of the tribal peoples they depict. Written in Russian, Nerkagi's *Aniko* reads more like an ethnographic account of an outsider who wishes to record the customs and traditions of the Nogo tribe for a predominantly Russian audience than it does a work written from the inside by a member of that tribe. It is not so much that Nerkagi chooses to write in the language of those who colonized and oppressed her people as that she places herself, whether consciously or not, in the position of ethnographer vis-à-vis her own people, thus estranging herself from them even as she attempts to record their traditions.

Silko too, despite her devaluation of the role of language in storytelling, nevertheless underscores the linguistic alienation of her protagonist from both the Gussuck and the Yupik worlds. The young woman yells profanity in English without knowing what it means, "probably swear words she'd heard from the oil drilling crews last winter," but ironically becomes a linguistic outcast from her own people as well, as her Yupik jailer, now coopted into the world of the Gussucks, refuses to speak to her in her own language. In one sense she is the reverse embodiment of Silko herself, who grew up speaking the language of the protagonist's jailers. But she is also the means by which Silko tackles the whole issue of language head on. The inability of this young woman to speak the Gussuck language is more than mere metaphor for her own alienation and estrangement. Rather it suggests that the issue of language may matter very much to Silko, for if she tells her story in English, her nameless protagonist intones hers in Yupik. Since telling the story in the white man's tongue risks imparting the knowledge and the secrets which form the sacred circle called tribe, speaking in the native language is a way to keep the truth safe and inviolable from the Gussuck world.

The issues of boundaries that inform Nerkagi's and Silko's works are in many ways the literary expressions of their geographic positioning in their respective countries. Silko comes from an area in New Mexico along the Rio Grande basin, long a crossroads where Hopi, Zuni, Spanish, Navajo, and Anglo cultures merged and mingled with the Laguna peoples. Because of their geographical placement among these various cultures, to be a Laguna is almost by definition to be a mixed breed. Silko voiced it this way:

> The white men who came to the Laguna Pueblo Reservation and married Laguna women were the beginning of the half-breed Laguna people like my family, the Marmon family. I suppose at the core of my writing is the attempt to identify what it is to be a half-breed or mixed-blooded person: what it is to grow up neither white nor fully traditional Indian. It is for this reason that I hesitate to say that I am representative of Indian poets or Indian people, or even Laguna people. I am only one human being, one Laguna woman. (Lincoln 233)

This highly specific construction of her own identity suggests that for both Silko and her readers the issue is not simply whether she is part Native American or Anglo, but whose voice she represents as a woman within her own tribe. It is this construction which allows her to beg the question of whether she can, as a half-white, speak compellingly for Native American issues.

Like Silko's, Nerkagi's own sense of tribal identity has been formed by geographical positioning. The Nentsy, the largest of the Samoyedic-speaking peoples inhabiting the central and western portions of Siberia, have, like the Laguna, long intermarried with the other native tribes of their region—the Komi, the Khanty, and the Selkup—and even with the Russians, who first began settling in northwestern Siberia as early as the fifteenth century. However, the particular area from which Nerkagi comes, the Yamal Peninsula, is sufficiently remote that it has experienced less intermarriage with the dominant Russian culture than some of the more populated areas to the south. Because of the historical lack of racial intermingling, the contact between Russians and the native peoples may well be more of an issue for Nerkagi than for Silko, who takes that intermingling to be part of what it means to be a member of her tribe. Boundaries between tribe and the outside are more clearly delineated in Nerkagi's work, one's infection by so-called foreign influences a source of much greater concern for her than for Silko, who builds imaginative bridges to her own tribe whether writing in Arizona, New Mexico, or, as in the case of "Storyteller," Alaska.

The question of boundaries between the two worlds in which Silko's and Nerkagi's protagonists each have a foot is also felt in the narrative structure each employs. Nerkagi's text is written according to traditional European notions of linear narrative with an omniscient narrator, thus highlighting the tension between a young woman's assimilation into a Russian world and her gradual recognition of her own roots. Although these notions of narrative are no longer adhered to by many authors in the West, whence they arose, they became a standard feature of twentieth-century Soviet literature, which was distinguished by its conservatism in matters of narrative technique. Thus Aniko's ultimate decision to return to the Russian world is suggested by the very structure of the narrative she may, in fact, unconsciously employ to tell her story.

Silko, on the other hand, plants herself more squarely in her own Laguna tradition by writing about tribal life from the inside. Although her nameless female protagonist is equally estranged from the two cultures between which she moves, the narrative itself adheres strongly to the Laguna tradition out of which Silko comes. Silko has often compared the art of tribal storytelling to a spider's web that weaves together its beginnings and its ends (1979, 54). At the end of "Storyteller" she brings us back to the incarceration of the young girl with which the story began. The notion of story as a spider's web deviates from standard Western notions of linear time and linear plot development. Silko plays with that linearity in the old man's final dream, recounted for us after he dies.

Similarly, her use of images reflects her tribal heritage: she will often leave events and descriptions unclear, as if assuming that the reader will understand her intent. The description, for example, of "something red in the grass" remains elusive when first mentioned. We come to understand that meaning later in the text as the story unfolds and with it the multiplicity of meanings inherent within the original image. Silko has said that among the Pueblo there is a belief that if you are just patient and listen, the meaning will be made clear.

Ironically, however, the narrative technique Silko draws out of her own tribal tradition has much in common with modernist and postmodernist narratives, which also play with temporality and indeterminate symbolism, evoking precisely the open interpretations that we mark as distinctly Indian in Silko's story. The distinction lies not in any explicit divergence in the two narrative techniques but in what motivates their usage. Whereas Silko seeks to incorporate and re-create traditional Laguna notions of time and meaning into her text, postmodernist writing makes use of these same techniques out of a desire to rebel against traditional narratology, thus ironically creating a structure of literary discourse not unlike the structure of many traditional Native American narratives.

As with the issues of boundaries that inform the symbolic worlds of these two writers, their narratives each chronicle literal voyages of displacement: Nerkagi's as her young protagonist Aniko journeys back to the camp that was once home, now as a complete stranger; Silko's as she follows the hopeless and helpless wanderings of her nameless protagonist, who moves uncertainly between the Gussuck and the Yupik worlds. Both authors examine closely notions of tribal identity in a world in which meanings and allegiances once formerly understood have become hopelessly blurred.

For Nerkagi, to be a member of the Nogo tribe is to pass through an invisible circle that delineates the tribal from the nontribal world. Once inside this circle one enters a space where rituals seem virtually unchanged from earlier time. It is Aniko who can penetrate that sacred circle because she is part of the Nogo tribe. In the world inside this circle, one's identity becomes indivisible from that of the clan. As the narrative makes increasingly apparent, however, Aniko is unwilling to merge herself with the people who live inside this circle.

Those lines of demarcation are less visibly drawn in Silko's story. Her nameless protagonist wanders silently from the Yupik village upriver to the Gussuck camp, equally abused and violated by both cultures. Her very wanderings between the two places suggest how fluid are the boundaries between the two worlds she inhabits. But whatever abuse she has suffered at the hands of her own tribe and her nominal grandfather, her identity is still powerfully formed by her tribal roots. She is meant to be nameless, as are the other characters in this story, for Silko is less interested in their personal identity than in the cycle of creation, violence, and survival they represent.

If the young woman's anonymity seems initially to reflect her own denigration at the hands of people who have misused her, it is also the means by which Silko lifts her story out of the confines of the personal into the archetypal. Identity in Silko's world is formed not by one's name nor by what sets the characters apart from one another but by what bonds the people together into a unified whole. And only the stories can do that. Silko's heroine gains an identity, a voice, through her ability to tell the old stories that conjoin her to the tribe. She herself becomes a character in the stories as she relives through them her parents' death and her own slow revenge. It is the stories, then, that finally link her to her own roots. They are the strong threads that remind her of who she is and where she came from in a world in which tribal identity is no longer so easy to come by or to define.

Questions of identity which inform both texts are inseparable from the subtle interconnections between the human and the natural sphere, which, as Silko has stated, could come undone at any moment (Danielson 342). The natural world dominates these two stories, not merely as the backdrop against which the lives of these northern people unfold but as the way both writers examine the complex web of relationships between the human and the natural world which lies at the heart of the stories they tell.

Silko's story is framed by the milk-white sky, which hovers over the white ice of the river as her protagonist stands looking at it from her jail cell. It is a bad omen, portending the arrival of the cold that cripples the big yellow machines belonging to the Gussucks. Significantly, the Yupik jailer pays no heed to the dangerous pale color of the sky; presumably, by aligning himself with the Gussuck world, he has forgotten how to read nature's signs.

It is the mark of her own deeply rooted tribal identity that Silko's heroine understands the foolhardiness of trying to tamper with nature. It is why she laughs at the attempts by the Gussucks to keep out the cold with their stringy yellow wadding and looks on knowingly as their big oil drilling machines sit motionless in the Arctic freeze. But there is more in this image than the domineering all-pervasive power and presence of nature that ultimately subverts all human endeavor. The natural and the human worlds in "Storyteller" constantly reflect upon each other, bringing the disharmony in one to bear upon the other. The sun whose pale stillness portends the hard freeze and the worsening cold reflects the disruption in the moral order of the Yupik and Gussuck communities, in which the young Yupik girl sits in jail while the Gussuck men who rape both women and land go free. Nature not only reflects the transgression of that moral order but responds to it, seemingly taking steps of its own to right corrupt values and wreak vengeance on its transgressors.

The subtle collision in this story between the two worlds extends to the process through which the protagonist's revenge is worked out. Traditional Anglo notions of revenge, guilt, and innocence take on a different cast when seen through the prism of the natural world. The moment during which the notion of revenge first takes shape in the girl's consciousness comes in the form of a story which the grandmother tells her about how her parents died ("They bought a tin can full of it from the storeman. Late at night. He told them it was alcohol safe to drink. They traded a rifle for it").

Putting together the pieces, invoking the moment of her parents' death, the girl transposes it onto the realm of nature, where she alludes to it through the image of "something red in the grass that morning." It is a dream in which the blood of their death mixes improbably with the blood of her own puberty, her own sexual yearnings merging with the image of the parents lying dead on the grass, victims of the Gussuck storeman who traded them bad alcohol for a rifle. Just as their moment of death mingles with images of the natural world, so is the slow act of revenge similarly worked out with the collusion of nature, as the ice gives way beneath the Gussuck storeman.

What, then, does it mean, this quiet collusion of revenge between woman and nature? So closely are the two entwined that the act of revenge becomes by implication part of the natural order of things, thereby rendering invalid traditional notions of guilt or innocence. The death of the girl's parents at the hands of the Gussuck storekeeper sets quietly and deliberately in motion something which, years later, will find its resolution through the same natural order whose unstated rules the Gussuck offended. Neither guilt nor expiation plays a role here, because the girl's act appeals to a set of constructs and values outside Gussuck consciousness. "Some village children had seen it happen," said the lawyer, "and said it was an accident. That's all you have to say to the judge: that it was an accident." The problem is that there are no true accidents in the world this girl inhabits and in the world out of which Silko writes. Things happen because they must. Yet to make such an affirmation is not to say that there are no accountabilities. Silko's protagonist is very much aware of her own part in what she has done: "I will not change the story, not even to escape this place and go home. I intended that he die. The story must be told as it is." Her way of thinking about this "crime" escapes the Gussuck mentality because it combines at once the notion of personal accountability with the equally compelling notion that things unfold and work themselves out through the silent partnership of the natural world, irrespective of human interference.

Nerkagi likewise uses the theme of revenge as a means to explore the intricate interplay between the human and the natural worlds. The cycle of revenge in *Aniko* was set in motion years prior to the beginning of Nerkagi's narrative, when the old wolf Lame Devil lost a leg to a hunter's trap. Revenge begets revenge and plays itself out until the old wolf, in a final irony, is killed by the dog he wished to destroy.

Like Silko, Nerkagi sees revenge as a natural and inevitable part of the order of things in the world of nature, but she also sees it as the force which divides the human and the natural world. In her efforts to idealize the tribal world from which she was estranged at the time *Aniko* was written, Nerkagi depicts the Nogo people as having freed themselves from the cycle of killing and revenge by depicting Seberui as deliberately backing off from dealing out that same rough justice to the wolf for killing his wife and daughter. Yet if Nerkagi seems to pit the two worlds against each other, she also avoids giving in to the notion that the human world is somehow of a higher order, suggesting instead that the wolf is only acting according to the laws of the tundra. She implies that those laws provide the same source of sustenance for those who perpetuate them as does the Nogo tribe's belief in the Idols as fundamental to their own tribal identity.

Nerkagi also uses the notion of revenge as a trope for the ambiguities inherent in the tribal world to which Aniko will ultimately return. In the final chapters of the novel, Lame Devil kidnaps the cub in an attempt to pass on the old hatreds to the next generation. In the final scene the cub returns to inspect the corpse of the old wolf, who lies alongside Buro, each the other's victim. As the cub stands surveying one of the tribesmen nearby, Nerkagi suggests that the old cycle of revenge may have played itself out at last, as wolf and man look at each other with new regard. The wolf turns and walks away, no longer sure of the world to which he is returning. In rejecting these old precepts the young cub breaks the cycle of violence and killing, yet in doing so also cuts himself off from a set of laws and precepts which have sustained the wolf clan for centuries. The ambiguity is that at the end, he is left an isolated and lonely figure, suggesting by his very stance that while his actions may be morally viable from the human standpoint, they also separate him from a way of life that long sustained his tribe. Like Aniko's father, the old wolf senses the necessity of having a community, a family, to whom to pass on the old laws, a fact which prompts his kidnapping of the young cub. It is likewise what motivates Aniko's father to beg her to stay and believe in the old gods: "You alone are the last of the Nogo tribe. Look, this is its master. Talk with him." If there is no one to whom to pass on the rituals and beliefs that are part of the community called tribe, then both the belief patterns and the tribe itself must ultimately vanish. The image of the wolf cub thus implicitly suggests the dilemma which Seberui and ultimately Nerkagi face, namely the necessity for change, for bringing the tribal world into the modern era, yet in so doing risking the destruction of the very things that sustained it and gave it its identity throughout the centuries.

How then, each of these writers asks, does one steer one's course between the conflicting claims of tribe and the so-called "civilizing" forces of the Gussuck and the Russian worlds which threaten to engulf the tribe? For Silko the question centers on how one retains one's ties to one's people while simultaneously freeing oneself from the abuse and victimization that have characterized tribal life. Caught in a world where there are no real exits, in which she wanders silently between the Gussuck camp and the Yupik village (that silence being a mark of her powerlessness), Silko's protagonist quietly finds a way of gaining power over the people and the structures that victimize her. Through laughter and through her ability to remember the old stories, she is able to subvert the systems of power in the two worlds. She laughs at the futility of the Gussucks' attempt to keep out the cold with yellow wadding, knowing that nothing can prevail against this kind of cold. She laughs aloud when the jailer translates the attorney's words for her, because she knows that the Gussucks will never understand the story the way it must be told. Her laughter comes at odd moments and catches people off guard, the more so because it is never accompanied by any kind of verbal explanation. In a sense she is like the Coyote figure in Native American tradition, the Trickster who confounds expectations regarding appropriate behavior. In doing so she not only mocks the Gussucks and their culture but simultaneously gains power over them (Danielson 345; Radin), for her laughter comes from a place they can neither rape, nor mine, nor exploit.

The young woman's ability to remember the old stories enables her to retain the best of what binds her to her culture, yet free herself from the worst of that tribal experience, namely her victimization at the hands of the old man. There is much that is powerfully self-reflexive here of Silko's own art of storytelling, for she has often said that if you just know the stories you will be all right (1977, 2). No matter where you are, you will know where you came from, you will know the cycle of relationships that have determined your life and how to judge them. The stories serve as the means by which the girl, and Silko herself, take power through memory over a world that has both nourished and abused them. Ironically, the young woman finds her own voice through the last story the old man tells before he dies, the tale of the hunter being stalked over the ice by a polar bear. The narrative prefigures his own death, which occurs at the moment when he must cede his power to the bear ("He felt a single muscle tremor in his hand that he could not stop, and the jade knife fell; it shattered on the ice, and the blue glacier bear turned slowly to face him").

We do not know who tells this story, for it is related after the old man has died. But, it is, in several senses, his story. It is also in a sense the girl's story, for in it the dropping of the knife, the steel blade, upon the ice signals the final emasculation of the old man as predator. As he loses his voice, she gains hers, and for the first time in Silko's narrative she speaks: "She did not pause or hesitate; she went on with the story, and she never stopped, not even when the woman got up to close the door behind the village men." Finding her own voice, she finds the power not only to remember and to tell the old tales but to free herself from the fetters of the world they come from. In so doing, she supplants the old man as a shamanic figure, one who literally *controls reality* by telling the stories that create it.

That the story of the polar bear is both the old man's and the young girl's suggests the complex nature of the affiliations and allegiances that lie at the heart of Silko's story. The very complexity of the protagonist's situation is illustrated by the fact that it is from him, her seducer, as well as from her grandmother that the girl inherits the stories that will keep her whole as she gravitates between two equally problematic worlds. In presenting us with this twofold inheritance, Silko may perhaps be suggesting the dual nature of the tradition which her protagonist inherits, a tradition which she wants to preserve on the one hand yet kill off on the other.

For Nerkagi, the possibility of steering one's course between the Russian and tribal worlds is more elusive, because neither Aniko nor her creator is ever fully able to find her own voice in this text. Aniko remembers that when she heard the news of her mother's death, what shocked her was not so much the death itself as the remembrance that she even had a mother. The most destructive part of her alienation from her tribe is that she no longer has control over her own memories—unlike Silko's protagonist, for whom story resurrects the memory of events either suppressed or misapprehended. The loss of those memories is also related to Aniko's loss of any connection to the old stories and songs (yarobtsy) of her people and to the understanding of them as part of her heritage. She does not, for example, comprehend why one of the Russian geologists living among the Nentsy is collecting their ancient stories and songs and why he wishes to preserve them. Her ties to her own tribe are thus irrevocably severed through her repression of her own memories and through her inability to sense the importance of song.

That Aniko is unable to build the necessary bridges back to her own tribe has much to do with Nerkagi's own repression and suppression of her own ambivalent relationship to these two worlds.[2] Given the time during which *Aniko* was written, much in this novel necessarily goes unsaid. A case in point is Nerkagi's own double displacement from the Russian world, which she would ultimately leave, and from her own tribe, to which she returned as an outsider. The story of Aniko is obviously meant on some level to mirror that displacement. The problem, however, is that it does so incompletely. If Aniko, named after her creator, experiences Nerkagi's own severance from her tribal roots, she incompletely embodies Nerkagi's response to the experience of living within a Russianized environment. Partially out of a tendency towards self-censorship so deeply embedded in writers during the pre-glasnost and perhaps even the post-glasnost era that one's personal response was frequently indistinguishable from political viability, Nerkagi stops short of using Aniko as a way of explicitly discussing her own displacement from the dominant culture. That she does so makes Aniko's defense of that culture largely artificial. Whereas the sense of anomie and alienation from the indigenous and the dominant cultures becomes a point of departure for Silko in her narrative, that same response remains repressed within the story of Aniko, as it does within its own author.

Border crossings are fragile things. I cross one trepidatiously as I presume to write about two cultures, neither of which is mine. For Silko that issue is made even more complicated by her recognition that those borders divide not only the tribal from the nontribal world but person from person within the tribe itself. For it is the grandfather who treads where he ought not, crossing that invisible but firmly delineated line separating him from the girl. Further, if it was once clear where one's tribe left off and the colonizer's world began, in "Storyteller" those boundaries have become blurred by the corruption of values each world shares. In order to survive, Silko's protagonist, like Silko herself, creates her own internal landscape with its own lines of demarcation by learning to tell the stories.

There is no internalization of those borders in Nerkagi's work. They exist as part of the external world. One is either a member of the tribal world or not. For Nerkagi there can be no compromise between these two. For her, one's survival as a member of the tribe has as much to do with one's active participation in its daily life as with the remembering of its songs. Silko holds the tribal world no less dear, but unlike Nerkagi she has internalized it, and thus is able to move away from it when need be. Finally, for her the issue is less a matter of one's physical positioning within the tribe itself than of one's ability to find the imaginative threads which bind one to that tradition, while simultaneously cutting those ties that have choked the life out of one's people.

Notes

1. Writers such as Vladimir Sangi, a Nivkhi, have taken a particularly active role in collecting the old legends and tales of their peoples and in reworking them for a contemporary audience. See the collection he edited, *Legendy i mify severa*. See also his epic poem *Chelovek ykhmifa*, based on ancient Nivkhi legends on the formation of the universe.

2. This tendency toward repression is particularly evident in the early writings of the Chukchi writer Yurii Rytkheu, who glorified the Bolshevik state in bringing his people out of the dark ages into the enlightenment of the socialist world. However, in his recent writings, such as *Magicheskie chisla*, Rytkheu has taken a more critical view of the effects these outside forces have had on traditional Chukchi life and culture.

Dialogue

ON SILKO AND NERKAGI

Katya: I feel, maybe because I'm "Soviet," that Nerkagi's thinking is more rational, more "Soviet," less tribal than Silko's. Maybe it's just that I don't see these things.

Adele: I think you're right that Nerkagi's story is much more like a typical Soviet work than a tribal narrative. I want to make that distinction, but what interests me in Nerkagi is how her work is at once very "Soviet" and yet also—maybe unconsciously?—subversive of the Soviet ideals Aniko seems to espouse. I think we need to remember that many Soviet works written before glasnost existed both inside and outside the system simultaneously.

Katya: Another thing: You write about modern literary traditions that are inclined to depict disintegration of links. You need to be aware that if you speak of Nerkagi, "modern tradition" means something different from what it does in the United States. For us it is Socialist Realism, which does not stress the disintegration but the strengthening of links. If Nerkagi deals with disintegration, it is only implicitly. You also think Silko's heroine is raped by the old man, but I think not. He's too old! [Laughter.] And, she carries on his story. If he were abusing her, why would she continue to live with him?

Adele: We really disagree on this point. I think that's why it's so complicated. She *does* carry on his story, and she continues living with him, because she has nowhere else to go. She has no place anywhere. It's part of the dilemma of tribal life. But I like your essay very much, Katya. I think you were more sensitive than I to Nerkagi's role vis-à-vis her own culture. But there are interesting differences, too. You say about the old wolf that his feelings are understandable and justified and that natural instincts propel him. In his fight with man, there was no one who was right or wrong, the more so because from Nerkagi's point of view, if anyone is guilty, it's the inventors of the traps. I think the animal world, much more than the human world, nurses its revenge. But I also see that revenge, from the tribal point of view, as acceptable and natural.

Susan: Adele sees the wolf as more anthropomorphic, Katya as more natural: wolves don't seek revenge in the sense that human beings might. In terms of fictional form, though, doesn't the wolf also become a symbolic parallel to the tribe, the trap an emblem of what technological society has done to indigenous peoples?

Maya: I have a question that concerns both papers: the development of the tribe and the individual. It's tragic that the modern world denied tribal cultures natural ways of development. The crime of the white man against those peoples is not that they were just forced to follow Western civilization, but that they were denied their own natural development, inherent in their cultures. As I understand it, tribal life, communal life, is just a stage in the development of any nation. It happened that Western civilization was brought face to face with the culture of American natives or Siberian peoples at a time when the distance between them was so great that the whites became the dominant culture, so there was no way for native people to evolve beyond this tribal life as they might have done otherwise. Even Western cultures developed out of tribal groups. Their natural development was allowed, but these other people had no chance. There's no telling how they would have evolved if they had. Because these tribal groups were brought into contact with European civilization so early in their history, they were given only two choices: to remain exactly as they were, fossilized, or to take the European way. To me, either way is tragic.

Susan: But are those the only two choices? When one speaks of the "natural evolution" of human cultures, I worry about the use of the term "natural." I agree with you that we have no idea how indigenous peoples might have changed over time had Western interventions not occurred, but it seems to me that some of the assumptions you're making about the direction of "natural evolution"—the very idea of what's "natural"—are culturally mediated.

Maya: That raises another question. In "Storyteller," Silko takes on the storyteller's role, but in what capacity? As a shaman? Or as a European storyteller, an individual, a "person" in the European sense? Both Adele and Katya speak of her as an individual, but how much of a "person" is she?

Adele: I see her in her role as storyteller, reaching back deeply into the past, in which one's link with the tribe was solidified by one's ability to pass on the old stories. Aniko is more Europeanized than the storyteller in Silko. Maybe this is because Nerkagi, even more than Silko, is writing for the dominant culture in her country, which is Russian. Most of the "native writers" of Siberia write in Russian, not only to reach a Russian audience but to reach their own people as well. Russian is the language of success—it's the key to a better life, to more pay, and thus among the native peoples there's not much impetus these days to write in their native languages. From what I gather, Nerkagi's situation was much like Aniko's. When she returned to her tribe after twenty years away, she could barely speak their language.

Maya: It's a mixture of choices, don't you think? It's not only selling out to Russian or American culture. It's also a natural development of the individual who evolves from the tribe.

Adele: Katya makes the point that Aniko's decision to leave is not simple. She resists it. But finally she can't submerge her will into someone else's—the father's.

Susan: And the father is the representative of the tribe. In all these discussions, I'm concerned that we not impose Western notions of individualism on cultures for which that concept may not be the most appropriate.

Maya: But don't we also impose these standards when we say to tribal peoples, "You stay just as you are, don't go beyond where you are now"—regarding them as exotics to be studied?

Susan: Yes, of course, but that's not what I'm saying. I'm not sure the issue of tribal change must be regarded in either/or terms, as you've construed it: *either* native peoples develop according to Western notions of cultural evolution, *or* they remain unchanging, static. I think all sorts of variations are possible relative to distinctive historical conditions, including the ways native cultures influence the colonizing groups as well as vice versa. In any case, as you're suggesting, *our* views of native peoples are hardly the ones that should prevail: we need to listen to their voices.

Afterword: Histories and Fictions

SUSAN HARDY AIKEN AND ADELE BARKER

The preceding chapters trace the history of our personal and critical journeys in composing this book. Here we turn to a larger narrative: the diverse histories of women in both cultures, the gender ideologies that have informed them, and the implications of these historical contexts for the writings of contemporary American and (ex)Soviet women. Obviously, adequate treatment of subjects so vast and complex would require volumes, and many such studies already exist, especially in America. During the past two decades Western scholars have minutely analyzed the interplay of gender and cultural history in relation to women's writing. The theories animating this enterprise have also exercised a formative influence on the thinking of American Slavicists interested in women's studies or gender theory, but because critics have generally viewed the situations of Russian/Soviet and American women as radically different, there has been little comparative analysis of the two traditions. Indeed, until recently relatively few Western scholars, and still fewer inhabitants of the former republics, were concerned at all with the import of sexual difference in Russian and Soviet society. Unlike the United States, where the feminist movement has had wide-ranging effects on contemporary women's lives and writings and where even nonfeminist or antifeminist critics have become increasingly cognizant of the import of gender in literature and society, most scholarship devoted to Russian and Soviet literature prior to glasnost, whether inside or outside the former Soviet Union, paid scant attention to these concerns.[1] Even in the glasnost era many Soviet scholars continued to equate all gender analysis with a reductive concept of so-called bourgeois feminism.[2]

That situation has begun to change; in the four years since we began this project, a number of important books on Russian, Soviet, and post-Soviet women have appeared in the West. Yet even with this abundance of new scholarship, much remains to be done: analysis of gender in Russian and Soviet society still lags far behind comparable work in the United States, and vast archival research will be required before we can develop anything approaching a complete history of women's writing in the pre- and post-revolutionary periods.[3] Thus, while this chapter refers to Western cultural contexts for comparative purposes, we focus primarily on the implications of gender in the history, literature, and sociopolitical order of Russia and the USSR. We by no means presume to be exhaustive or definitive; any summary risks oversimplifications, and some of the ground we cover will doubtless be familiar to specialists in American and Soviet studies or feminist theory. Rather, by comparing some of the dominant cultural discourses on sexuality and gender in America and the former Soviet Union, we hope to suggest the complexity of issues we can only touch on, as well as to indicate potentially fruitful areas for further exploration.[4]

Finding a Voice

Repression operated as a sentence to disappear, but also as an injunction to silence, an affirmation of nonexistence, and, by implication, an admission that there was nothing to say about such things, nothing to see, and nothing to know.—Michel Foucault, *The History of Sexuality,* vol. 1

"You can't live on 100 rubles a month. Either you become a prostitute or a thief."—Quoted in Attwood, "Sex and the Cinema," 1993

Though the social and political effects of feminism have remained limited in the former Soviet republics, one of the most notable consequences of glasnost was a freer circulation of feminist ideas. Yet even before the advent of glasnost, a few courageous women contested the gender ideologies and inequities which, despite the official rhetoric of equality, remained entrenched in the social and symbolic systems of the USSR. One of the most formidable of these pioneers was Tatiana Mamonova, who with her small group of colleagues made one of the earliest attempts to develop a sustained feminist critique of Soviet society. The founding editor of *Women and Russia*, the first Soviet feminist *samizdat* journal, Mamonova and the women who worked with her became targets of recurrent government harrassment and interrogation as the authorities sought to silence them. In 1980, having defied the orders of the KGB to cease publication, Mamonova and three of her coeditors were expelled from the Soviet Union. Other contributors were ultimately forced underground.[5]

Mamonova's ground-breaking work helped launch a movement that gained momentum under Gorbachev, and other feminist publications gradually began to appear. One of the most remarkable of these, because so much of it has been done singlehandedly, is *Zhenskoe chtenie (Woman's Reading)*, an underground journal edited by Olga Lipovskaia and published irregularly in St. Petersburg since 1988. Originally supported exclusively by Lipovskaia herself with the aid of funds from Western contributors, *Zhenskoe chtenie* prints articles by and about Soviet women, translations of Western feminist works, and literary texts by unknown or underground women writers (Engel 1989, 6–10).[6] In 1992 a new feminist magazine in English and Russian, *Woman and Earth* (*Zhenshchina i Zemlia*), designed as a forum for discussion between women in the former USSR and the West who wish to learn more about each other's lives and ideas, began publication in the United States and Australia under Mamonova's editorship. The same sort of cross-cultural dialogue has recently appeared in a bilingual Russian/English special edition of *Heresies: A Feminist Publication on Art and Politics* (1992) devoted to feminist issues in the former USSR. Among other current alternative publications are journals such as *Nabat*, published in Kharkov, and *Tema*, a gay and lesbian journal in Moscow. A recent issue of *Zhenskoe chtenie* was also devoted exclusively to lesbian concerns.

To American readers, many of these publications might seem anachronistic, recapitulating ideas long commonplace in Western feminist analyses. Yet it is hardly surprising that as women in Russia and the successor states begin developing the sorts of revisionary critique that have engaged contemporary Western feminism for over two decades, they may sometimes trace a comparable philosophical trajectory. Lipovskaia herself, for example, defines the purpose of her magazine as "consciousness raising" (Engel 1989, 7), recalling the widespread occurrence of that phenomenon—literally one of the formative events of contemporary American feminism—at the outset of the second wave American women's movement in the late sixties and early seventies.[7] And the projected 1992–93 publication list of Progress Publishers, the largest press in Russia, included Russian translations of some of the founding texts of contemporary Western feminisms—Simone de Beauvoir's *Le Deuxième sexe*, Betty Friedan's *The Feminine Mystique*, and the latest edition of *Our Bodies/Ourselves.*[8]

The plethora of new women's magazines begun in the wake of glasnost, with their predictable standard advice (resembling that of similar publications in America) on how to balance home and career, rear one's children, sew a better dress, or attract the man of one's dreams, have also begun including, for the first time, previously inaccessible information about women's bodies and birth control, even though much publication on the subject is still limited to letters of complaint from women regarding the appalling conditions in abortion clinics and the unavailability of reliable contraceptives.[9] The newspaper *Delovaia zhenshchina* (*Professional Working Woman*), which along with *Sovetskaia zhenshchina* (*Soviet Woman*) and *Rabotnitsa* (*Working*

Woman) often touches on feminist issues, recently published an article on linguistic sex discrimination (January 1992). Similarly, *Gazeta dlia Zhenshchin*, a periodical for women founded in 1991, offers information and advice on sex, as do a number of widely disseminated popular newspapers, such as *Moskovskii komsomolets*. Yet despite these signs of growing interest, most women's publications still give little attention to the politics of gender.

Women's discussion groups, not unlike the early consciousness-raising sessions of American feminism, have recently proliferated as well. Providing the matrix for investigating women's issues for years suppressed by the party, these groups deal with a wide variety of concerns: the appalling state of health and child care; diet (no trivial matter in a country plagued by chronic food shortages and lack of information on nutrition); sexuality; personal relationships; and work—especially the double burden (*dvoinaia nosha*) that (ex)Soviet women must assume as both full-time members of the labor force and de facto heads of families, responsible for all the time-consuming tasks of *byt*. But because most of these groups are still at the stage of attempting to mobilize women, to establish a workable organizational structure, and to seek funding for their activities and publications, they have only begun to explore the kinds of politically focused critiques characteristic of Western feminist organizations, which assume gender to be an inseparable component of all sociopolitical structures.

The past five years have also seen the proliferation of other kinds of women's organizations. In 1990, responding to pressure initiated by Anastasiia Posadskaia, an economist from the Institute of Socioeconomic Population Studies, the Academy of Sciences approved the establishment of a Center for Gender Studies (Tsentr gendernykh issledovanii) in Moscow, devoted mainly to research, information, and training and focusing on the social construction of sexuality.[10] Similarly, the Institute of Ethnography and Anthropology has begun research into gender stereotypes and the anthropology of the body, and the Institute of Philosophy in Moscow is currently entertaining plans to create the first women's studies course for university teachers. Many women from various professions, from cinematographers to writers, have organized themselves in order to survive the transition to a market economy (Lipovskaia 75–77).

At least two major conferences recently brought feminist activists, academics, and writers from the former Soviet Union, Europe, and America together to discuss women's issues: "Gender Restructuring—Perestroika in Russian Studies" (held in Helsinki, Finland, 20–22 August 1992) and "Women in Russia and the Former USSR" (held in Bath, England, 31 March–2 April 1993). And yet, as Lipovskaia has noted (79), most post-Soviet women's recognition of their society's entrenched gender inequality is still too limited to prompt them automatically to link their economic plight with larger political and social issues.

It would therefore be inaccurate to assume that all these new organizations unequivocally align themselves with Western women's movements. While some clearly support international feminisms, others fear what they see as a tendency among Western feminists to deprive women of their "essential femininity" (Goscilo 1991, 49). The recently expressed view of Galina Semyonova, the first woman to hold full membership in the Politburo, typifies the widespread Soviet and post-Soviet assumption that gender bears little relation to *realpolitik:* "We can talk in the high-flown terms of the international feminist movement, but we have very tough, very real problems that must be solved before we can speak of women's liberation in a philosophic or a political way." [11]

Official policy reinforces this position. Soviet and post-Soviet governments in the former republics have tended to regard feminism (when they regarded it at all) as a potential threat to the status quo: a state founded on the primacy of the family and, by extension, on woman's presumed proper role as its creator and sustainer.[12] As in the United States, the sacrosanct notion of the family is still regularly invoked to advance governmental agendas, and this propaganda has been so effective that it is difficult to separate what women have been socialized to believe from the desires they might otherwise feel. The new cult of femininity among Soviet women bears at least some relation to this contradictory dynamic, although, as Mary Buckley notes (1992c), Russian women's fascination with Western cosmetics is more a function of their desire to please themselves finally than a desire to attract men.

Women's extensive involvement in activities outside the home since the mid-1970s has been advanced as one reason for the alarming increase of depictions of violence against women both on the screen and in print. This notion that woman has strayed from her proper role as nurturer and protector of the family is shared not only by men but by women as well, thus eroding much of the work on gender inequality conducted by recently established women's organizations. In a recent interview Naina Yeltsin advanced the view that women are "weak, helpless, and defenseless and that social and political activity is not for us" (Liborakina 8). Yet at the same time, the very existence of these active organizations suggests a growing awareness of the gender inequities official policy systematically denies.

By Western standards the discussions of women's sexuality in Russia and the former republics also seem relatively circumscribed. On one level, this limitation is a sign of the tenacious grip traditional heterosexual ideologies have maintained on Soviet society since the Stalin era. For the greater part of this century, the party suppressed questions relating to female sexuality—

indeed to all sexuality—and attempted to harness the erotic in the service
of the nuclear family while simultaneously associating open expressions of
sexuality with decadent Western culture.[13] Since glasnost the situation has
changed radically. As a recent report put it:

> After years of pretending that it had no gays, no AIDS, and at times no sex,
> Soviet society is rushing to acknowledge its sexuality and struggling to deal with
> the consequences. Pamphlets full of earnest advice about condom use and dis-
> cussions of Freud, Shere Hite, and the Kinsey report have suddenly appeared at
> news kiosks, along with glossaries explaining terms such as "erogenous zones."
> Three weeks ago a letter that could have been written by Hugh Hefner, urging
> the creation of "palaces of free love," was printed in the official labor newspaper,
> *Trud* [Labor].[14]

Yet even now popular conceptions of what constitutes sexuality remain
strikingly limited. A notable exception is Igor Kon, the country's leading
sexologist, whose book *Introduction to Sexology (Vvedenie v seksologiyu)*
was finally published in 1988 after being banned for ten years. All 550,000
copies—a vast number by Soviet standards—sold out within weeks. But Kon
faces enormous cultural resistance and has stated in a recent article that to
this day he is often referred to in his own country as a "sexopathologist" (Kon
1993, 27). Consider his recent complaint that even when Russian television
dared for the first time to broadcast a program on sex education, the only
images of intercourse it used were drawn from ancient Chinese erotic art,
and "it proved to be impossible to find a single art historian who was willing
to go on television to talk about the history of the nude and erotic art."[15]

If, as Kon observes, "people here still don't completely accept the idea
that sexuality is a normal and important part of human nature," still less
do they accept the idea of homosexuality. Popular opinion commonly tends
to exclude, dismiss, or denigrate both lesbianism and male homosexuality,
which continue to be driven underground and constrained, even more than in
the United States, by widespread repression in both language and law. That
situation too is changing: in May 1990, for example, the first international gay
and lesbian conference was held in Tallinn, and for the first time some public
discussion of AIDS (SPID in Russian) is surfacing; moreover, in May 1993,
Article 121 of the Soviet criminal code was repealed, which outlawed consen-
sual sex between men. The fact remains, however, that the overwhelmingly
homophobic stance of the party and the repressive measures historically employed against homosexuals have had profound and abiding effects on public
opinion. Despite the efforts of some activists to change traditional ideologies, popular sentiment remains even more hostile to any deviation from
heterosexual gender norms than does popular opinion in the United States,

as doctors, psychologists, and the public continue the debate over whether homosexuality is an inherent variant of normal sexuality, a lifestyle, or an "illness" (Engel 1989, 7).[16]

Given the traditional Soviet suppressions of sexuality, the recent proliferation of pornography on the screen and in print seems all the more notable—a telling instance of the excess engendered by the return of the repressed. Admittedly, as recent debates in the United States have amply demonstrated, the issue of what constitutes pornography is itself complex and elusive.[17] As here, so in the former Soviet Union do artists and members of the intelligentsia often deploy representations that conservative observers regard as pornographic—representations which, in their deliberate violation of prescriptive social norms, proclaim the value of artistic freedom and challenge conventional aesthetic, generic, or ethical criteria. Yet the current proliferation of crudely misogynist pornography in Russia and the former republics can be explained not only as a response to the sudden lifting of censorship but also as an example of the more questionable effects of Western influence during the transition to a market economy that is inseparable, as in the West, from a sexual economy that traffics in women's bodies as prime consumable objects.[18] Films such as *Little Vera* (*Malen'kaia Vera*, 1988), *International Girl* (*Interdevochka*, 1988), or *Blown Kiss* (*Vozdushnyi potselui*, 1990), like their many Western analogues, titillate audiences for profit, depicting explicit sexual acts, nudity, and often rape, and focus primarily on the exploitation of the female body.[19] While most of these films are made by male directors, the few that are made by women, notably *Picnic on the Beach* (*Dikii pliazh*, 1990) by Natalia Kupakozova, fall prey to the same pattern, portraying women as passive victims or objects of violence (Attwood 1993, 82–83). Publications ranging from the Soviet version of *Playboy* to the more hardcore *Venera* (*Venus*), *Mr. X*, and *Krasnaia Shapochka* (*Little Red Riding Hood*) all edited by men, are for the first time widely available on newsstands throughout the former USSR. Yet the current prevalence of pornography there is hardly a mere artifact of Western influence. Like the intense nationalist and ethnic chauvinisms that have also burgeoned since the breakup of the Soviet Union, the misogynistic impulses that drive the production and consumption of most pornography were never absent from either Soviet or prerevolutionary Russian culture. Rather, they were less blatant than in the United States—muted, ironically enough, by strict official controls on free expression.

In both cinema and life a disturbing rise in rape and violence directed against women has occurred since the inception of glasnost. The figure of woman, once used to portray the moral perfectibility of the Russian land and people, is now deployed to represent the moral collapse of the Soviet Union. In glasnost and post-glasnost films such as *The Burn* (1988) or *Seven Days after Murder* (1990), female characters appear as symbols of the state. Such an association implies that male violence against women is exacerbated by a displaced desire to rape a government that over the past seventy years has symbolically raped them (Attwood 1993b.). In a recent essay on women in the mass media, Olga Voronina commented astutely on this phenomenon:

> The post-revolutionary participation of women in the social sphere was not really a form of emancipation. What happened was simply the replacement of one type of male dominance with another. If in pre-revolutionary Russia, it was Man who subjugated women, then in post-revolutionary Russia it was the Soviet State, which appropriated to its own ends the socioeconomic basis of male dominance. Actually, the patriarchy in Russia was never destroyed. Only its form has changed. Masculine ideology was always, in fact, the official state ideology in relation to women; only on the surface was it concealed by the myth of sexual equality. Men, formally deprived of their power over women, nevertheless lived and thought within the framework of a totalitarian masculine ideology. It is precisely because of this that the destruction of the totalitarian Soviet state and its patriarchal role in relation to women led inevitably to attempts to reconstruct the traditional system of male dominance. . . . This explains, in my view, the upsurge of aggression against women that we have been experiencing for the past seven years during the so-called "demokratizatsiia" of society. (Voronina 1993, 252)

The complex relationship between the circulation of female bodies, the lifting of social censorship, and the ongoing economic crisis in the former USSR has another dimension. Prostitution, officially outlawed even while unofficially tolerated under Soviet regimes, has burgeoned since the beginning of the transition to a market economy. As in other societies historically, such proliferation bears direct relation to the severity of economic conditions; a recent survey found, for example, that more than a third of Russian girls in secondary school professed themselves willing to exchange sex for hard currency in order to enhance their material circumstances during difficult times and to increase their chances of finding a foreign husband (Pilkington). And eager entrepeneurs have discovered a booming business in marriage bureaus that cater to Russian women seeking American husbands (no candidates over forty, please).[20]

The issue of prostitution is further complicated by the current usage of the term. In a society where women's sexuality is assumed to be tied inexorably to reproduction and mothering, "prostitute" serves as a pejorative designation for any young woman who does not conform to traditional gender codes (Waters 1989), and even otherwise progressive films still uncritically deploy the wife/whore dichotomy. "Prostitution" has also come to be used in recent films as a term for selling oneself in both a moral and a physical sense in order to ensure survival in Soviet and post-Soviet society. In *Interdevochka*

Tania, a nurse by day and a prostitute by night, is accused by her mother of such self-commodification. "Correct," she replies, "but how many of us do *not* sell ourselves?" (Attwood 1993a, 72–73). Yet though the exploitation of women persists in various ways, both obvious and covert, the complete rupture of Soviet society has also produced a vehement backlash against those who refuse to conform to conventional sexual stereotypes.

Nevertheless, despite these signs of refractory traditionalism, ripples of change have begun to stir the literary establishment. As in the West, where until the 1970s women's writing, with a few notable exceptions, was virtually excluded from traditional canons, so in the canons of Russian and Soviet literature women have historically been either absent or grossly underrepresented. But whereas feminist criticism in the West has dramatically altered the masculinist orientation of literary scholarship, the dearth of anything resembling a feminist revisionary analysis in mainstream literary criticism in Russia and the former republics has seriously retarded comparable possibilities there.[21] Ironically, even though the literary hierarchy of both pre- and postrevolutionary Russia deemed poetry a more "suitable" genre for women writers, poets such as Zinaida Gippius, Marina Tsvetaeva, and Anna Akhmatova had substantial troubles with the censors over subject matter and were only sporadically anthologized in the Soviet Union during their lifetimes. The genre of autobiography, with the notable exceptions of Evgeniia Ginzburg and Nadezhda Mandelshtam, remained largely male authored. And except for Vera Panova, and to a lesser extent Ol'ga Forsh, Marietta Shaginian, and Lidiia Seifullina, all of whom wrote about the construction of a new Soviet society, even female fiction writers remained in relative obscurity until the 1960s. In recent years, not only have more women begun to write prose fiction, but the literary establishment, however reluctantly, has also begun to accord their work a modicum of recognition. Since 1985, for example, partly because glasnost exposed Soviet readers to more contemporary critical theory from the West, several collections of women's narratives from the nineteenth and twentieth centuries have appeared, publications which suggest a growing awareness that women's fictions might constitute a category worthy of attention.[22] But as in the West, an inevitable paradox attends such publications; for even as they make available neglected texts by women, often for the first time, they also paradoxically help perpetuate the ghettoization of those texts rather than altering the fundamental configurations of received male-dominated canons.

To address the marginalization of Soviet women writers, a special women's section of the Writers' Union (Federatsiia pisatel'nits soiuza pisatelei) was founded in Moscow under the leadership of the poet Larisa Vasil'eva in December 1989. The Federatsiia was designed as a forum and conduit of women's views and a lobby for change in what had, till then, been quite literally an old boys' network (Vasil'eva 1989). This women's caucus now has branches not only in Moscow but in Irkutsk, Vologda, and Petrozavodsk, among others, and the Moscow branch has begun publishing its own almanac, *Pchela* (*The Bee*).

Yet for all these promising developments, the new thinking about gender has had only limited impact on the Russian literary establishment. Most contemporary writers would still agree with Tatiana Tolstaia's insistence that gender is irrelevant to authorship,[23] and even those who otherwise see themselves as radical critics of the establishment tend to ignore sexual politics. Thus Vasil'eva advocates the federation's commitment to the "feminine principle" (*zhenskoe nachalo*) in both literature and society; and though the April Committee, formed in Moscow in 1989 as a splinter group of the Writers' Union, has sought greater independence for Soviet writers, advocated wide dissemination of new ideas, and pressed for fundamental reforms of the status quo, it has said little about the concerns of women.[24] This tendency to ignore women's issues inspired a scathing critique by the Russian author Maia Ganina at the Eighth All-Union Writers' Congress during the summer of 1986, when glasnost was first enunciated for literature. Castigating Soviet leaders for failing to include more women in the party's upper echelons, Ganina noted wryly that "the Writers' Union treats women as an evil force. It pretends they don't exist, but in fact it is afraid of them" (Ganina 1986).

The disregard for women's writing exemplified by both writers and critics in the former USSR has a distinctive rationale, deeply embedded in Russian/Soviet history and ideology. Many of the early activists behind the October revolution of 1917 were women, and gender equality was one of the founding principles of Bolshevism. Prominent figures such as Alexandra Kollontai and Inessa Armand worked tirelessly on women's behalf, lobbying for legislation to assure their equal treatment and access to education and setting up a system of public kitchens and child-care facilities designed to liberate mothers from the confinements of traditional sex roles within the bourgeois family. Yet these reforms failed to transform deeply embedded gender codes; despite the party's official support for equality, many male Bolsheviks resented and resisted the social transformations it entailed, while women from the working and peasant classes tended to oppose it as a harbinger of the Russian family's dismemberment (Buckley 1989).

Varieties of these forms of resistance continue to the present day. Seventy-five years since the early Bolshevik reformers sought to secure women's emancipation, women in the former Soviet Union have yet to benefit fully from many of their egalitarian ideas.[25] Even as cataclysmic changes and movements for democratic reform have dismantled the USSR, women's situation has altered very little. At the time of the elections in June 1989, women made up fewer than 15 percent of those elected to the Congress of People's Deputies. And most representatives chosen by professional and social organizations have been men even when women dominated the professions in question. Thus although 74 percent of teachers are women, the Academy of Pedagogical Science and the Soviet Association of Pedagogical Researchers chose as deputies three men and only one woman. (Compare the situation in American public schools, where though women currently make up over 80 percent of the teaching staff, a disproportionate number of administrators are men.[26]) Further, though 66 percent of Soviet doctors were women (a statistic frequently cited as proof that Soviet and Russian women had better professional opportunities than their U.S. counterparts) eight of the ten delegates chosen from the Academy of Medical Science were men. Under Gorbachev the Soviet Union had only one woman ambassador, Zoia Novozhilova (appointed to Switzerland, the last country in Europe to give women the vote).[27] Currently no women hold ambassadorial posts.

Yet ironically, although significant gender inequities have persisted throughout Soviet and post-Soviet society as in the West, official policy, taking refuge in Leninist doctrine, has tenaciously resisted acknowledging their existence. Similarly, though voices protesting women's lot have been raised sporadically since the 1960s—the most obvious being Natalia Baranskaia's 1969 novella *Nedelia kak nedelia* (*A Week Like Any Other*), widely interpreted in the West as the first feminist exposé of woman's notorious double burden—for a variety of complex historical reasons the ideological underpinnings of that burden have received little sustained critique.

There are many reasons for this curious discrepancy between official claims and daily reality and for the widespread resistance to questioning the prevailing gender norms. On the most obvious level, protest has been deflected by a narrow definition of sex roles that focuses solely on access to job opportunities, and by a disregard for feminism—not unlike that of some of its Western opponents (see Faludi)—based on the simplistic notion that it is merely a movement to deny sexual difference and advance women's access to traditionally male positions and professions. Exhausted by the pressures they have endured as a result of their so-called equality with men—the notorious double burden of domestic maintenance combined with professional accountability—many (ex)Soviet women have understandably found the notion unappealing. Moreover, according to the common argument, women in the former USSR have achieved full equality because they took on traditionally "masculine" professional roles earlier than did most of their American counterparts. But this rationalization is patently misleading, for while less professional discrimination indeed existed at the lower and middle echelons in the republics than was the case in the United States until relatively recently, women still rose far more seldom and more slowly to the upper levels of the party and the professions than men, who have occupied almost all the highest administrative posts. Even now, as in the United States, the glass ceiling remains a powerful barrier, all the more insidious because of its invisibility.[28]

Other factors have reinforced this process of obfuscation, deterring the sorts of sustained critique that might effect social and ideological change. Most prominent was the platform of the revolution itself. The early Bolsheviks held that abolishing class inequities would also eradicate inequities of gender; women had been enslaved not by hierarchical sexual ideologies but by feudal and capitalistic systems. Thus, in analyzing the causes of woman's oppression prior to the revolution, the early revolutionaries seldom examined gender (Buckley 1989b, 48–49). Although the radical women of that era were all too aware of the fact that the revolution was not going to bring them the equality they so desired, they persisted in their support of the revolutionary agenda, believing that once the larger problems were solved, their own liberation would follow. Those larger problems, of course, never found solutions. The manmade (quite literally) cataclysms of this century in the USSR— the two world wars, the civil war, forced collectivization, the purges—persistently deflected attention from concerns about gender and women's status to concerns about survival, categories generally (mis)perceived to be unrelated.

Thus, despite early Bolshevik history and philosophy, only now are questions about sex/gender systems beginning to surface in Russia and the former republics with anything approaching the interest such issues have long inspired in the West. Given the potential impact of that surfacing, the government's reluctance to countenance these questions is hardly surprising. It is interesting to speculate on what might happen in the former republics should women gain even the limited voice they have acquired in the West. Because serious interrogation of traditional gender formations threatens a status quo predicated even now on some of the most deeply held beliefs of the past, the transformation of the dominant sex/gender systems of the former USSR might ultimately pose at least as great a threat to the stability of the new regimes as do the vicissitudes of the economy or of the leadership. As Tatiana Klimenkova of the Institute of Philosophy of the Russian Academy of Sciences recently said of the incipient women's movement in her country, "We are ruining a national mythology, so we are doing something utterly scandalous."

If there is a glimmer of hope in the official attitude towards women's issues, it is that concepts once considered completely taboo in the former Soviet state are now allowed expression. Established notions of masculine privilege have been called into question since the late 1980s through such terms as *muzhekratiia* (male-dominated bureaucracy), *printsipy muzhskogo prevoskhodstva* (principles of male superiority), and *muzhskoi mir* (man's world). If the woman question (*zhenskii vopros*) has yet to be taken seriously by the government, the fact that the terminology through which women's oppression is expressed is once again in use suggests a slow but steady movement toward official acknowledgment of this problem (Buckley 1992c, 214).

Mythographies and Misogynies

As in the West, much Russian and Soviet thinking about gender roles originated in traditional conceptions of "woman's nature."[29] Reinforced in both Western and Slavic cultures by religious doctrines, secular philosophies, and social codes and customs, the argument from nature holds that women's fundamental role is reproduction and that the biological capacity for childbearing inevitably entails the principal responsibility for child rearing. Despite the Soviet expectation that women should participate fully in the extradomestic realm of production, these postulates about the so-called primary female role extend, as in the bourgeois West, to domestic maintenance—that is, to all the daily drudgery and the familial management subsumed within the all-encompassing word *byt*.

This socially constructed feminine role has been sustained by the tenacity of mythologies identifying woman with the land, with nature, and with fertility—ancient associations which, while also pervasive in Western culture, assume their own distinctive configurations in Russian and Soviet history. It is no accident that the feminized and maternalized image of a country as motherland, so widespread in European traditions, finds one of its most intense expressions in the image of "Mother Russia" (*Matushka Rus'*), or that one of the most persistent Russian folk epithets invokes "the damp mother earth" (*mat' syra zemlia*). But as in the West, this link between woman and land is far from simple, evolving diversely in response to the shifting exigencies of specific historical pressures and contexts and seldom separable from pervasive male anxieties about women's subversive power.[30]

As many Western feminist critics have shown, symbolic alliances of woman with nature have complex consequences for female authorship. While on the one hand granting women a measure of potentially subversive power, such stereotypes also tend to relegate the feminine, as an embodiment of nature, to the position of obscurity, wildness, and muteness. Within this ideological context, men are construed as the makers of culture, the speaking subjects whose power over naming and language ratifies and perpetuates male-dominated sociosymbolic orders. Conversely, women become figures of what Freud called "those dim Minoan regions" of the unconscious—inert, in-articulable, and inarticulate—the embodiment of dangerous forces that must be superseded or suppressed in order for civilization to flourish.[31]

The drive to inhibit women's agency and to restrain their creative expression appeared not only in attempts by the Church in both Russia and Europe to supplant powerful female deities with the more submissive figure of the *Bogoroditsa* (Mother of God) or the Madonna, and in secular political appropriations of the mother/land symbolic nexus, but also in the later attempts, in Muscovite Russia, to denigrate women's position both socially and morally. Thus, for example, in the *Domostroi* (*Household Book*), a powerfully influential tract attributed to the monk Sylvester in the sixteenth century, women were enjoined to silence and to strict obedience to their husbands—injunctions that recall similar forms of silencing imposed on Western women.[32]

Of course, like white women in the West, women in Russia have also possessed to a greater or lesser extent certain legal and moral rights within the very systems that enforced their subordination, as well as various unofficial forms of power exercised through their ability to manipulate the respect conferred by age, social status, or sheer force of character. Yet even the demonstrable effects of these interventions could not override women's compulsory subordination within interlocking systems of state, religion, and family whose legitimacy and authority derived from firmly entrenched patriarchal notions of rulership, civic order, and public discourse.[33] In both Russian and Western traditions, these complex and often contradictory constructions of woman continued to shape the gender codes that helped constitute the social and ideological matrices of female authorship. Dominant gender ideologies posited women as inferior in both body and mind, requiring control by men in the name of law, order, and civilization. So pervasive were those views, so profound their internalizations in individual psyches, so thoroughgoing their reinforcements in prevailing legal, economic, social, and religious institutions, that only the most extraordinary women could break through their constraints.

Before returning to the implications of these cultural and symbolic matrices for women writing in Russia in this century, let us make a brief excursion into the history of women in England and America. Prior to the seventeenth century, only a few exceptional Western women would "attempt the pen," to borrow Anne Finch's telling locution. Not only were most women (like most men outside the clergy and the upper classes) illiterate (though we should not underestimate their probable, if untraceable, contributions to the shaping of oral folklore), but even those of privileged classes were usually barred from the classical educations their brothers could take for granted. Those rare women who did write for circulation to more than a tiny closet audience were often vilified, ridiculed, or dismissed as beneath serious consideration— social controls that worked with considerable efficiency to enforce silence.

Only in the seventeenth century did certain daring women in the Anglo-American tradition begin to write for publication, and even then, with occasional striking exceptions such as Aphra Behn, they usually did so apologetically and defensively. Whether these apologias were at least partially ironic, even parodic—a tempting reading from a contemporary perspective—is difficult to assess. One recalls the elaborate mea culpas of Anne Bradstreet, the first white American poet (*The Tenth Muse, Lately Sprung Up in America*, 1650), or the self-abnegating conclusion to Anne Finch's "The Introduction," a lament on the opprobrium women risked by seeking publication in the early eighteenth century. It is a measure of the effectiveness of the taboo on female authorship that Finch, Countess of Winchelsea, published her poetry anonymously. Her 1713 collection is entitled simply *Poems, by a Lady*—"lady" presumably connoting not only aristocratic social class but also the "good breeding" (as Finch puns in "The Introduction") required of women, who are expected to give birth to babies, not books, to remain decorously silent, and most certainly not to presume to advertise their own names on title pages. The outspoken "Introduction," significantly, would not see print until 1903.

But by the second half of the eighteenth century, as a result of converging historical phenomena that feminist scholars have analyzed extensively over the past two decades, an extraordinary transformation had begun in the West. To oversimplify a highly complex social, political, and demographic process, we might summarize by saying that from the late eighteenth through the nineteenth centuries, at the same time the bourgeois classes were gaining increasing civic power and literacy was spreading with the mass production of inexpensive books, newspapers, and journals, the gender structures of society were also slowly shifting, giving way to the processes of democratization that would eventually affect all levels of society. In this dynamic milieu, women from all classes and of various racial and ethnic backgrounds gradually began trying their hands at authorship.

Especially with the rise of the novel, which by the early nineteenth century was fast becoming the dominant literary genre in America and England, women began to make their impact on the literary scene. As Virginia Woolf remarks in *A Room of One's Own*, "a change came about which, if I were re-writing history, I should describe more fully and think of greater importance than the Crusades or the Wars of the Roses. The middle-class woman began to write." In England, by the end of the eighteenth century, white female novelists and novel readers outnumbered men, as they would do in the United States in the nineteenth century—a fact at once verified and vilified in Hawthorne's famous jab at the "d——d mob of scribbling women" who dominated the American literary market. It is no accident that critics have commonly regarded the Anglo-American novel as the woman's genre *par excellence* (e.g., Showalter 1977; Armstrong; Tompkins; and Davidson). Significantly, in a virtual reverse of the situation that prevailed in Russia, Anglo-American women poets faced more difficult obstacles than did their fiction-writing counterparts (Gilbert and Gubar 1978, 1979), a situation exacerbated in the case of women of color. Consider, for example, the eighteenth-century author Phillis Wheatley, the first black poet published in this country, who felt obliged to defend her racial heritage as well as her gender position; or the case of the innumerable gifted black women whose creativity was suppressed by state-enforced illiteracy.

As these examples suggest, women of color have inhabited significantly different, if overlapping, cultural milieux from those of white middle-class women in the West, and since the advent of Western imperialism have been subject to far more severe forms of oppression and repression. Only in recent years has the crucial archival work of retrieval begun in earnest to reclaim many lost or formerly unrecognized works by black women both before and after slavery (e.g., Gates) or to make sustained investigations of African American women novelists (e.g., Carby). Native American women, Latina women, and Asian-American women have also been grossly underrepresented in official literary histories and curricula, though in recent years the project of retrieval and revaluation has begun in those literatures as well (e.g., Fisher; Allen; Lim; Tatum; Rivero and Rebolleda; and Harjo). This scholarship is altering the face of received traditions, both white and male, in ways that have incalculable consequences for regnant assumptions about literary and cultural expression.

Throughout the nineteenth century, then, even when writing by women flourished in the literary marketplace, it remained severely constrained by social structures and strictures. Although more women than men produced fiction in the nineteenth century, a combination of ideological pressures, institutional controls, gender-based apprehension and misapprehensions, and critical or cultural censure still led many of them, including some of the most gifted, to publish under pseudonyms, prompting Virginia Woolf's wry observation in *A Room of One's Own* that "the desire to be veiled still possessed them." The male critic who, upon receiving the manuscript of *Jane Eyre*, suggested to Charlotte Brontë that she should stay at home and attend to the domestic sphere proper to a woman was unfortunately only too typical of both popular opinion and the politics of the publishing and academic establishments. Small wonder, then, that well into our own century the vast majority of texts accorded canonical status have been authored by white men.

Only late in the twentieth century has the American critical climate shifted sufficiently that women might write with a freedom approaching men's. Criticism over the past twenty years has amply demonstrated that it was not the lack of genius, but prevailing social systems and ideologies, that hindered women's production of literature throughout earlier periods. The workings of such pervasive instruments of repression, of course, are not only overt, as in legal, social, or religious codes that still systematically institute the subordination of women. More pernicious because less discernible are the covert mechanisms of discrimination, sustained through a process of acculturation and internalization that enforces conventional gender arrangements by socializing girls to think and act like women as the dominant culture defines that term—an ideology still widely sustained through familial patterns, educational systems, popular iconographies, and the media (Faludi). As in the former Soviet Union, it is this complex tacit psychosocial matrix, as much as explicit prejudices and deliberate exclusions, that impedes women's creativity and helps account for the dearth of attention accorded to women writers in Anglo-American traditions until very recent years.

In Russia, typologies of gender had equally far-reaching effects. As the pre-Christian link between maternity and the land continued to flourish among the peasantry and even, nostalgically, among many of the intelligentsia as they became increasingly urbanized and Westernized, so too did the topos of woman as the embodiment of potentially chaotic natural forces which men could not control. By the nineteenth century, women of all classes were brought up within the resulting cultural matrix, dominated by polarities of veneration and contempt, adoration and anxiety. What is remarkable, in fact, is just how stable those polarities remained despite the changing social structures and growing intellectual ferment that characterized the century (Engel 1983, Heldt 1987, Glasse).

Traditional configurations of women have persisted with striking tenacity even into postrevolutionary times, often with contradictory results. On the one hand, in an ironic confluence of mythology and historical reality, the Bolshevik Revolution produced a social order in which women were expected to become *Amazonki*—strong, self-sufficient, and as competent as any man. Ideology under Lenin stressed the withering away of the family and the entry of women into previously male-dominated professions as symbolic of the revolt against bourgeois capitalist society. Much of the early literature of Socialist Realism reinforced this view, representing female figures who mirrored in idealized terms the roles assigned to women outside the text (Waters 1991).

The tension between life and official ideology reached a climax after

World War II. As in postwar America, where women who had experienced their first real independence in "men's" jobs were expected to make a docile return to home and family, so when Soviet men came home from the front, the party exhorted the *Amazonki* to remove their leather jackets, their pilots' uniforms, and their engineers' caps and to become "feminine" once more— that is, wives and mothers primarily devoted to their men—while still working in the labor force at jobs that generally offered lower status and less professional satisfaction than those they had formerly occupied in the men's absence.[34]

The literature of the Stalinist era increasingly criticized those women who retained the Amazon characteristics for which they had been praised when such "masculine" assertiveness and independence served national ends (Dunham 214–24). The party once again sought to use women for state purposes, this time by making them pivotal figures in the rebuilding of the Soviet nuclear family, which had been decimated by the purges, the siege, and the war. Thus in official fictions (that is, those subservient to and sanctioned by the party), even women depicted as fulfilling traditionally male roles displayed "feminine" submissiveness and humility in personal relationships, particularly within familial contexts. Through such devices the party undermined many of its original promises of women's equality.

This pattern was exacerbated by the typologies of Socialist Realism, which dominated the canons of Soviet literature until the 1980s and recapitulated with surprising frequency earlier ideological constructions of femininity. It is indicative of the tenacity of these ideologies that even those writers whose works violated the tenets of Socialist Realism often remained conformist in matters of gender, constructing female characters, from Lara in Boris Pasternak's *Doktor Zhivago* to Matryona in Alexander Solzhenitsyn's *Matryona's House* (*Matrenin dvor*), who are stereotypically identified with the sacrosanct and inarticulate images of the fertile earth and of Mother Russia.

To what degree most Soviet women were willing to embrace traditional feminine roles is debatable. But insofar as the manmade catastrophes of the century had deprived women of what traditional ideology defined as a normal family life, and to the extent that they had internalized these values, many welcomed the opportunity to return to them.[35] This desire was intensified by practical pressures: the vaunted "equality" created by the revolution had in fact given women added professional responsibilities without relieving them of traditional domestic roles. Thus for most Soviet women the issue was not so much whether to enter the labor force or not—the latter was not an option— but rather whether they could sustain the crushing weight of a double burden (*dvoinaia nosha*) from which men remained exempt.

To this day, as we have seen, post-Soviet women's continued hostility to feminism reflects this cultural difference. Tatiana Tolstaia recently summarized the situation thus:

> For years women from Western countries who call themselves feminists have interviewed us in the same cold, rigid manner: "How do your men oppress you? Why don't they wash the dishes? Why don't they prepare meals? Why don't they allow women into politics? Why don't women rebel against the phallocracy?"
>
> Soviet women are dumbfounded. Not only do they not want to be involved in the depressing, nauseating activity called Soviet "politics" . . . they would much rather not work at all. In bewilderment they ask themselves: What do we need this ridiculous feminism for anyway? In order to do the work of two people? So men can lie on the sofa?
>
> A Soviet woman's dream is to not have to work—but work she must because salaries are very low. . . . A career is more likely to give power than money, but most Soviet women feel they have enough power as is (Tolstaia 1990, 5–6).

Postrevolutionary historical and ideological shifts were profoundly complicated under Stalin, whose personal background and psychological conflicts intersected in complex ways with the inherited mythographies of Russia's past on which writers drew. Stalin engaged in an elaborate reinterpretation of the myth of maternity, a project driven not only by contemporary historical pressures but by his own childhood relations to his parents—a harsh, tyrannical father who brutally abused his wife and subjected the son to years of "undeserved, frightful beatings," and a strong-willed but self-abnegating mother who took refuge in religion and wanted her son to become a priest (Rancour-Laferrière 1988, 36).

As historians and literary critics have suggested, these formative events affected Stalin's later rule, in which, in effect, he supplanted the aggressor who threatened him or whom he wanted to overcome—whether his own father or a public authority figure like Trotsky or Hitler—by symbolically identifying with him.[36] Having achieved sole power after Lenin's death, Stalin presided over the virtual dismantling of the Soviet family through a series of events from forced collectivization and the ensuing famine to the purges and ultimately the Second World War. In subsequent efforts to remediate what he himself had helped instigate, he promulgated the myth of the "great Soviet family," with himself as symbolic head, epitomized in the various grandiose epithets by which he was extolled: "Father of the Soviet People," "Uncle Joe," "Great Friend of the Children," "Friend and Teacher," "Great Helmsman," "Leader," or—perhaps the most spectacularly misleading of all—"Friend to Women." Propaganda images depicted him surrounded by happy children, whom he regards beneficently from paternal heights.

This history raises an insistent question: with Stalin as paterfamilias of a Soviet nation whose families he had helped decimate, what happened to the mother(s)? Given his tendency to reproduce, on a national scale, his own childhood pathology, no family could exist in his world with both a powerful father figure and a strong mother. On the one hand, Stalin officially resurrected the term *rodina* (motherland), thus changing Russia's sex once more to female in preference to the patriarchal locution *otechestvo* (fatherland) introduced by Peter the Great. Yet even as Stalin invoked the emotionally resonant sign of the "suffering mother earth" beloved by her children since time immemorial, he also simultaneously undermined the power of that image through figures that recalled his own childhood, speaking repeatedly of the centuries-long "beating" of Mother Russia by the Mongols, the Swedes, or other countries from Poland to Japan. This myth of masochism—the mother who is beloved in direct proportion to the intensity of her suffering—assumes a different configuration, however, when "mother" becomes "father": when referring to his country's strength, Stalin shifts to the term "fatherland." It was only the feminized, fetishized version of the land that could be abused; in its masculinized incarnation it would itself do the "beating," mastering all foreign aggressors.

This phenomenon may partially explain the resurgence of interest among both male and female authors, since Stalin's death, in resurrecting and re-sanctifying not only the image of the mother but that of the land as maternal. As we have seen, such a resurrection is not uncomplicated: the dominant images of the mother/land in post-Stalinist literature have represented "her" as long-suffering, desecrated, even mutilated. The typical Marxist representation of women as strong, self-reliant figures, then, often reverted to a vision of sacrificial womanhood rooted in archaic cultural formations. Those women who attempted to carve out a life for themselves on the pages of literature independent of these stereotypes frequently fell prey to self-inflicted guilt and victimization, in effect replicating the very myth they sought to undermine.[37] Either mythology—that of the superwoman who is presumed to do it all or the mother whose sanctity is inseparable from sacrifice—propounds an ideology that implicitly endorses, even sanctifies, woman's suffering and silence.[38]

Writing Otherwise

There are women's baths—
but women's literature?—Lydiia Chukovskaia

Throughout Russian literary history these cultural dynamics have complicated the fates of women writers. As in England, privileged or aristocratic women began producing literary works at least as early as the thirteenth century, women in court circles wrote sporadically during the seventeenth and eighteenth centuries (the most spectacular example being Catherine the Great), and women from the gentry had also begun to publish by the late eighteenth century. But it was not until the nineteenth century that Russian women began to write in any great numbers. While generalizations are problematic, especially since so little of their writing has yet been recovered, we can conclude that even then their acceptance by the (male) literary establishment was heavily dependent on their choice of genre. Like European women, they worked in every conceivable generic form, including some—diaries, letters, and memoirs—that were not considered literary genres at all; but in the early nineteenth century, if a Russian woman wished to become an author, she was more likely to find acceptance for either lyric poetry or sentimental fiction—both regarded as properly feminine forms.

The situation with autobiography and memoirs was more complex. One way Russian women's autobiography achieved acceptance from a male-dominated literary establishment was by focusing on political and social questions. Thus Catherine the Great or the twentieth-century Russian revolutionary Vera Figner stressed the "official self" and the burning issues of the day (Heldt 1987, 68). In contrast, most prerevolutionary women writers had no official self to stress. Those who did, as in the case of the Princess Dashkova, often preferred to focus on more private (hence less socially sanctioned) areas of their lives.[39] Not until the late nineteenth century did women's private experiences come to be regarded as worthwhile literary subjects (Rosenthal and Zirin).

With fiction it was otherwise. While nineteenth-century Russian women authors wrote and published novels aplenty, they never achieved canonization.[40] The novel originally entered Russia from the West, particularly England, in the late eighteenth century, with translations of works by Daniel Defoe, Henry Fielding, Samuel Richardson, Oliver Goldsmith, Ann Radcliffe, and Laurence Sterne, who exercised a formative influence on the Russian novelistic tradition. As this list suggests, men were perceived as the chief shapers of the novel, although women, as we have seen, were already its most prolific practitioners.

Similarly, many authors of the novel and novella in Russia were women—from Avdot'ia Panaeva, whose autobiographical novel *The Tal'nikov Family* (*Semeistvo Tal'nikova*, 1848) described her upbringing in the 1820s, through Karolina Pavlova's *A Double Life* (*Dvoinaia zhizn'*, 1848), about a thoughtful young woman trying to rise above the insensitivities of the society around her, to Sofia Khvoshchinskaia's *City and Country Folk* (*Gorodskie i derevenskie*, 1863), treating the hypocrisy of contemporary freethinkers[41]—but their works were not regarded as canonical. Ironically, women who wished to write fiction in nineteenth-century Russia were caught in a double bind: On the one hand, they were discouraged by prevailing gender ideologies from attempting subjects outside the "proper feminine" sphere of domestic/familial conditions, interpersonal relations, and social customs. Yet when they wrote of that domestic world, their work was deemed trivial by a literary establishment ostensibly concerned only with the "big themes"—by definition the exclusive property of male authors.

The possibility that domestic issues might in fact be profoundly political, a concept now commonplace among American critics, was foreign to critical thinking in nineteenth-century Russia. Thus the novels of such masters as Tolstoy and Dostoevsky, treating philosophical and psychological questions or matters explicitly regarded as political, were perceived as far more serious than novels by women about issues regarded as feminine. It is a measure of the biases evoked by gender that these same male novelists, especially Tolstoy, were also celebrated for treatments of the very domestic and familial worlds (e.g., *Anna Karenina*) for which women writers were denigrated. Further, it now seems obvious that women's works dealt as frequently with political and social issues as did male-authored texts of the time. Elena Gan, for example, long before the "woman question" became an issue, had written about the fate of talented women in bourgeois male-dominated society. Panaeva, under the pseudonym N. Stanitskii, had written stories critical of male attitudes towards women's emancipation. And by the end of the nineteenth century women's works focused increasingly on the revolutionary ferment of Russian society.

As these examples demonstrate, women's situation in nineteenth-century Russia was fraught with contradictions. On the one hand, they were expected to behave in properly "feminine" fashion, yet they were also extolled in male-authored literature from Pushkin to Dostoevsky as strong figures revered by several generations of passive, weak-willed male creatures. But when it came to authoring novels, women were persistently anathematized and discounted. Better, prevailing opinion implied, for a woman to remain pure and untainted—and unknown on the pages of fiction—than to stain herself by writing books.[42]

Even so, women did manage to get published in some arenas. From the 1830s throughout the century, Russia's leading journals, which frequently had trouble filling their pages, readily accepted women's works. But even the women who published in these journals often used male pseudonyms.[43] There were other forms of literary cross-dressing as well. Perhaps the most spectacular example was Nadezhda Durova (1783–1866), who disguised herself as a boy, served in the Russian forces during the Napoleonic invasions, and later wrote about her experiences using various pseudonyms, both male and female.[44]

As these stories suggest, the ability to break into print was not simply a function of gender and genre but also of class and patronage.[45] Durova was a member of the aristocracy, but most women who published in nineteenth-century Russia came from the mercantile classes and the gentry, which, over the course of the century, became increasingly impoverished. Beginning in the early 1860s, when the emancipation of the serfs and the ensuing social reforms forced many women to look for remunerative work for the first time, writing was one of the professions they pursued. This process accelerated as women achieved the right to university education later in the century, attaining for the first time a cultural literacy approaching that of their male counterparts.

In spite of these advances, however, the tendency to extol woman's image while trivializing women's writing has continued to the present. Most twentieth-century Russian and Soviet women writers, from Akhmatova and Grekova to Tolstaia, have been reluctant to align themselves with anything that might possibly be construed as "women's writing," since the official critical establishment continues to dismiss such productions as subliterary: lightweight, trivial, and beneath serious notice. This derogatory attitude shows up dramatically in some of the common epithets still used about women's writing: *babskaia literatura* (old broad's literature) or *zhenskie stishki* (women's little verses). (Ex)Soviet citizens both male and female, reared from birth within this ideological context, have internalized its underlying assumptions to a striking degree. Until recently women writers, responding to the implicit party mandate that they must, to be taken seriously, "write like men," have eschewed discussions of their own personal concerns *as women* altogether, not only suppressing their identification with other women but also scanting issues of crucial importance in Soviet society: gender inequities, the political dimensions of sexuality and maternity, and, until recently, the dissolution of domestic life.[46]

Now, as more women writers have begun to explore their own personal concerns, many of them have created female characters who seem to represent their author's own alienation from traditional feminine models. Ironically, some of these writers return to the recurrent image of the *Amazonki*, but others figure their own estrangement from tradition through female characters who wander between worlds, unable to find a viable identity, or indulge in self-blame because they can accede neither to the Amazon image nor to that of the all-nurturing mother/land.

Yet even under the reactionary pressures of the socialist canon, certain women writers throughout this century have continued to press for redefinitions of the feminine, elaborating a complex, nuanced interrogation of both orthodox Soviet ideology and traditional gender structures. Most notable among them, perhaps, was the poet Marina Tsvetaeva, who played with the notion of gender reversals by (re)figuring herself alternately as the *amazonka* of ancient legend or the pretender (*samozvanka*) usurping authority from the male political or literary establishment, and who engaged in an ongoing examination of the gendered construction of the artist in her society. Tsvetaeva anticipated many of the concerns of contemporary gender theorists, most strikingly the focus on the relation between the artist's body and the body of the text.[47] The poetry of Sophia Parnok also questioned prevailing gender constructs: in a tradition in which the audience, like the writer, was generally assumed to be male, Parnok addressed most of her verses to other women while employing Russian masculine grammatical forms when referring to herself—a gesture that reflected less the desire to conceal her own voice than her implicit acknowledgment of women's divided identities (Heldt 1987, 119; Burgin).

After the death of Stalin in 1953, depending on the current winds of reform, Soviet writers no less than the Soviet people as a whole engaged in a reevaluation of their society vis-à-vis its revolutionary and prerevolutionary past. While this is not the place to provide a detailed examination of how specific representations of women have changed (indeed, much needed work is only beginning to be done on this subject), it is evident that the best Soviet and post-Soviet writers of the last four decades, both male and female, have involved themselves in a far-reaching dialogue with many of the configurations they have inherited both from their prerevolutionary past and from the Soviet state. However, in the fiction of even the most distinguished male authors, despite their willingness to write about other sensitive political and social issues and to question official policy on many fronts, one is struck by the persistence of traditional images of the feminine. That these writers, from Valentin Rasputin to Vasilii Belov and Viktor Astafyev, enjoy widespread popularity and marketability suggests the tenacity of these traditional representations even today.[48]

In works authored by women, one finds many of these same images— but with a difference. For among women writers the dialogue with the past more obviously occurs at the level of their own distinctive gender concerns. Strikingly, as we have seen, most of these authors continue to deny their interest in questions of gender.

Yet despite their denial, and whatever the complexities of its origins, it seems clear that these writers are ineluctably drawn into an ongoing dialogue with the gendered myths and ideologies of the past. The kinds of writing these women are producing, no less than their attitudes towards themselves as writers, cannot escape the historical processes that have formed contemporary post-Soviet culture. Within their works one senses a genuine angst and confusion regarding gender. As our essays have suggested, there is often an ongoing intratextual dialogue between the representations of female characters or the configurations of gender which the authors apparently want to project and their own—perhaps subconscious—attachment to or reaction against the gender codes in which their society is enmeshed. The vision of despair that characterizes the world of Liudmila Razumovskaia, the humiliated female victims in the prose of Larisa Vaneeva, or the retreat into spirituality and religion in the texts of Olesia Nikolaeva suggest that even the most recent women writers are often treading on old territory, exploring, and in some cases exploiting, conventions elaborated in male-authored fictions.

Perhaps the two best-known exemplars of this tendency are Tatiana Tolstaia and Liudmila Petrushevskaia. Although Tolstaia has outspokenly repudiated the idea that writing is a gendered activity, and although she writes in a self-consciously literary style reminiscent of many of Russia's masters from Gogol to Nabokov, her fictions implicitly question and critique received constructions of gender. It is no accident that a number of her female protagonists—for example, Zoya in "Hunt for the Wooly Mammoth" ("Okhota na mamonta") or Nina in "The Poet and the Muse" ("Poet i muza")—fall prey to stereotypical gender codes that the larger narratives cast in an ironic light. In those stories in which her female protagonists live according to what they perceive as proper feminine behavior, Tolstaia relentlessly satirizes their values. In other stories, such as her classic (and her favorite) "Sweet Shura" ("Milaia Shura"), she draws a poignant and loving portrait of a woman whose entire life has been lived for men. What distinguishes Shura from Tolstaia's more modern philistine protagonists is that she, like Tolstaia herself, is an artist who creates her own text out of the raw material of her life and takes responsibility for her creation.

Petrushevskaia plays even more radically with inherited ideologies of gender, particularly through her use of the female body to figure the forms of oppression. In a recent analysis of this phenomenon, Helena Goscilo astutely dubbed Petrushevskaia "the patron saint of the New Physiology." Her works take to extreme the ironized perspective that has typified women's writings at least since the 1980s, supplanting traditional romanticized or idealized conceptions of the female body with somatic representations wherein bodies become sign systems that "document their owners' suffering and degradation" (Goscilo 1993, 74). It is indicative of this new poetics that the uterus and the lower extremities (in both senses) have displaced the heart as the privileged sites of women's experience. Other writers, notably Nina Sadur, Svetlana Vasilenko, Nina Gorlanova, and Liudmila Ulitskaia, similarly dismember or disfigure the bodies of their female protagonists in order to inscribe the debilitating circumstances in which most women are forced to live in Soviet and post-Soviet society.

Perhaps what most distinguishes the writing of contemporary women authors in the new Russia, however, is the expressionistic use of setting as a figure for the construction of the female subject. Whether the mise-en-scène is an overcrowded apartment, the streets of Moscow, a village in Siberia, an urban hospital, or an abortion clinic, women's fictions ultimately focus most acutely on internal landscapes. This double geography is hardly surprising, for even on the most obvious level the impulse to withdraw into psychological spaces is an understandable form of escape—from *byt*, from living amidst radical political upheaval, uncertainty, and instability, or from the desperate conditions to which quotidian life in Russia has been reduced. But the current focus on female subjectivity may also be read as an effort to reclaim voices previously silenced, to locate and define discursive positions previously denied or prohibited. This is so even when the narratives seem primarily focused on the obstacles to articulation. Petrushevskaia's female narrators, for instance, stand boldly before us ready to tell their stories. Yet the truth her texts reveal—apparent to the reader if frequently elusive to the narrators themselves—is that often they themselves do not understand what they have to tell, or have repressed the stories they most needed and wanted to narrate. In this Petrushevskaian paradox we might see a vivid metaphor for the problematic status of post-Soviet women writing within a system in which the very condition for articulation may be self-alienation: the denial of one's own female body and gendered being in the world.

There is little doubt that the dominant ideologies of the past seventy years have taken their toll on post-Soviet women writers. In denigrating the specificity of women's issues and "women's writing," implicitly positing that to write well is to write as—and for—"man," the dominant culture not only imposed conformity to official party policy but also suppressed women's expression, even perhaps their very consciousness, of their own distinctive and distinctively gendered visions. Perhaps this is less surprising than it might at first seem to Western readers. For if the history of Soviet literature has taught its writers anything, it has been how best to survive within the system. In that, of course, the situation of (ex)Soviet women writers bears comparison to analogous survival strategies evolved by American women of all races and classes throughout the post-Columbian history of this country.

Yet as events of recent years have shown, the censorship and censure women have endured for centuries is gradually giving way to a new generation of writers with their own distinctive voices, voices that have resisted all attempts to silence them. Writers such as Larisa Vaneeva, Elena Tarasova,

Nina Sadur, and Nina Gorlanova, among others, are creating experimental fictions, carving out a path for themselves and for other writers in a literature that has traditionally suppressed such attempts. Their work is flourishing. Increasingly, post-Soviet women are taking the liberties American women have assumed for several generations, though even American women still occupy a ground more fragile than many might wish to believe. Theirs too is a survival story. The freedom they currently enjoy—even those who would deny the difference gender makes for writing and for literary history—has been hard won.[49] For women in this country, as for most post-Soviet women writers now, there is no turning back. If comparison between these authors and their American counterparts can tell us anything, it is the story of those parallel survivals.

Notes

1. Heldt's *Terrible Perfection* (1987) was the first Western feminist analysis of Russia's women writers and the image of women in male-authored fiction. Other recent works include Sandler; Heldt 1989; Forrester; Gove; and Kroth. See also Göpfert 1992, *Dichterinnen und Schriftstellerinnen in Russland von Mitte des 18. bis zum Beginn des 20. Jahrhunderts* (Munich). Several valuable anthologies of Soviet women's writing have also appeared recently in the West (Goscilo 1989, 1993d; McLaughlin; Decter; Ledkovsky; and Bromfeld and Perova). For a recent revisionist history of Russian women's literature, including much new archival material, see Rosenthal and Zirin. Critical essays on Russian women's culture have also begun to appear. See Goscilo, ed., 1993c, *Fruits of Her Plume*; Costlow, Sandler, and Vowles, eds., 1993, *Sexuality and the Body in Russian Culture*; and Liljeström, Mäntysaari, and Rosenholm, eds., 1993, *Gender Restructuring in Russian Studies*; also see Andrew, *Narrative and Desire in Russian Literature* (forthcoming). See also the special issue of *Glas* devoted to Russian women's writing (Bromfeld and Perova, eds., 1992, *Women's View*); Goscilo, ed., 1992, "Skirted Issues: The Discreteness and Indiscretions of Russian Women's Prose," a special issue of *Russian Studies in Literature*, 28:2. As this book goes to press, so too does *A Dictionary of Russian Women Writers*, ed. Ledkovsky, Rosenthal, and Zirin (1993). In addition, see Nemec Ignashev, and Krive, comps., 1992, *Women and Writing in Russia and the USSR: A Bibliography of English Language Sources* (Garland).

2. In a recent special issue of *Russian Studies in Literature* entitled "Skirted Issues" (ed. Goscilo, 1992), devoted to the writings of contemporary Russian critics on the subject of women's writing, not one of the five critics represented saw a connection between writing and gender though most saw women's fiction as an "identifiably distinct entity." While virtually all these critics acknowledge women's inherent difference from men, that difference seems miraculously to evaporate the moment the woman writer in question sets pen to paper (3–17).

3. In the social sciences several pioneering books have recently appeared, notably Attwood 1990; Bridger 1987; Browning; Edmondson; and Waters 1991. Social science and humanities combine in Buckley 1992; Costlow et al.; and Edmondson. See also Shapiro. We are indebted to all these studies. The belatedness of studies of Russian and Soviet women is less a result of Western scholars' lack of interest than of the difficulty, until recently, of access to data and the party's problematic attitude towards the issue of women's place in Soviet society. See Engel 1987.

4. The diverse histories of U.S. women's writing are too numerous to cite, but see, for example, Faust et al.; Baym; Kelley; Tompkins; Davidson; Carby; and Zimmerman. For useful introductions and bibliographies of many American women authors, see Fisher; Evans; Gilbert and Gubar 1985; Allen 1989; Lim; Birkby et al.; Bulkin; Beck; and Rivero and Rebolleda.

5. The term *samizdat* (literally, "self-published") denotes the process of underground publication by which manuscripts unacceptable to the official political line were circulated prior to glasnost. Samizdat had its beginnings with the inception of the dissident movement in 1966. For an account of Mamonova's activities, see Morgan 1984, Foreword, and Mamonova 1984, Introduction to *Women and Russia*, ix–xxiii. See also Mamonova 1989, *Russian Women's Studies*, and Ruthchild on the split among Russia's feminists.

6. The original issues of *Zhenskoe chtenie* contained approximately 100–140 pages of text per issue in a circulation of thirty to forty copies. Plans are now underway for the magazine to be published through a professional publishing house with a circulation of five thousand to ten thousand.

7. While the phenomenon called "second-wave feminism" has had an especially dramatic impact on Western thinking and social formations since the late 1960s, women's movements of various sorts have of course existed in America at least since the late eighteenth century. While not all were explicitly devoted to extending women's rights—some would not even have identified themselves in those terms— together they helped create social and ideological conditions that made possible the extension of those rights (a situation that bears comparison with various radical women's movements in Russia which, though most would eschew the term "feminism," have nonetheless advanced women's rights and prerogatives). These efforts culminated with the achievement of U.S. women's suffrage in 1920. For a variety of social and ideological reasons still debated by historians, the momentum of U.S. women's liberation movements subsequently waned, so that feminism had to be virtually reinvented in the second half of the century, in the aftermath of the civil rights movement. (For analyses see Flexner; S. Evans; Lerner; Rosenberg; DuBois; Cott; Rupp and Taylor; and Chafe.) Women's movements also occurred in nineteenth-century Russia in response to the dissemination of Western ideas among the intelligentsia.

8. As of this writing those translations have yet to appear, partially because of the chronic paper shortage and the recent emergence of cost-accounting policies (*khozraschet*) and self-financing (*samofinansirovanie*), which have caused publishers to become excessively conscious of the projected market value of their manuscripts.

Significantly, however, a book like Alex Comfort's *The Joy of Sex* has been in print in Russia since 1991.

9. The oldest of the Soviet women's magazines, *Rabotnitsa* (*Working Woman*) and *Krest'ianka* (*Peasant Woman*), dating from the 1920s, have long dealt with serious political issues, unlike their counterpart publications in the United States. This recognition of the links between politics and domesticity, potentially progressive by comparison with American popular culture aimed at women, resulted in part from the practical realities of Soviet women's lives: since women bearing the double burden of work and domestic maintenance traditionally have had less time to read than men in the USSR, magazines designed only for women made a serious attempt to disseminate information to which they might otherwise not have access. On women's magazines prior to glasnost, see McAndrew 78–115.

10. Predicated on the conviction that "the woman question" has never been solved in the former USSR and that the patriarchal system of gender relations pervades every level of society, the Tsentr brings together scholars with strong feminist leanings who wish to keep up with developments in Western gender studies. It has just received a grant from the German Fraueneinstiftung to set up an information center for women with archives, database, and a library. Other outgrowths of Soviet women's activities were the first interdisciplinary Soviet-American symposium on women (Moscow, May 1991) and the First Independent Women's Forum (Dubna, 29–31 March 1991), whose program included presentations such as A. Posadskaia's on "Woman as an Object and Subject of Social Transformations" and O. Lipovskaia's on "Woman as an Object of Consumption," as well as a session devoted to the discrimination against women in patriarchal cultures. The Second Independent Women's Forum was held 27–29 November 1992, in Dubna, where the topic was "From Problems to Strategy." Other hopeful signs of women's activities include the founding in 1992 of the Petersburg Women's Center; a Feminist Orientation Center in Moscow which hopes to support research, consultation, and psychological training in feminist issues; "Nadezhda" (Hope), the first independent women's radio station in Russia and the CIS, which broadcasts out of Moscow; "Cherepakha," the first feminist publishing house; and a fund called "Ariadna," which has been set up in Moscow to support gender studies and conduct training programs for women. For information on the development of Soviet women's groups see *Women: East-West* (May and September 1990), ed. Zirin, a newsletter whose appearance in the fall of 1987 was itself a cause for celebration, a sign of the advances made possible by both glasnost and the American women's movement. See also the new Russian language newspaper for women, *You and Us* (*Vy i My*), published under the auspices of the National Council for Research on Women, intended for both Soviet and American women, and including information on the development of the U.S. women's movement, health care, reproductive rights, family, education, and organizational, managerial, and communication skills. Similarly, the Russian journal *Sotsiologicheskie issledovaniia* (*Sociological Research*), no. 5, 1992, recently devoted its entire discussion section, by both Russian and foreign scholars, to gender issues. Similarly, one of the most popular magazines in the

country, *Ogonek*, has agreed to begin a column of women's issues called "Zhenskii ugol" ("Women's Corner"). Our thanks to Helena Goscilo for this information.

11. *Los Angeles Times*, 22 June 1992, H5. Lipovskaia comments that Western feminists mistakenly assume that any women's organizations in the former Soviet Union must necessarily be feminist. In fact these organizations, both formal and informal, are often founded on some specific platform (for example, the Committee of Soldiers' Mothers, formed in 1989 to aid invalided veterans of the Afghanistan war), a situation not unlike some of the women's movements in America in the nineteenth century. The Club Maria, one of the first groups formed in the seventies to espouse women's concerns, was opposed to the tenets of Western feminists and instead stressed female spirituality and woman's return to her original role as selfless mother as the path to social change (Ruthchild 7). Though women's political parties have also been founded to espouse a radical restructuring of politics and society, they stop short of formulating specific platforms to implement their ideals and of linking political with gender restructuring. The Lithuanian women's group Sajudis lobbies for an independent Lithuania because its members believe that this would allow them to return to home, family, and childrearing. See Lipovskaia 1992, "New Women's Organisations," and Buckley 1992c.

12. For example, women in Russia have come under increasing pressure to produce larger families because of government fears that the Muslim population will outnumber the Russian population by the end of this century. As this book goes to press (July 1993), a new law is due for a vote in the Russian Congress, "On the Protection of the Family, Motherland, Fatherhood, and Childhood"—clearly designed to put women back into the home, which is assumed to be the only proper way for them to realize their "natural" potential. See Liuka 1992, "Vlasti Rossii." This situation is compounded by the fact that more and more women, according to Anastasiia Posadskaia, are deciding not to divorce because of the worsening Russian economy and the substantial difference in wages paid men and women. Conversely, women in Central Asia, where the birth rate has traditionally been high, are being exhorted to enter the work force, in the expectation that they will then have fewer children (Attwood 1990, 6; Holt 237–65).

13. In an important book, *The Keys to Happiness: Sex and the Search for Modernity in Fin-de-Siècle Russia*, Laura Engelstein explores the role of sexuality in late tsarist imperial culture, showing how Western ideas and attitudes towards sex were transformed within the Russian context, creating a situation in which the liberal intelligentsia was caught between a desire to emulate the West and the need to reject certain aspects of its liberal social codes. Engelstein concludes that had tsarism been succeeded by a more liberal regime, sexual mores in the Soviet Union would have come to resemble more closely those of the West. As it was, the sexual code under which the Soviets lived for the greater part of this century only recapitulated and deepened that propagated by the tsarist regime.

14. Specter 1990.

15. Ibid. Kon has long held that the traditional Soviet silence about sex is un-

healthy and that lack of sex education is one reason for the high divorce and abortion rates there. He launched *Eros,* a new journal dealing with the scientific study of sexuality, in 1991. See also *Sex and Russian Society,* ed. Kon and Riordan, the first comprehensive work dealing with sexuality in Russia. It is a telling instance of Russian standards of sexuality that only in 1990 was D. H. Lawrence's *Lady Chatterley's Lover*—which now seems relatively tame (not to mention sexist) by Western standards—first translated into Russian (*Liubovnik Ledi Chatterlei,* trans. Tatiana Leschenko [Moscow: Video-Ass., 1990]).

16. For examples of studies of gay and lesbian history or of the persistence and pervasiveness of homophobia in the United States, see Katz; Rich 1980; d'Emilio; Lorde; Anzaldúa 1987 and 1990; Duberman et al.; Wittig; and Faderman. On the development of lesbian fiction, see Stimpson 1981; and Zimmerman. After the collapse of the Soviet Union, some former republics (Russia not among them) revoked their anti-gay legislation. However, they supplemented their legal codes with vague articles against "perverted forms of gratifying sexual lust." In the draft of the Russian Criminal Code presented to President Yeltsin, homosexual relations between consenting adults were decriminalized, but there is now a reference to "perverted forms" of sexuality which, interestingly enough, was not even present in Stalinist legislation.

Perhaps the worst danger to homosexuality in Russia and the former republics is found less in the law than in popular opinion. Reflecting some of that thinking, the Russian nationalist writer Valentin Rasputin stated in an interview for BBC in 1991 that homosexuality had been imported into Russia, and that if gays and lesbians felt that their rights were being violated, they should emigrate! Similarly, the right-wing popular media from *Nash Sovremennik, Den',* and *Sovetskaia Rossiia* on down to the TV program *600 Seconds* actively propagate homophobia (Riordan 1993). Our thanks to Jim Riordan for much of this valuable information.

17. Consider, for example, the recent intense debates in the United States in Congress, the arts community, academia, and the media about government censorship of the arts, focusing on (but not limited to) the appropriateness of providing NEA support for what some regard as "pornography," a debate that led to the Bush administration's replacement, in 1992, of the director of NEA and the subsequent narrowing of official NEA definitions of what counts as art. For some examples of diverse U.S. feminist views of pornography, see Dworkin; Snitow et al.; Vance; and MacKinnon 1985.

18. See, for example, Rubin; Berger; Banner; Suleiman; Jacobus et al. 1990; and Wolf.

19. For more on the treatment of sex in glasnost films see Horton and Brashinsky; and Attwood 1993a, 1993b. Most current Russian films are replete with sex scenes but contain little eroticism. Our thanks to Vida Johnson for this insight.

20. *Washington Post* (23 August 1992), F1–4. On prostitution in the USSR, see Waters 1989, 1992. For excellent overviews of the problems and prospects women have faced since the advent of glasnost, see Buckley 1989a, 1992c; Goscilo 1991; and Heldt 1992. According to Heldt, current press coverage of prostitution condemns

the prostitute, not the male clients—a situation entirely familiar to Western women. Yet paradoxically, as in the United States, the commercial exploitation of women's bodies in beauty pageants or the advertisement industry fails to elicit comparable social condemnation (164). See also Banner; and Buckley 1992c, 221–22.

21. Analyses of women's relation to Anglo-American canons are too numerous to cite, but see, in addition to Showalter's groundbreaking *Literature of Their Own* (1977); Froula; Kolodny; Robinson 1985; Aiken 1985; Anzaldúa and Moraga; Carby; and Braxton.

22. See n. 1. Notable examples include Stepanenko and Fomenko, comps., 1989, *Zhenskaia logika (Woman's Logic)*; Vaneeva, comp., 1990, *Ne pomniashchaia-zla (The Woman Who Holds No Grudge)*; Shavkuta, ed., 1980, *Chisten'kaia zhizn' (A Pristine Life)*; Vasilenko, comp., 1991, *Novye Amazonki (The New Amazons)*; Sokolova, comp., 1991, *Abstinentki (The Abstainers)*; and the English-language text *Always a Woman*, ed. Kupriianova 1987. Collections of nineteenth-century writings include probably the most ambitious work to date—the three-volume collection of nineteenth-century women writers compiled by Uchenova (1986), as well as her *Svidanie* (1987), her *Tol'ko chas* (1988), and a collection of essays on women writers during Pushkin's era, M. Sh. Fainshtein, ed., 1989, *Pisatel'nitsy pushkinskoi pory: Istoriko-literaturnye ocherki*. See also Uchenova 1989, *Tsaritsy muz: russkie poetessy XIX—nachala XXvv*. Yet like anthologies of American literature until relatively recently, most anthologies of Russian and Soviet writing have slighted women writers. No women appeared among the thirteen authors represented in Proffer 1969, *From Karamzin to Bunin: An Anthology of Russian Short Stories*, nor among the seven in Proffer and Proffer, eds., 1982, *Contemporary Russian Prose*. Soviet collections of stories from both the nineteenth and the twentieth centuries show the same pattern. *Sovetskii rasskaz* (ed. Kramov 1975), a two-volume anthology of Soviet short stories, includes three women in a total of ninety-one selections. In *Sovremennaia povest'* (comp. Skalon 1985), a two-volume collection of contemporary novellas published in the eighties, all nine writers are male. Even in *Povesti o liubvi* (comp. Kuleshov 1988), a two-volume collection of stories on love, in which one might expect the old guard to turn a passing glance to women writers, the editor evidently assumed that not one woman had anything of worth to say on the subject.

23. Personal communication with Tolstaia, Tucson, Arizona, November 1989. See also her review of *Soviet Women: Walking the Tightrope* in the *New York Review of Books*, 31 May 1990, 3–7. For the generality of this view, as well as the sorts of bias that often sustain it, see Gurevich's sarcastic treatment, in "Lost in Translation," of a conference on Soviet and American women's writing held in the spring of 1991 at the New York Institute for the Humanities at New York University.

24. In the first and second issues of its journal *Aprel'* (1989–90), only eight women writers appear among the forty-eight contributors. For more about the committee's platform, see Garrard and Garrard 230–34. Other alternative publications, specifically *Lanterna magica*, first published in 1990, have done somewhat better in publishing works by women. See Heldt 1992, 171–72.

25. Gray provides an eloquent account of the resistance of Soviet women to

Western feminism. For a more historically and politically oriented analysis of the interrelationship between ideology and "the woman question" see Buckley 1989b and 1992a.

26. Citation of NEA statistics, 7 July 1992, "The MacNeil-Lehrer Report."

27. For more statistics on women's participation in the political process, see Buckley 1992a, 54–71.

28. On the limitations of women's access to the higher echelons of professions in America, see Kanter; Elshtain; Cockburn; Baron; and England. A survey in the late 1980s of Soviet party membership showed that women generally either deferred joining the party until they had completed rearing their children or abstained from active participation in the kinds of party work that led to promotion. If a woman came to active party participation late, her male colleagues often had a twenty-year head start on her. Recent statistics indicated that 14.1 percent of all Soviet men over eighteen were members of the party, as opposed to only 3.7 percent of all women. Since 1918 the percentage of women in the Central Committee was never higher than 4.2 (Fischer). For a more up-to-date account of women's participation in the political process, see Buckley 1992b, 1992c. High-ranking women in the party are rare. The first female member of the Politburo in Soviet history was appointed when Khrushchev made Ekaterina Furtseva minister of culture. Under Khrushchev's successors until Gorbachev, no women held positions on the Politburo. Under Gorbachev, Alexandra Biriukova became a corresponding (nonvoting) member, with responsibility for consumer affairs—a traditionally feminine arena because of its association with *byt*. Only subsequently did a woman receive a voting position: Galina Semyonova, formerly editor of the monthly women's journal *Kres'tianka*, who replaced Biriukova upon her retirement and has now returned to *Kres'tianka*. Significantly, Gorbachev stated that Semyonova would handle "the woman-family-children portfolio." Semyonova herself, however, went on record otherwise: "I simply refuse to be limited. I consider that my portfolio covers virtually everything that comes before the Politburo or party Secretariat" (quoted in Parks 1991, "Galina Semyonova: No Mere Token in Soviet Politburo," *Los Angeles Times*, 15 Jan., H5). Similarly, there has been a noticeable absence of women in the highest positions on editorial boards in the Soviet and post-Soviet media. The former editor in chief of one of the leading Soviet magazines, *Ogonek*, Vitali Korotich, never allowed women reporters to engage in journalism on subjects that he felt were "dangerous." Such statements might be read simultaneously as protective and paternalistic—not unlike the recent debates in the United States over women in the armed services participating in combat. The newspaper *Literaturnaia gazeta* apparently does not share Korotich's policy (Heldt 1992, 162).

29. The studies of this persistent, problematic category are too numerous to mention, but see Beauvoir; Ortner; Rubin; Cixous; and MacCormack and Strathern. For Anglo-American feminist critiques of the limitations of traditional Marxism to address gender oppression, see Hartsock and Sargent. For diverse examples of Western Marxist-feminist analysis, see Mitchell; Firestone; Barrett; Davis; and Robinson.

30. For treatments of the diverse mythologies and ideologies informing both historical and current constructions of "woman's nature" in Russia, see Hubbs; Barker

1985; Ivanitz; Atkinson; Pushkareva; Heldt 1987; Glasse; and Waters 1991. While the non-Russian peoples of the former USSR have their own distinctive traditions of gender roles and rights, the Russian republic has been most influential in shaping official policy, and Russian traditions have pervasively informed the cultural matrix which produced the Soviet writers we treat. Even Nerkagi was reared in a Russianized environment.

31. Analyses of these issues are too numerous to detail, but see Beauvoir; Ortner; Rubin; Irigaray; Cixous; and Pateman.

32. See Bell; Gilbert and Gubar 1979a, 3–20; and Showalter 1981. On female conduct books of the English Renaissance, see Jones; Beilin; Hull; Newman; and Brigham.

33. Pushkareva 29–43 suggests that through the sixteenth century women's responsibility for keeping the family intact guaranteed them a certain amount of power within that unit. On women's legal status in the West, see MacKinnon 1982; Okin; Elshtain; Pateman; and Williams.

34. Of the young Soviet women who were trained by Marina Raskova as bomber pilots in World War II, only one was accepted as a pilot for the Soviet airline Aeroflot after the war, a fact little noted in traditional histories of the period (personal communication between Adele Barker and former bomber pilots, Moscow, 1988). For a telling critique of comparable treatments of women in America after World War II, see Anderson and the classic film *Rosie the Riveter*.

35. See Holmgren's *Women's Works in Stalin's Time*, which discusses how both male and female writers during the Stalin era composed works reevaluating the notion of the domestic sphere.

36. See Rancour-Laferrière 1988; and Tucker, who argues (74–75) that the beatings Stalin witnessed and received engendered his lifelong fascination with and need to beat his enemies, both literally and figuratively: "the alienating force his father represented had somehow been internalized within him." Stalin was evidently fascinated by the Leninist question *kto kogo?* (Who will beat whom?) in the struggle of socialism and capitalism. Obviously Stalin carried the implications of that remark far beyond its original intent (cited in Rancour-Laferrière 1988, 38).

37. Recent fiction by Russian women writers provides telling evidence of this tendency. See, for example, Natal'ia Sukhanova's "Delos," which seems to plead for humane conditions for women during childbirth but in fact seeks to induce guilt about abortion. Larisa Vaneeva's stories are equally mired in women's self-blame: e.g., "Parad planeta" ("Parade of the Planets") and "Khromye goloby," translated into English as "Lame Pigeons" (Heldt 1992, 168–69).

38. Exceptions exist: for example, the stories of Maia Ganina, whose Amazonki live independent of male assistance; or Anatoly Kim, whose *Father Forest* (*Otets les*) depicts women who have lived in the country without men since the war, celibate as nuns—the secularized Christian version of Amazons.

39. Appointed by Catherine the Great as the director of the Academy of Sciences, Ekaterina Dashkova wrote her autobiography late in life (1804–5), after Catherine's

death, while living out her days in seclusion and obscurity. Other nineteenth-century women's autobiographies were those of Nadezhda Sokhanskaia (1823–1884), who wrote as an exercise for P. A. Pletnev, editor of the journal *Sovremennik* from 1837 to 1847, because he was tantalized by her provincial world. They were published posthumously in *Russkoe obozrenie* (1896) as part of the general recovery of her legacy (*Russkii biograficheskii slovar'*, vol. 19, 168–71); Heldt 1987, 87–93; Rosenthal and Zirin, 109–18). Similarly, Avdotiia Panaeva (1819–1893) wrote her memoirs in 1889, hoping to support herself after the death of her second husband. The text, which languished for years on booksellers' shelves, disregarded by the critical establishment, is today regarded as one of the finest accounts of literary life and personages in mid-nineteenth-century Russia (Chukovskii, in Panaeva, 10).

40. Many were published serially in journals such as *Sovremennik* (*The Contemporary*), *Otechestvennye zapiski* (*Notes from the Fatherland*) and *Russkoe slovo* (*The Russian Word*). Journals particularly hospitable to women were *Russkii vestnik*, especially in the late 1850s under the literary editorship of Evgeniia Tur, *Vestnik Evropy*, and Liubov' Gurevich's *Severnyi vestnik* in the 1890s. Thanks to Mary Zirin for this information.

41. To date only *A Double Life* has been translated (Heldt 1978). Other nineteenth-century women novelists were the Ukrainian Marko Vovchok (pseudonym of Mariia Aleksandrovna Markovich), Mariia Zhukova, Elena Gan (pseudonym Zenaida R-Va.), Mariia Krestovskaia, and Nadezhda Khvoshchinskaia (pseudonym V. Krestovskii).

42. Heldt 1987, chaps. 1–2. Cf. Woolf's similar observations about English women in *A Room of One's Own*.

43. By the end of the century women were again using their real names or female pseudonyms, a possible indication that the literary scene was becoming more open to female authorship (Rosenthal and Zirin, 111).

44. Durova's journals have been admirably translated by Zirin (1988). It is a tribute to Durova's compelling personality that even though her masquerade was uncovered after she had served only one year in the cavalry, she nevertheless received permission from Tsar Alexander I to work in the Hussars under the pseudonym Alexandrov, which the Tsar himself selected after his own name.

45. Although Barbara Engel does not deal with writers per se, *Mothers and Daughters* provides the best account to date of class as a determining factor in the lives of nineteenth-century women. That some of these women came from nobility or even gentry did not guarantee them economic privileges: only one percent of the population enjoyed the kind of aristocratic way of life one reads about in Tolstoy. While 10 percent of the nobility lived comfortably, the remaining 90 percent were so poor that often they lived no better than their own peasants (Engel 10).

46. Gray (127–28) quotes a common remark among the Soviet literati describing talented women writers: "This is fine writing, as if accomplished by a man's hand." The trivialization of women's writing is reflected in the low numbers of women holding executive posts in the former Writers' Union: 12, as opposed to 360 men, as of 1986.

The newly created Rossiiskii Soiuz Pisatelei, however, is headed by a woman, and one of its section heads is a woman. For more information on women's representation both political and professional organizations, see Buckley 1992b, 1992c.

47. Sandler 139–57. See also Forrester; Boym; Kroth; Gove; Goscilo 1992, 1993; Weeks. On "writing the body," see Cixous; Irigaray; and Forrester.

48. Ironically, that image which for centuries embodied male authors' notions of female perfectability has now become associated with some of the basest forms of nationalism since the inception of glasnost. Much male-authored literature renders woman "safe" by confining her to the unthreatening repository of the land, as in the stories by the Siberian writer Valentin Rasputin (e.g., "Farewell to Matyora" [*Pro-shchanie s Materoi*], "Vasilii and Vasilissa"), or by denigrating her altogether, as in the recent fictions of Vasilii Belov ("Vse vperedi" ["Everything is Ahead"]) or Viktor Astafyev ("Pechal'nyi detektiv" ["The Sad Detective"]). The most obvious exception to this rule is the Russian writer Viktor Erofeev, whose novel *Russkaia krasavitsa* (*Russian Beauty*) charts the adventures of a young woman whose image suggests the dialogue taking place in post-glasnost Russian culture. Erofeev has called his heroine, Irina Tarakanova, both "Gorbachev in a skirt" and "the first free person in Russia" (lecture given at the University of Washington, 29 April 1993).

49. For eloquent proof that many prominent American women authors persist in such denials, witness the ongoing debate in the "Letters to the Editor" sections of the *New York Times Book Review* in 1985, prompted by the review of Gilbert and Gubar's *Norton Anthology of Literature by Women*.

Selected Bibliography

Aiken, Susan Hardy. 1990. *Isak Dinesen and the Engendering of Narrative*. Chicago: U of Chicago P.

———. 1985. "Women and the Question of Canonicity." *College English*. 48.3 (March): 288–301.

Alexandrova, Ekaterina. 1984. "Why Soviet Women Want to Get Married." Mamonova 31–50.

Allen, Paula Gunn. 1986. *The Sacred Hoop: Recovering the Feminine in American Indian Traditions*. Boston: Beacon.

———, ed. 1989. *Spider Woman's Granddaughters: Traditional Tales and Contemporary Writing by Native American Women*. New York: Fawcett/Columbine.

Anderson, Karen. 1981. *Wartime Women: Sex Roles, Family Relations, and the Status of Women during World War II*. Westport: Greenwood.

Andrew, Joe. Forthcoming. *Narrative and Desire in Russian Literature, 1822–1849: the Feminine and the Masculine*. St. Martins P.

Anisimov, Evgenii. 1991. "Russia in Search of New National Ethos." *Kennan Institute for Advanced Russian Studies: Meeting Report*, 8.16: not paginated.

Anzaldúa, Gloria. 1987. *Borderlands/La Frontera: The New Mestiza*. San Francisco: Spinsters.

Anzaldúa, Gloria, ed. 1990. *Making Face, Making Soul-Haciendo Caras: Creative and Critical Perspectives by Women of Color*. San Francisco: Aunt Lute Foundation.

Anzaldúa, Gloria, and Cherrie Moraga, eds. 1981. *This Bridge Called My Back: Writings by Radical Women of Color*. New York: Kitchen Table.

Ariev, A. 1987. "Zhazhda otkrytosti." *Literaturnaia Rossiia* 12: 14.

Armstrong, Nancy. 1987. *Desire and Domestic Fiction: A Political History of the Novel*. New York: Oxford.

Atkinson, Dorothy. 1977. "Society and the Sexes in the Russian Past." *Women in Russia*. Ed. Dorothy Atkinson, Alexander Dallin, and Gail Warshofsky Lapidus. Stanford: Stanford UP. 3–38.

Attwood, Lynne. 1990. *The New Soviet Man and Woman: Sex Role Socialization in the USSR*. Bloomington: Indiana UP.

———. 1993a. "Sex and the Cinema." Kon and Riordan 64–88.

———. 1993b. "'Rodina-Mat' and the Soviet Cinema." Liljeström, Mäntysaari, and Rosenholm. 15–28.

Bachofen, J. J. 1967. *Myth, Religion, and Mother Right*. Trans. Ralph Manheim. Princeton: Princeton UP.

Baker, Houston. 1984. *Blues, Ideology, and Afro-American Literature: A Vernacular Theory*. Chicago: U of Chicago P.

———. 1987. *Modernism and the Harlem Renaissance*. Chicago: U of Chicago P.

Bakhtin, Mikhail. 1981. *The Dialogic Imagination: Four Essays*. Ed. Michael Holquist. Trans. Caryl Emerson and Michael Holquist. Austin: U of Texas P.

———. 1984. *Rabelais and His World*. Trans. Helene Iswolsky. Bloomington: Indiana UP.

Bambara, Toni Cade. 1981. "Foreword." Anzaldúa and Moraga vi–viii.

———. 1984. "Salvation is the Issue." Evans 41–47.

Banner, Lois W. 1983. *American Beauty*. New York: Knopf.

Barker, Adele. 1985. *The Mother Syndrome in the Russian Folk Imagination*. Columbus: Slavica.

———. 1992. "The Reluctant Artist: The Career of I. Grekova." Unpublished ms.

Baron, Ava, ed. 1991. *Work Engendered: Toward a New History of American Labor*. Ithaca: Cornell UP.

Barrett, Michele. 1980. *Women's Oppression Today: Problems in Marxist Feminist Analysis*. London: Verso.

Baym, Nina. 1978. *Women's Fiction: A Guide to Novels by and about Women in America, 1820–1870*. Ithaca: Cornell UP.

Beauvoir, Simone de. 1953. *The Second Sex*. Trans. H. M. Parshley. New York: Knopf.

Beck, Evelyn Torton. 1982. *Nice Jewish Girls: A Lesbian Anthology*. Watertown: Persephone.

Beilin, Elaine. 1987. "Redeeming Eve: Defenses of Women and Mother's Advice Books." *Redeeming Eve: Women Writers of the English Renaissance*. Princeton: Princeton UP. 247–85.

Bell, Susan Groag. 1973. *Women: From the Greeks to the French Revolution*. Rpt. Stanford: Stanford UP, 1980.

Berger, John. 1972. *Ways of Seeing*. London: Penguin.

Birkby, Phyllis, et al. 1973. *Amazon Expedition: A Lesbian Feminist Anthology*. New York: Times Change.

Blok, Liubov'. 1979. *Byli i nebylitsy*. 2nd ed. Bremen: Verlag K-Presse.

Borisova, Inna. 1989. "Posleslovie." L. Petrushevskaia, *Bessmertnaia liubov'*. Moscow: Moskovskii Rabochii. 219–22.

Boym, Svetlana. 1991. *Death in Quotation Marks: Cultural Myths of the Modern Poet*. Cambridge, MA: Harvard UP.

Braxton, Joanne M., and Andree Nicola McLaughlin. 1990. *Wild Women in the Whirlwind: Afra-American Culture and the Contemporary Literary Renaissance*. New Brunswick: Rutgers UP.

Bridger, Susan. 1987. *Women in the Soviet Countryside: Women's Roles in Rural Development in the USSR*. Cambridge: Cambridge UP.

———. 1992. "Women and Agricultural Reform." Buckley 39–53.

Brigham, Ann. 1992. "Renavigating Discursive Waters: The Contributions of Mothers'

Advice Books to Renaissance Constructions of Motherhood." Unpublished essay.

Bromfeld, Andrew, and Natasha Perova, eds. 1992. *Women's View*. Special issue, *Glas. New Russian Writing* 3.

Brooks, Peter. 1992. *Reading for the Plot: Design and Intention in Narrative*. Cambridge, MA: Harvard UP.

Brown, Deming. 1978. *Soviet Russian Literature Since Stalin*. Cambridge: Cambridge UP.

Browning, Genia. 1987. *Women and Politics in the USSR: Consciousness Raising and Soviet Women's Groups*. New York: St. Martin's.

Buckley, Mary. 1989a. "What Does Perestroika Mean for Women?" *The Soviet Revolution: Perestroika and the Remaking of Socialism*. Ed. Jon Bloomfield. London: Lawrence & Wishart. 151–75.

———. 1989b. *Women and Ideology in the Soviet Union*. Ann Arbor: U of Michigan P.

———, ed. 1992a. *Perestroika and Soviet Women*. Cambridge: Cambridge UP.

———. 1992b. "Political Reform." *Perestroika and Soviet Women*. 54–71.

———. 1992c. "Glasnost and the Woman Question." *Women and Society in Russia and the Soviet Union*. Ed. Linda Edmondson. Cambridge: Cambridge UP. 202–26.

Bulkin, Elly, ed. 1981. *Lesbian Fiction: An Anthology*. Watertown: Persephone.

Burgin, Diana Lewis. 1992. "Sophia Parnok and the Writing of a Lesbian Poet's Life." *Slavic Review* 51.2: 214–31.

Burks, Ruth Elizabeth. 1984. "From Baptism to Resurrection: Toni Cade Bambara and the Incongruity of Language." Evans 48–57.

Butler, W. E., and V. N. Kudriavtsev. 1985. *Comparative Law and Socio-Legal Systems: Historical and Sociolegal Perspectives*. New York: Oceana.

Butler-Evans, Elliott. 1989. *Race, Gender, and Desire: Narrative Strategies in the Fiction of Toni Cade Bambara, Toni Morrison, and Alice Walker*. Philadelphia: Temple UP.

Byerman, Keith. 1985. "Women's Blues: The Fiction of Toni Cade Bambara and Alice Walker." *Fingering the Jagged Grain: Tradition and Form in Recent Black Fiction*. Ed. Keith Byerman. Athens: U of Georgia P. 115–70.

Carby, Hazel. 1987. *Reconstructing Womanhood: The Emergence of the Afro-American Woman Novelist*. New York: Oxford.

Castro, Michael. 1983. *Interpreting the Indian: Twentieth-Century Poets and the Native American*. Albuquerque: U of New Mexico P.

Chafe, William H. 1991. *The Paradox of Change: American Women in the Twentieth Century*. New York: Oxford UP.

Chakovsky, Sergei, and M. Thomas Inge, eds. 1992. *Russian Eyes on American Literature*. Jackson: UP of Mississippi and A. M. Gorky Institute of World Literature.

Chances, Ellen, Emory Elliot, and Robert Maguire, eds. Forthcoming. *Culture/Kul'tura: Soviet and American Dialogues on Literature and Culture*. Durham: Duke UP.

Chodorow, Nancy. 1978. *The Reproduction of Mothering: Psychoanalysis and the Sociology of Gender*. Berkeley: U of California P.

Christian, Barbara. 1989. "But What Do We Think We're Doing Anyway: The State of Black Feminist Criticism(s) and My Version of a Little Bit of History." Wall 58–74.

Cixous, Hélène. 1986. "Sorties." Cixous and Catherine Clément, *The Newly Born Woman*. Trans. Betsy Wing. Minneapolis: U of Minnesota P. 63–132.

Clements, Barbara Evans, Barbara Alpern Engel, and Christine Worobec, eds. 1991. *Russia's Women: Accommodation, Resistance, Transformation*. Berkeley: U of California P.

Cockburn, Cynthia. 1985. *Machinery of Dominance: Women, Men and Technical Knowhow*. London and Dover, NH: Pluto.

Cohen, Stephen F., and Katrina Vanden Heuvel. 1989. *Voices of Glasnost: Conversations with Gorbachev's Reformers*. New York: Norton.

Colby, Vineta, ed. 1985. *World Authors, 1975–80*. New York: H. W. Wilson.

Costlow, Jane T., Stephanie Sandler, and Judith Vowles, eds. 1993. *Sexuality and the Body in Russian Culture*. Stanford: Stanford UP.

Cott, Nancy F. 1987. *The Grounding of Modern Feminism*. New Haven: Yale UP.

Danielson, Linda L. 1988. "*Storyteller:* Grandmother Spider's Web." *Journal of the Southwest* 30:3: 325–55.

Davidson, Cathy N. 1986. *Revolution and the Word: The Rise of the Novel in America*. New York: Oxford UP.

Davis, Angela. 1981. *Women, Race, and Class*. Rpt. New York: Vintage, 1983.

Dearborn, Mary V. 1986. *Pocahontas's Daughters: Gender and Ethnicity in American Culture*. New York: Oxford UP.

Decter, Jacqueline, ed. 1990. *Soviet Women Writing*. Introd. I. Grekova. New York: Abbeville.

De Lauretis, Teresa. 1984. *Alice Doesn't: Feminism, Semiotics, Cinema*. Bloomington: Indiana UP.

D'Emilio, John. 1983. *Sexual Politics, Sexual Communities: The Making of a Homosexual Minority in the United States, 1940–1970*. Chicago: U of Chicago P.

———, and Estelle B. Freedman. 1988. *Intimate Matters: A History of Sexuality in America*. New York: Harper.

Douglas, Mary. 1966. *Purity and Danger: An Analysis of the Concepts of Pollution and Taboo*. London: Routledge.

Drakulic, Slavenka. 1992. *How We Survived Communism and Even Laughed*. New York: Norton.

Duberman, Martin, Martha Vicinus, and George Chauncey, Jr. 1989. *Hidden from History: Reclaiming the Gay and Lesbian Past*. New York: New American Library.

DuBois, Ellen C. 1978. *Feminism and Suffrage: The Emergence of an Independent Women's Movement in America, 1848–1869*. Ithaca: Cornell UP.

Dunham, Vera. 1976. *In Stalin's Time: Middleclass Values in Soviet Fiction*. Cambridge: Cambridge UP. Rpt. Durham: Duke UP, 1991.

Durova, Nadezhda. 1988. *The Cavalry Maiden: Journals of a Russian Officer in the Napoleonic Wars*. Trans. and intro. notes Mary Zirin. Bloomington: Indiana UP.

Dworkin, Andrea. 1981. *Pornography and Silence: Culture's Revenge against Nature.* New York: Harper.

Eagleton, Terry. 1981. *Walter Benjamin: Toward a Revolutionary Criticism.* London: Verso.

Edberg, Rolf, and Alexei Yablokov. 1991. *Tomorrow Will Be Too Late: East Meets West on Global Ecology.* Tucson: U of Arizona P.

Edmondson, Linda, ed. 1992. *Women and Society in Russia and the Soviet Union.* Cambridge: Cambridge UP.

Edwards, Audrey, and Craig K. Polite. 1992. *Children of the Dream: The Psychology of Black Success.* New York: Doubleday.

Eikhenbaum, Boris. 1986. *O proze-o poezii: sbornik statei.* Leningrad: Khudozhestvennaia Literatura.

Elshtain, Jean Bethke. 1981. *Public Man, Private Woman: Women in Social and Political Thought.* Princeton: Princeton UP.

Engel, Barbara Alpern. 1983. *Mothers and Daughters: Women of the Intelligentsia in Nineteenth Century Russia.* Cambridge: Cambridge UP.

———. 1987. "Women in Russia and the Soviet Union," *Signs: Journal of Women in Culture and Society* 12.4: 781–96.

———. 1989. "An Interview with Olga Lipovskaia." *Frontiers* 10.3: 6–10.

———. 1992. "Engendering Russia's History: Women in Post-Emancipation Russia and the Soviet Union." *Slavic Review* 51.2: 309–21.

Engelstein, Laura. 1992. *The Keys to Happiness: Sex and the Search for Modernity in Fin-de-Siècle Russia.* Ithaca: Cornell UP.

England, Paula. 1992. *Comparable Worth: Theories and Evidence.* New York: Aldine de Gruyter.

Evans, Mari, ed. 1984. *Black Women Writers (1950–1980): A Critical Evaluation.* Garden City: Anchor/Doubleday.

Evans, Sara. 1980. *Personal Politics: The Roots of Women's Liberation in the Civil Rights Movement & the New Left.* New York: Vintage.

Faderman, Lillian. 1981. *Surpassing the Love of Men: Romantic Friendship and Love Between Women from the Renaissance to the Present.* New York: Wm. Morrow.

Fainshtein, Mikhail Sh. 1989. *Pisatel'nitsy pushkinskoi pory: Istoriko-literaturnye ocherki.* Leningrad: Nauka.

Faludi, Susan. 1991. *Backlash: The Undeclared War Against American Women.* New York: Crown.

Faust, Langdon Lynne, and Lina Mainiero, eds. 1979. *American Women Writers: A Critical Reference Guide from Colonial Times to the Present.* 4 vols. New York: Frederick Ungar.

Fetterley, Judith. 1978. *The Resisting Reader: A Feminist Approach to American Fiction.* Bloomington: Indiana UP.

Fiorenza, Elizabeth Schussler. 1983. *In Memory of Her: A Feminist Theological Reconstruction of Christian Origins.* New York: Crossroad.

Firestone, Shulamith. 1970. *The Dialectic of Sex: The Case for Feminist Revolution.* New York: Wm. Morrow.

Fischer, Mary Ellen. 1988. "Women." *The Soviet Union Today: An Interpretive Guide*. Ed. James Cracraft. Chicago: U of Chicago P. 327–38.

Fisher, Dexter, ed. 1980. *The Third Woman: Minority Women Writers in the United States*. New York: Houghton Mifflin.

Flexner, Eleanor. 1959. *Century of Struggle: The Women's Rights Movement in the United States*. Cambridge, MA: Belknap P of Harvard UP.

Flynn, Elizabeth, and Patrocinio Schweikart, eds. 1986. *Gender and Reading: Essays on Readers, Texts, and Contexts*. Baltimore: Johns Hopkins UP.

Forrester, Sibelan. 1992. "Bells and Cupolas: The Formative Role of the Female Body in Marina Tsvetaeva's Poetry." *Slavic Review* 51.2:232–46.

Freud, Sigmund. 1989a. *Vvedenie v psikhoanaliz (Introduction to Psychoanalysis)*. Moscow: Nauka.

————. 1989b. *Izbrannoe (Selected Works)*. Moscow: Vneshtorogizdat.

————. 1991. *Ostroumie i ego otnoshenie k bessoznatel'nomu (Wit [Humor] and Its Relation to the Unconscious)*. Moscow: Izvestiia.

Froula, Christine. 1983. "When Eve Reads Milton: Undoing the Canonical Economy." *Critical Inquiry* 10.2:321–47.

Fuss, Diana. 1989. *Essentially Speaking: Feminism, Nature and Difference*. New York: Routledge.

Gallop, Jane. 1982. *The Daughter's Seduction: Feminism and Psychoanalysis*. Ithaca: Cornell UP.

Ganina, Maia. 1986. "VIII S"ezd pisatelei SSSR." *Literaturnaia gazeta*. 2 July:8.

Garrard, John and Carol. 1990. *Inside the Soviet Writers' Union*. New York: Macmillan.

Gary, Roderick. 1992. "Stories of Uncommon Achievements." Review of *Children of the Dream: The Psychology of Black Success*, by Audrey Edwards and Craig K. Polite. *Arizona Daily Star*. 8 Mar.: E10.

Gates, Henry Louis Jr., ed. 1990. *Reading Black, Reading Feminist: A Critical Anthology*. New York: Meridian.

Gilbert, Sandra, and Susan Gubar. 1979a. *The Madwoman in the Attic: The Woman Writer and the Nineteenth Century Literary Imagination*. New Haven: Yale UP.

————, eds. 1979b. *Shakespeare's Sisters: Feminist Essays on Women Poets*. Bloomington: Indiana UP.

————, eds. 1985. *The Norton Anthology of Literature by Women*. New York: Norton.

————. 1988. *No Man's Land*. 3 vols. New Haven: Yale UP.

Glasse, Antonina. 1974. "The Formidable Woman: Portrait and Original." *Russian Literature Tri-Quarterly* 9: 433–53.

Göpfert, Frank. 1992. *Dichterinnen und Schriftstellerinnen in Russland von Mitte des 18. bis zum Beginn des 20. Jahrhunderts: Eine Problemskizze*. Slavistische Beiträge 289. Munich: Otto Sagner.

Gorbachev, M. S. 1987. *Perestroika: New Thinking for Our Country and the World*. New York: Harper.

Goscilo, Helena, ed. 1989. *Balancing Acts: Contemporary Stories by Russian Women.* Bloomington: Indiana UP.

———. 1991. "Russian Women under Glasnost." *New Outlook* 2.4 (Fall): 45–50.

———, ed. 1992. "Skirted Issues: The Discreteness and Indiscretions of Russian Women's Prose." *Russian Studies in Literature* 28.2 (Spring): special issue.

———. 1993a. "Inscribing the Female Body in Women's Fiction: Cross-Gendered Passion à la Holbein." Liljeström, Mäntysaari, and Rosenholm 73–86.

———. 1993b. "Body Talk in Current Fiction: Speaking Parts and (W)holes." *Stanford Slavic Studies* 7.

———, ed. 1993c. *Fruits of Her Plume: Essays on Contemporary Russian Women's Culture.* Armonk, NY: M. E. Sharpe.

———, ed. 1993d. *Lives in Transit: Recent Russian Women's Writing.* Ann Arbor: Ardis.

gossett, hattie. 1993. "billie lives! billie lives!" Anzaldúa and Moraga 109–12.

Gove, Antonina Filonov. 1977. "The Feminine Stereotype and Beyond: Role Conflict and Resolution in the Poetics of Marina Tsvetaeva." *Slavic Review* 36.2: 231–55.

———. 1978. "Gender as a Poetic Feature in the Verse of Zinaida Gippius." *American Contributions to the Eighth International Congress of Slavists.* Columbus: Slavica. Vol. 1: 379–407.

Gray, Francine du Plessix. 1989. *Soviet Women: Walking the Tightrope.* New York: Doubleday.

Grekova, I. 1967. "Real Life in Real Terms." *Moscow News* 24: 11.

———. 1981. "Zhenskii portret v inter'ere." *Literaturnaia Gazeta* 36: 13.

———. 1982. "Zamysel: zarozhdenie i voploshchenie." *Literaturnaia Rossiia* 28: 11.

———. 1990. "Introduction." Decter 9–14.

———. 1991. "God Solzhenitsyna." *Literaturnaia gazeta* 19 June: 10.

Gubar, Susan. 1981. "Blessings in Disguise: Cross Dressing as Re-dressing for Female Modernists." *Massachusetts Review* 22 (Autumn): 477–508.

Gurevich, David. 1991. "Lost in Translation." *American Spectator* (August): 28–29.

Harjo, Joy, ed. Forthcoming. *Reinventing Ourselves in the Enemy's Language.* U of Arizona P.

Hartsock, Nancy. 1983. *Money, Sex, and Power: Toward a Feminist Historical Materialism.* New York: Longman.

Heldt, Barbara. 1987. *Terrible Perfection: Women and Russian Literature.* Bloomington: Indiana UP.

———. 1989. "Men Who Give Birth: A Feminist Perspective on Russian Literature." *Discontinuous Discourses in Modern Russian Literature.* Ed. Catriona Kelly, Michael Makin, and David Shepherd. London: Macmillan. 157–67.

———. 1992. "Gynoglasnost: Writing the Feminine." Buckley, *Perestroika and Soviet Women,* 160–75.

Heresies: A Feminist Publication of Art and Politics. 1992. 7.2: special Russian/ English issue.

Herodotus. 1956. *The History of Herodotus.* Trans. G. Rawlinson. New York: Tudor Publishing Co.

Holland, Barbara, ed. 1985. *Soviet Sisterhood*. Bloomington: Indiana UP.

Holmgren, Beth. 1993. *Women's Works in Stalin's Time: On Lidiia Chukovskaia and Nadezhda Mandelstam*. Bloomington: Indiana UP.

Holt, Alix. 1985. "The First Soviet Feminists." Holland 237–65.

hooks, bell. 1990. *Yearning: Race, Gender, and Cultural Politics*. Boston: South End.

Horton, Andrew, and Michael Brashinsky. 1992. *The Zero Hour: Glasnost and Soviet Cinema in Transition*. Princeton: Princeton UP.

Hubbs, Joanna. 1988. *Mother Russia: The Feminine Myth in Russian Culture*. Bloomington: Indiana UP.

Hull, Suzanne. 1982. *Chaste, Silent, and Obedient: English Books for Women, 1475–1640*. San Marino: Huntington Library.

Ignashev, Diane M. Nemec, and Sarah Krive, comps. 1992. *Women and Writing in Russia and the USSR: A Bibliography of English Language Sources*. New York: Garland.

Irigaray, Luce. 1974. *Speculum of the Other Woman*. Trans. Gillian Gill. Ithaca: Cornell UP.

Ivanitz, Linda J. 1989. *Russian Folk Belief*. Armonk, NY: M. E. Sharpe.

Ivanov, F. 1990. "VAAP teriat monopoliiu-kto etogo priobretaet?" *Izvestiia* 29 Nov.: 3.

Ivanova, Natalia. 1988a. "Chem pakhnet tormoznaia zhidkost'." *Ogonek* 11: 25–28.

———. 1988b "Zvezda zheny soseda Mitrofana." *Ogonek* 34: 28–30.

Jacobus, Mary. 1986. *Reading Woman: Essays in Feminist Criticism*. New York: Columbia UP.

Jacobus, Mary, Evelyn Fox Keller, and Sally Shuttleworth, eds. 1990. *Body/Politics: Women and the Discourses of Science*. New York: Routledge.

JanMohamed, Abdul R., and David Lloyd, eds. 1990. *The Nature and Context of Minority Discourse*. New York: Oxford UP.

Jardine, Alice. 1985. *Gynesis: Configurations of Woman and Modernity*. Ithaca: Cornell UP.

Jones, Ann Rosalind. 1987. "Nets and Bridles: Early Modern Conduct Books and Sixteenth Century Women's Lyrics." *The Ideology of Conduct: Essays on Literature and the History of Sexuality*. Ed. Nancy Armstrong and Leonard Tennenhouse. New York: Methuen.

Kamuf, Peggy. 1982. "Replacing Feminist Criticism." *Diacritics* 12 (Summer): 42–47.

Kanter, Rosabeth Moss. 1977. *Men and Women of the Corporation*. New York: Basic Books.

Kashkin, I. 1958. *Faulkner W., Sem' rasskazov*. Moscow: Izd. inostrannoi literatury.

Katz, Jonathan, ed. 1975. *Lesbians and Gay Men in History and Literature*. New York: Arno.

———. 1976. *Gay American History: Lesbians and Gay Men in the USA*. New York: Crowell.

Kelley, Mary. 1984. *Private Woman, Public Stage: Literary Domesticity in Nineteenth Century America*. New York: Oxford UP.

Kelly, Catriona, ed. 1994a. *An Anthology of Russian Women's Writing, 1772–1992*. Oxford: Oxford UP.

————. 1994b. *A History of Russian Women's Writing, 1820–1992*. Oxford: Oxford UP.

Kolodny, Annette. 1985. "The Integrity of Memory: Creating a New Literary History of the United States." *American Literature* 57 (May): 291–307.

Kon, Igor. 1979. *Brachnost', rozhdaemost', semia za tri veka: sbornik statei*. Moscow: Statistika.

————. 1988. *Vvedenie v seksologiyu*. Moscow: Meditsina, 1988.

————. 1989. *Psikhologiia rannei iunosti. Kniga dlia uchitelia*. Moscow: Prosveshchenie.

————, and James Riordan, eds. 1993. *Sex and Russian Society*. Bloomington: Indiana UP.

————. 1993. "Sexuality and Culture." Kon and Riordan. 15–44.

Koreneva, Maya. 1990. "Faulkner's Short Stories." Paper presented at the Faulkner Conference, Summer, University of Mississippi.

Kramov, I. N., comp. 1975. *Sovetskii rasskaz*. Moscow: Khudozhestvennaia Literatura.

Kristeva, Julia. 1980. "Motherhood According to Giovanni Bellini." *Desire in Language: A Semiotic Approach to Literature and Art*. Trans. Thomas Gora et al. Ed. Leon S. Roudiez. New York: Columbia UP. 237–70.

————. 1981. "Women's Time." Trans. Alice Jardine and Harry Blake. *Signs: Journal of Women in Culture and Society* 7 (Autumn): 13–35.

————. 1987. "Stabat Mater." *Tales of Love*. Trans. Leon S. Roudiez. New York: Columbia UP. 234–64.

Kroth, Anya M. 1979. "Androgeny as an Exemplary Feature of Marina Tsvetaeva's Dichotomous Poetic Vision." *Slavic Review* 38: 563–82.

Kuleshov, F. I., comp. 1988. *Povesti o liubvi*. 2 vols. Minsk: Vysheshaia Shkola.

Kupriianova, Nina, comp. 1987. *Always a Woman*. Moscow: Raduga.

Lakshin, V. 1991. "Predislovie k: Dmitrii Vitkovskii. Polzhizni." *Znamia* 6: 90–91.

Lawrence, D. H. 1990. *Liubovnik Ledi Chatterlei [Lady Chatterley's Lover]*. Trans. Tatiana Leschenko. Moscow: Video-Ass.

Ledkovsky, Marina. 1991. *Russia According to Women*. Tenafly, NJ: Hermitage. *Rossiia glazami zhenshchin: Literaturnaia antologiia*. 1989.

Ledkovsky, Marina, Charlotte Rosenthal, and Mary Zirin, eds. 1993. *Dictionary of Russian Women Writers*. Westport: Greenwood Press.

Lerner, Gerda. 1979. *The Majority Finds Its Past: Placing Women in History*. New York: Oxford UP.

Liborakina, Marina. 1992. "Ia prosto zhena prezidenta: Opyt feministskogo prochteniia odnogo interv'iu." *Nezavisimaia gazeta* 28.10: 8.

Likhachev, D. S. 1979. *Poetika drevnerusskoi literatury*. Moscow: Nauka.

Liljeström, Marianne, Eila Mäntysaari, and Arja Rosenholm, eds. 1993. *Gender Restructuring in Russian Studies*. Tampere: Slavica Tamperensia 11.

Lim, Shirley Geok-lin, ed. 1989. *The Forbidden Stitch: Asian American Women's Anthology*. Corvallis, OR: Calyx.

Lincoln, Kenneth. 1983. *Native American Renaissance*. Berkeley: U of California P.

Lipovskaia, Olga. 1992. "New Women's Organisations." Buckley, *Perestroika and Soviet Women*, 72–81.

Liuka, Gabi. 1992. "Vlasti Rossii reshili zaniat'sia det'mi i roditeliami." *Nezavisimaia Gazeta* 5 June: 6.

Lorde, Audre. 1984. "Scratching the Surface: Some Notes on the Barriers to Women and Loving." *Sister Outsider: Essays and Speeches*. Trumansberg, NY: Crossing.

Losev, Lev. 1984. *On the Beneficence of Censorship: Aesopian Language in Modern Russian Literature*. Trans. Jane Bobko. Munich: Otto Sagner.

Lowe, David A. 1993. "The Book Business in Postcommunist Russia: Moscow, Year One (1992)." *Harriman Institute Forum* 6.5.

McAndrew, Maggie. 1985. "Soviet Women's Magazines." Holland 78–115.

MacCormack, Carol, and Marilyn Strathern. 1980. *Nature, Culture and Gender*. Cambridge: Cambridge UP.

McDowell, Deborah E. 1989. "Reading Family Matters." Wall 95–97.

MacKinnon, Catharine. 1982. "Feminism, Marxism, Method, and the State: An Agenda for Theory." *Signs* 7.3 (Spring): 515–44.

———. 1985. "Pornography, Civil Rights, and Speech." *Harvard Civil Rights & Civil Liberties Law Review* 2: 1–70.

McLaughlin, Sigrid, ed. and trans. 1989. *The Image of Women in Contemporary Soviet Fiction*. London: Macmillan.

Mamonova, Tatiana, ed. 1984. *Women and Russia: Feminist Writings from the Soviet Union*. Trans. Rebecca Park and Catherine A. Fitzpatrick. Boston: Beacon.

Mamonova, Tatiana. 1989. *Russian Women's Studies: Essays on Sexism in Soviet Culture*. New York: Pergamon.

Melikhova, E. 1989. Letter to the editor, *Rabotnitsa*. Quoted in *Soviet Women* 15.

Miller, Nancy K. 1981. "Emphasis Added: Plots and Plausibilities in Women's Fiction." *PMLA*: 36–48.

———. 1982. "The Text's Heroine: A Feminist Critic and Her Fictions." *Diacritics* 12 (Summer): 48–53.

———. 1986. "Arachnologies: The Woman, the Text, and the Critic." *The Poetics of Gender*. Ed. Nancy K. Miller. New York: Columbia UP. 270–95.

Mischenko, A. 1985. "Nerka." *Literaturnaia Rossiia* 29: 14.

Mitchell, Juliet. 1971. *Woman's Estate*. New York: Pantheon. Rpt. New York: Vintage, 1973.

Morrison, Toni. 1988. *Beloved*. New York: Knopf.

Morgan, Robin. 1984. "Foreword." Mamonova. ix–xi.

Newman, Karen. 1991. *Fashioning Femininity and English Renaissance Drama*. Chicago: U of Chicago P.

Nikolaeva, Olesia. 1990. *Kliuchi ot mira: Povesti*. Moscow: Moskovskii Rabochii.

O'Brien, Mary. 1983. *The Politics of Reproduction*. Boston: Routledge.

Okin, Susan Moller. 1979. *Women in Western Political Thought*. Princeton: Princeton UP.

Olsen, Tillie. 1965. *Silences*. New York: Delacorte.

Omelchuk, Anatolii. 1987. "The Writer Whose Home Is the Tundra." *Soviet Literature* 5: 122–28.

Ortner, Sherry. 1974. "Is Female to Male as Nature is to Culture?" Rosaldo and Lamphere 67–87.

Pagels, Elaine. 1979. *The Gnostic Gospels*. New York: Random.

––––––. 1988. *Adam, Eve, and the Serpent*. New York: Random.

Panaeva, A. Ia. 1986. *Vospominaniia*. Moscow: Pravda.

Parks, Michael. 1991. "Galina Semyonova: No Mere Token in Soviet Politburo." *Los Angeles Times* 15 Jan.: H5.

Pateman, Carole. 1980. "The Disorder of Women." *Ethics* 91: 20–34.

––––––. 1988. *The Sexual Contract*. Stanford: Stanford UP.

Pavlova, Karolina. 1978. *A Double Life*. Trans. Barbara Heldt. Ann Arbor: Ardis.

Petrushevskaia, Liudmila. 1988. "Bessmertnaia liubov'." *Bessmertnaia liubov'*. Moscow: Moskovskii Rabochii. 108–11.

––––––. 1988. "Doch' Kseni." *Bessmertnaia liubov'*. Moscow: Moskovskii Rabochii. 81–86.

Phillips, John A. 1984. *Eve: The History of an Idea*. San Francisco: Harper.

Pilkington, Hilary. 1992. "Going Out in Style: Girls in Youth Cultural Activity." Buckley, *Perestroika and Soviet Women*, 142–59.

Pipes, Richard. 1989. "What is to be Done?" *National Review* 41.10: 42–43.

Popovskii, Mark. 1985. *Tretii lishnii: on, ona, i Sovetskii rezhim*. London: Overseas Publications, Interchange.

Proffer, Carl R., ed. 1969. *From Karamzin to Bunin: An Anthology of Russian Short Stories*. Bloomington: Indiana UP.

Proffer, Carl and Ellendea, eds. 1982. *Contemporary Russian Prose*. Ann Arbor: Ardis.

Pushkareva, N. L. 1991. "Women in the Medieval Russian Family of the Tenth through Fifteenth Centuries." Clements et al. 29–43.

Radin, Paul. 1972. *The Trickster: A Study in American Indian Mythology*. New York: Schocken.

Rancour-Laferrière, Daniel. 1988. *The Mind of Stalin: A Psychoanalytic Study*. Ann Arbor: Ardis.

––––––. 1991. "Freud Returns to the Soviet Union." *Report on the USSR* 3.38: 4–11.

Rich, Adrienne. 1979. "The Anti-Feminist Woman." *On Lies, Secrets, and Silence: Selected Prose 1966–1978*. New York: Norton.

––––––. 1980. "Compulsory Heterosexuality and Lesbian Existence." *Signs: Journal of Women in Culture and Society* 5.4 (Summer): 631–60.

Richmond, Alexander. 1973. *A Long View from the Left: Memoirs of an American Revolutionary*. Boston: Houghton Mifflin.

Riesman, David. 1950. *The Lonely Crowd: A Study of the Changing American Character*. New Haven: Yale UP.

Riordan, James. 1993. "Sexual Minorities: The Status of Gays and Lesbians in Russian-Soviet-Russian Society." Paper presented at Conference on Women in Russia and the Soviet Union, 31 March–2 April, Bath, England.

Rivero, Eliana, and Tey Diana Rebolleda, eds. 1993. *Infinite Divisions: An Anthology of Chicana Literature*. Tucson: U of Arizona P.

Robinson, Lillian. 1978. *Sex, Class, and Culture*. Bloomington: Indiana UP.

———. 1985. "Treason Our Text: Feminist Challenges to the Literary Canon." *The New Feminist Criticism: Essays on Women, Literature, and Theory*. Ed. Elaine Showalter. New York: Pantheon. 105–21.

Rosaldo, Michelle, and Louise Lamphere, eds. 1974. *Woman, Culture, and Society*. Stanford: Stanford UP.

Rosenberg, Rosalind. 1982. *Beyond Separate Spheres: The Intellectual Roots of Modern Feminism*. New Haven: Yale UP.

Rosenfelt, Deborah. 1981. "From the Thirties: Tillie Olsen and the Radical Tradition." *Feminist Studies* 7.3 (Fall): 371–406.

Rosenthal, Charlotte, and Mary Zirin. 1992. "Russia." *Bloomsbury Guide to Women's Literature*. Ed. Claire Buck. New York: Prentice-Hall. 109–18.

Rubin, Gayle. 1975. "The Traffic in Women." *Toward an Anthropology of Women*. Ed. Rayna Rapp Reiter. New York: Monthly Review. 157–210.

Rupp, Leila, and Verta Taylor. 1987. *Survival in the Doldrums: The American Women's Rights Movement, 1945 to the 1960s*. New York: Oxford UP.

Russkii biograficheskii slovar'. 1909. Vol. 19. St. Petersburg: Izd. Imp. Russkogo Istoricheskogo Obshchestva.

Russo, Mary. 1986. "Female Grotesques: Carnival and Theory." *Feminist Studies/Critical Studies*. Ed. Teresa de Lauretis. Bloomington: Indiana UP. 213–29.

Ruthchild, Rochelle. 1983. "Sisterhood and Socialism: The Soviet Feminist Movement." *Frontiers: A Journal of Women Studies* 7.2: 4–12.

Rytkheu, Yurii. 1986. *Magicheskie chisla*. Leningrad: Sovetskii Pisatel'.

Sadoff, Dianne F. 1982. *Monsters of Affection: Dickens, Eliot, and Brontë on Fatherhood*. Baltimore: Johns Hopkins UP.

Sandler, Stephanie. 1990. "Embodied Words: Gender in Cvetaeva's Reading of Pushkin." *Slavic and East European Journal* 34.2:139–57.

Sangari, Kumkum. 1990. "The Politics of the Possible." JanMohamed and Lloyd 216–45.

Sangi, Vladimir, ed. 1985. *Legendy i mify severa*. Moscow: Sovremennik.

Sangi, Vladimir. 1986. *Chelovek ykhmifa*. Moscow: Sovremennik.

Sargent, Lydia, ed. 1981. *Women and Revolution: A Discussion of the Unhappy Marriage of Marxism and Feminism*. Boston: South End.

Shagin, Igor. 1989. Review of L. Petrushevskaia. "Seraia noga, ili vstrecha druzei!" *Sovetskaia dramaturgiia* 2: 72–74.

Shapiro, Judith. 1992. "The Industrial Labour Force." Buckley, *Perestroika and Soviet Women*, 14–38.

Shavkuta, Anatoly, ed. 1990. *Chisten'kaia zhizn'*. Moscow: Molodaia Gvardiia.

Showalter, Elaine. 1977. *A Literature of Their Own: British Women Novelists from Bronte to Lessing*. Princeton: Princeton UP.

———. 1981. "Feminist Criticism in the Wilderness." *Critical Inquiry* 8: 179–205.

Silko, Leslie Marmon. 1977. *Ceremony*. New York: Penguin.

———. 1979. "Language and Literature from a Pueblo Indian Perspective." *English Literature: Selected Papers from the English Institute*, ed. Leslie A. Fiedler and Houston A. Baker, Jr. Baltimore: Johns Hopkins UP. 54–72.

———. 1981. "Story from Bear Country." *Storyteller*. New York: Seaver. 204–9.

Skalon, A. V., comp. 1985. *Sovremennaia povest'*. 2 vols. Moscow: Sovetskii Pisatel'.

Smith, Valerie. 1987. *Self-Discovery and Authority in Afro-American Narrative*. Cambridge MA: Harvard UP.

Snitow, Ann, Christine Stansell, and Sharon Thompson, eds. 1983. *Powers of Desire: The Politics of Sexuality*. New York: Monthly Review.

Sokolova, Olga, comp. 1991. *Abstinentki*. Moscow: Gum. fund im Pushkina, seriia andegraund.

Soviet Women. 1989. *Canadian Woman Studies/Les cahiers de la femme*. 10.4 (Winter): special issue.

Specter, Michael. 1990. "Amid New Sexual Freedom Soviets Face Public Health Perils." *Washington Post* 29 April: A29.

Spender, Dale. 1980. *Man Made Language*. London: Routledge.

Spillers, Hortense. 1984. "Interstices: A Small Drama of Words." Vance 73–100.

Spivak, Gayatri Chakravorty. 1987. *In Other Worlds: Essays in Cultural Politics*. New York: Methuen.

———. 1990. *The Post-Colonial Critic: Interviews, Strategies, Dialogues*. New York: Routledge.

Stallybrass, Peter, and Allon White. 1986. *The Politics and Poetics of Transgression*. Ithaca: Cornell UP.

Stepanenko, L. V., and A. V. Fomenko, comp. 1989. *Zhenskaia logika*. Moscow: Sovremennik.

Sternburg, Janet, ed. 1980. *The Writer on Her Work*. New York: Norton.

Stimpson, Catharine R. 1981. "Zero Degree Deviancy: The Lesbian Novel in English." *Critical Inquiry* 8.2 (Winter): 363–79.

———. 1984. *Where the Meanings Are: Feminism and Cultural Spaces*. New York: Methuen.

Stone, Merlin. 1976. *When God Was a Woman*. New York: Harcourt Brace Jovanovich.

Sukhanova, Natal'ia. 1988. "Delos." *Novyi mir* 3: 69–84. Trans. Charlotte Rosenthal. *The Wild Beach: An Anthology of Contemporary Russian Stories*. Ed. Helena Goscilo and Byron Lindsey. Ann Arbor: Ardis, 1992. 147–71.

Suleiman, Susan Rubin, ed. 1986. *The Female Body in Western Culture: Contemporary Perspectives*. Cambridge, MA: Harvard UP.

Sulimirski, Tadeusz. 1970. *The Sarmathians*. Southampton: Thames and Hudson.

Svobodin, Alexander. 1989. "What to do with Petrushevskaya?" *Moscow News Weekly* 19–26 Mar.: 12.

Tate, Claudia, ed. 1983a. *Black Women Writers at Work*. New York: Continuum.

———. 1983b. "Toni Cade Bambara: An Interview." Tate 12–38.

Tatum, Charles. 1992. *New Chicano/Chicana Writing*. 2 vols. Tucson: U of Arizona P.

Tokarev, S. A., ed. 1980–82. *Mify narodov mira: Entsiklopediia*. 2 vols. Moscow: Sovetskaia Entsiklopediia.

Tolstaia, Tatiana. 1990. "Notes from Underground." Review of *Soviet Women: Walking the Tightrope. New York Review of Books*. 31 May: 3–7.

———. 1991. "In Cannibalistic Times." *New York Times Book Review*. 11 April: 3–6.

Tompkins, Jane. 1985. *Sensational Designs: The Cultural Work of American Fiction 1790–1860*. New York: Oxford UP.

Traylor, Eleanor. 1984. "Music as Theme: The Jazz Mode in the Works of Toni Cade Bambara." Evans 58–70.

Trifonov, Yurii. 1985. "Net, ne o byte—o zhizni!" *Kak slovo nashe otzovetsia*. Moscow: Sovetskaia Rossiia. 101–7.

Trinh, T. Minh-ha. 1989. *Woman, Native, Other: Writing, Post-Coloniality and Feminism*. Bloomington: Indiana UP.

———. 1991. *When the Moon Waxes Red: Representation, Gender and Cultural Politics*. New York: Routledge.

Tucker, Robert C. 1973. *Stalin as Revolutionary, 1879–1929: A Study in History and Personality*. New York: Norton.

Uchenova, V. V., comp. 1986. *Dacha na Petergofskoi doroge*. Moscow: Sovremennik.

———. 1987. *Svidanie*. Moscow: Sovremennik.

———. 1988. *Tol'ko chas*. Moscow: Sovremennik.

———. 1989. *Tsaritsy muz: russkie poetessy XIX—nachala XXvv*. Moscow: Sovremennik.

Vainer, Viktoria. 1989a. "An Interview with Liudmila Petrushevskaya." *Theater* 20.3 (1989): 61–64.

———. 1989b. "Ludmilla Petrushevskaya, the Dramatist." *Soviet Literature* 3: 72–79.

Vance, Carole S., ed. 1984. *Pleasure and Danger: Exploring Female Sexuality*. Boston: Routledge.

Vaneeva, Larisa, comp. 1990. *Ne pomniashchaia zla*. Moscow: Moskovskii Rabochii.

Vaneeva, Larisa. 1991. "Lame Pigeons." Trans. Rosamund Bartlett. *Dissonant Voices: The New Russian Fiction*. Ed. Oleg Chukhontsev and Nina Sadur. New York: Harvill.

Vangen, Kate Shanley. 1984. "The Devil's Domain: Leslie Silko's 'Storyteller.'" *Coyote Was Here: Essays on Contemporary Native American Literary and Political Mobilization*. Ed. Bo Scholer. Aarhus, Denmark: Seklos. 116–23.

Vasilenko, Svetlana, comp. 1991. *Novye Amazonki*. Moscow: Moskovskii Rabochii.

Vasil'eva, Larisa. 1989. "Zhenshchina. Zhizn'. Literatura." *Literaturnaia gazeta* 20 Dec.: 7.

Voronina, Olga. 1993. "Obraz zhenshchiny v sredstvakh massovoi informatsii: rekonstruktsiia pola posle 1985 goda." Liljeström, Mäntysaari, and Rosenholm. 243–53.

Wall, Cheryl A., ed. 1989. *Changing Our Own Words: Essays on Criticism, Theory, and Writing by Black Women*. New Brunswick: Rutgers UP.

Wallace, Michele. 1978. *Black Macho and the Myth of the Superwoman*. Rpt. New York: Verso, 1990.

———. 1990. "Variations on Negation and the Heresy of Black Feminist Creativity." Gates 52–67.

Warner, Marina. 1976. *Alone of All Her Sex: The Myth and Cult of the Virgin Mary.* Rpt. New York: Pocket, 1978.

Washington, Mary Helen, ed. 1975. *Black-Eyed Susans/Midnight Birds: Stories By and About Black Women.* New York: Anchor/Doubleday, 1990.

Washington, Mary Helen. 1977. "The Blues Women of the Seventies." *Ms.* 1 July: 36–38.

Waters, Elizabeth. 1989. "Restructuring the 'Woman Question': Perestroika and Prostitution." *Feminist Review* 33 (Autumn): 3–19.

———. 1991. "The Female Form in Soviet Political Iconography, 1917–1932." Clements et al. 225–42.

———. 1992. "Victim or Villain: Prostitution in Post-Revolutionary Russia." Edmondson. 160–77.

Weeks, Laura D. 1990. "'I Named Her Ariadne . . .' The Demeter-Persephone Myth in Tsvetaeva's Poems for Her Daughter." *Slavic Review* 49.4 (Winter): 568–84.

Whitney, Craig R. 1991. "Union of Soviet Writers is also Breaking Apart." *New York Times* 14 Sept.: 13.

Williams, Patricia J. 1991. *The Alchemy of Race and Rights.* Cambridge, MA: Harvard UP.

Wittig, Monique. 1992. *The Straight Mind.* Boston: Beacon.

Wolf, Naomi. 1991. *The Beauty Myth: How Images of Beauty Are Used against Women.* New York: William Morrow.

Woolf, Virginia. 1929. *A Room of One's Own.* Rpt. London: Granada, 1977.

Yalom, Marilyn, ed. 1983. *Women Writers of the West Coast: Speaking of their Lives and Careers.* Santa Barbara: Capra.

Zimmerman, Bonnie. 1990. *The Safe Sea of Women: Lesbian Fiction, 1969–89.* Boston: Beacon.

Zirin, Mary, trans. 1988. *The Cavalry Maiden: Journals of a Russian Officer in the Napoleonic Wars.* Bloomington: Indiana UP.

Zwinger, Lynda. 1991. *Daughters, Fathers, and the Novel: The Sentimental Romance of Heterosexuality.* Madison: U of Wisconsin P.

Index

Left to right: *Maya Koreneva,*
Ekaterina Stetsenko, Adele Barker,
and Susan Aiken

SUSAN HARDY AIKEN is a professor of English at the University of Arizona and a member of the faculties of Comparative Cultural and Literary Studies and of Women's Studies. She is the author of *Isak Dinesen and the Engendering of Narrative* and the coeditor of *Changing our Minds: Feminist Transformations of Knowledge.*

ADELE MARIE BARKER is an associate professor of Slavic languages and literatures at the University of Washington, Seattle. She is the author of *The Mother Syndrome in the Russian Folk Imagination.*

MAYA KORENEVA is a senior researcher in the Department of European and American Literature at the A. M. Gorky Institute of World Literature in Moscow. She is the author of *Franklin's Autobiography* and *Eugene O'Neill and the Development of American Drama.*

EKATERINA STETSENKO is a researcher in the Department of European and American Literature at the A. M. Gorky Institute of World Literature in Moscow. She is the author of *The Fate of America in the Modern U.S. Novel.*